BRAHMS

JOHANNES BRAHMS

BRAHMS

by

WALTER NIEMANN

TRANSLATED BY

CATHERINE ALISON PHILLIPS

NEW YORK

COOPER SQUARE PUBLISHERS, INC.

1969

Originally Published and Copyright © 1929
by Alfred A. Knopf, Inc.
Published by Cooper Square Publishers, Inc.
59 Fourth Avenue, New York, N. Y. 10003
Standard Book Number: 8154-0310-0
Library of Congress Catalog Card No.: 79-92028

Printed in the United States of America
by Noble Offset Printers, Inc., New York, N. Y. 10003

If ever our German nation is passing through a phase of national mourning and tribulation — which God forbid for long years to come, though, as the history of the past teaches us, this becomes necessary in the course of ages, as a result of external and internal enemies, in order to restore national balance — then shall the children of Brahms's muse, like holy angels, droop their lily wands over mankind in its affliction, pouring a healing balm into their wounds, and thus aid in directing our mission in the life of nations towards new and glorious aims. God grant it may be so!

RUDOLF VON DER LEYEN

(Johannes Brahms als Mensch und Freund)

The translator's most grateful thanks are due to Miss Agnes Bedford, for her kind assistance in the musical sections of the book, to her husband, Professor W. Alison Phillips, for his advice and help, and to Messrs. J. and W. Chester, for the special facilities which they were so good as to give her for consulting the works.

PREFACE

When we glance at the array of works on Brahms forming the bibliography of this book, or recall Max Kalbeck's monumental biography in several volumes, it is hardly possible to believe that there is any material need for a new life of Brahms. And yet such a material need does exist, as well as what we may call an intrinsic necessity. What has been most seriously lacking hitherto has been a comprehensive biography of Brahms in one volume, which should sift out what is most essential in the vast mass of purely biographical material collected by Kalbeck, and combine it with a critical account of Brahms's works, and a commentary upon them. What has been written about Brahms up till now — and the mass of it is almost overwhelming — bears the stamp of an official and unqualified admiration, which is either utterly uncritical, or else based upon a hostile reaction against neo-German and modern art.

And this brings me to the question: What is there in this book that is new, and how does it meet the need alluded to above, in both form and content? The first new feature is the critical attitude which I have adopted towards Brahms's art — in all love and reverence — in venturing to point out not only those respects in which he appears to be immortal, but also those in which he appears to be mortal; and the second, the manner of presenting Brahms's life, in which a critical review of the biographical material is combined with the purely biographical element. In this sense my book is the first critical biography of Brahms. Another new and essential point is the stress laid upon the Low German characteristics in Brahms both as man and as artist — and that not in any narrowly regional sense, but in such a way as to explain and throw light upon those qualities of his temperament which have a " Nordic " tinge, a North German and Low German char-

ix

acter, in contradistinction from that of Southern and central Germany. This has occasionally made it possible to draw certain free parallels between Brahms and Hebbel, Storm, and other modern poets of Schleswig-Holstein. The last new and essential contribution, arising directly out of this "regional" point of view, may perhaps be considered permissible in one coming from the same part of the country: namely, the upsetting of the one-sided estimate of Brahms as invariably "harsh" and "hard," and an equally strong, though in no wise exaggerated or partial insistence upon his tender qualities, which had their origin in the emotional *milieu* of the middle classes of his day.

The outward form of the book aims at a clarity and plasticity like those of Brahms: short, clearly defined chapters, as much direct narration as possible, passages from actual letters, recorded opinions, reminiscences, etc., in order to heighten the living reality of the impression. The first section, dealing with the life of Brahms, does not consciously make any new contribution to the subject, but presents familiar facts in a new form. The centre of gravity of the book is situated entirely in the second part, which deals with the works. In this section I may claim to have gone far beyond the accepted interpretations of Brahms's works, in spite of the great difficulties due to the fact that it is impossible to include more than a few musical citations.

My most cordial thanks are due to the Leipzig publishing houses of Messrs. Peters, Simrock, and Klemm for the kind assistance which they have lent to my work.

Leipzig, March 1920   W. N.

CONTENTS

APPENDICES

PART ONE

BRAHMS'S LIFE

EARLY YEARS (HAMBURG)

I

"TWO THALERS AND DRINK *AD LIB.*"

To a Southern or central German ear the name " Brahms "
("Brahmst," "Brams," perhaps from *"Bram,"* one name for the
yellow broom or genista) has a certain "Nordic" ring — that is
to say, North German, and in particular Low German. It is especially familiar in Schleswig-Holstein, Oldenburg, and Hanover.
The composer's great-grandfather, Peter Brahms, was of Han-
overian descent, and worked as a carpenter at Brunsbüttel, where
what is now the Nord-Ostsee Canal joins the yellowish grey
waters of the lower Elbe, as it flows on towards the North Sea,
already a broad, mighty stream. By his marriage with Sophie Uhl
— and who can help being reminded by this name of the proud
Ditmarsh peasant stock of the Uhls in Gustav Frenssen's *Jörn
Uhl,* a romance of peasant life in Schleswig-Holstein? — he had
a son, Johann Brahms (1769–1839), our composer's grandfather.
Johann started as an innkeeper and small tradesman at the sign of
the "Neuer Krug" at Wöhrden, in Northern Ditmarsh (Dith-
marschen), to the east of what is now the watering-place of Büsum
on the North Sea, and quite near the shallow Wattenmeer. At
the age of twenty-three he married Christiana Magdalena Asmus,
who was the same age as himself, the daughter of Jürgen Asmus,
a burgess of Heide, in the Eiderstadt peninsula, and went to ply
his double calling in this hospitable town of Northern Ditmarsh,
the native place of Claus Groth, whose *Quickborn* is one of the
greatest masterpieces of Low German folk-poetry. He died at
the age of sixty. His eldest son, Peter Hoeft Hinrich (1793–1863),
who married Christina Ruge of Bennewohld in 1813, left five
children, and there are still some descendants of a collateral branch
of the Brahms family flourishing in Heide — respectable crafts-
men, tanners, and innkeepers who have inherited their father's

occupations of innkeeper, dealer in antiquities, and pawnbroker. It was his second son, Peter Hoeft's brother Johann Jakob (1806–72), who was the father of our composer.

Old Peter Brahms was a passive dreamer of the true Low German type, who, as Claus Groth tells us, used as an old man to sit puffing at a short pipe in front of his son's inn. Peter Hoeft Hinrich was an active, hard-working tradesman, but he too, like a good Low German, was already pursuing a nice little hobby, the collecting of antiquities. But " old Brahms," as Johann Jakob was afterwards called in Hamburg, was the type of the light-hearted and jovial German musician. While still quite a lad, what he liked best was to wander about the open country-side in the rich Marshlands or the rugged, sterile hill-country; he was fond of playing truant in order to learn " music " — that is to say, how to play the chief instruments — from the band who played dance-music at his father's inn; and soon he would go round the neighbouring villages playing the fiddle. The artistic resources of Heide, then a sleepy little country town of Holstein, with some five thousand inhabitants, soon became too narrow for him, just as those of Wesselburen, a still smaller town near by, did to the poet Friedrich Hebbel, pining in the subaltern drudgery of a parish clerk, and since he was bent upon being a musician and nothing else, he " twice," as his son Johannes afterwards wrote to Claus Groth, " ran away from his parents' house out of a pure passion for music." The first time it was to the capital of Southern Ditmarsh, to Meldorf, the nearest town-musician, who is well known to us from Gustav Frenssen's novels, and who gave him lessons on the stringed instruments, horn, and flute; the second time it was to Theodor Müller, the " privileged and official musician " of the town-band of Wesselburen; and it was " not till the third time " that he was pronounced by his masters free to go out into the world as their " pupil Johannes Brahmst " and, having been dismissed on December 16, 1825 with a " certificate of apprenticeship (*Lehrbrief*)" in due form, after studying for two years with Müller, was sent out into the wide world by his still reluctant parents, " with their blessing, some bedding, and the rest."

He naturally went straight off to Hamburg, the great capital of Lower Germany. Here " Father " Brahms worked his way up from the very bottom of the ladder with iron industry. A capable double-bass, with a good practical knowledge of the 'cello and horn — which he was able to turn to good use as bugler and afterwards *Oberjäger* in the green uniform of the Hamburg civic guard, until it was disbanded in 1867 — a musician of distinguished talents and versatile ability, he climbed step by step the steep ladder of his modest career as a musician. The first step consisted of the lowest sailors' taverns round about the port. The next already advanced him to the sextet in the old, fashionable Alsterpavillon on the Neuer Jungfernstieg, in which Johann Jakob took part as a deputy from noon till towards midnight, from 1831 onwards, as "horn-player who handed round the plate," being permanently engaged on the death of the double-bass in 1840 as his successor. His next step upwards was to become double-bass in the Carl-Schultze Theatre in the suburb of St. Pauli, and he at last reached his highest position as double-bass at the Stadttheater (Municipal Theatre) and in the Philharmonic Orchestra.

Eduard Marxsen, Brahms's master at Hamburg, speaks of " Father " Brahms as a " thoroughly upright character, of limited intellect, but great good nature." Chrysander, whose account of him is also based upon personal knowledge, remembers him as a shrewd, amiable, humorous man of the lower middle class. A youthful portrait of him, which bears a surprising resemblance to Lortzing as a young man, shows us a pleasing face with vivacious, mischievous dark-grey eyes, brown hair, and a finely cut mouth. He was attached by the most affectionate ties to his *" Kunterbass,"* as he called it in his Hamburg *patois,* and the Hamburgers of the day had a constant source of laughter in the latest anecdote about " Father " Brahms, in which he would stand up for the honour of his double-bass as a man and artist with comical pride and a delightfully ready wit. Thus on one occasion, when the conductor found fault with him for being slightly out of tune, he replied in genuine Hamburg *patois* (" *Missingsch* ") : " Herr Kapellmeister, a pure tone on the double-bass is a pure chance (*en reinen Ton up den Kunterbass is en puren Taufall*)"; or, when the same conductor told him to play a little louder, his answer was: "Herr Kapellmeister, this is *my* double-bass; so I can play on it as loud as I like (*dat is min Kunterbass, da kann ick so laut up spelen, als ick mag*)."

On June 9, 1830, Johann Brahms — now a smart *Oberjäger*, who had risen to the position of a citizen of Hamburg — married Johanna Henrika Christiane Nissen of Hamburg (1789–1865), who was seventeen years older than himself, and lived with her married sister Christina Friederika Detmering in the Ulricusstrasse, a short side-street cutting across the Valentinskamp in the north-western portion of the inner town, where they kept a shop and sold what were known as Dutch goods (small ironmongery). Christiane kept house for her sister, her brother-in-law, and the lodgers, and Johann Jakob, who at once took up his quarters there as a boarder, must certainly soon have found out what a tidy housewife and a tidy room mean to an untidy young bachelor musician.

According to the testimony of Marxsen, our Johannes's mother was "also of an upright character; of no education, it is true, but, as the saying goes, with more mother wit than her husband." It is no wonder, then, that Johannes clung with the deepest love and tenderness to this gentle, refined, much-tried woman, with her simple piety, the soulful, childlike eyes, which Johannes inherited from her, and the fair hair, who was both a good housekeeper and a clever needlewoman.

Three children were born of this marriage — Elisabeth Wilhelmine Louise (1831–92) and two sons, Friedrich Fritz (1835–85) and Johannes, the subject of our biography — but it was not at all a well-assorted one, and in later years the parents lived apart. His sister Elise, who married the watch-maker Grund of Hamburg, caused her brother Johannes much anxiety and sorrow throughout his life. His strong, characteristically Low German family feeling prevented him from becoming quite estranged from her; on the contrary, he supported her up to the time of her death, even after she had married, against his wishes, a widower sixty years of age, and with six children.

His brother, Fritz, known in Hamburg as "the wrong (*falsche*) Brahms," did not come up to the high hopes which Johannes had based upon his remarkable musical gifts. At the instance of Johannes he also became a pupil of Marxsen, but in spite of his brother's constant, helpful encouragement and admonitions, he did not, like him, possess the vast force of will and untiring industry which would have enabled him to achieve anything remarkable and concentrate on his work ("*drauf los zu studieren*"). His health was delicate during his whole life, and after a considerable period of residence in Caracas, Venezuela, from 1867 to 1870, he worked in Hamburg as a capable pianist and teacher, being much sought after and charging good fees. After many years of estrangement — due to the fact that he refused to contribute towards the support of their father — he was reconciled with his brother at their father's death-bed. A portrait of him dated 1863 shows us a languid young man with fine, but rather weary, drawn features, not much expression, and introspective, dreamy eyes.

At first Johann Jakob Brahms boarded with the Detmerings in the Ulricusstrasse. After the birth of their little daughter the young couple moved to the Specksgang near by, to No. 24 Schlütershof (now No. 60 Speckstrasse), in what is called the "Gängeviertel" of Old Hamburg, and here they lived modestly, on very small earnings. The name "Schlütershof" reveals the fact that the house did not stand in the row of houses fronting on the narrow alley, where a man can only just pass, but a few yards back, on a still narrower passage between what are now Nos. 59 and 61. The Specksgang lies about half-way between the Gänsemarkt and the western part of the ramparts surrounding the Altstadt; it runs roughly from south to north and connects the Neustädter Strasse with the Caffamacherreihe. The house is a typical old Hamburg timbered building, tall and five-storied, with the windows opening outwards and set very close together, low under the eaves, with pots of flowers, canaries, parrots, and white

curtains of a cleanliness worthy of Holland, and thronged with
people and children. The Brahms family occupied a low-ceiled
doll's house of a three-roomed apartment in this building, probably on the first " *étage* " or " *Sahl,*" a kitchen with one window,
a living-room with two windows, and a tiny bedroom or " alcove,"
looking on to a steaming, evil-smelling courtyard — a miserable
haunt of mass poverty which might have been situated in the
poorest East End quarter of Dickens's London just as well as in
Hamburg.

It was there, in the very heart of the Old Hamburg Gängeviertel, round whose lower-middle-class life Gustav Falke has cast
such a soft aureole of humble romance in his novel *Die Kinder
aus Ohlsens Gang,* in the very heart, too, of the populace of Hamburg, sound and hard-working to the core, and as robust and
tough as they are good-hearted, humorous, and kindly, that our
composer, Johannes, was born on May 7, 1833. He was baptized
by Pastor von Ahlsen on May 26 of the same year in the splendid
Michaeliskirche, built by Sonnin in the middle of the eighteenth
century in the finest late-baroque style, and known as " *der Alte
Michel* " to seafarers, who can see it towering on high, a mighty
mass. His godfathers were his grandfather Johann Brahms,
his uncle Diederich Philipp Detmering the lighterman, and
Catharina Margaretha Stäcker.

In 1866, only a year after the death of his wife Christiane, his
father married again. This time he married a widow, Caroline
Schnack, whose maiden name was Paasch, belonging to a family
coming from Neustadt on the bay of Lübeck in Holstein, and
eighteen years younger than himself. She was a true wife and
helpmeet to " Father " Brahms. Throughout his whole life the
composer was on terms of the tenderest and most devoted affection, not only with his parents, but also with his step-mother and
her son by her first marriage, the watch-maker Fritz Schnack of
Pinneberg, between Altona and Elmshorn on the Hamburg-Kiel
railway, and with his sisters and brothers.

Little Johannes grew into a stocky, tough, healthy boy. He
easily shook off all the usual diseases of childhood. From the age

of six he attended a bad private school kept by Heinrich Friedrich Voss by the Dammtorwalle, near his home, and afterwards the " superior " lower-middle-class school kept by Johann Friedrich Hoffmann in the A-B-C-Strasse, a good popular school, where he spent his last three years; and there he learnt industriously and conscientiously what little such schools could then offer. At Christmas 1846 he was even able to wish his parents the compliments of the season in French.

It was at school that the Bible first came into his hands, and the deep and powerful impression which it made upon this typically Lower Saxon child — quiet, thoughtful, and dreamy, yet with a deep, sensitive, and imaginative nature — contributed in large measure towards that uncommon devotion to the Bible and knowledge of it which characterized the future composer of the *Deutsches Requiem*. It was during these early school years that the foundations of Brahms's austerely North German and Protestant view of life and art were firmly laid, together with his deep-rooted love for the true Protestant chorale and Protestant church music, implanted in him by Pastor Geffcken of St. Michaelis. For the rest, Brahms, like so many great German composers, had a long, hard struggle to obtain a good education. By the time he was fifteen, he had mastered the usual rudiments, together with religious knowledge and a little French. The education which he continued to acquire later in life, even in his old age — and, quite apart from music and musical history, it was amazingly extensive, particularly in the literary sphere — was won by his own efforts and by a rigid self-discipline.

At the age of ten he was run over by a carriage, and suffered considerable injuries, but his life was spared by a beneficent Providence. The same protection was extended to the Specksgang, the Schlütershof, and the tall old timbered house in which his parents lived, when a terrible fire, which raged from May 5 to 8, 1842, reduced a third of the Altstadt of Hamburg to ashes. All that Friedrich Hebbel, then a blond, slender young poet of twenty-nine, was able to save from the popular fury and destruction — for he was taken for an Englishman and an incendiary — was, as he wrote in his autobiography, published by Brockhaus in 1852, his "Low German speech." The catastrophe produced a deep and terrible impression on the sensitive and impressionable mind of little Johannes, as it did on Hebbel, and it was nothing but a fortunate change in the wind that saved his parents' house from the destruction which was approaching threateningly near.

The young Hebbel! The greatest poet and the greatest musician of Lower Germany were both living in its capital, Hamburg, one as a young man and the other as a child, yet neither was aware of the other's existence, nor did they come in contact with each other even in later years. It is curious that the name of Brahms does not once occur in Hebbel's diaries and letters, though Brahms was already thirty at the time of Hebbel's death, and there is a leaf from one of the poet's albums in the Hebbel Museum at Wesselburen, dated April 30, 1863, with the following epigram, entitled "Consolation (*Trost*)," dedicated to the composer:

Perlen hast du gesä't, auf einmal beginnt es zu hageln,
Und man erblickt sie nicht mehr; hoff' auf die Sonne, sie
   kommt!

(Pearls hast thou sown, but lo! on a sudden the hail-storm begins, and hides them from sight; only wait, soon will the sunshine return.)

Again, it seems more than a mere accident that the great poet and the great musician of Lower Germany should both have found their second and true home in Vienna. At that time, it is true, young Hebbel was writing poetry and going hungry beneath Madame Amalie Schoppe's protecting wing in his room in Mamsell Elise Lensing's house. He lived for two periods in Hamburg; firstly (1835-6), while preparing for the universities of Heidelberg and Munich; and secondly, on his return from his terrible journey on foot from Munich through the Thuringian Forest to Hamburg (1839-42). At this time Brahms was a child. The lasting fruit of Hebbel's stay in Hamburg, so far as human relations are concerned, was his tragic liaison — a struggle between poverty and love — with the faithful, self-sacrificing Elise

Lensing. The permanent poetic fruits were the two great youthful dramas *Judith* and *Genoveva,* in which Hebbel first appeared as a writer of tragedies. Both Hebbel and Brahms had a hard and struggling childhood and youth, for both of them alike rose from the humblest lower-middle-class surroundings; but Hebbel's lot was the harder, for his mother was no longer at his side to encourage him by her love.

In 1848, at the age of fifteen, Johannes was confirmed by the excellent pastor of St. Michaelis, Johannes Geffcken, the distinguished hymnologist, who was one of the collaborators in the *New Hamburg Hymn-book.* By the same year "Hannes" had finished his musical studies with his father and acquired enough proficiency on the violin, 'cello, and horn to be able to act as a stopgap when necessary.

"Father" Brahms had early recognized the exceptional musical talent of his "Jehannes." Whether little Johannes liked it or not — and he generally did not — he had to play his earliest efforts at composition to their admiring friends and acquaintances and lend stout assistance to his father in the routine of his musical craft. Composition was a matter of very secondary importance to Papa Brahms: there was no money to be earned by it. But to little Johannes it was absolutely supreme. "I was always composing," he told Widmann, his Swiss friend, in later years. "My finest songs would come to me early in the morning, while I was cleaning my boots." Or again: "I was already composing even then, but only in great secrecy and in the earliest hours of the morning. All day long I was arranging marches for brass bands, and at night I would be seated at the piano in taverns." Or again: "I had invented myself a stave before I knew that such a thing had long been in existence." But to Father Brahms this musical journeyman's work was of far greater importance; so nobody can blame him for having tried in the first place to turn his son's musical talents to practical use, in his immediate surroundings, to relieve him of some of his own burdens. His son had to start helping to earn money very early. He accompanied his father not only when he went to play second violin lustily in private orchestras, but also to play at dances; and in this connexion there is a nice anecdote. Late one evening a gentleman's servant came knocking at old Brahms's door. "*Wecker is doar?* (Who is there?)" replied Father Brahms in his broad accent. " Open the door, you there! Johann has got to play." "Where?" "At the Schröders' on the *Burstah.*" "What'll they pay?" " *Twee Daler un duhn* (Two thalers and drink *ad lib.*)." And Johann was dragged out of bed and had to go and play at a ball at the Schröders' on the " Burstah " for two thalers and unlimited alcohol. He had often done the same thing before, and his fame had even travelled far beyond the bounds of Hamburg. He used often to play dance-music for two thalers like this on Sunday afternoons at the country inn " Zur schönen Aussicht " at Bergedorf, between Hamburg and Friedrichsruh. It was there, we read in an article by A. Steiner in a New Year issue of the Zürich Allgemeine Musikgesellschaft's proceedings, that he was heard by Christian Miller, afterwards a piano-teacher of some repute in Hamburg, who was so enthusiastic over his playing that he asked him as a favour to be allowed to make music with him. On the next Sunday the two young men went out to Bergedorf together and entertained the unsuspecting public by playing piano duets to them — and very likely some piece of good, serious music, some march by Schubert, or Mozart sonata, occasionally found its way in among the ordinary Viennese or Berlin waltzes. During the walks which they would take together almost every day — and which went on until Miller entered the Leipzig Conservatoire — " the conversation does not seem to have been very animated; as a rule Brahms did not speak a word, but walked along humming to himself, usually carrying his hat in his hand, as he loved to do throughout his whole life."

Thus, like a true musician's child, young Johannes first learnt his art by practical experience on the piano, horn, violin, and 'cello, and he seemed to be going the right way to end his days as a mere ballroom player, in the same narrow middle-class surroundings, both material and artistic, as his parents. His life and studies followed the same course as that of countless talented musicians of Lower Germany. To them art was a business, as, for instance, the orchestra run by an honest municipal conductor of Ditmarsh; they were for the most part highly capable musicians, with a solid academic training, who had almost always mastered several instruments and were also quite familiar with the organ, and to them, as to the sober, materially minded Lower Germans in general, with their minds always set upon good living, art was in the main a practical matter: a means of earning money, a profession — in fact, a calling like any other.

This should constantly be borne in mind if we are to see these early years of Johannes Brahms's life in the right light. Harsh as this premature drudgery and exploitation of his exceptional musical talents by his father may seem, yet his father's intentions towards his Johannes were sincerely good; this subaltern musical activity was thoroughly suited to the practical career of a good North German musician, and Brahms's parents had not the means to endow their son, of whom they were so fond and proud, with " anything better " in music either. On the other hand, we cannot too much insist upon what a real advantage this practical employment in his father's calling was to the future composer. It is not for nothing that the simplest and most popular musical forms — song, dance, or variations — play such a large part in Brahms's works, and that not only during his youth: his mastery of song, dance, and variations alike was gained while he was still a boy, and it was thanks to his father's calling and his own that these forms came naturally to him from the first. As a composer, too, Brahms served in the ranks, as a man of the people, and from this firm ground of solid routine, this complete mastery of his simplest, most natural, and most popular forms of expression at the earliest possible age, golden fruit was to spring.

II

FROM COSSEL TO MARXSEN

All the same, Father Brahms certainly realized at an early
date that the extraordinary talent of his Johannes made it his
moral duty to do all that lay within his power to develop and
train his son's talent, and he was further impelled to do so by
the pressure of his brother musicians. And so one day he went
with the seven-year-old boy to the pianist Otto F. W. Cossel, a
pupil of Eduard Marxsen, the Altona composer, who was an
admirable teacher. But even now, for practical reasons, he tried
to set precise limits to his future curriculum. "My Johann is to
learn as much as you, Herr Cossel; then he will know enough.
He wants very much to be a pianist."

Cossel agreed and soon discovered to his great joy what an
extraordinary talent had been entrusted to his musical training.
The nine-year-old Brahms, who on January 1, 1842 addressed to
his "beloved master" a beautifully written New Year's letter
of thanks, in which he pledged himself to respond to his wishes
"by attention and obedience," already felt irresistibly drawn
towards musical knowledge and training; he would take musical
works of some size and score them from the parts, and thus
became his own master in the rudiments of musical theory.
Julius Spengel describes how Cossel, who was entirely bent upon
training Brahms, with unselfish devotion, to become a pianist
of note, was not altogether edified by these aberrations of his
young pupil's. "It is a pity," he said once. "He might be such
a good pianist, but he will not leave this everlasting composition
alone."

Cossel, who taught Brahms the rudiments, was an idealistic,
thorough, and conscientious music-teacher, and in later days
Brahms would often say that he had never met such an admirable

master. Of course even he could offer Brahms no more than the ordinary piano exercises current at the time, the range of which was limited, in the main, by the names of Czerny, Clementi, Cramer, Kalkbrenner, and Hummel — as is still the case even nowadays in this modern age of mass-training at musical colleges. But he would now and then let him try his hand at a piece by Johann Sebastian Bach and has the decided merit of having initiated his young pupil into the great world of piano music from the beginning. This cannot have happened without a certain preliminary struggle with Father Brahms, for in his eyes the piano was an "unnecessary" instrument, since much better money was to be earned by the horn, 'cello, and violin. But Cossel must also be credited with a far more important service: he protected little Brahms from any premature exploitation as a child prodigy. At the age of ten the boy played a study by Herz, among other pieces, at a subscription concert to which the great public was not admitted. A concert agent heard him and at once wanted to book the boy and Father Brahms for a concert tour in America. The parents almost yielded to the temptation, but Cossel made strong representations through Marxsen, and little Johannes was allowed to stay in Hamburg and go on with his studies quietly and industriously. He was grateful to Cossel for this all his life.

It is the impressions, developments, and events of childhood which play the most decisive part in determining the course of a man's life. In the case of Brahms two marked characteristics of his achievement as a man and artist had already come into strong prominence during his childhood and adolescence: namely, a pure deep love of nature as the eternal fount of all sound human and artistic endeavour; and an overmastering bent towards knowledge and culture.

The mighty symphony of labour with which the harbours of Hamburg resounded even at that time, the cathedral aisles of beeches in the Sachsenwald, the little romantic "piece of Italy" along the lower Elbe, Blankenese with the Süllberg, the pleasant idyllic scenes of the Alstertal, the mighty Elbe with its protecting dikes, the cherry-orchards of Stade in blossom time — what an effect all these great beauties in near or more remote proximity to the proud old Hanse town must have produced upon the deep and receptive spirit of the young musician! And then his native city itself, with its skies usually melancholy and heavy with clouds, and its frequent rain and fog. In the letters which he wrote to the *Ostdeutscher Post* during his travels in 1853, Hebbel has traced in a few sentences a wonderfully vivid picture of old Hamburg, which is still true of it today; and since it was there that Brahms wandered as a child, a boy, and a young man, they may well be quoted here. " Hamburg," he says, " is and remains one of the most interesting cities in Germany! Outwardly, surprising as this may sound, it simply reminds one of Venice. On a lovely summer evening the Alster, with its brightly lighted boats, from which float sounds of singing and music, is really not very inferior to the Riva or the Grand Canal. Those who can compare the two from their own observation will be amazed at the resemblance. But the Altstadt, too, huddled together and gloomy in mediæval fashion, also offers certain features which might have been brought straight from Venice. One need only stand by one of the dark-green canals which glide through it with intricate windings, and then ask oneself the question. To left and right, piles are driven into the canal, which once, perhaps, grew up as proud oaks in a forest in Schleswig-Holstein and now humbly support the Hamburg warehouses; here and there a bridge spans the canals, and over the mirror-like water — or, rather, swamp — the heavily laden lighters float slowly on their way to their destination at some wharf. It is true that a more or less broad street always runs alongside of them, but even in Venice he who has neither the desire nor the money to sit in a gondola may go on foot. Essentially, however, the old Hanse town has not the slightest affinity with the former queen of the seas, and that is what enhances the oddity of the impression; the alembic is the same, but how different is the resultant compound! "

There were times when, like every true Hamburger, little Johannes could not be torn from the harbour, and like all true

Germans, as well as Hamburg boys, at the age when their feeling for nature and love of adventure are developing, he also read that classic, Campe's *Robinson Crusoe*. But this feeling for nature only affected his inner self. During his whole life Brahms never felt drawn towards "representing" the phases and phenomena of nature in the modern impressionist sense, by characterizing them in sound or painting them in tone-colour. His art was always enriched by nature and grew out of nature in the sense that man's soul and mind are ennobled and enriched by it. The port of Hamburg drove his brother Fritz out westward across the ocean, but Johannes was drawn ever more towards the south, farther and farther away from the sea.

The longing for knowledge and culture awoke in little Johannes equally early. Even as a young lad he was far from content with what school could offer him. He steeped himself in the proud history of his native city and at an early age became acquainted with Johann Mattheson, that biting musical ironist, a critic as vain as he was remarkable, reading about his "duel" with young Handel, and the early Hamburg operas by him and Keiser; while equally early he took a liking to Johann Sebastian Bach's most meritorious son, Philipp Emanuel, "the Hamburg Bach," a notable composer of piano sonatas, who wrote that classic the *Versuch über die wahre Art, das Klavier zu Spielen* (*Inquiry into the Right Method of Piano-playing*). He acquired a respectful reverence, if no more, for Gotthold Ephraim Lessing, author of *Emilia Galotti* and *Minna von Barnhelm* and of the *Hamburgische Dramaturgie,* with its acute criticism; and he loved to pass by the house where Felix Mendelssohn-Bartholdy was born. During early years spent in Hamburg he also acquired the taste — perhaps inherited from his grandfather — which in later years made him a book-lover and collector of literary curiosities. His precociously ardent longing for culture and knowledge made him frequent every antique bookseller and second-hand dealer, as well as those itinerant venders of books such as still haunt the streets, bridges, and squares in that part of the Altstadt, especially the Gänsemarkt, with the Dutch barrows which are such a typical sight in Hamburg. Thus even during these early years he laid the foundations of that wide reading which embraced a more extensive sphere than that of mere music, including more especially literature and art, and of an already imposing library, which betrayed what a passionate collector he was to become in future — at that time, we regret to say, quite a rare thing for a German musician. Books, too, were Brahms's favourite present to his friends of both sexes, and those unaware of his book-loving propensities must indeed be amazed at the taste and sure judgment which, for instance, at the age of twenty, made him select Eichendorff's *Taugenichts* and Bernardin de St. Pierre's *Paul et Virginie* as a birthday present for little Maria Schumann.

Cossel must soon have recognized, however reluctantly, the exceptional creative genius of his young pupil. Though he could train him to become a pianist, for the future composer a more important master of the art was needed. And this could be none other than Eduard Marxsen (1806–87). Together with Friedrich Wilhelm Grund, the founder of the Hamburg Singakademie and for years conductor of the Hamburg Philharmonic concerts, Marxsen was the most important musical personality of a Hamburg which had outgrown the musical Philistinism of the thirties and forties. Marxsen too had had to fight a hard fight for music's sake. Born in the picturesque little town of Nienstedten, on the north bank of the Elbe between Altona and Blankenese, and the son of an organist, who was the first to teach him music, young Marxsen had been intended for the ministry; it was not till he was eighteen that he abandoned theology for music, and then for years on end he had to tramp to and fro on the long road between Hamburg and Nienstedten in order to pursue his musical studies under Johann Heinrich Clasing (who composed oratorios, choral works, and operas, and organized the first great musical festivals in North Germany), subsequently completing them in 1830 under Seyfried and Bocklet in Vienna. He next settled down in Altona as a composer and music-teacher of the solid old Viennese school of piano-playing and succeeded in making a success of this too, thanks to his dogged, Low German, conscientious endurance. Nowadays we are perhaps inclined to lay the chief stress upon the admirable training of Brahms's character, his lofty and austere striving after the great in art, his unflagging energy and self-reliance in pursuing the aim of his life, his spirited enterprise in making his way out of the narrow musical conditions of his home; and we must add that this splendid man and artist must have been just the right master for the rising young composer. For in him, too, the same struggle towards the light was repeated in a somewhat different form, but starting from the same social conditions. Hence it was of the highest importance and greatest value that the young lad's mentor should have been a man of such sound moral principles as Marxsen, nurtured in the eternal classical ideals, who had experienced and surmounted the same hardships and privations in life and so grown to ripe maturity as man and artist, combining character, intellect, and culture with the most thorough technical equipment. But Marxsen was not only an excellent man; he was also an admirable artist, with great erudition and a thorough mastery of his profession, whose works had attracted the notice and recognition of the best authorities of his day and, indeed, were not wanting in a tinge of genius which was in advance of his time, at any rate in the choice and working-out of his poetic and intellectual ideas. Marxsen wrote some seventy works: among them were some in the greater forms — symphonies and overtures, sonatas and variations; there were also some excellent arrangements and adaptations. He had a great veneration for Beethoven, of which he gave practical proof by a considerable foundation at the Vienna Conservatoire. But none of his works made such a sensation in his own day as his orchestral arrangement of Beethoven's Kreutzer Sonata, of which he gave a performance in Hamburg in 1835, and the great orchestral composition *Aux manes de Beethoven,* which is scored with a splendour of instrumentation worthy of a Berlioz. Ritter von Seyfried alluded to it in the *Neue Zeitschrift für Musik* as "a moving dirge on the loss of the immortal singer, as brilliant in its conception as in its execution." His piano music paid decided homage to the fashionable ideals of the thirties by all kinds of "Hommages," as they were called, dedicated, among others, to Hummel, Dreyschock, Jenny Lind, and Clara Schumann. Marxsen, with Kalkbrenner, was one of the first to enrich this curious and sensational, rather than necessary department of piano music with studies and short pieces, some of which, indeed — for instance the Three Impromptus (op. 33) — attracted the notice of Robert Schumann, though, owing to his dislike on principle for all unnecessary "one-hand" work in piano-playing, they did not meet with his approval. However that may be, Marxsen's piano-pieces for the left hand are excellent and ingenious, repaying study as regards both form and content, and are based upon the same foundations as the rest of his music: namely, the classical, late classical, and early Romantic work of Beethoven, Hummel, Kalkbrenner, and Spohr. When Marxsen is paying a tribute to the memory of great men, or mournfully brooding over the destinies of nations — for he was an ardently patriotic Schleswig-Holsteiner — the musical idiom in which he prefers to express himself is that of Spohr, embellished with chromatic figures and descriptive passages in the romantic style. An instance of this is to be found in the *Trauerklängen Schleswig-Holsteins* (*Schleswig-Holstein's Knell*), after the luckless defeat by the Danes at the battle of Idstedt, the subject of which is borrowed from a poem of Zeise, and which is dedicated to his fatherland in the narrower sense of the word.

Young Brahms was ten years old when he came under Marxsen's care. Cossel himself took him to the master with cheerful, unselfish self-sacrifice, and Father Brahms made successful representations to him in favour of his "Hannes." Let us hear the account of Brahms's arrival and studies given by the excellent man in later years to La Mara, the Leipzig authoress of the *Musikalische Studienköpfe:* "In the year 1843 my pupil Cossel — an excellent teacher for technique, and as such greatly esteemed and beloved — brought me the ten-year-old boy (who was at that time attending the ordinary popular school, which he continued to do up to the time of his early confirmation), so that I might test whether he really possessed musical aptitudes. He played me a few studies from Cramer's first volume thoroughly well. Cossel praised his diligence and wanted me to give him lessons if I saw ability in him. At first I refused, for the instruction which he had hitherto received was most competent and would be sufficient for some time to come. A few months later the boy's father came to me to repeat the request in his own and Cossel's name; whereupon I so far consented as to agree to devote an hour a week to the boy, on condition that he was to continue his lessons with Cossel as usual. And so things happened; but less than a year later, Cossel pressed me to undertake the boy's entire instruction from that time onwards, for he was making such progress that Cossel could not trust himself to criticize him in any way. His progress was indeed remarkable, but not such as to give evidence of exceptional talent, only of the results of great industry and unremitting zeal. Accordingly, from that time onwards I undertook his whole instruction, and that gladly, for two reasons: on the one hand, because I had already taken a liking to the boy, and on the other, out of consideration for his parents, who were unable to make any sacrifices to continue his education. His studies in the practical side of playing made excellent progress, and his talent became more and more evident. But later on, when I started teaching him composition, he exhibited a rare acuteness of mind which enchanted me, and, insignificant though his first attempts at original creation turned out to be, I was bound to recognize in them an intelligence which convinced me that an exceptional, great, and peculiarly profound talent was dormant in him. I therefore shrank from no effort or work in order to awaken and form it, that I might one day rear a priest of art, who should preach in new accents what was sublime, true, and eternally incorruptible in art, and that by acts as well as words."

It was this firm and lofty faith, too, that later led old Marxsen to say, on hearing the news of Mendelssohn's death: "A great master of the musical art has gone hence, but an even greater one will bloom for us in Brahms."

He had already had astonishing experiences with the boy, as

he once related to Claus Groth: "On one occasion I had given him a piano work of C. M. von Weber to study and had gone through it with him in detail; when he came back the next week, he played me the sonata so faultlessly and so perfectly in accordance with my intentions that I praised him for it. He then said: 'I have also practised it in accordance with another interpretation,' and played it to me in such a way as to bring out the melody in the lower part."

Marxsen's idealistic attitude towards life and art had an influence on Brahms's development which cannot be rated too highly. Thanks to the example of his master, Brahms was from the first won over to the moral in music, and the classical in art. His earliest compositions already show this with the utmost clearness. The main lines of his character as a man and an artist were already laid down in the years that he spent as a pupil under Marxsen's training. The fact that Marxsen initiated him into Bach, Beethoven, Weber, etc., as early as possible confirmed this. It was quite an exceptional thing at that Philistine period of uninspired virtuosity, when the foremost figures both in concert-room and opera-house were such artists as Thalberg, Paganini, Charles Mayer, the Herzes and Hüntens, Kalkbrenner, Döhler, and Rosenhain. Bach, Beethoven, and the classic masters of Vienna were not then the first and last word in the curriculum of a young artist thirsting for knowledge, as they are in these modern days of mass instruction in musical colleges. In later days Brahms certainly discerned more and more clearly what a decisive bend this capable and modest master gave to his art, which was in the noblest sense "post-classical." The fact that he dedicated his Second Piano Concerto, in B flat major, one of his greatest and most characteristic works, to Eduard Marxsen, "my faithful friend and master," and that it was he who prompted Simrock to print and publish, without his knowledge, Marxsen's *Hundred Variations on a Folk-song* — an attempt to combine in one piece all the different varieties of touch and rhythm — show that throughout his whole life he was bound to his old master by the same cordial and grateful affection.

And he had reason enough for this, for eternal credit is due to Marxsen for having been a strict and capable, but never a reactionary or pedantic musical pedagogue to him. Brought up in the classical ideals of the post-classical school of Vienna, less in sympathy with Schubert, and hardly at all with the romantic masters Schumann and Chopin, he was, owing to his tolerance, the right — indeed, the predestined — teacher for a great talent pointing the way towards the future. He hated all attempts at "levelling" artistic genius, or imposing any constraint upon it, and allowed a great talent like that of Brahms, with its strongly original stamp, to develop, not indeed lawlessly and regardless of rule, but freely and unhampered by the letter of the law and dry theoretical precepts. And he had yet another gift to bestow upon his young and brilliantly gifted pupil by his teaching: namely, a respect for the austere North German conception of art as applied to music, a conception concerned with form rather than colour, contrapuntal and polyphonic rather than homo phonic. If we now call Brahms the greatest of the classicists, the most important post-classical composer in the history of nineteenth-century music, by so doing we are involuntarily recognizing that art (*Kunst*) is based upon "cunning" in the old English sense of the word (that is, trained skill), and that it is this quality which appears to us to find its purest and most perfect expression in the works of the great pre-classic and classical masters. It was Eduard Marxsen who laid the immutably firm foundations of this conception of life and art in young Brahms, and we must never forget to give credit for this to that excellent artist, whose outlook upon life was quite as gentle, sentimental, and sleek as that of any Philistine of his day.

Even during these days when he was being taught by Marxsen, Brahms was faced with the daily anxieties of earning a livelihood. Towards the end of his life he confessed this in the following terms: "See now, I have given lessons ever since I was twelve years old, and you will certainly believe me when I say that such a young lad was hardly likely to have pupils entrusted to him who could give him any particular pleasure. And yet I stood it all well enough; indeed, I would not on any account have missed this period of hardship in my life, for I am convinced that it did me good and was necessary to my development." But, as Gustav Frenssen said of Jörn Uhl, our young pupil and teacher always found " those who helped him " in his day of need. When he was fourteen years old, Adolf Giesemann, a friend of his father's who owned a paper-mill, invited him to his house in the country at Winsen on the Luhe in the Lüneburger Heide, between Hamburg and Lüneburg, so that he could get a good " breath of air." In return for this he was to give piano lessons to Giesemann's little daughter Lieschen. But here too Johannes's recreation took a different form from that of other people: he acted as conductor to the Winsen male-voice choir, composed it some choruses for men's voices, continued his studies diligently, and paid a weekly visit to Marxsen at Altona for his lessons.

Young Brahms made his first public appearance as a pianist. His debut, as we have seen, took place, also as a pianist, at the age of ten, when he was a pupil of Cossel. " Brahms gave the first concert arranged by himself," wrote Marxsen, again to La Mara, " at the age of fourteen. Besides works of Bach, Beethoven, and Mendelssohn the program also included a number composed by himself: some charming variations on a folk-theme, one of which consisted of a most successfully worked-out canon."

A hopeless confusion prevails with regard to what Brahms played at the two concerts which he gave on his own account in Herr Honnef's hall (the " Alter Rabe ") by the Dammtor on September 21, 1848 and April 14, 1849, and what he played at others at which he assisted, as we again learn from Marxsen, " partly by solos, partly by accompanying songs." This much at least is certain, that amid a dead level of trivialities and elegant, fashionable concert-music — as represented, for instance, by fantasias on operatic airs by Thalberg and Döhler, and studies by Herz and Mayer for the piano, or by the airs and variations of Donizetti, Mollenhauer, and others, for the voice, horn, and flute — young Brahms had the courage to introduce a couple of works rising like lonely and " inacessible (*unzugänglich*) " rocks above the stagnant waters: a fugue by Johann Sebastian Bach and Beethoven's Waldstein Sonata. Nor did he forget his old teacher Marxsen, whose Serenade for the left hand was included in the program. At first he even continued to pay tribute to the taste of the day in his own compositions, by a fantasia for pianoforte on a popular waltz-air, which was given an honourable reception as evidence of " unusual talent." We need not over-estimate the small attempts that he made to break away from the musical fashions of the day, and should ascribe them in great part to Marxsen's initiative; but they do already to a certain extent bear clear witness to an early departure on Brahms's part from the dead-level taste of the period.

"During the last few years before he left Hamburg," as we once more learn from Marxsen's communications to La Mara, " he did not appear in public, for his time seemed to me too precious, as interludes of this kind often upset a man's studies very considerably. At any rate, the press always spoke of these first attempts with great appreciation."

All the more eagerly must young Brahms have taken part in the animated musical life of Hamburg in the forties, through Marxsen's agency, as a young and enthusiastic listener. Friedrich Wilhelm Grund (1791–1874), the leading Hamburg musician of the Philistine period before Marxsen, and during his life, conducted the choral concerts of the Singakademie, which he had founded, and the orchestral concerts of the Philharmonic Society; Karl Voigt was director of the Cäcilienverein, founded by him in 1843; Otten conducted the orchestral concerts of the Musikalische Gesellschaft, which he had called into being in the same year. From 1843 onwards the Good Friday concerts at the Stadttheater won a great reputation. Hector Berlioz conducted there on his great concert tour through Germany, his *Requiem* being performed under his conductorship on a second visit in the same year. Chamber-music found zealous exponents at the evening concerts of quartets and trios given by Haffner, Goldschmidt, and von Königslöw. Famous artists came and went: Liszt, Thalberg, Dreyschock, and Litolff, among pianists; Ernst, David,

Joachim, Vieuxtemps, and Ole Bull, the " Norwegian Paganini," among violinists; Jenny Lind, the " Swedish Nightingale," and Sontag, among singers; and many others.

In spite of favourable criticisms, Brahms's first Hamburg concerts could not expect more than a passing success. The reasons for this must be sought, on the one hand, in the political upheaval caused by the Revolution of 1848, which diverted the attention of most people from artistic matters; and, on the other hand, in Brahms's own musical idiosyncrasies and his attitude towards the musical taste and type of program current in his day. At these first concerts given on his own account he had, indeed, to do homage to the taste of the age, which tended towards superficial " tunyness," sentimental gush, " *pluies de perles*," and the fireworks of virtuosi, but he already perceived plainly that his genius and the bent of his creative faculty forbade any repetition of these concessions wrung from him by necessity: after this Brahms but rarely gave concerts of his own.

And so for yet a little longer his material and artistic drudgery continued. Brahms gave piano lessons at a mark each, played at dances, played *entr'actes* behind the scenes at the Stadttheater, or accompanied the virtuosi on the platform. He toiled at transcriptions and arrangements for publishers, signing the arrangements " G. W. Marks," and his own free compositions " Karl Würth." In the midst of all this he still found time to continue his own education by unwearying study, composing not only some hundred and fifty fantasias on waltz-airs in the style of the one which he had played with success at his own concert in 1849, but also all kinds of serious works; for instance a duet for 'cello and piano, and a piano trio which was performed on July 5, 1851 at a private concert given to celebrate the silver wedding of the Schröders! And now, during these youthful days, came the powerful musical stimulus of what we may describe, in the words used by Brahms himself to Joachim, as a " very chaos of emotion (*recht chaotisches Schwärmen*) " which the visit of that great artist to Hamburg set up in the young man. It is significant that even at this time the classical had a powerful attraction for him, while the romantic, as represented in its greatest master, repelled him at the outset. His deepest musical impression was the performance of Beethoven's violin concerto by young Joseph Joachim, at which Brahms was present, as "certainly the most enthusiastic listener," at a Philharmonic concert on March 11, 1848; while he was first made to feel the stinging pain of a slight — unintentional, it is true — by Robert Schumann, the romantic composer whom he revered so deeply in later days, who had the rising young composer's manuscript, which had been sent him at his hotel, returned unopened.

Brahms had spent a childhood and youth whose hardships and painful difficulties had been made tolerable to him only by the devoted love of his parents. Yet, as Albert Dietrich said later when Brahms was twenty years old, "in this school he had learnt much and gained in strength of character." " Few can have had so hard a time as I," Brahms said in Vienna when he was fifty years old to his only personal pupil, Gustav Jenner. At this time it almost seemed as though Brahms's life, like that of young Hebbel, was to remain stranded like a boat on the mud-flats of sordid want. Then came the year 1849, and with it a totally unexpected rescuer, who was quite a stranger to him.

III

THE FIRST CONCERT TOUR

In the year 1849 some political refugees and other persons involved in the Hungarian revolution appeared in Hamburg, and among them the Hungarian violinist of Jewish extraction Eduard Reményi (Hoffmann). The ground was well prepared for him. At that time there were detachments of Hungarian regiments stationed at Altona, in readiness to take part in the attack on Denmark, and Reményi may have been on good terms with some of the officers. He gave it out that he was going to America; but the Hamburgers took so much interest in this young political martyr, this temperamental son of the *puszta,* that they crowded to his "farewell concert," at which, with young Brahms at the piano, he electrified everybody by his "imaginative rendering of his national dances." The box-office receipts were so splendid that Reményi let America alone for the time being and resolved to cultivate the productive soil of Hamburg more intensively. And so he remained in Hamburg after the departure of his fellow-countrymen, till 1851 — when he does seem to have spent a year on the other side of the Atlantic, returning to Hamburg in the winter of 1852-3 by way of Paris. A second concert met with the same extraordinary success as the first. Young Brahms was dazzled by the romance of Reményi's roving, gipsy-like artist's life and offered himself as his accompanist. Reményi, who had at once recognized his extraordinary talent, accepted, and engaged him for an improvised concert-tour through Hanover (Winsen, Lüneburg, Celle), after which he intended to take him to Joseph Joachim, whose acquaintance he had made at the Vienna Conservatoire. On April 19 they started out on their tour; the three concerts, at which the program was the same (including Beethoven's Violin Sonata, op. 30, in C minor), swelled to seven, always marked by the same struggles with abominable grand pianos and pianos appallingly out of tune. " Brahms's memory," to quote a letter from Marxsen to La Mara, " is so amazing that it never occurred to him to take any music with him on his concert tours. When he started out into the world on his first tour, as a young man of twenty, the works of Beethoven and Bach, besides a large number of modern concert-pieces by Thalberg, Liszt, Mendelssohn, and others, were indelibly impressed upon his mind." Proof of this vast memory and rare presence of mind, which were also vouched for in after years by his astonished friends at Zürich, was already forthcoming at Celle, for there, as La Mara tells us, he had to transpose the above-mentioned C minor Sonata into C sharp minor "from memory," thanks to the fact that the piano was tuned to the wrong pitch, a little preliminary exercise for the tour de force that, according to Dr. Schubring's account in the *Allgemeine musikalische Zeitung* for 1868, he accomplished at Göttingen with Joachim, when, owing to the low pitch of the piano, he transposed Beethoven's Kreutzer Sonata from A to A sharp. In other respects, too, this first concert tour was most romantic; a moonlight serenade which our Johannes gave to a noble lady with an enthusiasm for music, at Hildesheim, assisted by Reményi, who improvised a violin fantasia on themes from *I Puritani,* and a few students, had as its result a brilliant audience at the second concert, and was, if not pure Spitzweg, at any rate " pure Eichendorff."

In his book *Die Zigeuner* (*The Gipsies*) Franz Liszt celebrates the memory of the Hungarian violinist Eduard Reményi, who was one of the most brilliant virtuosi of his native land. He had studied at the Vienna Conservatoire and, during the years immediately preceding his meeting with Brahms, had developed into a fine violinist, and he was now, at the age of twenty-three, at the height of his fame as a virtuoso. His name is closely bound up with Liszt's life and struggle for recognition as a composer, which Liszt acknowledged by dedicating to him the violin solo in the *Benedictus* of his Coronation Mass. Liszt also assisted him

in his political and artistic struggles during his whole life, with
all the disinterested kindliness of a great and noble heart, and a
trust that was in no wise diminished by disappointment in
Reményi's unstable character. He found that artist a good position as solo violinist in the royal orchestra and as court violinist
to Queen Victoria in London. In the year 1875 Reményi next
settled in Paris, from whence he started out on his great tours
all over the world, on one of which he died, at San Francisco,
California, in 1898.

To Reményi is due the credit for having brought about the
first meeting between Joachim and Brahms, in Hanover, thus
laying the foundations not only of a deep and faithful friendship that lasted for life, but also of a close artistic alliance between
two great personalities, both of whom were devoted to the same
classical ideals in art. Joachim had attended Waitz's and Ritter's
lectures in history and philosophy at the University of Göttingen,
but at the age of twenty-two, when Brahms, who was two years
younger, first met him in Hanover, young Joachim was already
a famous artist. This brilliantly gifted young German-Hungarian,
a protégé of Mendelssohn's, had already gone through his artistic
baptism of fire at the Leipzig Gewandhaus and the Crystal Palace,
London, with brilliant success. As conductor of the court orchestra he had been in close relation with Liszt and his circle
at Weimar for a few years, but even at that time he had become
more and more alienated from the neo-German spirit. Since
1853 he had been working as conductor to the royal orchestra at
the noble capital of the art-loving King of Hanover, and was
bound to regard Brahms, quite rightly, as the great coming
prophet and creative artist who was to give life to his own classical
views of art.

Joachim's first meeting with Brahms took place at Joachim's
house in Hanover. The impression produced on him by young
Brahms, both personally and as an artist, was like a revelation.
He was delighted with young Johannes's " nature, of a kind
which could only develop in its full purity in the most secluded
retirement from the world; pure as a diamond, and soft as snow."

As regards Brahms's artistic qualities, Joachim at once discerned in his playing "an intense fire, and what I might almost call a fateful energy and inevitable precision of rhythm which proclaim the predestined artist; while his compositions," Joachim concedes, "already give evidence of remarkable qualities such as I have never yet met with before in any young artist of his age." At the unveiling of the Brahms memorial at Meiningen, on October 7, 1899, Joachim specially referred to the deeply moving impression made upon him on that occasion in Hanover by Brahms's now world-famous " *O versenk' dein Leid, mein Kind* " (*Liebestreu,* from op. 3) in the following terms: " Never in the whole of my artistic career have I been overcome by a more joyful astonishment than when my fellow-countryman's almost shy-looking fair-haired accompanist played, with a noble, uplifted expression, the movements of his sonata, of an originality and power which nobody would have suspected. It affected me like a revelation when I then heard the song ' *O versenk' dein Leid* ' for the first time. Add to this his piano-playing, so tender, so imaginative, so free, and so full of fire, that it held me absolutely spellbound." Besides this and other songs, " Johannes Kreisler, junior " — as he signed himself on the manuscript, after the romantic fashion — submitted to him a sonata for violin, a string quartet, the piano sonatas in C major and F sharp minor, and the E flat minor Scherzo for piano.

Joachim at once saw that some drastic steps must be taken on behalf of his new young friend, so soon as he had parted from the companion with whom he was unequally yoked, in order to obtain due encouragement and recognition for the talent with which he was gifted. He therefore presented him to his sovereign, the art-loving King of Hanover, who commanded him to play at a court concert with Reményi, and nicknamed him " little Beethoven." Above all, he next drew Franz Liszt's attention to him, and also held earnest consultations with Brahms as to the order in which his first works were to be published.

Brahms spent a few more days full of artistic delights in Hanover with his celebrated new friend, and was hardly aware of the gathering storm-clouds which threatened himself and Reményi: Wermuth, the Chief of Police, scented the demagogical mischief that might arise from the presence of the wild Hungarian, and tried to remove him beyond the frontier to Bückeburg with all possible speed, together with his young German accompanist. It was only thanks to the good offices of Heinrich Ehrlich, the pianist and music-teacher, who was living in Hanover at the time, that the order was cancelled, and they were able to pursue their way to Weimar, the court of the Muses, without hindrance.

Reményi was of decided importance to Brahms as a composer. He must early have directed his young North German partner's attention towards Hungarian folk-music, and thus probably implanted in his mind the first germ and the first impulse which resulted in his later pianoforte settings of Hungarian dances, and in many of the fiery finales of his chamber-music compositions with a Magyar tinge.

IV

WEIMAR

The visit of Brahms and Reményi to the Altenburg at Weimar lasted for six weeks. Though Brahms was no longer a young Parsifal who would be in danger, both to his body and to his soul, in such a distracting garden of lovely flower-maidens — by which I mean the key-thumping or key-stroking pupils of Liszt, that wizard Klingsor among musicians — his unflinching honesty with himself and the severe criticism to which he was in the habit of subjecting himself and his works from youth upwards — enabling him to meet even such enchanting visions as these with the cool, practical caution of a Low German — made him feel that his further stay there would become impossible sooner or later, and that both his personal and his artistic relations with Liszt and the " neo-German music of the future " were bound in time to reach breaking-point. This would be due to his artistic ideals and convictions, which were becoming more and more firmly established during these years of youthful " storm and stress," with their ferment of development.

For a time, indeed, the break was made difficult for him. Liszt received the young Hamburger, who was lodged in the house of the Princess Wittgenstein, with all the magnanimous eagerness to be of service, the humane and artistic sympathy and easily kindled enthusiasm, which he and he alone has ever been capable of displaying with such overflowing cordiality and kindliness, up to our own day, when art has become so commercial, self-seeking, and vain. Liszt sat down at the grand piano and played the great E flat Scherzo, op. 4, from a most illegible manuscript at sight, with dazzling precision and complete mastery of a musical idiom which was already thoroughly personal, novel, and intractable, and he was so delighted that he repeated it twice. It

was followed by the first and second piano sonatas in C major
(op. 1) and F sharp minor (op. 2) and a sonata for violin and
piano which is now lost. He was frankly enthusiastic! At first
sight this seems surprising; but it becomes quite credible if we remember the precise character of these youthful works of Brahms.
In them, if anywhere, it is possible to speak of a certain " storm
and stress " in the young Brahms indicative of genius. The E flat
minor Scherzo, like the C major and F sharp minor sonatas, is a
genuinely youthful work, eminently romantic and full of turmoil
and vehemence. In true romantic fashion, a flood of richly varied
and animated fancy bursts all the dams and dikes of form; the
wealth of pictures and images from saga, legend, and history in
the sonatas, the wild and tangled humour of the Scherzo, rough
and uncouth, approximating both to Schumann and to E. T. A.
Hoffmann, the rugged, healthy, and concentrated strength which
found expression in them both, and, according to Schumann,
promised a new young " Beethovener " — all this was bound to
appeal to Liszt's most deeply rooted tendencies. After these first
essays he expected to see a wonderfully gifted young man
grow up to maturity in his own intellectual and artistic ideals,
free in both content and form, fantastic, neo-romantic and " neo-
German " — indeed, he thought he had already found him. He
kindly took pains to have Brahms soon received as an acquaintance and friend by his own faithful followers.

Brahms seems to have become especially intimate with that
splendid fellow " Peterl," the poet-composer Peter Cornelius, who
enriched the German people with the pensive Christmas Songs
(Weihnachtslieder) and Bridal Songs (Brautlieder); and with
Joachim Raff, who was forced by necessity to become so versatile
and eclectic, and, like Joseph Rheinberger, was so affectionately
overrated by Hans von Bülow. They can scarcely have afforded
him much stimulus or opportunity for clarifying and developing
his own genius. They were too different, and, with the exception
of Cornelius, too much of " mere musicians " — too much of their
own generation, both as men and as artists, to have discovered
bonds of common intellectual interest, which, in any case, were not

strong at that time. So that Raff, like a true "musician" and hunter for "reminiscences," at once discovered that the form and scheme of the E flat minor Scherzo displayed considerable points of resemblance with those of the great Chopin scherzos for piano, which Brahms could only counter by the assurance that he was totally unacquainted with the Polish master's scherzos. This was quite true, for as late as November 1853 Albert Dietrich wrote from Düsseldorf to Ernst Naumann at Leipzig: "The most wonderful thing about Brahms is that, living in complete isolation at Hamburg, he knew nothing until lately of Schumann, Chopin, and others, and yet the ground trodden by these modern writers is quite his own native soil; indeed, compositions of his early childhood already rise to quite exalted heights."

Meanwhile Liszt was becoming more and more familiar with these early poetical piano-works, so full of grandeur and genius in their tendency towards the ultra-romantic and fantastic, recalling Schumann and Hoffmann, with their care-free, youthful freshness, closely related in character to the free style of Beethoven's latest piano sonatas, and rich in truly dæmonic traits; and, as was his ungrudging, unselfish way, he was not backward in praising them in the highest terms to his friends. Bülow received an enthusiastic letter about the C major Sonata.

Yet, in spite of all, the same thing happened to Brahms at the Altenburg at Weimar as to my father and so many other artists, in whom personal acquaintance with the weaknesses in Liszt's creative work caused doubts and hesitation with regard to his neo-German ideals, especially when, as with these men, a classical training in music was added. As a pianist, indeed, Brahms was enchanted by Liszt's "incomparable piano-playing," but as a composer he soon felt that his own efforts tended towards a different goal from that of Liszt and the neo-Germans; and his inexorable self-criticism, his already settled character, his acute artistic discrimination and superior intelligence soon left him no doubt on this head. Besides, the slight touch of rhetoric and pose, the whole worldly and artificial atmosphere of Weimar court life and of the artistic coterie surrounding Liszt, the flattering and often hypocritical and servile apotheosis of the master, may have been antipathetic to this simple, straightforward North German, who was capable of illusions about everything save himself and others.

And now Brahms began to lose personal touch with Liszt as well. Liszt's consummate and well-bred courtesy naturally prevented an open breach. But he was far too accustomed to being flattered and spoilt by everybody not to perceive at once that his reliance upon the unqualified adherence of his young protégé had been misplaced. Their relations became cool and formal; the faint sparks of personal sympathy and artistic esteem which still glowed beneath the ashes of Liszt's buried hopes of Brahms were afterwards extinguished by the latter's own act in signing the unfortunate manifesto against the neo-Germans. Brahms saw that his stay at the Altenburg could hardly be prolonged any further, and about a fortnight later he disappeared unobtrusively from Weimar.

V

SCHUMANN'S ARTICLE: *"NEUE BAHNEN"*

For the time being, Reményi stayed on with his master at Weimar. His name only makes one more appearance in this book, in the second part, devoted to Brahms's works, and this time, unfortunately, not in the most pleasant way. When Brahms published the two volumes containing his masterly Hungarian Dances "arranged (*gesetzt*) " for piano duet, it was actually Reményi and Kéler-Béla (Albrecht Keller) who accused him of an act of musical piracy, instead of being grateful to him for winning the composers of the dances certain immortality by his version of them.

Brahms received a cordial invitation to Göttingen for the summer from Joachim, who, true to his motto, " Free, but alone (*Frei, aber einsam*)," was enduring the boredom of Hanover; and he responded to the summons. Here he spent two months of joyous " student life." They played chamber-music at the house of Wehner, the musical director, attended lectures, arranged a students' concert, and caroused manfully with the *" Sachsen"* (students' clubs); and Brahms joined untiringly in the splendid students' songs, some of which he noted down and treasured up for the musical tribute which he was afterwards to offer to German student life: the *Akademische Festouvertüre*. The faithful Low German made many valuable friendships during this and the other summers which he afterwards spent at Göttingen. In 1864, for instance, he made the acquaintance, through Grimm, of Philipp Spitta, then a young student, and is said to have advised him to confine himself entirely to the study of musical history. Spitta followed his advice and became one of the most erudite of German writers on music; it is he and his great colleagues Hermann Kretzschmar and Hugo Riemann who have made some of the most important, acute, and profound observations on Brahms.

Moved, perhaps, by the love of travel and change which possessed him throughout his whole life, perhaps by a delight in grand, or at any rate romantic, natural scenes, the young composer at last tore himself away from Göttingen, and, by Joachim's advice, paid a visit to the Rhine. But the shrewd Joachim took longer and more far-reaching views than this; it was important to keep this young man of the highest promise, who was now forewarned and forearmed against all the siren voices of neo-Germanism, true to the classical ideals of music by bringing him into touch with the greatest " *Beethovener* " among the Romantics, Robert Schumann and his circle.

The wonderful, soft, romantic poetry of the Rhine seems, indeed, to have produced quite a different effect upon the serious young North German from that which it produced, for instance, upon Eichendorff as a young man; but it certainly made him quite as contented and happy and produced in him a lighter and more cheerful mood. At any rate, in the freshness of his youth, he was not so " incapable of enjoyment and subject to ill humour " as his great fellow-countryman Hebbel in his mature years, to whom the glories of the Rhine were not revealed till 1857, near the end of his life, during a great tour which he made of the whole of Germany. Brahms stayed in the hospitable house of the musical Deichmann family at Mehlem, near Bonn, wandered up the Rhine and the valleys of its loveliest tributaries, the Ahr and the Lahn, with their three young sons, and could not write enthusiastically enough to Joachim about his " heavenly visit," and those " splendid people " the Deichmanns, so irrepressible were his delight in and instinctive appreciation of the comfortable security of a highly cultivated home after his roving and often bohemian professional travels. He soon made the acquaintance of Franz Wüllner, the 'cellist Reimers, and the " delightful " Herr Wilhelm Joseph von Wasielewski, Schumann's biographer, who was afterwards, unfortunately, to become so strangely susceptible to reactionary and narrow-minded prejudices against the beloved master of his choice. Wasielewski, who was then almost thirty, must have shown Brahms so much about Schumann's music that he came to regard a visit to Schumann, not only as a duty that could not be omitted, but also as a welcome necessity. Up to that time he would hardly have been quite ready for it. In the first place, Marxsen's classicism and Schumann's romanticism were two conceptions that were hardly compatible in his eyes; besides, though it was certainly unintentional, he had not yet forgotten the severe disappointment and slight which he had suffered when Schumann sent back his composition unopened owing to press of work during his visit to Hamburg. Moreover, his own wish was to go to Leipzig, so as to obtain as much work there as possible, and then spend a quiet, busy winter at Hanover doing it. But the delight and enthusiasm of his new circle of friends on the Rhine at his compositions — which were those that had won him Joachim's friendship: namely, the first and second piano sonatas, the Scherzo, op. 4, and the songs, op. 3 — and Wasielewski's urgent representations finally overcame his hesitation and decided him to present Joachim's introduction to Schumann at Düsseldorf in person.

On September 30 of this fateful year, 1853, the young Hamburger paid his first visit to Schumann at Düsseldorf, thus becoming acquainted with one of the loveliest German garden-cities of the lower Rhine, whose fame as a leading centre of German literature, art, and music is for ever established, thanks to Heine and Immermann, Mendelssohn and Schumann, and the Düsseldorf school of painters, which was then world-famous. Schumann had been living there since the beginning of September 1850, when he had been summoned from Dresden to the lower Rhine as municipal conductor and director of music of Düsseldorf. The three years which he had spent at Düsseldorf had produced a terrible psychical change in him; he was increasingly tormented by the premonitory symptoms of that incurable derangement of which his attempted suicide from the Rhine bridge at the end of February 1854 was the first alarming manifestation — these symptoms taking the form of attacks of gloomy melancholy, insomnia, auditory hallucinations, and fits of nervous irritation. He had never been a born conductor, and in the long run he could no longer be depended upon for the discharge of his duties at Düsseldorf. The concert committee, while sparing his feelings as much as possible, had proposed to Schumann that he should allow Herr Tausch to take his place as conductor of the concerts. Clara, with her energetic nature and innate tendency to stand strictly upon her rights, had turned the latent conflict into an open one, and urged her husband to give formal notice of his intended resignation.

This was at the beginning of November 1854 — that is to say, a good year after Brahms's visit. But as early as the summer of 1852 Schumann had felt so ill at ease in his Düsseldorf post that he was seriously entertaining ideas of a move. These had become increasingly fixed upon Vienna. It was in the midst of this anxious, troubled time, and the preparations for a great concert tour in Holland, that young Johannes's visit took place, and, together with his Dutch triumphs, it was the last great joy of Schumann's life. His diary first mentions Brahms on September 30, 1853, in the words: "Herr Brahms from Hamburg." On the next day it notes: "Brahms to see me (a genius)." Then: "Much with Brahms." And finally: "Brahms" every day. The impression produced upon him by Brahms, both as man and as artist, was, as Wasielewski tells us, "absolutely like a spell." He never tired of informing his friends: "One has come from whom we may expect all kinds of wonders. His name is Johannes Brahms." From the first he was enchanted with such a natural, modest, pure, and amiable man. In a letter to Joachim he compares him to a " young eagle, who has descended upon us from the Alps so suddenly and unexpectedly," or to "a splendid river, which, like the Niagara, shows itself at its finest when it rushes roaring from on high with a rainbow playing on its waters, with butterflies fluttering round it on the bank, and accompanied by the song of nightingales "; and he adds with perfect certitude: " This is he who was to come." But he admits to Joachim with equal candour — and this seems to me not unimportant in arriving at a just estimate of his subsequent article on Brahms, "*Neue Bahnen*" — that he is "afraid he is still too much influenced by his personal liking to be able to distinguish clearly between the dark and light feathers of the eagle's pinions." With the sure, lightning instinct of a remarkable creative mind, Schumann recognized that this man would grow up to be one of the elect. As he wrote to Joachim, "Johannes is the true apostle, and he too will write Revelations, the secret of which many Pharisees will still be unable to unravel even centuries later." Johannes had hardly played a few bars on the piano when he interrupted him with the words: "Clara must hear this"; and as she entered the room, he said: "Here, dear Clara, you shall hear music such as you have never heard before. Now begin the piece again, young man." And Kreisler junior continued to play — perhaps indeed, as at his farewell visit on November 2, it was the F minor Sonata, which Schumann liked so much for its dreamy long movement. There is a nice little story to the effect that in his kind-hearted, shy way Schumann placed his purse at the disposal of his young friend, who was not as yet very well provided with money, invited him to their midday meal, and, when he was too shy to appear, had him fetched by Clara, after a long search, from his very modest little inn; and from that moment Brahms became like one of the family at the Schumanns' house.

Weeks of unclouded joy on the Rhine, both personal and artistic, followed for Brahms, who was, in Dietrich's words, "thoroughly happy in the anticipation of better times and in the enjoyment of the splendid, free present." He was introduced to the families of some painters of the Düsseldorf school, to Lessing, Schirmer, Sohn, Gude, etc., to the Eulers and Lesers, and won the most cordial sympathy and admiration everywhere, as much for himself as for his playing. On October 14 Joachim was to come to Düsseldorf for the Musical Festival of the Lower Rhine, and introduce to the public Schumann's *Phantasie*, op. 131, with the composer himself conducting. On this occasion, at Schumann's suggestion, they revived in merry mood the old fashion, which was also characteristic of the Romantics, of the musical pasticcio, or joint composition: Schumann, Albert Dietrich — his noble, enthusiastic, faithful young fellow Saxon, who composed a fine D minor symphony — and young Brahms joined forces in a violin sonata for their mutual friend the famous violinist, the first movement (*allegro,* in A minor) being allotted to Dietrich, the intermezzo (F major) and finale (A minor, ending in A major) to Schumann, and the C minor scherzo, based on a motif of Dietrich's in the first movement, to Brahms. At the end of the performance Joachim, in consultation with Clara Schumann, was to guess the author of each movement, which he managed quite successfully. Of all these Joachim handed over only the scherzo for publication after Brahms's death, keeping back Schumann's contributions, which showed clear traces of his approaching mental derangement, out of pious consideration for his memory. Schumann wrote the title-page, which by another of his romantic fancies bore young Joachim's motto, *Frei aber einsam,* the initials of which, F, A, E, form the principal theme of the sonata, and ended with the words: " In anticipation of the arrival of our revered and beloved friend Joseph Joachim this sonata was written by Robert Schumann, Johannes Brahms, Albert Dietrich."

This wild enthusiasm and unqualified appreciation of an outstanding young talent — perhaps, indeed, as always happens when the heart is concerned, too unqualified if we consider its effect upon the public — by the ageing and deeply suffering Schumann has something unusually touching and endearing about it. None but a noble, warm-hearted man and a great artist would have been capable of shaking off the increasing taciturnity and melancholia which had grown almost into apathy during these years when an inevitable doom was hanging over him, in order to smooth the way for his young protégé by the weight of his name and judgment, and that publicly. The following pronouncement, which he read to his friends on October 13, appeared on October 23, 1853 in the Leipzig *Neue Zeitschrift für Musik,* and bore the title:

"NEW PATHS"

" Years have passed by — almost as many as I spent in editing
these pages in past days: namely, ten — so that I might well have
turned my attention to such a fertile source of reminiscences.
I have often felt impelled to do so, in spite of my own intense
productive activity; many new and remarkable talents have appeared, a new force in music seemed to be foreshadowed, as
many of the artists of recent days bear witness by their high
aspirations, even though their productions are known to quite
a restricted circle. (Note: I have in mind Joseph Joachim, Ernst
Naumann, Ludwig Norman, Woldemar Bargiel, Theodor Kirchner, Julius Schäffer, Albert Dietrich, not to mention that profound
writer of religious music C. F. Wilsing, with his devotion to the
highest art. Niels W. Gade, C. F. Mangold, Robert Franz, and
Stephen Heller should also be mentioned as active heralds of
this new tendency.) As I followed the career of these clever talents
with the greatest interest, I thought that, after such a prelude,
there must and would suddenly appear one whose destiny should
be to express the spirit of our age in the highest and most ideal
fashion, one who should not reveal his mastery by a gradual
development, but spring, like Minerva, fully armed from the head
of Jove. And now he has come, a young creature over whose
cradle the Graces and heroes have kept watch. His name is
Johannes Brahms; he comes from Hamburg, where he has
worked in quiet obscurity, though trained in the most difficult
rules of his art by the enthusiastic solicitude of an admirable
master (Note: Eduard Marxsen of Hamburg), and recently introduced to me by a revered and well-known artist. Even in his
outward appearance he bore all the distinguishing signs which
proclaim him one of the elect. Sitting down to the piano, he
began to open up regions of wonder. We were drawn more and
more into charmed circles. Add to this a technique of absolute
genius, which turned the piano into an orchestra of wailing or
exultant voices. There were sonatas — which were rather veiled
symphonies — songs whose poetry one could have understood

even without knowing the words, though a deep singing melody runs throughout them — some detached piano-pieces, some of a dæmonic nature, though most graceful in form — then sonatas for violin and piano — quartets for stringed instruments — and all so different from one another that each seemed to spring from a different source. And then it seemed as though, rushing onward like a river, he combined them all as though in a water-fall, with the rainbow of peace playing on its downward streaming waters, while butterflies flutter round it on the banks, accompanied by the song of nightingales.

" If he would only point his magic wand to where the might of mass, in chorus and orchestra, lends him its power, yet more wondrous glimpses into the mysteries of the spirit world await us. May the highest genius give him strength for this! And indeed there is every prospect of it, since another genius, that of modesty, also dwells within him. His comrades hail him on his first journey out into the world, where wounds perhaps await him, but laurels and palms besides. We welcome him as a stout fighter.

" Every age is dominated by a secret coalition of kindred spirits. Do ye who are its members draw the circle closer, that the truth of art may shine ever more brightly, spreading joy and blessing on every side.

" R.S."

VI

LEIPZIG

The effect of this weighty proclamation of Schumann's, rendered still more powerful by his previous silence of ten years as a writer on music, was immense. It extended far beyond the professional musical circles for which it was intended, and is still familiar today, even to the non-musical, as Schumann's fine and noble literary testament both as man and as artist. At the same time, however, we should take into consideration the fact that it was the most advanced German musical review of the day that published this article, that in those days a musical paper represented a far greater power, and that its judgments carried far greater weight than today, in the age of our modern newspapers, which daily discover fresh geniuses and trumpet forth their fame by quite other methods. But if the effect was at the same time to produce dissension, by at once ranging musicians and musical amateurs in two opposing camps, for and against Brahms, that is to be explained by the following reasons: Schumann's unique importance and capacity for discrimination in what he wrote about music were far from being as justly appreciated at that time as they are today. It is true that Schumann often went astray, and in the warm-hearted impulsiveness of his artist's nature greatly overrated such talents as those, for instance, of Ries, Hummel, Sterndale Bennett, or Henselt, of whom his contemporaries had rightly formed a decidedly cooler estimate. But his wonderful artistic instinct, his sure flair for character in music, his fine critical sense, developed by wide reading in æsthetic, literature, and philosophy, never betrayed him when, as in the case of Brahms, it was a question of discovering a new and exceptional talent. And so it came about that many musicians — and not bad ones, either; as we said, Bülow was among their number — thought that " we have only to wait quietly; we scent another Bennett case." But further — and this was the most solid reason — the news of Schumann's steadily increasing mental derangement had been slowly spreading everywhere since the beginning of the fifties and naturally deprived his prophecies of much of their weight. Their " morbid exaltation," in the opinion even of that very important musical scholar Wilhelm Ambros, rendered caution and discretion doubly necessary, especially as young Brahms had as yet done nothing which justified proclaiming him as a new musical Messiah. Schumann's oracular pronouncement was a severe blow to the very numerous disciples of Mendelssohn, who had only recently died. How could they, who had already found it hard to tolerate Schumann and had turned their chosen master's lukewarm friendship for him into positive coldness, so soon allow him to impose upon them an heir to their master's throne, who might perhaps — horrid thought! — even put their master in the shade? Never! It was for them to treat him with contempt from the very outset, and, as we shall see below, the Mendelssohn clique at Leipzig took good care to do so. The " neo-Germans " in Liszt's camp were bound to be equally hostile to Schumann's " young eagle"; it had for long been no secret to them that, during his visit to Weimar, young Brahms had paid the tribute of his highest admiration to Liszt as a great pianist, but had shown his dislike for him as a composer in a way which was, moreover, quite unintentionally offensive. This young man who had despised Liszt was now set up in opposition to their master by the " reactionary " camp as a future antipope, and, what was more, accompanied by the provocative rallying-cry of " *Neue Bahnen* (New Paths)." As though Schumann's, or any other future tendency which, as here, was manifestly building upon existing foundations, could ever appear " new " in their eyes! Of all the covert or open currents of opposing criticism which this warm and magnificent outburst of feeling was bound to produce, by a natural reaction, this " neo-German " one became the most dangerous in the course of years and was unfortunately widened into a deep and open breach by the deplorable manifesto against the neo-Germans which followed it. However this may be, the germs of the Brahms-Wagner, Brahms-Bruckner, and Brahms-Wolf controversies, which seem to us so senseless nowadays, were already latent in Schumann's oracular article.

There was only one person who was not surprised at Schumann's clarion call to battle, and that was Brahms's old master Marxsen. " I knew," he wrote in later days to La Mara, " of what Brahms was capable, how wide and thorough was his knowledge, with what a noble talent a kindly Providence had endowed him, and how magnificently it was unfolding itself in bloom. But at the same time Schumann's recognition and admiration were a very, very great joy to me too; for thanks to them I had the rare satisfaction of knowing that, as his master, I had found the right way to preserve the individual quality of his talent and thus train it up to independence."

And so the situation remained for the time being; this thunderbolt hurled Jove-like on the smoking earth by Schumann on behalf of Brahms, the young favourite of the gods, produced a powerful and fruitfully stimulating effect, though, contrary to his intentions, it proved to a certain extent destructive and confusing. But what was its effect on Brahms himself? Many have expressed the opinion that Schumann's prophecy turned a spontaneous young composer, exulting in his youth, whose element of " storm and stress," in the Brahmsian sense of the word, was already in almost every case subjected to the restraints of form, into an earnest, laborious, academic musician who spent his whole life in the effort to justify Schumann's tremendous expectations by his achievement. Stated in this extreme form it is of course untrue, but there is certainly an element of truth in it. For all the youthful light-heartedness of these years, Brahms had served too hard an apprenticeship and was of too serious a nature and too inclined to make the highest demands upon himself not to feel the whole weight of responsibility laid upon him by this prophecy, in addition to the joy of it. We know this from Theodor Kirchner, who more than once in Switzerland saw him weighed down by rare but oppressive moods of discouragement. We also know it now from Rudolf von der Leyen, who in the spring of 1884, while they were awaiting the Duke of Meiningen and his wife at the Villa Carlotta on the Lake of Como, could easily say of Brahms, who was his travelling-companion: " He has had such a hard time, and takes his work and his genius so seriously, that the poor fellow no longer knows what joy is "; and he adds Brahms's own words: " People sometimes think that I am merry when I seem to join in the laughter and jollity in society; I need not tell *you* that inwardly I am not laughing." At first, perhaps, Brahms only *felt* the weight of Schumann's prophecy. Realization of what it involved was left for a later day, when he was *fighting* for his art and artistic convictions in his mature years. Fortunately it did not have the effect upon him which might have been expected of such a challenge — that of making him conceited, vain, and proud, and causing him to lull himself with the false belief that he had nothing more to learn. Though young Brahms had been brought at a single bound into the full glare of publicity, he remained, on the contrary, the " thoroughly modest fellow " of whom Schumann was so fond, who could thank him in the following words: " May you never regret what you have done for me; may I become entirely worthy of it! " and wrote to Joachim in the following year: " God grant that my wings may yet grow vigorously! "

He spent a few unclouded, happy weeks at Düsseldorf in daily intercourse with the Schumanns; how deeply he won Schumann's love and admiration is shown in that composer's heart-rending letters to him and Clara after the blow had fallen upon him, when he was living in the asylum at Endenich. He calls Brahms " my dear," or " my true friend "; sometimes Brahms is " Johannes," called by the intimate " *Du*," sometimes by the more formal " *Sie* "; Schumann talks enthusiastically, in difficult and complicated terms, of Brahms's sonatas and variations, recalls with delight his own performance of them, longs to be with him, stands before the picture of Brahms given him by Clara and done at his request by the French artist Laurens, hanging below the mirror; then sums it all up to his wife, as though in an ecstatic leitmotiv of blissful memory: " I am also writing to Brahms myself. Is the drawing of him by de Laurens still in my study? He is one of the finest and most brilliantly talented young fellows. What a delight it is to me to recall the glorious impression which he made on me the first time with his C major Sonata, and later on with the F sharp minor Sonata and the Scherzo in E flat minor! Could I but hear him again! I should like to have his Ballades too." Or a fortnight later, to his young friend himself: " Dear friend! Could I only be with you at Christmas! I have just received your picture from my wonderful wife — the well-known picture — and well do I know the right place for it in my room — under the mirror. I still cheer myself with your (*Deine*) variations; I should like to hear many by you (*Dir*) and my Clara. . . ." And lastly, on March 10, 1855, to Joachim: " And so I am getting deeper into Johannes's music. The First Sonata was quite without precedent for a first published piece, and all the four movements formed a single whole. And in the other works, too, one gets deeper and deeper, as in the Ballades, like which, again, nothing has ever appeared before. If only he would now do as you do, my honoured friend, and turn to big masses, to the orchestra and chorus; that would be glorious."

At the beginning of November 1853 Brahms again visited Joachim at Hanover, where he read Schumann's article for the first time and expressed his gratitude to him in the following letter, which is more than ordinarily characteristic of him in its mixture of warm, youthful feeling, gratitude, self-criticism, and conciseness:

" Honoured Master:

" You have made me so unspeakably happy that I cannot attempt to thank you in words. God grant that my works may soon show evidence of how much your affection and kindness have uplifted and inspired me! The public praise which you have lavished on me will have raised public expectation of my achievements so extraordinarily that I do not know how I am at all to come up to it. Above all, it makes the greatest caution incumbent upon me in the choice of the things which I am to publish. I do not propose to publish any of my trios, but to choose the sonatas in C (major) and F sharp minor as op. 1 and 2, songs as op. 3, and the Scherzo in E flat minor as op. 4. You will find it natural that I should try with all my power to disgrace you as little as possible.

" The reason of my long delay in writing to you is that I had sent the four works I have named to Breitkopf, and intended to wait for the answer, in order to be able to report the result of your recommendation to you immediately. From your last letter to Joachim, however, we now learn the same thing, and so I have only to write to you that, as a result of your advice, I am going to Leipzig in the next day or two (probably tomorrow).

" I should further like to tell you that I have written out my F minor Sonata and made considerable modifications in the finale. I have also improved the violin sonata. I should also like to thank you a thousand times for the dear portrait of yourself which you sent me, as well as for the letter which you wrote my father. By so doing you have given the utmost delight to a couple of good people, and to yours for life,

" BRAHMS.

" Hanover, 16 November 1853 "

We learn from this letter that Schumann, who had already, perhaps at the request of Joachim, discussed the choice and order of the first works to be published by Brahms, had done still more and written to the world-famous Leipzig house of Breitkopf and Härtel recommending his works for publication. In so doing he proposed to them that they should pay the young composer " a fee only moderately proportionate to the merits of the works," but after an interval, say, of five years, if the sales came up to their expectations, " to grant him a share in the profits to be determined later." But at the same time he tried to smooth Brahms's way as a pianist into the great world by way of Leipzig and added: " His playing is an essential part of his music; I do not remember

ever to have heard such individual effects of tone." At the beginning of November Brahms had sent the manuscripts selected
to Härtel from Hanover, with a short letter, in which he says
modestly and judiciously: " It is not my own boldness, but rather
the desire of artistic friends, to whom I communicated the manuscripts, that has led me to take this step of seeking publicity for
them. And so, honoured sir, will you kindly excuse these lines in
case their contents are unwelcome to you."

The Leipzig publishers were well able to appreciate the value
of a recommendation from Schumann, couched in such an unusual form. They wished to make the acquaintance of the " new
John the Baptist or Messiah " and to hear him play. A letter was
sent to Brahms through the agency of Joachim asking him to
come to Leipzig. The young master shuddered " at this Leipzig,"
and the change " from the hills of the Rhine to the offices of
Leipzig " seemed to him " far too abrupt." But it was the leading
musical centre and fortress of musical romanticism at that time,
not only in Germany, but in the whole world of music, that must
pronounce the first judgment on him, which would decide the
whole of his future career as a composer. Here, in the intellectual
centre of central Germany, with its broad, old-established musical
culture, both in the home and in the concert-hall, not only the
good effects of Schumann's challenge, but the bad ones too, were
bound to show themselves for the first time; it was here that his
" first wounds awaited him." And both these things happened.
At first young Brahms found nothing but sunshine. In the first
place, from the point of view of " business," " I have to thank
your warm recommendation for my kind reception in Leipzig,
which has exceeded all my expectations, and, more particularly,
my deserts. Härtel's declared themselves ready to print my first
attempts with great pleasure. They are as follows: op. 1, Sonata
in C major; op. 2, Sonata in F sharp minor; op. 3, songs; op. 4,
Scherzo in E flat minor. I handed the following to Herr Senff
for publication: op. 5, Sonata in A minor for violin and pianoforte; op. 6, six songs," he was soon able to write to his beloved
" Mijnheer Domine " Schumann. Thus the two trios were for the

present struck off the first list of the works ripe for publication by Breitkopf and Senff — only that in B major, op. 8, was left for a later date — and the opus numbers no longer correspond to the order in which the works were composed; for the E flat minor Scherzo is the oldest of all, and the Sonata in F sharp minor, except for the *andante,* is older than that in C major. But Brahms acted in agreement with Joachim, after mature consideration, and allowed himself to be guided by his friend in the matter of the dedications as well: the first piano sonata is dedicated to his friend Joachim, the second to Clara Schumann.

But socially, too, he basked in the sunshine of Leipzig, then the leading musical centre, which set the fashion for all Germany. In one of the musical salons he soon made the acquaintance of the young Livonian Julius Otto Grimm and they became so intimate that they " might have been doubles in their similar views on art, and they soon took fire from each other's works " (Ludwig); indeed, long before this first meeting, Grimm had displayed curious Brahmsian traits and idiosyncrasies in his works, which, though late Romantic and Schumannesque, had a North German fondness for an erudite contrapuntal substructure. In Heinrich von Sahr — the composer of the *Stimmen der Nacht* for pianoforte, and a disciple of Schumann — who devoted himself to him in Leipzig with the greatest unselfishness, he found a faithful and most enthusiastic friend and apostle of his art. Brahms candidly admits to his friend Albert Dietrich that he spent only one night at a hotel, and Sahr took this " divine fellow," his " old fellow (*Kerl*)," his " ideal of an artist," round to the houses of Härtel and Senff, of Moscheles and David; while Grimm introduced him to the Countess Hohenthal, and others of the best Leipzig families. Among those who made his acquaintance were Hedwig Salomon (von Holstein), Rietz, the caustic old Friedrich Wieck (Robert Schumann's father-in-law) and his daughter Marie, Brendel, at that time editor of the *Neue Zeitschrift für Musik,* and, among the North German group, Hans von Bronsart and Karl Klindworth; and he was received by them all with open arms and open-eyed amazement at his talent. David played his violin sonata at Sahr's house, Brahms himself played his C major Piano Sonata, and the admiration for them knew no bounds. Liszt was also staying in Leipzig for Berlioz's concerts, and earnest attempts seem to have been made by the neo-German group to win over the brilliant young composer of the piano sonatas, whom even a Berlioz could still understand with entire consistency and embrace with delight. But in vain. With North German straightforwardness and honesty Brahms was heartily glad to make it up with that " wonderful fellow " Liszt; but with North German conservatism he refused him all allegiance as a great artist and would have nothing to do with his noisy host of followers. Let us hear his own words to Joachim on the subject:

" Liszt was at Berlioz's concert with all his apostles (Reményi among them); it has done him endless harm. The exaggerated applause of the Weimar clique called forth determined opposition. I am nervous about his own concert on Monday. In spite of the vehement efforts of a few Leipzigers (Sahr and others) to prevent it, my first visit on Friday was to Liszt. I had a very friendly reception. From Reményi, too, I was careful to avoid all that might suggest ideas and memories of the past. Reményi has changed very much for the worse. Liszt also called upon me, with Cornelius and others. On Friday I went to see David, as well as Liszt, Berlioz, etc. On Sunday I even went to see Brendel, in spite of the wry faces pulled by the Leipzigers. . . . Berlioz praised me with such infinite warmth and cordiality that the others humbly followed suit. Yesterday evening at Moscheles's he was equally friendly. I ought to be very grateful to him. On Monday Liszt is coming here again (very much to the disadvantage of Berlioz)."

For the rest, he felt highly delighted at the " endlessly kind reception " which he received in Leipzig, " far beyond " his " deserts," took the liveliest interest in the rich musical life of the old concert centre, as much as was possible during these

four eventful weeks, and heard for the first time at the Gewandhaus Franz Schubert's great C major Symphony, so belatedly
discovered by Schumann.

On December 17, 1853 he played his C major Sonata and his
E flat minor Scherzo at the Gewandhaus, at an evening concert
of chamber-music given by the David Quartet. Here his inex-
perienced youth for the first time made the acquaintance of the
critical, lukewarm spirit of caution, scepticism, and cool neutrality
towards all new artists and works of art, which has remained
typical to this day of the conservative, cultured musical society
of Leipzig, rendered doubly exacting by a very excess of the
choicest music, and overburdened with intellectual interests: his
success both as a composer and as a pianist was only moderate
and partial. Personally he was received, without exception, with
the courtesy and amiability of the kindly and adaptable Saxons;
as a composer he aroused interest and esteem, especially in those
circles where, to quote the lady who was afterwards to become
the wife of Franz von Holstein, the Beethovenesque quality of
his music, its "great seriousness," its "immense power and
depth," could be set up as a welcome contrast with the neo-
German "revolutionaries." Besides, people did not dare openly
to give the lie to Schumann. But at that time it was only quite
a small circle of friends and acquaintances in Leipzig who recognized what was dormant in Brahms. The Mendelssohn clique
and the "neo-Germans" were already equally opposed to him,
and the public, which was perplexed by Schumann's prophetic
utterances and expected far too much, saw in him, now a second
Mozart or Beethoven, now a second Schumann, now a neo-
German "revolutionary," and in any case was for the most part
not qualified to class Brahms's art clearly and unequivocally
either as classicistic or as "neo-German"—which was still not
necessarily impossible at that time. Thus the success of Brahms's
Leipzig début was on the whole negative rather than positive;
he was merely accumulating the inflammable material which
was to cause such a terrific explosion six years later on the first
performance of his D minor Piano Concerto in the same spot.

VII

THE DEATH OF SCHUMANN

The publication of Brahms's first-fruits went on apace. " Even before Christmas I shall probably receive copies of my first things," wrote the young composer to Schumann. Next he was overcome with joy at once more joining his parents in Hamburg at Christmas — and how should it have been otherwise? " With what emotions I shall see my parents once more, after an absence of scarcely a year! I cannot describe my feelings when I think of it." How everything had changed for the better as regards his happiness and fame during this one year, 1853! How proud his old parents might now be of their " Johannes "! " I was overjoyed to see my parents and master again and spent a most happy time among them," he wrote to Schumann; and to Joachim: " My parents, my master, and I are as blissful as though we were in heaven " — these simple words of the young composer speak volumes. At the same time he enjoyed the first great happiness of the creative artist: that of seeing his works in print. He sent his friend and master Schumann these first foster-children, who owed him their position in the world, in great anxiety as to whether they would still be able to enjoy the same love and solicitude from him who had stood sponsor for them, adding, in the true spirit of youthful romanticism, the comment that " in their new form they look to me far too orderly and pains-taking — indeed, almost Philistine. I cannot yet get used to seeing these innocent children of nature in such a respectable guise."

By January in the next year Brahms, who, like a true early riser, had always made light of all the fatigues of travel and social life from youth upwards, was once more in Hanover, at Joachim's house, this time with Grimm. The three friends became more and more intimate as time went on. The days were spent in serious work; in the evenings they would report progress to each other, or discuss, with the exuberant spirits of artists, who was worthy to be admitted into the newly-founded " *Kaffernbund* (League of Stupid Asses) " of chosen artists which they had just founded. On January 4 Hans von Bülow became personally acquainted with young Brahms on the occasion of a concert at Hanover. In accordance with his intellectual but sceptical nature, always prone to extremes and paradoxes, Bülow had hesitated a long time before he would believe in or espouse the cause of the new young Messiah of music, who had first been enthusiastically recommended to him by a letter from Liszt and then publicly by Schumann. On November 5, 1853, fresh from the impression of Schumann's " *Neue Bahnen* " article, he had written to Liszt: " My peaceful slumbers are not at all troubled by the Mozart-Brahms or Schumann-Brahms controversy. Some fifteen years ago Schumann spoke in equally high terms of the ' genius ' of W. Sterndale 'Benêt' (= blockhead; Bennett)." But shortly afterwards, in a letter to his mother from Hanover, he says: " I have got to know Robert Schumann's young prophet Brahms fairly intimately; he has been here two days and is always with us. A very charming, candid nature, with really quite a touch of divine grace (*Gottesgnadentum*) about his talent, in the best sense of the word! " On March 21, 1854 he played the first movement of the C major Sonata at Hamburg, became more at home with the " brooding Brahms," and afterwards took a particular interest in the F minor Sonata. And so Brahms became a " made man " as a composer for the piano.

His acquaintance with Bülow was quite accidental; their meeting in Hanover had had a different object: Joachim was then conducting a series of orchestral concerts, and the Schumanns were expected from Düsseldorf for a performance of *Paradies und Peri,* arranged by Hille, the musical director, which, however, was unfortunately a failure. It was their last professional concert tour together before the catastrophe overtook them. They had a cordial reception. Clara played Beethoven's E flat major Concerto, so

Wasielewski informs us, at a subscription concert given by the court orchestra; while her husband's last symphony was performed, and his *Phantasie* for the violin, which was played by Joachim. The art-loving court received the Schumanns with distinction, and Clara had to play there twice. The friends spent happy hours together, making music sometimes at the Schumanns', sometimes at Joachim's, and meeting every evening for refreshment at the pleasant old station café. Brahms, who struck Clara as being unusually silent, wrote to Dietrich after their departure: "What festive times we have had, thanks to the Schumanns! What can I say about it? Since then everything here seems to me thoroughly alive, and that speaks volumes. For in Hanover nothing is alive. Give my heartiest greetings to the glorious creatures (*die Herrlichen*)." None of the friends dreamt that it was the last time they were to see their beloved master free from the gloomy shadow of the doom which threatened him; for, though extremely neurasthenic, he was to all appearance in good health and the best of spirits as he recalled his triumphs in Holland.

After the performance at Hanover the Schumanns returned to Düsseldorf, and Robert set to work quietly and busily to prepare his collected writings for publication. Then the terrible news fell like a thunderbolt upon his friends and the whole musical world, that the noble master, in a fit of insanity, had thrown himself into the Rhine at midday on February 27, 1854. He was saved by some boatmen, and now his rich artistic life ended in a phantom existence tormented by the deepest melancholy and all the hallucinations of insanity. Brahms remained faithful to him even in misfortune. He came to Düsseldorf, as Dietrich wrote to Ernst Naumann, "the moment he heard the terrible news." Grimm and Joachim too were quickly on the spot, and in the midst of her grief the distracted Clara was able to write to her friend Emilie List: "Brahms is my dearest, truest support; since the beginning of Robert's illness he has never left me, but has gone through everything with me and shared my sufferings." On March 4 Schumann was removed to Dr. Richarz's private

asylum for the insane at Endenich, near Bonn. Here he lived for
another two years in a state of complete mental and physical
collapse, sustained by his memories and a scanty correspondence
with those he loved. Brahms, who had meanwhile written his
great piano Trio in B major, op. 8, was wholly one of them. Indeed, his visits — for Clara was not allowed to see her unhappy
husband — produced a peculiarly calming effect upon the poor
sufferer, and, musically, were even most stimulating, for the two
played duets together. As we have already seen above, nothing
could be more touching or heart-rending than the few letters
which he wrote to Brahms from the asylum during these last
two years. Brahms requited this to the best of his power. Indeed,
since all misfortune at the same time steels the energies and
reveals deep, latent moral forces, during these very years Brahms
learnt for the first time, not only to venerate his master and friend
as an artist, but also to love him as a man more than he had ever
done before. Never again in his life did Brahms write such warm
and heart-felt letters. "This year," he writes to Schumann from
Hamburg at the beginning of December 1854, "I spent from the
spring onwards at Düsseldorf; I shall never forget it; I have
learnt to revere and love you and your splendid wife more than
ever. Never- have I looked forward so gladly and with such
security to the future, or believed so firmly in a glorious future, as
now. How I long for the beautiful time to come quickly when
you will be entirely restored to us. Then I can never leave you
again, I shall try more and more to win your dear friendship."
How delicately he passes over the black Shrovetide Monday of
the catastrophe by the word "spring"; with what fine feeling he
leads the patient's memory back to his wife by his affectionate,
respectful mention of Clara, to whom, to her sorrow, Schumann
had not sent a single word or line for the first six months! Thus
he always managed to place Clara's love and care in the brightest
light and to withdraw himself into the background: " On Christmas Eve," he writes on December 31, 1854, "I returned here; how
long the separation from your wife seemed to me! I had become
so accustomed to her inspiring company; I had spent the whole

summer so delightfully near her, and learnt to admire her and
love her so deeply, that everything seemed colourless to me,
and I could only long to see her again." Or: "For one beautiful
word in your last letter, for the affectionate '*du*,' I must especially
thank you from the bottom of my heart; your wife, who is so
kind, also delights me now by this beautiful, intimate word; it is
the highest proof to me of her affection, I shall always try to be
more worthy of it." Or lastly, in March 1855: "Your wife has
just written to me so happily about your letter; she meant to send
you some beautiful note-paper. I have been prompt, but not so
tender; it is only women who do everything promptly, and beautifully and tenderly at the same time." But like a good physician
of souls he never omits to hold out hopes of a quick recovery and
return to his master and friend in his letters. His ever-recurring
refrain is: "So we shall go on seeing you oftener and in better
circumstances, until we have you with us again." Whoever is able
to read between the lines will see something else tacitly expressed
in these letters of Brahms to Schumann — namely, a tender and
affectionate bond of friendship between the young man of twenty-
two and Clara, who was fourteen years older. Here, too, the
venomous tongue of gossip has been busy — *cui bono?* — for did
not Brahms himself once write to Clara in 1855: "I grow more
and more joyful and peaceful in my *love* (*Liebe*) for you, I miss
you (*Sie*) more every time, but my longing for you is almost
joyful, it really is, and I have known the feeling before, and never
was my heart so warm"? Or again: "I wish I could write to
you (*Dir*) as tenderly as I love you, and do all the kind and
loving things that I desire for you. You are so infinitely dear to
me that I simply cannot express it. I should like to keep calling
you darling and everything possible, and never weary of saying
caressing words to you." Or again: "Your letters are like kisses
to me"; or again: "I hope you (*Du*) will hear something beautiful and endearing in this; I think a true spirit and a heart aglow
with love can make itself heard in music. . . . Think of me with
love." But in the previous letter, of the end of August 1859, from
Hamburg, we read: "I feel more and more convinced of it, and

it makes me happier and happier that you (*Du*) are my friend, and you will feel this and believe it anew."

In course of years this love became an inseparably close intellectual friendship. And whoever reads the correspondence between Clara Schumann and Brahms attentively and without prejudice will soon recognize that it was an ideal friendship of *artist for artist;* in which Brahms was the giver, and Clara, who loved him with a maternal feeling, as a son, and delighted with jealous pride in possessing his love, remained the receiver. In the first place, she was his incorruptible artistic conscience. There was not a song, not a symphony, that he did not first submit to her with a request for an unflinchingly honest opinion on it, which was always joyfully granted. " How unhappy I should perhaps be," wrote Brahms to her once, " if I had not you! It is from you that I am constantly learning that one cannot obtain vital force (vitality of creation) out of books, but only out of one's own soul. One must draw inspiration not from without, but from within." Brahms requited her throughout his whole life with the most unselfish solicitude, and if at times Clara had rather difficult negotiations with publishers — for instance, with the Härtel brothers, over the complete edition of Robert Schumann's works — he would throw himself into the breach and give her exhaustive directions, dictated by great worldly wisdom and knowledge of men, and always succeeded in bringing the matter to a happy issue by his calm and prudent discretion. We should know from Brahms's Third Piano Quartet, if from nothing else, that Brahms fought a hard and long fight with his love; but he, the truest friend and helper of this woman of strong character in her deepest misfortune, passed through even this terrible ordeal victorious in purity and strength. But his affectionate friendship for Clara Schumann remained unchanged for life. In the opinion of Widmann, he honoured in this " splendid woman " the noblest of her sex, and once said to him: " When you write anything, always ask yourself whether a woman like Frau Schumann could look upon it with approval. And if you have to doubt this, strike it out." What Brahms honoured and

loved above all in Clara Schumann — as we learn from Eugenie
Schumann's *Erinnerungen* — was her great heart, her friendship
for him, which always remained the same, the truest, the most
grateful, and the most affectionate. During his thirties especially,
Brahms did not always make it easy for her to preserve this
friendship for him with unshaken constancy. At that time he
tormented her, and especially her children, so much by his
brusquerie and aggravating ways, his ill humour and suspicion,
that nothing but the angelic kindness of Clara's letter of October
15, 1868, full of a woman's unerringly subtle instinct, which
enabled her to understand and forgive the discouragement and
irritable susceptibilities of a creative artist, could have broken
down the "wall" between them. But Brahms's own great, good
heart, overjoyed by her "wonderfully gentle smoothing away of
the difficulty," suffered even more severely from these uncontrolled moods of his, and at such times he could never do enough
to paint Clara's noble qualities to her children in the most splendid
and radiant colours, and was jealously anxious that not the
slightest shadow should be cast upon them. On June 11 Clara
brought into the world her seventh child, a son called Felix, to
whom Brahms stood godfather. So as to be near at hand to help
the Schumanns by both word and deed, Brahms had to make
arrangements for a temporary removal to Düsseldorf, for Frau
Clara was frequently kept at a distance from Düsseldorf by her
concert tours. He escorted Clara to Rotterdam, helped her to
move to a new house on her return, and, having been a " book-
worm " from childhood, spent a glorious time arranging the
library. " I have seldom been so happy as now in this library,"
he admitted with a smile to his friend Dietrich. The " meetings "
of the three friends, who were now joined by a new recruit, the
engraver Allgeyer, were now resumed round Clara's newly-
inaugurated coffee-machine, and so, too, were their innocent
birthday festivities — as, for instance, when Grimm offered his
beloved Brahms a " Zukunfts-Brahmanen Polka," based on the
notes represented by the letters of his name " Brahms," as a
musical " birthday cake."

Robert Schumann's condition underwent a change. In August 1854, while Clara was on a visit to the seaside at Ostend, Brahms was encouraged by passing symptoms of improvement, which were, however, deceptive, to take a little trip with Grimm up the Rhine by boat to Mainz, and then, by way of Heidelberg, up the valley of the Neckar to Heilbronn and by way of Esslingen to Ulm. But he got no farther; for he was soon driven back to Düsseldorf by a homesickness which Grimm could not understand, and by his longing for the Schumanns, passing through Endenich, where, concealed behind an open window, he could watch his beloved master unseen. In the autumn he spent a short time in Hamburg; then he visited Hanover, bringing back Joachim with him, and returned to Frau Clara to celebrate the Christmas festivities.

It was not long before the dark day arrived which prepared even the unhappy wife's mind for the fact that her beloved and suffering husband's end, though perhaps still distant, was inevitable. Clara was now faced with the hard necessity of making her way in the world alone, with a family of five, and no resources save her art and teaching. Brahms, too, was forced to seek some provision for the time being, if he was to stay near Clara at Düsseldorf. And now the sober calculation and dogged enterprise of the Low German showed themselves in him. He first tried to obtain lessons, acted as deputy for Clara Schumann, and solicited the position of director of music to the city of Düsseldorf, vacated by Robert Schumann. In spite of Clara's zealous advocacy, it was refused him, partly because he was still considered too young, partly because he was regarded as too closely bound by ties of friendship to Schumann. It was promised to Julius Tausch, who had already acted as Schumann's substitute at the request of the committee. And since music lessons are not lucrative enough, Brahms was forced, even before the death of Schumann, to make up his mind to an energetic step, and once more make his appearance as a pianist, which he always did with extreme reluctance throughout his whole life. But in order to help Clara, who had already in October 1854 resumed her concert-

work "with admirable fortitude" (Dietrich), he also formed
an artistic alliance with her and Joachim. After a short visit to
his parents at Hamburg, where they now lived at No. 7 Lilien-
strasse, Brahms started out in November on his concert tour.
They played at Danzig, Hamburg, Altona, Kiel, Bremen, and
Leipzig. At his native city Brahms played Beethoven's E flat
major Concerto, at Leipzig the G major Concerto. He was never
a great pianist, or, rather, virtuoso, who carried audiences away
by his fire; fortunately his small success only confirmed the young
composer in his original violent antipathy for the career of a
concert pianist.

At Hanover, where the concert tour came to an end, Brahms
for the first time made the acquaintance of the great pianist
Anton Rubinstein, who happened to be giving a concert there.
Much as he admired his genius as a pianist, Brahms's thoroughly
efficient nature was repelled by Rubinstein's brilliant but careless
and slipshod methods of composition. "At times insignificant, at
times abominable, but even then sometimes clever," as he says
to Clara Schumann. Rubinstein, who seems to have had the same
feelings as Liszt, but was less able to hide them than the well-
bred Liszt, and who, of the three friends Joachim, Brahms, and
Grimm, was by far the most interested in the first, expressed
himself to Liszt on the subject of Schumann's young Messiah in
no friendly fashion: "As for Brahms, I hardly know how to
describe precisely the impression which he has made on me; he
is not supple enough for the drawing-room, not fiery (*fougueux*)
enough for the concert-room, not primitive enough for the
country, not universal (*général*) enough for the town — I have
little faith in such natures." Throughout his whole life, as we
learn from Goldmark's *Erinnerungen,* Rubinstein could never
get over this "inveterate" dislike of Brahms — as also of Wagner
and everybody else who outshone his own works. Brahms made
other acquaintances of decisive importance for his whole life at
the two Musical Festivals of the Lower Rhine in 1855 and 1856.
At the former, with Jenny Lind in the title rôle in Schumann's
Paradies und Peri, Liszt appeared as a visitor, but met with a

very cool reception from the Schumann circle. At the two musical festivals Brahms met young Eduard Hanslick, afterwards his intimate friend and a clever musical journalist, writing for the *Neue Freie Presse* of Vienna, Professor Otto Jahn, author of the standard biography of Mozart, Theodor Kirchner, the composer of romantic miniature pieces for piano in Schumann's style, his beloved friend, the much-fêted singer Julius Stockhausen, and Claus Groth, a native of his own parts and author of *Quickborn,* that classic of Schleswig-Holstein poetry. Nearly all these acquaintances became lifelong friends; Hanslick championed Brahms with his pen, Stockhausen by singing his songs; Kirchner played a most important part in winning the Swiss public for Brahms; and to Groth's poems we owe the words of many of his songs.

The seal was set on his new friendship with Stockhausen by a concert which they gave together at Cologne. Then Clara Schumann returned from her great concert tour in England in the spring of 1856, and Brahms could only report to her that all the efforts he had made, at her request, to find a better asylum for Robert in South Germany had been in vain. She had always been distrustful and anxious about the right treatment of her unhappy husband, and doubtful as to its suitability, and now she had to endure the severest of her trials; on July 28 she and the faithful Brahms spent the whole day at the side of the dying man, who suffered terrible agonies, and on the 29th, at four o'clock in the afternoon, death gently released him. It was the first time that death — and death in such a terrible form — had approached Johannes.

On a still, summer afternoon, July 31, the master was laid to rest in the graveyard beautifully situated outside the Sternentor. Brahms's account of it is as follows: " I carried the wreath before him, Joachim and Dietrich walked beside me, the coffin was carried by members of a choral society, there was a band and singing." The warm-hearted, sympathetic, art-loving Rhinelanders followed in a great concourse. Schumann's death meant the break-up of Clara's circle of friends at Düsseldorf, for in future she was constantly forced to undertake great concert tours. Clara herself moved to Berlin, Joachim returned to Hanover, Grimm as director of music to Göttingen, and afterwards to Münster, Dietrich to Bonn in succession to Wasielewski, who was going to Dresden, and Brahms, after a considerable tour in Switzerland, which was urgently necessary for Clara's health, betook himself on October 21 to Detmold.

VIII

DETMOLD AND HAMBURG

How did Brahms come to Detmold, the quiet, pleasant little princely capital by the Teutoburg Forest? Princess Friederike of Lippe-Detmold, a pupil of Clara Schumann's, had made Brahms's acquaintance in 1855 at the Musical Festival of the Lower Rhine at Düsseldorf. In the following year Fräulein von Meysenbug, whose mother was an admirable pianist and wife of the Prime Minister at Detmold, also took lessons from Clara Schumann. These two ladies prepared the ground so well at the court of Lippe-Detmold that, in September 1857, Brahms was summoned to Detmold in a sort of unofficial capacity. Apart from the court etiquette, to which he also was naturally expected to conform, the burden of his new musical functions was not heavy; he only discharged them during the winter months, from September to December, and for the rest the young composer found in plenty at Detmold what he most longed for after the violent agitation of the last two years: namely, quiet and leisure for his own creative work. And here we must once again loudly sing the praises of the art-loving little German princely courts of the eighteenth and nineteenth centuries, which encouraged the arts, while respecting the justifiable desire of the artist for freedom, both outward and spiritual. Young Brahms was allowed an entirely free hand for his creative work and treated with unvarying generosity and understanding, leave being granted him for travel and study, in order that he might take steps on behalf of his works in person.

From the purely external point of view, the Detmold episode represents this introspective North German's first "flight" from the "great world," just as his time at Vienna, which occupied almost two-thirds of his life, stands for the second and permanent one; for about ten years Brahms spent his whole life either in the most lively intercourse with a small intimate circle of friends and admirers, or in memories of it; musically it was dominated by Clara Schumann, Joachim, and Stockhausen. It was not till 1868 that he was rediscovered by the great public as the composer of the *Deutsches Requiem.*

Brahms rapidly became accustomed to the court society of the little capital, which was at first strange to him, and, as director of the newly-founded court choir, soloist at the court concerts, and piano-teacher to the Princess Friederike and many Serene Highnesses, very soon felt quite at home in his comfortable lodging at the Hotel zur Stadt Frankfurt. The capital had a little opera-house, sacred to the name of Lortzing. The conductor of the Prince's orchestra and director of the subscription concerts was August Kiel. Before long, Brahms divulged to Joachim that he got on " rather better than not at all " with this unassuming romantic, once a favourite pupil of Spohr's, an admirable violinist and a capable conductor and teacher. For the rest, the Serene Highnesses left Brahms an entirely free hand. Thanks to his modest but secure emoluments, providing him with " money for all the year round," he was able, during these three years which he spent between Detmold and Hamburg, to devote himself almost undisturbed to his own studies and creative work, besides satisfying his passionate love of nature by rambling about the well-wooded heights and glorious forests of the Teutoburg hills to his heart's content. The works which he wrote or brought to maturity at Detmold bear in their very form the traces of tranquil comfort and sequestered self-communion; with the two Serenades, op. 11 and 16, he took the first cautious step in the direction of orchestral composition. He completed the First String Sextet, in B flat major, op. 18, and the dæmonic First Piano Concerto, in D minor, op. 15, begun during recent years at Düsseldorf, originally sketched out as a symphony, and next planned as a sonata for two pianos. His practical experience of choral singing was turned to account in a succession of exercises and studies in strict vocal style in the form of short choral works, most of which were not completed till he reached Hamburg; in the front rank of them may be mentioned the tender *Ave Maria,* op. 12, for female choir, string orchestra, wood-wind, and two horns; the *Gesänge,* op. 17, for female voices, with two horns and harp; the gloomy *Begräbnisgesang,* op. 13, for choir and orchestra; the *Marienlieder,* op. 22, for mixed choir; *Psalm XIII,* for three-part female choir; the *Gesänge,* op. 42, for unaccompanied six-part choir; the *Lieder,* op. 41, for four-part male choir; and the two motets, op. 29, *Schaff' in mir, Gott,* and *Es ist das Heil uns kommen hier.*

The character and style of these Detmold works proclaim an important internal development in Brahms's creative work: the " *Beethovener* " and composer of the first piano sonatas, the tragic artist of the first piano Ballades, reveals himself as an idyllic and exalted religious composer. This fruitful friend of Schumann, a young romantic of Schumann's school, was enjoying quiet communion with himself just at the right time; with his sound instinct he found in the classics the true sources and foundations of music, and, setting aside all imitation of Schumann, once more went to school to the strictly classical masters. The result of these years at Detmold, which were outwardly so calm, but inwardly so full of fruitful activity and so highly important for Brahms's development — quite apart from his accumulation of practical experience as a conductor — was, then, an instinctive, impassioned quest for the eternal and primal foundations of music in the classics, the discovery of these, and a thoroughly individual recasting of them. As late as 1854 Johannes Kreisler junior, the late Romantic, was still hankering after the school of Schumann, while, on the other hand, the neo-German clique would still have liked to claim him as in part their own on the ground of his youthful works; but, as he himself wrote to Clara Schumann: "I have a perfect terror of all that smacks of Liszt," and while at Detmold he finally broke entirely away from them and became the great neo-classic master Johannes Brahms. We can also see this from the strictly classical repertory of his court choir, and the piano-pieces which he himself contributed to the court concerts:

Bach, Handel, the old Italians, Mozart, Haydn, and Beethoven. As a mere child and a lad he had learnt to know the hardships of life at first hand in his parents' house, and though Schumann's prophetic words might smooth his path, yet they could not spare him the struggle for a livelihood and its anxieties with which he was now for the first time face to face; and now, in his thirties, he developed into mature manhood. During this period, which forms as a rule the decisive turning-point in every life, in both outward circumstances and inward development, he gradually secured a lifelong career of undisturbed creative work, in circumstances which became increasingly easy and free from care, thanks to the connexion which he formed about 1860 with the publishing-house of Simrock, thus putting an end to his original connexion with Breitkopf and Härtel and Bartholf Senff at Leipzig, and with the Swiss house of Rieter-Biedermann which followed.

In his calm retirement at Detmold, Brahms spent his time absorbed in industrious and eager study of the early classical and the classical masters. With inward satisfaction he felt that he was making progress: "I really believe, dear Clara, that I am growing!" And again: "How fine it is to create with unimpaired strength!" And again: "How laboriously I had to climb and toil over many things which I now feel that I can take in my stride!" Such are a few of his remarks to Clara Schumann from this Detmold period. His tranquillity, and the lack of artistic stimulus, produced in him a reminiscent mood, for the most part "as tender as it was melancholy," as he thought of the beautiful past with its wealth of activity, and this drove him "to turn inwards for his musical inspiration, and to do and think everything by himself alone." Later, however, at Hamburg he admitted to Clara Schumann: "I do not know; I was rather bored all the same at Detmold. I felt regularly tired and flat; now I am gradually recovering my freshness. I had really a good deal to do there; it was dull and monotonous, and when I was alone, I always had to make an effort to rouse myself from my apathy." So it is no wonder that, fond of travel as he always was, he went off in all directions during his generous allowance of free time. In spring and summer he usually spent a few months on the Rhine. Here the old friends Brahms, Joachim, Stockhausen, and Sahr met for the first time in the summer of 1857, at Bonn in Dietrich's house, or at Düsseldorf, in Clara Schumann's house, for the Musical Festival of the Lower Rhine, and passed a sunshiny artists' life in the wonderful spring of the Rhineland, with lovely excursions into the Siebengebirge close by, to St. Goarshausen, making chamber-music in company with Otto Jahn at the house of the artistic Kyllmann family, or at the Dietrichs' — for Albert had married the daughter of Carl Sohn, a professor at the Düsseldorf Academy. Brahms had brought the most important of his Detmold compositions with him: the First and the Second Serenade, the *Ave Maria* for female choir, the *Begräbnisgesang* for mixed choir, the *Lieder und Romanzen,* the First Piano Concerto, in D minor.

During these years, from January 1858 onwards, a second residence besides Detmold and another sphere of activity began to shape themselves for Brahms — namely, his native city of Hamburg. Here he lived for a year and a half, from 1861 onwards, not with his parents, at No. 74 Fuhlentwiete, opposite the Neustrasse, but, in order that he might be entirely undisturbed for his work, in "extraordinarily attractive" quarters, half an hour east of the city, in what was then still the countrified suburb of Hamm, in a pretty villa belonging to the widow of Dr. Rösing, an artistic old lady, whom the young composer had come to know and love in the house of her relatives the Völckers family. Everything required for undisturbed creative work was to be found in her old-fashioned turreted country-house, a quiet study, a large drawing-room with a piano, and verandas opening off it, a beautiful garden with quiet walks and fragrant syringas and laburnums, among which Johannes loved to pace up and down, with his hands clasped behind him, meditating and creating. A ladies' quartet was soon formed in the adjoining garden out of the female choir which Brahms had heard under the direction of the Hamburg composer and director of the Singakademie, Karl

G. P. Grädener, at a wedding for which he had acted as organist at the church. The quartet consisted of Frau Rösing's young nieces, two Fräulein Völckers (afterwards married to Professor Boie at Altona and Herr von Königslöw at Bonn respectively), and their two friends Fräulein Garbe and Fräulein Reuter. Brahms now wrote all kinds of four-part compositions for female voices — among them the *Geistliche Chöre,* op. 37 — and arranged old Italian church music for female choir. His new quartets for female voices were sung for the first time to his friend Avé Lallemant beneath the lofty beeches of the Sachsenwald. He was so pleased with the musical achievements of these ladies that, when Grädener went to Vienna in 1862, this ladies' quartet became the nucleus of a small female choir which he organized. Thus his practical experience of choral music at Detmold underwent a further profitable development at Hamburg. In the autumn of 1859, radiant with delight, he reports to Clara Schumann: "But above all I must also tell you about my fascinating Hamburg ladies' choir. O my dear girls, where are you? I shall certainly not stare about me when you are here singing me the pretty things which I have written for you; all forty of you shall stand before me, and I shall see you and hear you in my mind's eye. I tell you that one of my most endearing memories is this ladies' choir, and only think of its nice graduated arrangement, like a funnel: first the full choir, next a smaller one, for which I arranged three-part folk-songs which I made them practise; and then a still smaller one, which only sang me songs for solo voices and presented me with red ribbons."

Brahms invented the motto "*Fix oder nix* (Up to the mark or nothing) " for his little choir, and promised his ladies a lot of beautiful new music if only they would attend regularly, for in the autumn there was to be a short performance in St. Peter's Church as the crowning finale of their practices. But now that he was so deeply immersed in the study of the great old masters of choral composition, he also drew up some nice statutes for his new society in the style of the period. They are so delightfully comical and such incontrovertible proof that Brahms had really become thoroughly familiar and at home with early instruction books that they shall be inserted here in full "to rejoice the hearts (*zur Gemüthsergetzung*)," as they would have said, "of connoisseurs and amateurs."

Avertimento

Whereas it is absolutely conducive to *Plaisire* that it should be set about in right orderly fashion, it is hereby announced and made known to such inquiring minds as may desire to become and to remain members of the most profitable and delightful Ladies' Choir that they must sign *in toto* (*partoute*) the articles and heads of the following document before they can enjoy the above-mentioned title and participate in the musical recreation and diversion.

I ought in sooth (*zwaren*) to have dealt with the matter long ago, but whereas during spring's fair preamble (*præambuliret*), and until summer end (*finiret*), there should be singing, it should now be timely for this opus to see the light of day.

Pro primo be it remarked that the members of the Ladies' Choir must be present.

As who should say: they shall bind themselves (*obligiren*) to attend the meetings and practices of the society (*Societät*) regularly.

And if so be that anyone do not duly observe this article and (which God forbid!) it were to come to pass that anyone were to be so lacking in all decorum as to be entirely absent during a whole practice (*Exercitium*):

She shall be punished with a fine of 8 shillings (Hamburg currency).

Pro secundo it is to be observed that the members of the Ladies' Choir are to be present:

As who should say: they shall be there precisely (*præcise*) at the appointed time.

But, on the other hand, whosoever shall so transgress as to make her due reverence and attendance at the society a whole quarter of an hour too late shall be fined 2 shillings (H.C.).

(In consideration of her great merits in connexion with the Ladies' Choir, and in consideration of her presumably highly defective and unfortunate constitution (*Complexion*), a subscription shall now be established for the never enough to be favoured (*favorirende*) and adored (*adorirende*) Demoiselle Laura Garbe, in accordance with which she need not pay the fine every time, in lieu of which a moderate (*moderirte*) account shall be presented to her (*præsentiret*) at the end of the quarter.

Pro tertio: the moneys so collected shall be given to the poor, and it is to be desired that none of them get too much.

Pro quarto it is to be observed that the manuscript music (*Musikalien*) is largely confided to the discretion of the ladies. Wherefore it shall be preserved in due love and all kindness by the honourable and virtuous ladies, married or unmarried, as being the property of others, and shall also in no wise be taken outside the society.

Pro quinto: That which cannot join in the singing is regarded as neutral (*Neutrum*); to wit: listeners will be tolerated, but be it observed, *pro ordinario,* in such wise that the due usefulness of the *exercitia* be not impaired.

The above-mentioned due and detailed proclamation is herewith made public to all and sundry by the present *General Rescript* and shall be maintained in force until the Ladies' Choir shall have reached its latter end (*Endschaft*).

And you shall not only observe the above without fail, but also use your most earnest endeavours that others may in no wise or ways act or behave in a manner contrary to it.

To whom it may concern: such is our opinion and we await your judicious and much-to-be-desired approbation thereof.

In expectation whereof, in deepest devotion and veneration, the willing scribe of the Ladies' Choir, who always keeps time and is at all times theirs to command,

JOHANNES KREISLER, JUN.
(alias BRAHMS)

Given this Monday the 30th of the month Aprilis, A.D. 1860

Brahms made no small demand upon his ladies: "My young ladies have to write out all the parts themselves and this must always be done in a few days by sending them round among themselves." But he performed his artistic work without remuneration, purely for the love of the thing, and so the ladies requited him with extra devotion, not to speak of a silver ink-stand at the last performance in St. Peter's Church. A charming jesting correspondence now took place, in which he humorously admitted that there was "really a regular cult" of him in Hamburg, that "at any rate he always wrote in better spirits," and that his mind was so full of music "that something divine really ought to come out of it sooner or later"; and amid all these "merry doings" he assured them, in thanking them for their handsome presentation: "Now that is the kind of present for which I like to work; how I wish and long that there were no other sort of honorarium!"

The stiff society of Hamburg had no attraction for Brahms; the house which he most often frequented was that of his friend and fellow artist Avé Lallemant, where a number of gentlemen of mature years used to meet for the pursuit of literature, rather than music. He obtained a footing in the musical life of Hamburg only very slowly, and that as director of his ladies' choir and as a pianist rather than as a composer. His Detmold works were received with approval. On the whole the years of his second Hamburg period may be placed in contrast with his vocal "choral period" at Detmold as a sort of parallel period of instrumental composition, a "period of chamber- and piano-music." It was in Hamburg that a few of Brahms's important larger works belonging to these categories came into being; the two piano quartets, the string quintet (afterwards the F minor Piano Quintet), the First String Sextet, the Handel Variations for piano solo, and the Schumann Variations for piano duet. It is a rich harvest. But it was garnered with great labour — "Alas, how difficult everything still is to me!" he confesses to Clara Schumann at that time — and, beneath the melancholy northern skies of Hamburg especially, there occurred at times many hours of inward doubt, grievous discouragement, and dark moods, such as always visited him with particular severity in his native city: " But when one is well on in the thirties and feels as feeble as I do, one is glad to lock oneself up and stare at the walls in despondency." Or, as he says still more bitterly to Clara: ". . . and rail against all the ugly sounds and the boredom and one's halting artificiality and coldness of inspiration."

The many holiday or concert tours which he made during these years at Hamburg took him far afield. In Berlin he visited Clara Schumann and her friends at the house of her step-brother Woldemar Bargiel, the earnest, enthusiastic desciple of Schumann, and Hermann Grimm. At Hanover and Göttingen he passed many happy hours in the circle of Joachim, Grimm, and the latter's wife and father-in-law, Ritmüller, and knew the pains and pleasures of a serious passion for Agathe von Siebold, the charming young daughter of a professor at the university. Between whiles he would visit the Rhine, Leipzig, and other places.

These years spent between Detmold and Hamburg were darkened by a black cloud: the failure of the D minor Piano Concerto at the Leipzig Gewandhaus. Nowadays we laugh at the paltry critics who felt it incumbent upon them to reject it at the time. But we should remember in justification of them that it has very little in common with the ordinary conception, spirit, and form of the instrumental concerto, that it makes demands on both player and audience which it was impossible to satisfy between the fifties and sixties of the last century, when the after-effects of the style of Mendelssohn and Schumann were still in full force; and that, in spite of all the flashes in the mighty tempest of the first movement which recall Beethoven and Bach, it is not so much retrospective as markedly progressive in style. In this concerto, if in any of Brahms's youthful works, it is possible to speak of " new paths." Brahms presented it to the world in person in 1859, first on January 22 at Hanover, with Joachim as conductor, and then, on January 27, at Leipzig, with Rietz conducting. At Hanover it met with a respectable, though only partial, success, for even his friend Joachim speaks of a " success which

does credit to both the public and the artist "; but the " blasé "
Leipzig public, to quote Joachim, gave themselves " a testimonial
for mean-spiritedness and heartlessness," and inflicted a sensational fiasco upon the composer-pianist, by a crushing, absolute
silence at the rehearsal and by hissing him outright at the performance, at which, as he reported to Clara Schumann, " not
three people took the trouble to applaud." In the sacred halls of
the augustly conservative Leipzig Gewandhaus the impression
created by the titanic " storm and stress " of the first movement
of this concerto must have been particularly " revolutionary." No
wonder, then, that this time the neo-Germans found much to
praise in Brahms and his new work, while on the other hand the
rigidly conservative *Signale* group raised an outcry about it as
" a production — now given decent burial — of truly unrelieved
dreariness and aridity, three quarters of an hour of ranting and
raging, pulling and tugging, patching together and ripping
apart of phrases and embellishments," an undigested mass with
" screaming dissonances and discordant noises in general as a
dessert."

At first, indeed, his reverse at Leipzig thoroughly disheartened
even Brahms himself, though he would not admit it to anybody;
but it did not discourage him for long or turn him aside from
what he rightly recognized to be the true path in concerto composition. On the very next day he was able to write to his friend
Joachim with philosophic composure:

" For the rest, this failure makes absolutely no impression upon
me, and the little touch of poor and depressed spirits passed off
afterwards, as I listened to a Symphony in C major by Haydn
and the *Ruins of Athens*. In spite of all, the concerto will yet
meet with approval when I have improved its structure, and a
second one shall sound quite different.

" I think this is the best thing that can happen to anyone, it
compels one to collect one's ideas thoroughly and braces one's
courage. I am still experimenting and groping my way. But the
hissing was surely excessive."

But the failure at Leipzig was a serious hindrance to the printing and circulation of the work. The score did not appear till fifteen years later, and then only when Clara Schumann, indignant at its rejection by her fellow townsmen (" the critics in Leipzig were only less stupid than the public, and *spiteful* as well! " as she wrote later to Brahms on the subject of the malevolent Leipzigers), won a personal *succès d'estime,* which even then was not unanimous, by her playing of it in 1873 at the Leipzig Gewandhaus, with Reinecke as conductor. It was only very slowly that it won its way into the repertory of leading pianists, and the united efforts were necessary of artists such as Mary Krebs, Wilhelmine Clauss-Szarvády, Theodor Kirchner, Theodor Leschetizky, and, above all, Hans von Bülow and Eugen d'Albert, who were afterwards his two greatest apostles, before it finally carried the day even in Leipzig, after thirty long years. The fact that Brahms placed his name at the head of the list of signatures to the unfortunate protest against the neo-German school is as a rule represented as the immediate result, the direct expression of his suppressed resentment at the fiasco of his D minor Concerto at Leipzig, which was attributed to the machinations of the neo-German clique. This is not correct, for it was not the neo-Germans, of all people, who could have repudiated this concerto, the " reforming " character of which bore witness to a " storm and stress " spirit far in advance of his time. But it may have been partly this work that prompted the Leipzig *Neue Zeitschrift für Musik,* the official organ of progressive ideas in music at the time, to declare that all the important musicians of the time had accepted the tenets of the " music of the future (*Zukunftsmusik*)." Brahms felt bound to enter a vigorous protest against this, and, as is now established, Joachim seems to have played the principal part in stirring up and promoting it. He and Bernhard Scholz seem to have drawn up the text of the declaration. It was as follows:

" The undersigned have for long past followed with regret the activities of a certain party whose organ is Brendel's *Zeitschrift für Musik*. The said periodical constantly disseminates the opinion that serious musicians are fundamentally in accord with the tendencies which it champions, and has recognized the compositions of the leaders of this movement [the reference is above all to Liszt and Berlioz, but *not* to Wagner, as Brahms expressly admitted to Joachim — Author's Note] as works of artistic value; and that in general, and especially in North Germany, the controversy for and against the so-called " music of the future " has already been fought out, and settled in its favour. The undersigned consider it their duty to protest against such a distortion of the facts, and declare that, so far as they themselves are concerned, they do not recognize the principles which find expression in Brendel's *Zeitschrift,* and can only deplore or condemn as contrary to the most fundamental essence of music the productions of the leaders and disciples of the so-called ' neo-German ' school, some of whom put these principles into practice, while others keep trying to impose the establishment of more and more novel and preposterous theories.

" JOHANNES BRAHMS. JOSEPH JOACHIM. JULIUS OTTO GRIMM. BERNHARD SCHOLZ."

A circular letter was appended, asking for signatures to be sent to Brahms's address, 74 Hohe Fuhlentwiete, Hamburg. A whole series of leading artists had pledged themselves to sign it. While their names were being collected, a copy with none but the four names given above happened to be printed prematurely in the Berlin *Echo.* The point of the protest was thus destroyed, and unfortunately all its wider practical effect was frustrated. For a stream of hatred, mockery, and ridicule now poured down on these four from the neo-German camp, and for the rest of their lives Brahms, Joachim, Grimm, and Scholz were on the index of the Weimar clique.

We must pause a moment over this matter if we are to understand the deeper significance of this document, and the motives which induced Brahms to sign it. He had clearly realized the serious dangers threatened by the neo-German party of the Allgemeine Deutsche Musikverein, grouped round their master Liszt,

who was cosmopolitan and un-German to the core, and by the
subversive force of the modern spirit in German music. He had
foreseen what was coming, and what has actually made its way
into German composition in the course of the generations immediately following his: that is to say, the means have been taken
for the end, and, in their quite understandable blindness, men
have placed the new methods far above the personality which
makes use of them, thus bringing about a colossal confusion in
artistic ideas, in which we are still plunged today, perhaps even
more than ever. It was this conviction to which he gave the
clearest expression in his characteristically straightforward and
honest way by signing the manifesto.

Those who condemn party politics in music as harmful and
deplorable are bound to disapprove of this party manifesto. But
the fact that the document failed of its effect cannot but be deplored by those who grasp the fact that by it young Brahms
merely intended to bring about a coalition, which was absolutely
necessary at that time, between those holding the same opinions
as himself, against the serious dangers of a childishly rigid and
autocratic " party of progress," the aim of which was innovation
at all costs by means of an excessively one-sided overrating of
mere methods, which is destructive of art; and to set up an
opposition party, which should seek to put its aims into practice
on the firm artistic basis of an intensive study of the classical
and early classical writers. In his mature years Brahms may indeed
have regarded this as a " youthful peccadillo," which was at any
rate inspired by idealism and serious intentions.

The attitude of Brahms's native city of Hamburg towards
his D minor Concerto, which he performed there too in person, at a concert given by Otten's Musikalische Gesellschaft on
March 24, was very much the same as that of Leipzig. Once
again the first movement narrowly escaped a fiasco, and Brahms
was with difficulty prevailed upon by the conductor to play the
rest. Far friendlier was the reception given four days later to
his First Serenade at a concert of his own in collaboration with
Joachim and Stockhausen; and so at a Clara Schumann concert on

January 15, 1861 Brahms was able to present to the Hamburgers his songs for female choir, with harp and two horns, and the Second Serenade, without having to dread a hostile reception.

As early as August 1860 Brahms, who had all the Low German's independence and love of liberty, had firmly resolved to give up his safe, remunerative post at Detmold and shift his headquarters from Detmold to Hamburg, for the former, though pleasant, was naturally narrow and entirely lacking in the artistic and intellectual stimulus of a great city. The most important reason why he decided to take this step was a deep, if unexpressed, desire that, through the good offices of his friend Avé Lallemant, he might obtain the post of conductor to the Hamburg Philharmonic Society. But the cold reception of his D minor Piano Concerto by his fellow townsmen was only the prelude to a still colder welcome home. Once more the intellectual and artistic capital of Lower Germany was true to the traditional Low German character, which is really tragic in its hereditary failing — namely, a slow-moving and reactionary conservatism, always clinging to established usages — so that it will never recognize its own remarkable creative geniuses in time and bind them to it by secure appointments, but always prefers strangers, especially central or South Germans or Austrians; on this occasion, when Hamburg could have appointed its young composer Brahms, who was already famous throughout the great world of musical Germany, to an important musical post, it let him go and appointed Stockhausen to the directorship of the Philharmonic concerts, though he occupied the post only till 1866.

Joachim, who had strained every nerve to help his friend to obtain the post, sums up the choice in a letter to Avé Lallemant in a way which is not very flattering to the Hamburgers of the day, though it is absolutely justified:

" You know I have the highest esteem for Stockhausen's talent as a singer, and he is certainly the best musician among singers; but, with my limited musician's understanding, I fail to conceive how, when the choice lies between him and Johannes as director of an institution for giving concerts, anyone can decide in favour of the former! I have the highest possible opinion of Johannes, precisely as a man upon whom one can depend, thanks to his talents and will-power. There is nothing that he cannot grasp and master by his serious qualities. You know that as well as I do — and if all of you on the committee and in the orchestra had received him with confidence and affection (as you have always done privately and as a friend) instead of with doubt and patronizing looks, it would have smoothed away the asperity of his nature, for in spite of all his Hamburg patriotism (which is almost touchingly childlike) it is bound still further to embitter him to see himself set aside. I cannot think of it without feeling sad that his fellow townsmen have thrown away the opportunity of making him more contented and less harsh, and capable of giving more enjoyment by the products of his genius."

Brahms felt the choice of Stockhausen deeply, little though he might show it, for, like all Low Germans, he was a faithful son of his native city. We hardly hear anything of it directly, but we feel it all the more indirectly. After that time Brahms only paid flying visits to Hamburg, mostly during Bülow's tenure of the post, when he was fond of railing good-humouredly at the proverbial Hamburg "*Mudd*" and "*Sott*" (mud and soot), its rain, fog, and dirt. But he was always faithful to Hamburg and his friends at home, and the subsequent conferment upon him of the freedom of his native city, his election as an honorary member of the Tonkünstlerverein (Musicians' Club), and the invitation to conduct the Philharmonic concerts which he at last received in 1894, and naturally declined, may have gone far to heal the smart of this first aching wound — caused by the fact that his native city, to which he clung "as to a mother," and in which he would most have liked to find a permanent home, should have misunderstood and rejected him.

Having found that the prophet was without honour in Germany and met with less than none in the Low German regions of the north, Brahms carried into effect the longing which

Schumann had felt during his last years of fatal mental disease as he recalled the happy memories of his stay in Vienna: he decided to follow Grädener's example and, being saved from absolute want by a small sum which he had put by during his years of travel, to visit the home of the four great classical and romantic composers, Haydn, Mozart, Beethoven, and Schubert, the great Austrian Imperial city of Vienna.

The migration took place gradually and in the desultory way which Brahms preferred, by informal concert tours and pleasure trips. During the last two years of his residence in Hamburg he played Beethoven's G major Concerto before an enthusiastic audience at Oldenburg — performing his new Handel Variations before the assembled court orchestra on the previous evening — and passed happy days at Dietrich's house and in the society of Oldenburg. In June 1862 he visited the Musical Festival of the Lower Rhine at Düsseldorf, and it appears that the distinguished Viennese singer Louise Dustmann-Meyer succeeded in doing what little Berta Prorubsky of the Hamburg Ladies' Choir had failed to do, and filled the young composer with an out and out enthusiasm for the "holy city of musicians." First he joined Clara Schumann and Dietrich for the summer in the Nahetal, at Münster am Stein, near Kreuznach, at the foot of the Ebernburg in the Bavarian Palatinate. Here, "where Franz von Sickingen died and Ulrich von Hutten wrote," he completed the two books of the *Magelone-Lieder,* which he had started in Hamburg, and sketched out the first draft of the first movement of the C minor Symphony. In the day-time they were tempted into glorious excursions; in the evening they spent hours making music at Frau Clara's house. Brahms was in his most exuberant and sportive mood. When Clara left, he went off with his friend Heinrich von Sahr on a little impromptu trip to Spires and Karlsruhe, on a visit to the Düsseldorf painters Lessing, Schirmer, and Schrötter, who had been appointed to posts at the Kunstakademie there.

On September 8, 1862 he visited Vienna for the first time, and there, as we shall see shortly, gave his inaugural concert on

November 29. He was back in Hamburg for Christmas, and about the New Year was at his friend Dietrich's at Oldenburg, with the D minor Piano Concerto and his luckless offspring the F minor String Quintet, afterwards recast as the Piano Quintet.

In January 1863 he went to Vienna for good; at first he was tormented by a deep homesickness and left a loop-hole open for a return: " How long I shall stay," he wrote to Dietrich, " I naturally do not know; we will let things take their course, and hope to see each other in the winter after all."

MATURITY (VIENNA)

IX

DIRECTORSHIP AT THE SINGAKADEMIE

His removal to Vienna, which was at first only temporary, divides Brahms's life into two main parts. His years of apprenticeship and travel were at an end; he was now fully qualified as a master. The following years, too, are *Lehrjahre,* in the sense that Brahms never finished learning, and they are also *Wanderjahre,* in that Brahms never travelled more often, or to greater distances, than during these very *Meisterjahre.* But they are the concert and holiday tours of one now settled and at home in Vienna — however much he may have felt at first that he was "a stranger there and had no rest," as he writes to Clara Schumann — of a great artist to whom self-expression in the conducting or performance of his own works was as natural and as much a necessity of his inner nature as travel, or even the enjoyment of nature and art. From now onwards, so far as external circumstances are concerned, the master's life was indissolubly bound up with Vienna, and, though simple, was one of comfortable independence and tranquillity.

When Brahms reached Vienna, it still shone with all its old musical brilliance. The Imperial Opera numbered the most eminent names among its conductors and singers. Its orchestra had always been among the foremost in the world. Its eight annual Philharmonic concerts, founded as early as 1841 by Otto Nicolai, the composer of *Die Lustigen Weiber von Windsor (The Merry Wives of Windsor)*, had already become world-famous. The conductors of them steadily rose in brilliance and international reputation: from Nicolai, Esser, Eckert, Dessoff, and Herbeck, the standard rose to the level of Richter, Mahler, Weingartner, and the great visiting conductors Safonoff, Schuch, Mottl, R. Strauss, and Nikisch. These concerts were always attended by all the intellectual and artistic élite of the art-loving concert public of Vienna. As a pendant to the Court Opera-house and the more recent Philharmonic concerts, there was the old Gesellschaft der Musikfreunde (Society of Musical Amateurs), founded in 1812, which had numbered Beethoven and Schubert among its members, with its Conservatoire, founded in 1817, and subscription concerts. It was a great institution which had done good service to the musical life of Vienna, and was run by non-professionals, in the sense that its business affairs were managed with the most devoted zeal by enthusiastic amateurs. Its close connexion with the Singverein (Choral Society) of the Gesellschaft der Musikfreunde, founded by Johann Herbeck in 1859, made it possible to produce great choral works and oratorios, in addition to symphony concerts with the best of soloists. When Brahms arrived in Vienna, the ambitious and restlessly active Herbeck had been the artistic director of this honourable old society for three years. Besides the Singverein, and in keen competition with it, there also flourished the more recent Singakademie, founded by Ferdinand Stegmayer, director of the chorus and instructor in choral singing at the Conservatoire. Chamber-music at Vienna during these years was dominated by that caustic wit Joseph Hellmesberger the elder — " old Hellmesberger," as he was called — who until 1859 had been artistic director of the concerts of the Musikfreunde and the Conservatoire. On the appointment of Herbeck as conductor of the concerts, the two offices which had been united in his person were separated. Hellmesberger continued to be director of the Akademie, and at the time of Brahms's arrival in Vienna he was professor of the violin at the Conservatoire (since 1851) and first violin (*Konzertmeister*) in the orchestra at the Court Opera-house (since 1860). His string quartet, founded in 1849 (including besides himself Durst, Heissler, and Schlesinger), enjoyed the reputation of being the first and best in the Austrian capital.

Such, in broad outline, was the musical life of Vienna about 1862 and 1863. It was a unique musical centre, of European fame, and it was certainly extraordinarily difficult for a " northern

stranger " to score a triumph there. The Hamburg composer
bravely faced the tough struggle which was inevitable and on
November 16, 1862 made his first appearance before the Viennese
public at the first concert of the Hellmesberger Quartet, with
Carl Tausig and Fräulein Bettelheim. " Piano Quartet in G minor
(first performance): Herr J. Brahms at the piano," runs the
program. On November 29 he gave the first concert on his own
account, in the hall of the Gesellschaft der Musikfreunde. " As a
courtesy to the giver of the concert " the Hellmesberger Quartet
also took part, playing his Second Piano Quartet, in A major,
besides Frau Passy-Cornet, a professor at the Conservatoire, who
sang some of his songs, and Professor E. Förchtgott, who played
the *Balladen*. Brahms's artistic conceptions and tendencies are
summed up in the fact that he played Bach's F major Toccata,
Schumann's C major Fantasia, op. 17, and his own Handel Variations and Fugue.

His success was great and complete. Let us hear the happy
excitement with which the modest young composer wrote to his
parents:

" My dear parents:
" I was so happy yesterday, my concert went off splendidly,
far better than I had hoped.

" After the quartet had been received most favourably, I had
an extraordinary success as a pianist. Every number met with the
greatest applause, I think there was absolute enthusiasm in the
hall.

" I could certainly give some very good concerts now, but I
have no wish to do so, it takes up too much of my time, so that
I can get nothing else done. But, for the rest, I understand that I
have covered the costs of this concert; the hall was naturally
filled with free tickets.

" I played as freely as though I had been sitting at home
among friends, and certainly this public is far more stimulating
than our own.

" You ought to have seen how attentive they were, and heard
the applause!

" For the rest, I also want to say that Hr. Bagge seems to have been the only one who wrote about my quartet with disapprobation, the rest of the dailies here praised me very highly at the time.

" I am very glad that I gave the concert. . . .

" I think my Serenade will be performed next Sunday.

" At my concert yesterday I wanted some of my songs to be performed, which caused me a terrible amount of running about and unpleasantness, that is the chief reason why I mean to have peace at last. . . . The publishers here, especially Spina and Lewy, have been pressing me for things ever since the quartet; however, there are many things that I like better in North Germany, and particularly the publishers, and for the present I had rather go without the few extra Ldrs. [louis-d'or] which they might perhaps pay me. . . .

" Write soon and think lovingly of

" Your JOHANNES.

" My cordial greetings to Herr Marxsen and, do not forget, on Bösendorfer's account."

On the advice of Hanslick, Brahms gave another concert by himself on January 6, 1863, at which Richard Wagner was present. He himself played his F minor Piano Sonata, some Bach and Schumann; Marie Wilt sang a few of his songs. Herbeck included his First Orchestral Serenade in one of his programs, Dessoff the Second; the First String Sextet produced an extraordinary impression; and a year later the F minor Quintet, in its new form as a sonata for two pianos, was received with great esteem when performed by Brahms and Tausig. Brahms began to arouse more and more interest in Vienna as a composer, though only indirectly, through his piano-playing. The best Viennese artists, particularly Julius Epstein, the pianist, and the best of the neo-German group — for instance, Tausig and Cornelius — vied with one another in their anxiety to be of service to him. Gradually, too, he won firmer ground in society, and, thanks to the amiability, cordiality, and gaiety of the art-loving Austrians,

with their easily kindled emotions — though the shrewd Clara
Schumann remarks that this fire which blazes up so quickly
is only a " fire of straw " — he came to feel increasingly happy
and at home in Vienna.

Thanks to his clear-sighted pursuit of his aim, and his acute
and detached judgment, this letter, palpitating with joy, summed
up once for all what he intended to do: that is, to give up the
career of a concert pianist and return to quiet creative work, while
maintaining a permanent connexion with the North German
music-publishing house of Simrock.

The success achieved by Brahms at his inaugural concert in
Vienna should be rated highly, but not too highly. Exactly the
same thing happened to Brahms in Vienna as to his great fellow-
countryman Friedrich Hebbel, and indeed the similarity between
the outward features of the careers of these two great Low Germans, who unfortunately never came into personal touch with
each other, forces itself upon us more and more. As for Hebbel, on
his arrival in Vienna from Italy on November 4, 1845 and his
marriage with Christine Enghaus, the great actress at the Burgtheater, his terrible early years of bitter need and poverty were
at an end, and with them the everlasting bondage of his tragic
liaison with Elise Lensing. To Brahms, though of course in a
much less degree than to Hebbel, his migration to Vienna stood
for the same thing as compared with the dark hours, days, and
years that preceded it: it was his " port after stormy seas," after
the manifold storms and struggles of his life. Except that, just
as Hebbel was in conflict all his life with Heinrich Laube, the
director of the Burgtheater, so Brahms was always at odds with
the great Wagner party, represented by Anton Bruckner, and
indirectly by Hugo Wolf. The greatness and importance of both
Hebbel and Brahms alike were at once recognized by the serious,
genuine, and unprejudiced element even in Vienna, but the appreciation of the artistic world in general had always to be won afresh
for each separate work, and in this their rugged North German
virility and deeply reserved and retiring nature were naturally
more likely to hinder and mislead than to help them. For

Viennese life is not only light and gay, but also quick to change, and, as with the Rhinelanders, its motto is often: " Out of sight, out of mind."

In spite of all his successes, Brahms continued to hesitate between Vienna and Hamburg. "I sit here, but with a touch of homesickness for Hamburg," he writes to Joachim; and again: " It is quite nice here, but, all the same, I am glad to go back to Hamburg." On May 1, 1863, being " very old-fashioned in such matters," he went to see his parents in his native city, and, on his way through Hanover, visited Joachim and his young bride, Amalie Weiss. Disappointment after disappointment awaited him at Hamburg. Stockhausen was conductor at the Philharmonic, and there was dissension in his home. Brahms took a lodging at lovely Blankenese on the lower Elbe, in order to compose *Rinaldo,* and once again spent happy days with the Dietrichs at Oldenburg. His thirtieth birthday brought him a great joy: Vienna offered him the position of conductor of the choir at the Singakademie. Brahms's old love for choral singing revived, though his strong Low German sense of independence made the burden of a fixed post repugnant to him. " It is a grave decision, to give up one's liberty for the first time," he writes to the Singakademie on May 30. He accepted the position, stayed in Baden-Baden till the end of September, with Frau Clara Schumann, to recover fresh strength, and, some two months before Hebbel's death (which took place on December 13), moved to Vienna for good. He did not do so without a North German consciousness of responsibility: "I am terribly timid at putting my talent in this department to the test in Vienna, of all places," he wrote to Dietrich. On September 28 he joyfully and gladly entered upon his first appointment at Vienna, and conducted the practices with punctilious and earnest zeal in the discharge of his duty. His vocal material, as everywhere in South Germany, and particularly in Austria, was exceptionally fine, and his art-loving singers of both sexes were for the most part highly musical. He could therefore venture to devote himself to a systematic cult of Bach, and at the same time get up performances of the larger choral

works of Handel, Beethoven, Schubert, and Schumann, which
were rarely heard. The very first concert, which took place on
November 15, 1863 in the Grosse Redoutensaal, began with Bach's
cantata *Ich hatte viel Bekümmernis,* Beethoven's *Opferlied,* three
four-part arrangements of folk-songs by Brahms, and Schubert's
Requiem für Mignon. The next concert, on January 4, 1864 (at
which the program included, among other things, Beethoven's
Elegischer Gesang, Gabrieli's *Benedictus,* Bach's cantata *Mitten
wir im Leben sind,* and his motet *Liebster Gott, wann werd' ich
sterben?*), came to grief owing to the difficulties of unaccompanied singing. The third concert, on April 17, the first " Brahms
Evening," in which he was assisted by Tausig and the Hellmesberger Quartet, failed to redress the balance. " My winter will
soon be over, and I have now to make up my mind whether I
intend to spend the next in the same post, which will be very
hard for me, though it will give great pleasure to the Academy
and the orchestra," he confesses. With the inexorably severe self-
criticism which always characterized him, he saw that no laurels
awaited him in the sphere of choral conducting; indeed, that the
inevitable struggle against the competition of Herbeck would do
harm rather than good to his reputation as a composer. Though
he was re-elected in May for three years, in accordance with the
statutes, he resigned his position in July, and all attempts to
induce him to continue his work as a conductor were fruitless.
He was succeeded by Dessoff. And now began a fresh period of
travel for Brahms and a fresh sphere of activity.

X

COMPOSITION OF THE *DEUTSCHES REQUIEM*

It started, however, under quite different auspices from those of his previous *Wanderjahre*. He was no longer a partner and dependent of Reményi, and a protégé of Schumann, but a composer enjoying a growing independence, whose tours were no longer undertaken with a view to earning a livelihood, but to promoting and broadening his creative work and studies, or else for recreation, for purposes of health or intellectual development. But during all his ensuing travels and temporary changes of residence Vienna remained his headquarters. During the following ten years or so, while he had no fixed employment, Brahms made repeated attempts to become acclimatized in one place or another. But time after time he returned to the lovely blue Danube.

After resigning his first post at Vienna, Brahms, who had already composed the Second String Sextet, once more started off on long travels to beautiful regions and towns which could offer him undisturbed calm for his work and plenty of stimulus for his imagination. In the spring of 1864 he left Vienna, visited his parents — who had in the mean time separated and were living apart — and once more travelled by way of Göttingen to Baden-Baden. He was particularly fond of this lovely cosmopolitan watering-place in the Black Forest, and from 1862 to 1872 would join Clara Schumann and their friends here every summer. "The house known as Lichtental No. 316 — more correctly, 136 —" writes the composer to Frau Bertha Faber at Vienna, in May 1865, "lies on an eminence (the Cäcilienberg), and from my rooms I look out on three sides at the dark, wooded mountains, the roads winding up and down them, and the pleasant houses." His rooms at Baden were as simple as can be

imagined: a little uncarpeted, blue-papered attic, the "Blue
Room," and a bedroom. It was there, among the great fir-woods
of the Black Forest, early in the sixties at least, that many of
the finest of Brahms's works, among them the romantic Horn
Trio, op. 40, in its original form, came into being. On every
visit he would make an expedition to Karlsruhe, where he had
two dear friends in the person of Hermann Levi, afterwards
court conductor at Munich, and Julius Allgeyer, the engraver,
an enthusiastic admirer of Anselm Feuerbach, the great neo-
classic German painter — the one being as sanguine, vivacious,
and restless as the other was low-spirited, cautious, and deliberate.
The weekly performances of the Karlsruhe opera company in
Baden filled Brahms with schemes for operas; we shall see later
that they never materialized, and why. In August there was a
visit to the third congress of musicians at Karlsruhe, of which he
sent a sarcastic account to Joachim. Early in February 1865
Brahms accompanied his dearly loved mother to her last resting-
place at Hamburg, and in the spring he was back again in Baden
and made the acquaintance of Anselm Feuerbach through the
good offices of Allgeyer.

As soon as the Karlsruhe horn-player had "practised the
Horn Trio for a week or two," Brahms presented it to the public
at a court concert at the beginning of December with him playing
the horn part. At the beginning of November he had played
some Schumann and his D minor Piano Concerto at a concert
at the Museum, and, to his surprise, the latter had not "disgusted" the Karlsruhe public at all (" *gar keinen Verdruss
gemacht* "). Between the two concerts came a short visit to
Switzerland. At Basel he gave a concert on his own account; at
Zürich he conducted his First Serenade and played Schumann's
A minor Concerto and Bach's Chromatic Fantasia and Fugue.
It was on this occasion that a most amusing incident took place,
as afterwards reported by A. Steiner in the New Year's number
of the Allgemeine Musikgesellschaft of Zürich for 1898: "In
the first movement of the [Schumann] concerto Brahms brought
off a delightful musical joke. The oboist had made a mistake in

the well-known phrase of the melody, which is afterwards repeated on the piano, by sounding F sharp instead of G as the
grace-note on D; Brahms thereupon reproduced the passage with
the same mistake, for the sake of consistency, as he said, and so
as not to put the oboist in the wrong." From Zürich he went on to
Winterthur, where he exchanged courtesies with the Rieter-
Biedermanns and gave an evening concert of chamber-music with
Kirchner and Hegar. After a second concert at Karlsruhe, Brahms
continued his concert tour northwards, both conducting and
playing the piano, by way of Mannheim, Cologne, and Oldenburg to Hamburg. Here he made the acquaintance of his step-
mother, Caroline Schnack, whom " Father " Brahms had married
in March 1866, about a year after the death of his first wife; after
which Johannes returned to Karlsruhe.

In the spring of 1866, by the advice of Theodor Kirchner, he
took up his quarters in Zürich with a view to a long stay, and
for the first time made the acquaintance of the enthusiastic
musical amateur Theodor Billroth, a very able surgeon of the
school of Dr. Langenbeck, who lived near Hegar on the Plat-
tenstrasse. They had much in common, sharing the same gloomy,
pessimistic view of life, and soon formed a true and cordial
friendship, which lasted for life. The surgeon was a very clever
pianist, far more than a mere dilettante, and a capable viola-
player, who was in demand by Eschmann for the quartet which
used to play at his house; and he occasionally contributed musical
reviews to the *Neue Zürcher Zeitung.*

Brahms profited extremely by his stay at Zürich for purposes
of quiet composition. Besides working at the *Deutsches Requiem*
he also found time to put the finishing touches to the Horn
Trio, the *Magelone* song-cycle, and the *Vier Gesänge,* op. 43,
containing two gems, *Von ewiger Liebe* and *Die Mainacht.* He
spent a short time at Winterthur, staying with his publisher
Rieter-Biedermann. Then he went travelling in Switzerland, and
by June was back again at Zürich with Billroth. To the horror
of the classically minded Billroth, he played some symphonic
poems and symphonies of Liszt's with Kirchner, on two pianos:

"Horrible music! *Dante, Mazeppa, Prometheus. . . .* In the *Dante*," relates Billroth, " we only got as far as the ' *Purgatorio* '; I then interposed my veto from the medical point of view, and we purged ourselves with Brahms's new sextet, which has just been published. . . ." And Hegar told Steiner that " Brahms also visited frequently at the Wesendoncks' [Richard Wagner's friends] and showed a lively interest in everything that could be heard there about Wagner. Frau Wesendonck possessed the first drafts of *Tristan und Isolde* and a manuscript piano sonata; Herr Wesendonck, Wagner's autograph score of *Das Rheingold*. Brahms would look at these things with a certain awe, and indeed at that time he always spoke of Wagner with great respect." For the rest, the whole of his stay at Zürich was devoted to working at *the* great work which was soon, in the following year, to make Brahms's name popular, in the noblest sense of the word, and win him a decisive victory, a position of incontestable weight with the great public, far more than after the publication of the sextets, the *Magelone-Lieder,* the piano quartets, the Piano Quintet, and the Handel Variations for piano: namely, the *Deutsches Requiem.*

According to Kalbeck, the first sketches of the *Requiem* must have been written as early as 1861 at Hamm (Hamburg). This would at any rate dispose of the generally accepted view that the death of Brahms's mother was the direct occasion of its composition. On the contrary, Kalbeck produces convincing evidence that the *Deutsches Requiem* was " intended as a last great funeral rite for Robert Schumann." In any case, Brahms wrote the greater part of the *Deutsches Requiem* in his lodging at Zürich in the house of Kuser, the former town-clerk of Fluntern, below the so-called " Forster " on the Zürichberg, with a glorious distant view of the lake and the Alps, and, as Steiner relates, " In order to put together suitable words for it out of the Bible, he dragged up to the Zürichberg the *Great Concordance* — an alphabetical classification of all important passages in the Bible — from the municipal library." The score was completed in 1866, the year of the war with Austria, and consisted of six movements, a seventh movement not being added till later. At the end of May 1867 Billroth obtained an appointment at Vienna as professor and first director of the Operationsbildungsinstitut (Institute of Operative Surgery) at Vienna. In the autumn he moved from Zürich to Vienna, and Brahms accompanied him, perhaps already with the almost certain intention of shortly following this friend of whom he had become so fond to the Austrian capital, which had long been dear to his heart.

For the present, prospects seemed otherwise, and Brahms's life continued to run its curious zigzag course, divided between south-west Germany, Switzerland, and Austria. After a summer spent in Baden, and a fresh concert tour through Switzerland, he arrived in Vienna at the end of November 1866. To celebrate his reappearance he gave two concerts of his own, on March 17 and April 7, at which he himself played the Handel and Paganini Variations. His father had at once to be told that their success exceeded his expectations: " My piano-playing impresses them here well enough, and certainly I am not losing ground. . . . It is so long since I had played here that people had no idea what to expect, and meanwhile the evening went off splendidly." These two concerts played a decisive part in Brahms's subsequent decision to settle in Vienna for good. In April followed a tour in Hungary (Pressburg, Pest), and in November, with Joachim, to Vienna, Graz, Klagenfurt, and Pest.

On December 1 of that year Herbeck gave a first performance of the first three movements of the *Deutsches Requiem* at a concert of the Gesellschaft der Musikfreunde in the Grosse Redoutensaal. As was to be expected, it was not altogether appreciated. On the contrary, after the third movement in particular, with the mighty surge of the final fugue above the pedal-point on D, there was, as Richard von Perger, who was Brahms's friend and sponsor at the Vienna Tonkünstlerverein, reports, a nice burst of hissing on the part of some who wanted a " row," and Perger, who had been a Brahms enthusiast for thirteen years, narrowly escaped being assaulted by them. Hanslick severely dissociated himself from such expressions of disapproval in his *Neue Freie Presse* article:

"While the first two movements of the *Requiem,* in spite of their sombre gravity, were received with unanimous applause, the fate of the third movement was very doubtful. Brahms need not take this to heart — he can wait. It is comprehensible that a work so hard to understand, and dwelling on nothing but ideas of death, should not expect a popular success and should fail to please many elements of the great public. But we should have thought that even its opponents would have had some slight idea of the grandeur and seriousness of the work and felt bound to treat it with respect. This does not seem to have been the case with half a dozen bald-headed fanatics of the old school, who had the bad manners to greet the applause of the majority, and the appearance of the composer in response to it, with continuous hissing, thus performing a 'requiem' over decorum and good breeding in a Vienna concert-hall, which was a most unpleasant surprise to us."

But even Hanslick, enthusiastic as was his praise of the sincerity and importance of the *Requiem* in general, took particular exception to this third movement and confessed, among other things, that "during the concluding fugue of the third movement, surging above the pedal-point on D," he "experienced the sensations of a passenger rattling through a tunnel in an express train."

But this dubious success in Vienna was most brilliantly made up for at Bremen. Karl Reinthaler, the cathedral conductor, to whom Dietrich had shown the score in manuscript, rapidly made up his mind and fixed the performance of this work, of which he at once recognized the importance, for Good Friday, April 10, 1868, in the cathedral. Brahms, who had again been staying in Hamburg since January, and had played Schumann's Piano Concerto and his own Handel Variations and Fugue at the concert of the Oldenburg court orchestra at the beginning of April, made frequent visits to Bremen from Hamburg for the practices of the

Requiem (at that time still consisting of six movements), which was being rehearsed with devoted care by Reinthaler. Clara Schumann also arrived from Baden-Baden just in time, and surprised Brahms in the cathedral. Instead of the fifth chorus (" *Ich will Euch trösten* "), which was still lacking, Frau Amalie Joachim sang, in a wonderful medley of styles, the aria " I know that my Redeemer liveth," from *The Messiah,* and Joseph Joachim played Schumann's *Abendlied.* The success of the *Requiem,* which was splendidly performed, was so striking and profound that as early as April 28 it had to be repeated at the Union with Reinthaler as conductor. There was a little celebration afterwards at the old Ratskeller, where the Schumanns, Joachims, Dietrichs, Reinthalers, Stockhausens, Grimms, Max Bruch, Richard Barth, Rieter-Biedermann, who afterwards published the *Requiem,* and others — in all some hundred persons — gathered at a festive supper, fêted him cordially, and even tried to ensnare him into making a speech of thanks in response to Reinthaler's address, which he eluded with dignity and the assurance that " the gift of speech was certainly not his to command."

In the summer of this year the fifth movement (with soprano solo), composed after the rest of the work, was inaugurated on the occasion of a fresh visit to Switzerland, where he had accompanied his father, at the old Zürich concert-hall near the Fraumünster. The performance of the *Deutsches Requiem* at Bremen was followed in the next year by its production at Basel, Leipzig (both at the Gewandhaus and at the Riedelverein), Hamburg, Oldenburg (twice), Karlsruhe, Zürich (Good Friday, 1869), and Münster, and from this time onward it went the round of all the important large towns, wherever the German language is spoken — Berlin first made its acquaintance in 1872 (two performances), Halle and Königsberg in 1874 — and it met with the same admiration and affection everywhere. By 1868 Brahms, who had hardly been known as a composer hitherto, had become at a single bound a name of undisputed eminence in the musical world in the wider sense; his obscure years of effort and struggle for recognition were now followed by a period of collecting and maturing his forces and of rich fruition, throughout which he retained the same modesty, the same iron self-discipline, artistic conscience, and severe self-criticism, accompanied by the same steady, tranquil reflection and untiring work.

XI

DIRECTORSHIP OF THE VIENNA GESELL-
SCHAFT DER MUSIKFREUNDE

THE LARGER CHORAL WORKS

Brahms was now at the height of his slowly and hardly won fame, enjoying the plenitude of his creative power. In the spring of 1868 he again met his intimate friends at Cologne, at the Musical Festival of the Lower Rhine. The summer was devoted to bringing out the *Deutsches Requiem.* In his quiet villa at Bonn on the Kessenicher Weg, with its garden, he further completed his setting of Goethe's *Rinaldo,* composed another song-cycle (op. 43 and 46–9, including *Die Nachtigall* and the *Wiegenlied*), gave a concert at Neuenahr with Rosa Girzick, a pupil of Stockhausen, and entered into stimulating and frequent intercourse with the philologist Hermann Deiters, a pupil of Otto Jahn, who has won distinction as an able writer of the classical school on Beethoven, Schumann, and Brahms and as editor of Jahn's biography of Mozart and Thayer's life of Beethoven. *Rinaldo* was soon followed, still at Bonn, by the work *par excellence* which, with the *Requiem* and the *Ungarische Tänze* (Hungarian Dances), first made Brahms's name really popular: the *Liebeslieder-Walzer,* for piano duet, with vocal parts. During these fruitful years, 1868 and 1869, two of Brahms's finest choral works on a large scale also came into being: a setting of Hölderlin's *Schicksalslied* for chorus and orchestra, and the *Alto Rhapsody* ("*Aber abseits, wer ist 's?* ") from Goethe's *Harzreise im Winter,* for alto solo, male choir, and orchestra. At that time Goethe's *Harzreise* had stirred Brahms to his depths. He lost no time in making the acquaintance of Reichardt, "my honoured predecessor," through Deiters, and we know from Dietrich how he conceived the psychological relation between his *Rhapsodie* and the *Liebeslieder-Walzer:* " Poor recluse (*Abseiter*) that I am! Have I yet sent you my epilogue to the *Liebeslieder?* " The first idea for his *Schicksalslied,* so Dietrich informs us, came to Brahms while looking at the sea: " In the summer Brahms again came [to Bremen], to make a few excursions in the neighbourhood with us and the Reinthalers. One morning we went together to Wilhelmshaven, for Brahms was interested in seeing the magnificent naval port. On the way there our friend, who was usually so lively, was quiet and grave. He described how early that morning (he was always an early riser), he had found Hölderlin's poems in the bookcase and had been deeply impressed by the *Schicksalslied.* Later on, after spending a long time walking round and visiting all the points of interest, we were sitting resting by the sea, when we discovered Brahms a long way off sitting by himself on the shore writing. It was the first sketch for the *Schicksalslied,* which appeared fairly soon afterwards. A lovely excursion which we had arranged to the Urwald was never carried out. He hurried back to Hamburg, in order to give himself up to his work."

We see that, with Baden-Baden, Karlsruhe, Zürich, Bonn, Hanover, and Oldenburg, Hamburg keeps reappearing as one of his regular resorts outside Vienna during these years, if indeed we can speak of regular resorts at all where Brahms is concerned. From the artistic point of view, he may perhaps still have been drawn to his native city by the tacit hope of being appointed to some honourable official musical post there; but, as he soon admitted to Joachim: " Once again I have cause to deplore the fact that the sympathy of my friends here has waned." There was another reason of a personal order, as we saw just now, which may well have induced him to make frequent short visits to Hamburg: " Father " Brahms had married for the second time, in 1866, his second wife being Caroline Schnack, and Brahms became very fond of his step-mother and her son by her first marriage, Fritz Schnack, the watch-maker.

In the spring Brahms gave a number of concerts with Stockhausen and Rosa Girzick, and conducted his *Deutsches Requiem* at Karlsruhe. The summer of this year was again spent at Baden-Baden. Brahms was gradually becoming disgusted with this wandering life and wanted a regular post. "It goes without saying that I should like a post — that is to say, an occupation," he admitted to Max Bruch. Hamburg was now definitely out of the question; he therefore made up his mind to wait for a post in Vienna and to choose the Austrian capital as his permanent residence. From this time onwards he divided his life between intense periods of creative work, concert tours on which he conducted his own larger works, and considerable travels for recreation in the spring or winter.

Meanwhile the decisive moment was approaching in Vienna. "I am being spoken of more or less openly," he wrote to Joachim, "in connexion with the directorship [of the Singverein] of the Gesellschaft [der Musikfreunde]. But I almost dread an official offer and the subsequent business of making up my mind; for, much as I desired some such occupation, this position has too many elements of doubt, and my wisest course would be not even to try the experiment." These scruples on the part of a great creative artist about sacrificing his freedom, though divined rather than clearly defined, are just the same as those he felt before accepting the post at the Singakademie. Meanwhile everything remained in uncertainty; in the summer of 1870 Brahms paid a visit to Munich, Upper Bavaria, and Salzburg. The Franco-German War now broke out. Brahms watched events with passionate excitement. "How I long to come to Germany!" wrote this great patriot to Reinthaler. And to Dietrich: "I am shortly going to Germany, and I almost dread it. We outsiders have grown accustomed to doing nothing but rejoice over what is happening; but you have the seriousness and terror of this fine and great period terribly close, before your very eyes, and you may well contemplate it with some solemnity." To Gernsheim he writes: "You can imagine what a great joy and distinction it is to me that my requiem is being performed in honour of the victims of these great days. The thought of it moves me so deeply

that I almost shrink from speaking about it." To Levi he says:
" You are right; I simply had to come to Germany. I must have
my share in the rejoicings, I could no longer bear it in Vienna.
Long live Bismarck! That is my supreme expression of the
emotions that are stirring us so deeply."

The artistic fruit of the Franco-German War was the grand
music of his *Triumphlied,* written to words from the book of
Revelation during the winter of 1870-1 to celebrate the triumph
of the German arms. By the good offices of Joachim it was dedicated to the victorious Emperor William, and coldly acknowledged by a short, curt official letter of thanks. On Good Friday,
April 7, 1871, in Brahms's presence, Reinthaler conducted the
original performance of the first chorus of this work in Bremen
after the *Requiem.* On June 5 Brahms heard the first performance
of the complete work, conducted by Levi at Karlsruhe. It was
not till December 1872 that he himself presented it to the public
of Vienna as " artistic director " at the first special (*ausserordent-
lich*) concert of the Gesellschaft. The jubilation was naturally
indescribable at the time. In the year 1874 followed Leipzig,
Munich (with Franz Wüllner as conductor), Cologne (at the
Musical Festival of the Lower Rhine), then Basel and Cassel (on
the occasion of the jubilee of their choral societies), Zürich (at
the Musical Festival), Breslau and Berlin (with Stockhausen as
conductor). The work and the composer, who conducted it, were
everywhere received with wild enthusiasm.

Meanwhile it did not seem for the present as if the desire that
he had expressed to Dietrich as early as 1869 for " constant connexion with both chorus and orchestra " were likely to be realized
at Vienna. Herbeck was appointed to the Court Opera-house.
The Gesellschaft der Musikfreunde chose first Hellmesberger,
then Rubinstein, as their " artistic director." It was not till after
the retirement of the latter that Brahms was at last thought of.
There is an obvious note of annoyance at these typically Viennese
tactics of procrastination in his letter of August 1, which was
intended in part as an ultimatum. But it had its effect; in September 1872 Brahms entered upon his new appointment. He suc-

ceeded in securing the acceptance of his own conditions, sharply formulated in his own clear, vigorous, and uncompromising fashion, with regard to the number of concerts, his emoluments, and his own sole and unqualified personal responsibility for the choice of works and the invitation of soloists. The three years of Brahms's directorship form one of the most brilliant epochs in the history of this venerable and famous artistic institution. The new conductor and director of the choir — " artistic director " was his official title — who, like every outstanding artistic personality in Vienna, at once had strong currents of opposition and intrigues to fight against, established the concerts from the outset on a firm and solidly classical basis. The choir of the Singverein, whose three hundred or so members had always been recruited from the most select and musical amateur singers in Vienna, was spurred by Brahms to the most consummate achievements. Masterpieces of earlier periods, such as Handel's *Saul* and Dettingen *Te Deum* — with which he opened the first concert, which he conducted on November 10, 1872 — produced the most extraordinary impression. Billroth wrote in the following enthusiastic terms to Lübke about Brahms's conducting:

" He is rehearsing Handel's (Dettingen) *Te Deum,* and *Saul,* two Bach cantatas, his own *Triumphlied,* etc. For the present he is quite fired by conducting the Gesangverein and is in a constant state of delight at the voices and musical talent of the choir. If his success is encouraging, I think he will continue. A single failure is enough to dishearten him, so that he loses pleasure in it. . . . Brahms is extremely active as director of music here; he has achieved some incomparably fine performances, and meets with the fullest recognition from all who are well-disposed towards art. His *Triumphlied* made a wonderful impression here with organ and a colossal choir; great masses are suited to it, it is monumental music. Its effect is to give one every sort of pleasant musical 'creeps' (*Gänsehaut*) uninterruptedly, and withal it is lucid, in the most grandiose alfresco style. . . . At the last concert Brahms ventured on a Bach cantata, to Luther's words ('*Christ lag in Todesbanden*'), which had never been performed

before. It was damned stiff music, but imposing in its effect
in places. The Viennese accepted even that with amiable readiness, at the hands of a composer whom they respect as they
do Brahms. It was followed by two unaccompanied folk-songs
(by Brahms), which really provoked a perfect storm of applause
and made one quite anxious lest the house might collapse. The
old King of Hanover was so intoxicated by the music that he was
half mad . . . and indeed one is really drunk with the beauty
of this choir's tonal effects; its *crescendo* and *diminuendo,* its
forte and *piano* produce the effect of being sung by a single
voice; Brahms manages them like Renz putting a horse through
its paces."

In his treatment of Handel, Brahms based himself from the
first — that is, as early as 1872! (and this cannot be strongly
enough impressed upon the consciousness of many of our so-
called "great conductors" of the anti-Chrysander school) — on
the safe and firm foundation of historical fidelity and adherence
to the style of the original even in the instrumentation. " As
regards Handel too," he writes to Hegar, who was intending to
perform the *Joshua* at the Zürich Musical Festival in July, " I will
just tell you, briefly and hastily, that I perform him as closely as
possible to the original score, and I am better pleased with this
every time I try it. Naturally with the addition of organ and
piano. I modify the trumpet parts a little as required; in the
Te Deum, for instance, I used three trumpets and a cornet, in
such a way that the latter only took over a few notes in case of
need, and on the whole the trumpet tone remained as it was."
Of his own works he selected for these concerts the *Deutsches
Requiem,* the *Triumphlied,* the *Schicksalslied,* the *Alto Rhapsody,*
from Goethe's *Harzreise,* and a few unaccompanied songs.

Again in the winter of 1874-5 Brahms, to use Billroth's words,
" is so popular and so much fêted everywhere (though rather un-
discriminatingly) that he might easily become a rich man by his
compositions, if he were prepared to take his art lightly. Luckily
that is not the case." But by the beginning of 1875 a change took
place. Herbeck fell into disfavour in exalted quarters and retired

from his post as director of the Court Opera-house. A new position had now to be found for him. The choice fell on the directorship of the Singverein; so Brahms had to go too. With the practised aid of the poet Mosenthal, who had a particular grudge
against the " northern intruder," the artistic intrigues for which
Vienna is famous of old proceeded to lay their snares, which it
was impossible to elude, and Brahms fell into the trap. He was
no fighter, and once again he was far too easily discouraged by
a few small failures at certain concerts, just as he had been as
chorus-master at the Singakademie; so with characteristic dignity
he abstained from all counter-intrigues and counter-attacks, gave
notice of his resignation, and after the performance of Bruch's
Odysseus on April 18, 1875 retired from the directorship of the
concerts. It was Levi who first discovered who was really re-
sponsible: " Herbeck! Nothing has happened yet, but the prospects are not reassuring and I should be glad to go. I refuse either
to squabble with him or to wait till he ousts me." But there was
another victim too, as Billroth complained to Lübke: " Brahms
has had . . . very interesting programs, and so has Dessoff. Unfortunately we have lost them both as conductors. Both have been
squeezed out — both squeezed out by Herbeck." Herbeck once
more assumed the conductorship, only to fall a victim to inflammation of the lungs in November 1877, when he was no
more than forty-six years old.

XII

THE SYMPHONIES

With his resignation from the directorship of the choral concerts of the Gesellschaft der Musikfreunde Brahms definitively
renounced for the future all the burdens and prestige of an official
appointment. Three times he was approached with a view to
a "regular post." The first occasion was in November 1876,
when he was offered the position of director of music at Düsseldorf; the second in 1879, when the cantorship of St. Thomas's,
Leipzig, was vacant; and the third in the spring of 1884, when he
was offered the directorship of the Cologne Conservatoire and
Konzertverein. The negotiations with Düsseldorf dragged on till
February 1877, those with Leipzig never reached an acute stage,
and the Cologne proposal went no further. The reasons which
he gave for declining the Düsseldorf offer are humorous and at
the same time significant: "My chief reasons against it are of a
childish nature and must be passed over in silence (for instance,
the good taverns in Vienna and the bad, coarse tone on the Rhine,
especially in Düsseldorf), and besides — in Vienna one can remain a bachelor without comment. In a little town an old
bachelor is a figure of fun. I no longer intend to marry; yet, all
the same, I have some reason to be afraid of the fair sex." His
real reasons were not revealed till his more seriously worded refusal of the Cologne proposal: "I have remained too long out
of such a post, and grown too much accustomed to quite a different way of life, not to have become, on the one hand, rather
indifferent to many things in which, in such a position, I ought
to feel the most lively interest; and, on the other hand, out of
practice and awkward in matters which require to be handled as a
matter of routine." The loss of his yearly salary from the directorship at Vienna (three thousand gulden, Austrian currency) caused

him no material embarrassment. His publisher and friend Simrock had already, with exemplary generosity — and at the same
time with an eye to his own advantage — seen to it that Brahms
should be able to live in peace and independence so as to be free
to compose. His parting from the Gesellschaft der Musikfreunde
took place on the most amiable terms, and Brahms remained an
active honorary member of the committee.

Perhaps a sad change which took place in his family also had
something to do with his resolve to settle in Vienna for good, and
finally give up Hamburg. On February 11, 1872 Brahms had to
enter in his diary: "Death of my good father." This was seven
years after the death of his mother. At the end of January Brahms
had already hurried from Vienna to Hamburg, and now accompanied him to his last resting-place. This severed the last bond
with his parents, but not with his step-mother and step-brother.
In the year 1880, on the contrary, Brahms writes to a friend of
his youth, Frau Elise Denninghoff of Hamburg, the mother of
Agnes Denninghoff, the singer, and mother-in-law of Bernhard
Stavenhagen, the distinguished pianist and pupil of Liszt: " My
father and mother have long been dead. My father married again
and was very happy. He could not have lived alone (or with me),
and so our good step-mother really took care of him during his
last years. Moreover, during these latter years he saw a good deal
of the world, with the greatest enjoyment, in my company or that
of his wife. He went to the Rhine and the Danube, Switzerland,
the Harz, and goodness knows where besides! My sister has been
happily married for many long years to Grund, a watch-maker.
She and my brother Fritz are living in Hamburg, and I see them
all every year in passing through." Thus " Father " Brahms lived
to see with pride his " Jehannes " slowly but steadily rising to
fame, and with true filial affection his son repaid him as richly
as was in his power for all the want and hardships of his hard-
working life. As early as 1867 he was able to write from Hamburg
to his friend Dietrich: " I have had the great joy of having my
father with me for a few weeks. We have made a nice tour
through Styria and Salzburg; imagine how I enjoyed my father's

happiness, he had never seen a mountain and had hardly ever
been outside Hamburg." He often repeated these summer travels
with his father during the years that followed. But it is an open
secret that good, simple "Father" Brahms was sedentary rather
than roving in his tastes, and was always frankly glad when he
had escaped from the high mountains, which oppressed him and
made him anxious, and was happily back again in his room at
Hamburg. His touchingly devoted son did not notice this; now
that his father was dead, he lamented to Reinthaler: "But how
sad it is to me that it was not granted to us two happy creatures
to be together longer; that he could not enjoy a comfortable old
age longer after his long and toilsome life!"

After a few years had elapsed, this new phase of Brahms's life
was also marked by a visible sign: he gave up his old quarters
in the more low-lying Leopoldstadt, to which he had been attracted by the proximity of the Prater, with its glorious walks,
and in 1878 moved to the higher and more healthful suburb of
Wieden, on the third story of a comfortable house in the Karlsgasse, No. 4.

Concert tours, on which he performed or conducted his own
works, now occupied more and more of the composer's life. When
he appeared in his double capacity as conductor and pianist, as
a rule he conducted some new orchestral or choral work at the
first concert and played the piano part in some chamber work
at the second.

We have already followed the progress of his *Triumphlied*
from 1871–4, from Bremen to Karlsruhe, Leipzig, Munich, Cologne, Basel, Zürich, and Berlin. But this section is headed: "the
symphonies." Under this title are comprised the four jewels in
the crown of Brahms's work, which form the object and point
of all his concert tours from this time onwards. "A symphony
is no laughing matter nowadays," as he once wrote. Thanks to
his extremely severe self-criticism and artistic conscience, it was
not till after his two Serenades for orchestra and his orchestral
Variations on a Theme by Haydn that Brahms felt justified in
presenting his deeply pathetic First Symphony, in C minor, to the

musical world, which had been waiting for it for long years past. The first drafts of its first movements, as we have seen, go back a very long way, to the summer which he spent at Münster am Stein in 1862. It was finished in September 1876 at Baden-Lichtenthal, and on November 4 the original performance took place at Karlsruhe, with Dessoff conducting. In the same year followed Mannheim (with Brahms conducting), Munich, and on December 17 Vienna, with Herbeck as conductor, at a concert of the Gesellschaft, and on January 18, 1877 Leipzig. Its success everywhere was impressive; in Munich alone it was poor — for in spite of the devoted propaganda of Levi and Wüllner, South Germany in general, and its capital in particular, is, not unnaturally, unfavourable soil for the works of the North German composer, even nowadays.

The pastoral, idyllic Second Symphony, in D major, came into being in the summer of 1877, during Brahms's first stay at lovely Pörtschach on the Wörther See in Carinthia. Its first performance at Vienna by the Philharmonic Orchestra, on December 30 of that year, was Brahms's first triumph in symphony, and it was, beyond a doubt, a great one.

Between the Second Symphony and the Third, in F major, with its heroic vigour, there is an interval of six years, during which we again feel that Brahms was collecting his forces and was fully conscious that in his next symphony he must produce something quite special and individual. He finished it in the summer of 1883, when, after the Musical Festival at Cologne, he went for a change to Wiesbaden and the Rheingau and paid his respects to Frau Germania in the Niederwald. The success of its orginal performance at Vienna on December 2 of this year, with Hans Richter as conductor, surpassed even that of the Second Symphony, and was confirmed by the first performance at Berlin, on January 4, 1884, with Brahms conducting, and at Düsseldorf in the spring of the same year, at the sixty-first Musical Festival of the Lower Rhine.

In the same year he began to sketch out the two first movements of the deeply elegiac Fourth Symphony, in E minor. He completed it in the summer of 1885 at Mürzzuschlag (in Styria). Its original performance, in the same year, had been secured by Hans von Bülow and his Meiningen orchestra; Brahms conducted it on October 25. It was not till January 17, 1886 that it was first performed in Vienna, with only partial success.

Among the larger instrumental works produced in the intervals between the four symphonies were the Violin Concerto in D major, dedicated to his friend Joachim, and introduced by him to the public at the New Year concert at the Leipzig Gewandhaus in 1879 — an exquisite product of his third summer at Pörtschach — the incomparable pair of overtures composed at Ischl in the summer of 1880, the *Akademische* and the *Tragische,* and the Second Piano Concerto, in B flat major, the first drafts of which dated from years before and which was finished at Pressbaum in the summer of 1881. The *Tragic Overture* did not make much impression at its first performance in Vienna by the Philharmonic Orchestra under Hans Richter; the *Academic,* as we shall see below, was produced by Brahms himself at the beginning of 1881 in the great hall of Breslau University. The Second Piano Concerto he first brought out in person in Vienna and Budapest, Marie Baumayer performing it in public for the first time afterwards at Graz. In addition to these great instrumental works, there were also the two last great choral works: his settings of Schiller's *Nänie,* in memory of the death of Anselm Feuerbach (1881), and Goethe's *Gesang der Parzen* (1883). The *Nänie* was originally performed on December 6, 1881 at Zürich, with Brahms conducting, and performed for the first time before the great public on January 6, 1882 at a concert of the Vienna Gesellschaft. The *Gesang der Parzen,* composed during the summer of 1882 at Ischl, was originally performed on December 10, 1882 at a concert of the Allgemeine Musikgesellschaft at Basel, with Brahms as conductor, and performed for the first time in Vienna on February 18, 1883, with small success.

The performances of these great vocal and instrumental masterpieces of Brahms's maturity gave rise to innumerable concert tours. It would merely be a meaningless and unprofitable geo-

graphical and statistical game, and terribly wearisome to my
gentle readers, if I were to bundle them into the train at this
point and send them off with Brahms on all these unending
journeys in every direction up and down central Europe — for
at that time there were no *trains de luxe* or restaurant cars. I prefer
to confine myself to the most important points, by conducting
them to the general centres of Brahms's activities, which gradually
became more and more clearly defined, rising like islands in a
variegated sea of towns.

In Austria-Hungary the two capitals, Vienna and Budapest,
naturally formed such centres. Brahms had often given concerts
in Pest, either alone or with Joachim. From this centre he went
with his friend in the spring of 1879 to southern Hungary and
Transylvania, and in the spring of 1880 northwards to Bohemia
and Galicia. His first great centre in Germany was the Rhineland. Three of its cities were already particularly sacred to Brahms,
owing to their association with his friends the Schumanns —
Düsseldorf and Bonn, where Robert had first made his acquaintance, lived, and suffered; and Frankfurt, where Clara worked till
her death. There was hardly a winter concert season for Brahms
which did not include a visit to the Rhineland; there was never
a Musical Festival of the Lower Rhine at Cologne or Düsseldorf
without Brahms and his works; nor did he ever return to Vienna
without staying some time with Clara Schumann in Frankfurt,
where his new chamber-music works were as a rule inaugurated
strictly in the family circle, or as at the New Year 1880, when
weighty consultations took place over the complete edition of
Schumann's works which Frau Clara was bringing out. Bonn
continued to be the holy city sacred to the memory of Schumann;
here as a rule Brahms met his intimate friends, and here he conducted the performance in memory of Robert Schumann on the
occasion of the unveiling of the fine monument to him designed
by A. Donndorf, on May 2, 1880. In Coblenz Brahms performed
with Hermine Spies at a musical festival held to celebrate the
seventy-fifth anniversary of the foundation of the Musikinstitut
there. On January 20, 1880 he held a concert of his own works

to celebrate the foundation at Krefeld of a society whose devotion to him was peculiarly enthusiastic and heart-felt — namely, the Konzertgesellschaft, with Grüter, the director of music, at its head. The concert was at the house of Rudolf von der Leyen — the third of that name, who has left affectionate reminiscences of Brahms. His intimate circle was composed of the Leyens and their relations-in-law the von Beckeraths, the Grüters, Richard Barth, the first violin, Gustav Ophüls, the meritorius compiler of the *Brahms-Texte,* the violoncellists Schrempels, Schwormstädt, and later C. Piening, and others. There was no town or chorus in which Brahms took such an unvarying pleasure as at Krefeld. He gave concerts there several times, in 1881, 1883, and 1885. In North and South Germany important centres for Brahms's music sprang up at Hamburg (the Philharmonic), Berlin, Bremen (Reinthaler), Oldenburg (Dietrich), Hanover (Joachim), Münster (Grimm), Breslau, and Königsberg. He acknowledged the honorary doctorate conferred upon him by the University of Breslau by conducting before the assembled Rector, Senate, and Faculty of Philosophy his new *Akademische Festouvertüre,* which he had dedicated to them. At the jubilee celebrations of the foundation of the Hamburg Philharmonic, Brahms met his intimate friends Clara Schumann, Joachim, Reinthaler, Grimm, Henschel, Claus Groth, etc. By the year 1880, thanks to the propaganda of his friend Hans von Bülow, Meiningen became a sort of Brahms stronghold in central Germany. At the first Brahms concert at Meiningen, on November 27, 1881, the composer played his Second Piano Concerto; on October 25, 1885 he conducted the original performance of his Fourth Symphony. Between these dates and after them there were a number of Brahms concerts, which the composer generally attended with alacrity, being cordially fêted by Bülow and the art-loving Duke and his wife. During Brahms's life Leipzig lagged behind Meiningen as the second great Brahms centre in central Germany, though this was certainly not so after his death. No musical stronghold in Germany cost Brahms so much time or effort to win as Leipzig and its Gewandhaus. But they made amends after his death by the greatest fidelity, the most thorough understanding, the greatest and most reverently devoted veneration for his art. Nowadays, indeed, Leipzig may lay claim to the honourable title of *the* German Brahms city *par excellence,* thanks, by no means least, to the late Arthur Nikisch, incomparably the greatest conductor of Brahms at the Gewandhaus. There is no other city in Germany today whose leading concert institution can venture to present regular Brahms cycles every winter, performed with a perfection unknown elsewhere, before a public better schooled in the understanding of Brahms than any other.

Among other countries Holland and Switzerland may boast themselves above all others to be " Brahms countries." The great Brahms centres in the former are Amsterdam, Rotterdam, and The Hague, and in the latter Zürich and Basel. It was in 1876 that the wealthy, enthusiastic musical country of Holland gave the same triumph to the composer and pianist, at the age of forty-three, as it had done a generation earlier to Schumann, at the age of forty-four, and he returned there repeatedly — for instance, in 1880, with Richard Barth as the interpreter of his violin concerto. The composer, who was akin to the Dutch in race and nature, always enjoyed visiting the country, and in Verhulst of Amsterdam and Hol of Utrecht he found two admirable conductors, who were at the same time true friends and admirers. The Tonhallegesellschaft of Zürich and the Allgemeine Musikgesellschaft of Basel were the centre of the Brahms cult in Switzerland, which was intensified by the personal influence of a large circle of friends, whose acquaintance we shall shortly make. Zürich could early boast of being called by Hegar the Brahms city of Switzerland. It was here that Brahms himself conducted the original performance of the *Nänie* on December 6, 1881, and here that he first played his Second Piano Concerto from the manuscript.

For twenty years Brahms spent every winter in a concert tour which he called his " *Konzertwinter.*" It was not till the middle nineties that these ceased, owing to his failing health. Vienna fêted him as a conductor for the last time at the twenty-fifth

anniversary of the foundation of the Gesellschaft der Musikfreunde, on March 18, 1895 (when he conducted the *Akademische
Festouvertüre*), and as a pianist on January 11, 1895, when he
played his F minor Clarinet Sonata with Mühlfeld. Leipzig saw
him for the last time on January 31, 1895, when he conducted
the two piano concertos, played by Eugen d'Albert at the Gewandhaus; Frankfurt in the middle of February, Zürich in the autumn
of the same year, Berlin on January 10, 1896, at a concert of
d'Albert's.

XIII

SUMMER QUARTERS

In contrast with these concert and professional tours, which started as a rule in the second half of the winter, after the New Year, the long summer months, usually from May till well into the autumn, were devoted to recreation and quiet creative work. To Brahms, as to every true son of the Low German north, travel and the enjoyment of nature were a necessity of life. But, in contrast with his winter tours, we should not here speak of summer tours, but of long periods of summer residence. What Brahms liked for his summer quarters was a quiet, settled centre, where, like all intelligent men, he found recreation not in indolent idleness or restless touring about, but in concentrated creation and tranquil enjoyment of nature. On these holidays what he always tried to find were, for preference, "from two to three nice peasant rooms with plenty of windows and not much furniture" (Eugenie Schumann), which might indeed offer but modest comforts, but all the more "air, light, and room to move about."

In the early sixties the scene of Brahms's summer residence changed from year to year; then from 1877 onwards he spent three years in succession at Pörtschach, an equal number at Thun from 1886 onwards, and from 1889 onwards, after two previous trials, he always returned to Ischl. But with the sole exception of the summer which he spent at Rügen, in 1876, his summer residences were never in his native Low German north, but in the Austrian Alps, Switzerland, the Rhine, Bavaria, or Upper Bavaria.

May 1873 saw his arrival at Tutzing on the Starnberger See in Upper Bavaria. The peculiarly attractive beauty of these Bavarian foot-hills of the Alps enchanted this subtle appreciator

of nature: " Tutzing is far lovelier than we had previously imagined. Just now we had a splendid storm; the lake was almost
entirely black, with a glorious green on the shores. Usually it is
blue, but a lovelier, deeper blue than the sky. One never tires
of gazing at it and the chain of snow-covered mountains." Here
he worked at the orchestral Variations on a Theme by Haydn
and the songs, op. 59, and at the string quartets. Artistic stimulus
was provided by his friendly intercourse with the Vogls, both
of whom were distinguished singers, who, like true Bavarian
artists, were themselves " planting their cabbages " in good peasant fashion; and if the weather was bad, Paul Heyse and the
art-collections of Munich were there to attract him to that city
near by.

From the beginning of June to the end of September 1874
he spent a long summer holiday in a chalet near the " Nidelbad "
by Rüschlikon, high above the Lake of Zürich. He exchanged
frequent visits with the poet Gottfried Keller, made the acquaintance of Widmann, who afterwards became his friend, saw a great
deal of G. Eberhard, who at that time wrote the musical reviews
in the *Neue Zürcher Zeitung,* and indulged in his favourite recreation by composing the new series of *Liebeslieder-Walzer,* op. 65,
the vocal quartets, op. 64, and the *Lieder und Gesänge,* op. 63,
with the glorious *Meine Liebe ist grün wie der Fliederbusch.*

In the spring of 1875 he visited the Neckar, on Feuerbach's
account, and stayed with Hanno, the portrait-painter, in " abso--
lutely fascinating " quarters (as he wrote to his step-mother) at
Ziegelhausen, on the right bank of the Neckar, a little above
Heidelberg and opposite Schlierbach, and absorbed himself in
working at two quartets (the Third Piano Quartet, op. 60, in
C minor, and the Third String Quartet, op. 67, in B flat major),
the *Duetten,* op. 66, and the *Lieder,* op. 70 (including *Abendregen*). The composer felt thoroughly happy: " I am delightfully lodged and pass my time delightfully. Only too well; with
Heidelberg, Mannheim, and Karlsruhe all quite close at hand.
You know the country, people, and inns of Baden and can sing
their praise." In May, Dessoff, the court conductor, performed

the *Neue Liebeslieder-Walzer* at Karlsruhe; in August, Brahms
visited Mannheim for the performance of Goetz's *Der Widerspenstigen Zähmung* (*The Taming of the Shrew*), conducted
by Frank, the court conductor. In the quiet country near the
Neckar, at Baden-Baden, he again met Frau Clara Schumann,
who was taking a short rest at Heidelberg in the middle of July,
on her way from Kiel to Klosters, welcomed his friend Dietrich,
the Feuerbachs, the Dessoffs, the Steinbach brothers, Frank, and
others, spent equally sunny hours both with the devotees of the
Muses at Heidelberg, and with the young villagers of Ziegelhausen,
and had delicious pancakes, made with six eggs, cooked for him by
Bertha, the splendid cook at the " Adler," rewarding her at her
special request with a waltz, about which the fat Bertha used
afterwards to say wonderingly: " And when he played, one
couldn't see his hands! "

The next summer, that of 1876, was spent at Sassnitz, on the
island of Rügen, with George (now Sir George) Henschel, afterwards conductor of the Boston Symphony Orchestra, teacher of
singing at the Royal Academy, London, and composer. In his
personal reminiscences of Brahms, written in English and published in 1907, Henschel has given a charming account of how
happy Brahms was on Hertha's northern island with its wealth
of legend and the submerged city of Vineta, how " gloriously
beautiful " he found it, and how eager and glad he was to practise his " beloved Low German dialect " there again.

Towards the end of the seventies, in 1877, he discovered lovely
Pörtschach on the Wörther See in Carinthia, southern Austria,
and visited it twice more in the two following years, with occasional excursions into the Val d'Ampezzo, in the Dolomites.
He describes his new summer quarters in his old jesting way:
" Pörtschach is most exquisitely situated, and I have found a lovely
and apparently pleasant abode in the Schloss! You may tell everybody just simply this; it will impress them. But I may add in
parenthesis that I have just two little rooms in the housekeeper's
quarters; my piano could not be got up the stairs, it would
have burst the walls." His crowds of visitors and professional

colleagues — among them Ivan Knorr, the South Russian, then aged twenty-five, later the biographer of Tschaikowsky, professor of theory and director of Dr. Hoch's Conservatoire at Frankfurt am Main — forced him to descend to the lake next summer, and also, though only occasionally, to accept the tempting invitations of the Herzogenbergs, who had settled near by at Arnoldstein in the Gailtal. His three summers at Pörtschach were particularly rich in artistic achievement: the Second Symphony, two motets (op. 74), the Violin Concerto, two Rhapsodies for piano (op. 79), and the First Violin Sonata, in G major.

On May 22, 1881 he went to Pressbaum, in the country on the line going westward from Vienna, and there completed the Second Piano Concerto and the *Nänie,* in the garden of a house there belonging to a Frau Heingartner, No. 12 Brentenmais-strasse, in the charming Pfalzautal.

In the summer of 1883 he went to recuperate at Wiesbaden, staying at No. 19 Gaisbergstrasse, rising steeply from the Taunus-strasse, in " perfectly fascinating quarters " (in the house of Frau von Dewitz), and wrote to his friend von der Leyen that he wished his summer travels might bring him to Wiesbaden, " for no mere steel pen can describe anything so pretty " as he represents this lovely, hot, cosmopolitan watering-place on the Taunus as being. It was here that he finished the Third Symphony.

In the years 1884-5 the composer ensconced himself in a " perfectly delightful summer abode " at Mürzzuschlag (Styria) on the Semmering railway. Friends would come over from Vienna near by, or he would go on many a long excursion far into lovely Styria, where, happy in the preservation of his incognito, he paid a visit to Peter Rosegger, the amiable folk-poet, who wrote the *Waldbauernbuben,* or he would give Frau Clara ecstatic descriptions of the enchanting moonlit evenings on the Semmering. It was here that the Fourth Symphony came into being.

The three summers from 1886 to 1888 he spent quietly at Hofstetten, near Thun, on the Lake of Thun, in Switzerland. It was only his desire to go to Switzerland again that decided him to undertake this long and troublesome journey; as he confesses to his friend Joachim: "I am spending this summer most agreeably at Thun, which I had rather dreaded, but to my joy I have been pleasantly disappointed." This pleasant disappointment soon changed to absolute rapture. He writes to Dr. Richard Fellinger, to whom and to whose wife, Marie, a highly talented sculptor, he had been attached for many years in Vienna by the most cordial and sympathetic friendship, that he had " found an absolutely fascinating abode " and " must only be careful not to praise everything possible here far too highly." " Here are the most lovely greetings from Hofstetten near Thun," he writes to Max Kalbeck, " and the only reason why I do not take a sheet of note-paper is so as not to praise things too highly. But I congratulate myself on my decision; it is simply glorious here. I only say quite in passing that there are crowds of beer-gardens — actually beer-gardens — the English are not at home in them! That is no small addition to my comfort." Brahms had quite a fine lodging here on the first floor of the house belonging to the merchant Johann Spring, with a shop on the ground-floor, close by the glass-green Aar and opposite the well-wooded islet ("Inseli") of Scherzligen, made famous by Kleist's stay there in 1802. According to the account given by the musician Künzelmann, now settled at Rostock, who was then playing the viola in the casino orchestra under the Bern conductor Theil, almost every afternoon of this summer at Thun in 1886 Brahms would sit in the casino garden, always alone, silent and absorbed, with his beer and cigar, his broad-brimmed hat lying beside him, and listen to the music; during the interval he would good-naturedly help the young musicians by giving them francs to stake at Rössel (petits-chevaux), but none the less rejoiced slyly on one occasion, when he had noticed, after it had been performed, that a waltz described on the program as by Roth was not by Roth, but by a better composer, old Lammer! Every Sunday afternoon regularly he would go off, with a leather satchel stuffed with borrowed books, to spend a day or two with his friend Widmann at Bern, where he felt completely at home in the family of " his Johanna's father " — for he used jestingly to call Widmann's

youngest little daughter his fiancée — and was well able to appre-
ciate the solid bourgeois midday meal. Widmann's hospitable
house was frequented by the leading artistic amateurs of Bern and
Brahms's Austrian and German friends — Hanslick and Kalbeck
from Vienna, Professor Wendt, a prominent educationalist, from
Karlsruhe, Claus Groth and the black-and-white artist Hermann
Allers from North Germany, and perhaps Gottfried Keller from
Thun besides, and his biographer Professor Bächtold from Zürich,
Carl Reinecke from Leipzig, the classic exponent of Mozart's
piano music in Germany — a merry meeting indeed. In June 1888
our "one and only, our splendid, golden Brahms" met the masterly interpreter of his songs Hermine Spies — "Herminchen,"
as he called her — at Widmann's, and then Brahms would sit
down to the piano, play some Bach "in his incomparable fashion,"
or accompany his own songs, or perhaps the whole of the Schumann *Dichterliebe,* and the most lovely private concerts and
"miniature musical festivals" would be improvised on the spot,
with Brahms's latest works. Once, in September 1886, he met
there the poet Ernst von Wildenbruch, with whom Brahms, with
his strong, sound emotions and ardent patriotism, naturally became friendly at once. But so surely as the weather was fine, the
Widmanns would come over to Thun, and Brahms, who had
already a tendency to *embonpoint,* would light-heartedly let himself be led off on glorious excursions into the Alps, to Mürren,
Kandersteg, the Oeschinensee, or even up the Niesen.

His three summers at Thun bore a rich artistic harvest. The
first enriched us with the "tranquil happiness" of the tender, intimate Second Violin Sonata, known as the "Thun Sonata,"
op. 100, in A major, the Second 'Cello Sonata, op. 99, in F major,
and the Third Piano Trio, op. 101, in C minor; the second with
the Double Concerto for violin and 'cello with orchestra, op. 102,
and the *Zigeunerlieder,* op. 103; the third with the Third Violin
Sonata, op. 108, in D minor, the five choral songs (*Chorgesänge*),
op. 104, and the *Lieder,* op. 105–7.

But it was at Bad Ischl that the composer felt most comfortable in the summer. He discovered the enchanting beauty of

its scenery for the first time in 1880, and repeated his visit in 1882. Perhaps it was owing to the abominable weather on both occasions — which he had to thank for a bad chill in his ear the first time, and which greeted him the second time with wintry snow-squalls even in the middle of May — that there was a pause of seven years in his visits to Ischl. From 1889 to 1896, however, he was back again in his pleasant old summer quarters at No. 51 Salzburger Strasse. "But I must give high praise to Ischl," he wrote in June 1880 to Billroth, "and though I am only threatened with one thing — the fact that half Vienna is here — I can be quiet here — and on the whole I do not dislike it." And this was indeed true; half Vienna and the whole circle of Brahms's friends and acquaintances would gather here round the master as years went by, and so at rainy Ischl he felt quite secluded, and yet with much to stimulate him. He was particularly fond of making an excursion from Ischl to the lovelier, but even rainier, Gmunden, where he would visit his faithful friend Viktor von Miller zu Aichholz and his wife, Olga, in their splendid villa, surrounded by a great park. Here he would meet Goldmark, Eduard Hanslick, and other friends and colleagues from Vienna, or would bury himself in the great library with black coffee and his well-known enormous cigars, and he was treated by the Millers as one of the family. But wherever he spent the summer, the composer sought refreshment after his intense creative work (which often occupied him during his walks in the open air) in friendly, sociable intercourse with a small, cheerful circle of friends and in a reverent enjoyment of nature.

At Ischl a series of Brahms's finest masterpieces came into being: the two overtures, the *Gesang der Parzen,* the two string quintets, the Clarinet Quintet, the two clarinet sonatas, the *Fest- und Gedenksprüche* (festival and commemorative pieces) for chorus, and many others.

A great part of the composer's summers was devoted to his "old love" the Rhine, including Düsseldorf, Krefeld, Cologne, Bonn, and Godesberg, at all of which he stayed as often as possible with dear friends and gave himself up to old and beautiful

memories. Among these places was the charming villa at
Rüdesheim belonging to Rudolf von Beckerath, Rudolf von der
Leyen's uncle, who was often visited by Joachim and Frau Clara
Schumann, Stockhausen, Bruch, and others, and whose son Willy
has left us perhaps the most characteristic drawings and sketches
of Brahms. Every year, if possible, he had a happy meeting with
his oldest and most faithful friend, Clara Schumann. In summer
or autumn he preferred it to be at Baden-Baden, where he usually
stayed at the comfortable " Bär " in the Lichtentaler Allee, and
once, in 1889, entertained his friend Widmann there too. As he
grew older, from about the beginning of the nineties, he postponed it almost entirely to Frankfurt am Main. If there were no
public concerts or chamber-concerts of Brahms's works there —
where he had a large circle of admirers — they would first try
through for the first time the composer's latest chamber and piano
works of recent years. In this way the *Klavierstücke,* op. 116-17,
the two clarinet sonatas, the Clarinet Trio, or the Clarinet Quintet,
but also, and more frequently, Robert Schumann's *Fantasiestücke*
for clarinet, were played with the great Meiningen clarinettist
Richard Mühlfeld, among a small circle of friends and colleagues
at Clara Schumann's house in the Myliusstrasse, No. 32, which
was " so dear " to Brahms. Her grandson Ferdinand, who was
then a young man, has left a fascinating diary full of notes on
this musical circle of Brahms's at the house of the famous piano-
teacher, who was then seventy-seven. Here were to be found the
most distinguished members of the staff of the two great Frankfurt *conservatoires,* and cordial admirers of Brahms, such as Herr
Lazzaro Uzielli and his wife, Julia, Ivan Knorr and his wife,
Ernst Engesser, Hugo Heermann, Hugo Becker, Naret Koning,
Anton Urspruch, Gustav von Erlanger, Johannes Hegar (son
of the Zürich musician), who was at that time studying the
'cello under Becker, and Dr. Rottenberg, conductor of the
orchestra at the opera-house, and a native of Vienna. Here
the Heermann Quartet (consisting of Heermann, Bassermann,
Welker, and Becker) would meet to rehearse for matinées at
Frankfurt, or the Joachim Quartet would meet at the house of

Ladenburg, the banker, to perform Brahms's quartets in the presence of the composer. Or they would go to the house of Louis Sommerhoff, Clara Schumann's son-in-law, or Dr. Spies, of the public health department, president of the Frankfurt Museumsgesellschaft, the musical director of which was G. F. Kogel, and there improvise afternoon and evening concerts of Brahms's works. Friends and interpreters of Brahms always found Frau Schumann's house open to them as they passed through Frankfurt am Main: the Joachims, Mühlfeld, the Herzogenbergs, the Stockhausens, Ferdinand Kufferath (Brahms's venerable old apostle in Brussels), Rudolf von der Leyen, and so on. But whenever Brahms himself was passing through, he never omitted to pay a short visit, if only from the afternoon till the next day at noon, to his oldest friend, whom he loved with all his heart so long as she lived.

XIV

TRAVELS IN ITALY

A separate chapter in our composer's life must be devoted to his Italian travels. We are perhaps better informed about them than about almost any other part of his life, a fact which we owe especially to the charming reminiscences of Brahms left by his Swiss friend and travelling-companion J. V. Widmann in his *Johannes Brahms in Erinnerungen* and *Sizilien und andere Gegenden Italiens; Reisen mit Johannes Brahms.*

Why did Brahms go back to Italy time after time in his mature years? He shared in the northerner's longing for the sun, the south, and beauty, and for unsophisticated, unconstrained, and care-free life, the instinctive and overmastering attraction of German artists towards what will counterbalance and supplement German seriousness, correcting northern intellectuality and lack of sensuousness by southern gaiety and sensuous delights, by elemental nature in both life and art. Both as man and as artist he felt the recreation, relief, and healing afforded by the contemplation of unmixed nature, the purely animal, instinctive life, and natural passion, to be an inner necessity of his nature. The artist in Brahms was attracted to Italy in the first place by the pictures, and only lastly by the music. He was as much at home with Burckhardt and Gregorovius as with Gabrieli and Palestrina; and the masterpieces of Italian art, in both painting and architecture, produced a direct and elemental effect upon him; their most splendid creations were capable of moving him to tears of the deepest emotion. Widmann justly conjectures that it was chiefly in the works of the Italian Renaissance that he found the ideal and prototype of his own art. The harmony between content and form, the painstaking care and conscientiousness even in the smallest and most obscure details, the " humility

in the presence of superior genius" referred to by Hebbel in his
Michelangelo — all these were things of whose value he was
profoundly conscious.

Brahms loved Italy and the Italians to such an extent that
he simply refused to see the many dark blots on the radiant
escutcheon of that glorious land and its highly talented people:
the poverty, ignorance, and servility, the religious subjection and
dirt of the lower classes, the cruelty to animals, the scandal of
the bandits in southern Italy and Sicily, the corruption, the professional beggars, and the laziness of the *lazzaroni*. His Italy was
the ideal, much-belauded artistic land of promise, which lavished
on him nothing but happiness, sunshine, and beauty.

During the last twenty years or so of his life it was his custom
to start out in spring on his Italian tour, and it would almost
appear from his words to Hegar: " provided only we are safe in
the depths of the Abruzzi by May 7, or somewhere else where
we are sure that nobody can get at us," that he regarded it at
the same time as a particularly welcome means of slyly eluding
any birthday celebrations with which he might be threatened in
Vienna.

The prelude to his Italian travels was invariable: Brahms
looked round for a suitable travelling-companion, for he had not
sufficient command of Italian — nor, indeed, of any foreign
language — to be able to keep up a conversation in it by himself.
And so, shortly after the New Year, some such cautious, delicate
tentative inquiry as the following would flutter down upon his
friend Widmann's writing-table: "In case you might be thinking of ever such a modest little promenade beyond the Alps this
spring, just ask yourself whether yours very truly might not
perhaps accompany you." Or this, of a later date, in a more jesting form: "If, my dear friend, you have really liberal views and
principles, you can arrive at an idea of how much money I am
saving and have in reserve for an Italian tour — unless I get
married during the summer or buy myself a libretto for an
opera! Cannot we do the trip together? I cannot get on very
well alone in Italy."

Brahms was eight times in Italy. The first time was in 1878, with Billroth and Goldmark, when he rushed hurriedly through southern Italy (Rome, Naples) and Sicily and had a heart-rending meeting at Palermo with his god-child Felix Schumann, who was hopelessly consumptive. Next in 1881 through central and southern Italy and Sicily (Venice, Florence, Siena, Orvieto, Rome, Naples, Palermo, etc.), with Billroth, Dr. Adolf Exner (professor of law at Vienna, the successor of Jherings and the friend of Gottfried Keller), and Nottebohm (the expert on Beethoven, who dropped out as early as Venice, where he was held fast by the sweet Cyprus wine). In the spring of 1884 he combined a visit with Rudolf von der Leyen to the Villa Carlotta on the Lake of Como, belonging to the Duke of Meiningen, with a little tour through southern Tyrol (Trent, Roveredo) and by way of the Lake of Garda through northern Italy (Milan, Genoa, Turin). In the autumn of 1882 he made a "jolly, leisurely tour" with Billroth through northern Italy, from Lucerne by the St. Gotthard to the Italian lakes, Bergamo, Brescia, Milan, and Venice. The fifth Italian tour, in the spring of 1887, with the old friend of his youth Theodor Kirchner and the publisher Simrock, took him from Innsbruck over the Brenner to northern and central Italy (Vicenza, Verona, Venice, Bologna, Florence, Pisa, Genoa, Milan). From his sixth long tour in Italy, in the spring of 1888, onwards, his Swiss friend Widmann was his regular companion. It led him from Venice, through Bologna, Rimini, the "postage-stamp republic" of San Marino, Ancona (Loreto), and the Umbrian Apennines (Spoleto, Terni), to Rome (Frascati — where he visited the poet Richard Voss at the Villa Falconieri and admired the ancient Greek theatre in company with him — Tivoli, Porto d'Anzio, Nettuno); and he returned home by way of Florence, Turin, and Milan. The seventh tour, in 1890, was confined to northern Italy: the Lake of Garda, Parma, Bergamo, Cremona, Brescia, Vicenza, Padua, Verona. But the eighth, through Italy and Sicily in 1893, was the longest and most extensive of all, including Genoa, Pisa, Rome, Naples, Palermo (Monte Pellegrino, Monreale), Girgenti (where he visited the ruins of the temple),

Catania, Syracuse (where he visited the amphitheatre, the quarries, and the Anapus), Taormina, Messina, and a return home by way of Naples. In addition to Nottebohm — "*il Giovanastro,*" as they dubbed him in Rome — Goldmark — "*il re di Saba* (the King of Sheba) " — Billroth, Kirchner, Simrock, von der Leyen, and Widmann accompanied him on the last tour, when at Sorrento Brahms joined Hanslick and the pianist Schulhoff, the excellent musician Friedrich Hegar, whose friendship with him dated from Zürich days, and the German-Hungarian pianist Robert Freund — whom they dubbed the "*Romforscher* (explorer of Rome)," a most amiable, cultured young man and a professor of the piano at Zürich. On the way home he usually chose the St. Gotthard route, and enjoyed paying another visit to his Swiss friends at Zürich and Bern, with a fairly long stay on the Lake of Thun.

In Italy Brahms always preferred a good old-fashioned *albergo* to the great cosmopolitan caravanserais and took pains not to be in any way outdone by the innate tact, natural dignity, and graceful politeness of the Italians, while all the time, as was the charming habit of this man of the people, he was never at a loss with simple people in particular. In the evening, at the inn, he would go about in stockinged feet rather than keep a poor servant waiting for his boots; or, though a great smoker, he would not so much as light a cigarette before asking permission of any lady who might happen to be present; and, though a convinced Protestant, he would never enter a Catholic place of worship, even in Italy, without dipping his fingers in the holy water and making the sign of the cross. All these are charming little traits due to the delicate tact and gentle nature of this man whom some would have us believe to have been so "harsh" and "rough."

For those, it is true, who liked to travel comfortably and at leisure Brahms was not precisely a pleasant travelling-companion. As Widmann tells us: "The good wine and food of the genuine Italian cuisine, the excellent coffee, the ample, really princely beds in the lofty, airy rooms, had cast a spell upon him. Apart from

the fact that, in the Phæacian luxury of Vienna, he had grown
accustomed to the best of everything and liked a good table, in
other respects he was little addicted to luxury and was content
on occasion with the most modest night-quarters in the most
miserable dens; yet southern *joie de vivre* was sympathetic to
him. . . . But in spite of all this the alert mobility of his untiring intelligence could tolerate no self-indulgent revelling in
material pleasures. . . . His mind, accustomed to work and
making the best use of his time, was always longing for fresh
activities, and often, when I proposed travelling at a rather more
leisurely pace, he would jestingly cut me short, asking whether
I imagined I was travelling for pleasure in a land where there
was infinite variety and novelty to see at every step." In short,
this inveterate early riser was, as one of his travelling-companions
once said with a groan, "like a pet elephant rolling on us." In
Italy what he liked best was to avoid all travelling by rail; he
deplored the fact that the railway ran past such old Umbrian
mountain fastnesses as Fabriano, Gubbio, and Trevi, saying that
"one ought to ramble through all these parts on foot!" In a
letter to Widmann he sets the widest possible limits to his desires,
which extended from north to south: ". . . indeed, it is lovely
everywhere in that glorious land. Padua would be quite to my
taste, and you simply must see Orvieto, and I should like to go
to Perugia too, and you ought to visit Palermo as well." The
ineffable loveliness of Sicily was particularly near to his heart.
Palermo, with its cathedral and memories of the Hohenstaufen,
Girgenti, with the ruins of its wonderful ancient Greek temple,
Syracuse, with its quarries and the grave of the poet Platen, were
his chief stopping-places. But most of all he loved Taormina.
Let us hear what Billroth has to say to Hanslick on the subject:
"Five hundred feet above the murmuring sea! A full moon!
The intoxicating fragrance of orange blossom! The red-flowered
cactus on picturesque, colossal rocks, in masses like moss at home!
Groves of palms, oranges, and lemons! Moorish castles! A Greek
theatre in beautiful preservation! Add to this the wide, long,
snow-covered slopes of Etna, and her pillar of fire! Add to this

a wine called 'Monte Venere'! And to crown it all, Johannes in ecstasy! I, in drunken impudence, improvising fantasias to him on his quartets! . . . if only you were with us, dear Hans!"

As we see, Brahms's demands were not small. He had a thorough knowledge of the history and art of Italy — not only the contrapuntal unaccompanied vocal music of the great old Venetian and Roman masters of the sixteenth and seventeenth centuries, but also the painting — and never wearied of enjoying and assimilating it all from six o'clock in the morning till late in the evening. His gift, which Albert Dietrich already comments upon in his youth, of taking a nap at a moment's notice anywhere, even upon the hardest stone bench, was " a just compensation of nature " for this. Inexorable though he was in his desire that his companions should adapt themselves to his ways of travel and recreation, he was just as ungrudgingly self-sacrificing if his help was required. Thus on his last tour to Italy and Sicily, when Widmann was laid up in a hotel at Naples with a broken ankle (a fortunate misfortune, for when within an ace of falling into the hold of the *Asia,* off Messina, he had remained hanging with one foot in the link of a chain), Brahms acted as his nurse, and afterwards wrote jestingly from Ischl that he had never been so pleased at any misfortune as at Widmann's broken ankle, and the sixtieth birthday, which he had passed in quiet seclusion by his friend's sick-bed, since " a far worse fate had come so alarmingly near."

Perhaps, after all, Widmann was a little scared by this mishap, or else in future he could not keep up with the pace of Brahms's Italian holidays so well. For when in 1895 Brahms again wanted to have him as his companion in a journey to the south, he had to decline on grounds of health, not without receiving a caustic jest from Brahms in answer: " However, you will too often be reminded of the fragility of our ' machine,' and one cannot blame you for having no great opinion of the resurrection of all flesh."

XV

FRIENDS AND FOES

After resigning his post as director of concerts to the Gesellschaft der Musikfreunde, Brahms never held any other official appointment, except for the fact that, with Hanslick, he remained one of the experts on the examining board for the award of State scholarships; he performed this unobtrusive " office," which later enabled him to discover the wonderful creative talent of Anton Dvorák, with that strict artistic conscientiousness, impartiality, kindliness, and justice which characterized him in all musical matters. With every year of his long residence in Vienna, as his artistic successes increased, a growing and more and more select band of friends and admirers gathered round the great composer, both there and in Germany, though, like a true Low German, he was not easy of access. We shall see what sort of friend Brahms was to them when we come to know him better as a man.

Throughout his whole life he was bound by ties of the most heart-felt and loyal friendship to the old friends of his youth, whom he had known as he worked his way up to fame. Among these early friends whom he made before he came to Vienna were: Clara Schumann, his oldest and dearest woman friend, who from 1878 till her death devoted her life to teaching and giving concerts, being in charge of the highest class at Dr. Hoch's Conservatoire; Joseph Joachim, his dearest and most intimate friend; Albert Dietrich, Julius Stockhausen, Julius Otto Grimm, Theodor Kirchner, Franz Wüllner, Hermann Levi, and Hermann Deiters. His friendship with Levi, one of his most enthusiastic admirers in earlier days, grew cooler in later years, and finally ended in a complete breach, when, on visiting Munich, Brahms found that Levi took no further interest in his works. The true causes of the breach lay deeper; we may conjecture that Levi's fervent veneration for Wagner was unsympathetic to Brahms and appeared to him exaggerated.

Two of Brahms's friendships had a decisive influence on him as a composer: those with Eduard Hanslick and Hans von Bülow. The able musical critic of the *Neue Freie Presse,* who was at that time, as it were, the musical pontiff of Vienna, and author of a biased, formalistic treatise on æsthetic, *Vom Musikalisch Schönen* (*On the Beautiful in Music*), made Brahms a success in Vienna and beyond; while the equally able conductor at Meiningen won him success both there and in wider circles. Hanslick proclaimed himself an apostle of Brahms in 1867, and subsequently, having come to be on such brotherly terms with Brahms as to address him by the intimate " *du*," he was regarded in Vienna as the brilliant critical protagonist of the " Brahms clique (*Brahms-gemeinde*)," who adhered to classical ideals. As we have seen, Bülow approached Brahms's art with characteristically critical and sceptical caution. But there was a sudden change at the end of October 1877, after he had worked at Brahms's First Symphony. It is now certain that this acute master of musical analysis, who spent his time in critical extremes, jumping to conclusions and formulating witty paradoxes, hindered rather than helped the unprejudiced reception of Brahms's first symphonic work by ranking it as the " tenth symphony " of the new " classic," and by his paradox of the " three great B's " in musical history (Bach, Beethoven, Brahms). But this prophet and pioneer of Wagner and Liszt was won over for good by the First Symphony to the art of " the heir of Luigi [Cherubini] and Ludwig [Beethoven]," of the " great master " as a conductor and composer; and for the rest of his life acted as a systematic propagandist on behalf of Brahms, with all the resources of his outstanding artistic ability and with the equally steadfast loyalty, uprightness, and devoted enthusiasm of his great, high-minded, and noble nature — and in no way as a " substitute for his lost Wagner."

The *Berliner Börsen-Courier* once described at that time how Bülow, Brahms, and Meiningen came to be associated: In November 1881 Johannes Brahms, at the instance of his friend Bülow, was invited for the first time to Meiningen as the guest of the Duke, and took part in the great Brahms concert given by the court orchestra on November 27 as the fourth of its series, as pianist (playing the Second Piano Concerto, in B flat major, from the manuscript), as composer (*Tragische Ouvertüre* and Haydn Variations), and as conductor of his *Akademische Festouvertüre* and First Symphony. The musician's interesting personality made such an exceptionally sympathetic impression upon the Duke and Frau von Heldburg, and, on the other hand, the true, genuine love of art, and simple, humane amiability of the Duke and his wife made such a deep impression on Brahms, that an intimate bond was at once formed between the prince and the artist, which was only severed by death. During the last fifteen years of his life Brahms visited the castle at Meiningen as a most welcome guest, and his friends Widmann, whom he presented there in 1891 and 1893, and von der Leyen, who was invited to Meiningen in November 1891, give really charming accounts in their reminiscences of how happy the composer felt there, in spite of the demands of court etiquette, which were considerably relaxed for his benefit. He joined eagerly in the musical life of the court, which "often began with morning concerts, and went on again till late in the evening in the Duke's private apartments," with Joachim, Hausmann, Wirth, and Mühlfeld taking part. He wore his high order at gala banquets with justifiable pride and consciousness of his distinction, beamed with good temper, merriment, and delight at all kinds of jests and pranks, and sunned himself with the comfortable contentment of an artist in the solid splendour which surrounded him in both castle and chamber. He gave expression to his hearty liking and deep esteem for the Duke, not without a certain slight touch of piquancy which will easily be detected if we consider the subject of the poem — namely, the nothingness and transiency of all earthly fame and splendour — by dedicating to this exalted personage one of his most moving compositions, the *Gesang der Parzen*, which was performed at Meiningen for the first time on the Duke's birthday, April 2, 1883. Brahms's first meeting with Bülow

and the ducal ménage at Meiningen was due to his Second Piano
Concerto. " It was a graceful act of Bülow's," writes Billroth to
Lübke, " to invite Brahms to Meiningen, so that he might work
at his concerto with the orchestra in absolute leisure there, with
no public, and without any view to a concert. Brahms accordingly
returned perfectly enchanted with Bülow and the Duke." The
Duke at once realized what manner of man he had before him,
and what his masterly conductor Bülow and his master-clarinettist
Mühlfeld might mean to the composer: " Whenever you would
like to have leave, and Brahms is in question, you may leave
Meiningen without asking me first," he intimated to Mühlfeld.

The chapter " Brahms at Meiningen " also has its Italian
idyll, when Brahms and his friend Rudolf von der Leyen visited
the Duke at the Villa Carlotta on the Lake of Como in May 1884.
It reminds one of the age of the Italian Renaissance. The exalted
personages were late risers, for reasons of health. Brahms and his
friend lived for a good while like Tasso and the Duke of Ferrara,
" quite solitary and gloriously alone, as though in an enchanted
castle," and when the Duke and his wife were there, there would
be improvised concerts on two pianos with the new Third Symphony, or they would listen to a Neapolitan band, and in the
wonderful starlit night, " in a perfect intoxication of bliss,"
Brahms's austere northern art became harmoniously fused with
the soft, extravagant luxuriance of exuberant southern nature.

From now onwards Meiningen was the main stronghold of
Brahms propaganda in Germany. The Meiningen court orchestra
was the authorized instrument, consecrated by direct, personal
tradition, for the performance of Brahms's works, under Bülow
and his successor, General Music-Director Fritz Steinbach —
Brahms's " *Lieber Herr General.*" Brahms's larger instrumental
works, the serenades, the Haydn Variations, symphonies, overtures, and piano concertos, are to be found in every program of the
" *Meininger.*" On February 3, 1884 the Third Symphony was
heard twice at the same concert — by a characteristic idea of
Bülow's; on October 25, 1885 the Fourth Symphony started its
career at Meiningen, being conducted by Brahms and repeated

on November 1 by Bülow. It was Bülow who conducted Brahms's
First Symphony in unexpansive Leipzig and played his First
Piano Concerto, in D minor, here, as also at a concert of the
Berlin Philharmonic on March 4, 1889, "without conductor."
And eight years after their first meeting, Brahms dedicated his
Third Violin Sonata (D minor) to "his friend Hans von Bülow."

Brahms was bound by ties of the most cordial friendship, based
upon thorough-going mutual esteem, with his contemporaries
the artists and musical scholars of Vienna, and it made no
difference even if their artistic tendencies and activities were in
the greatest possible contrast with his own, provided only that
they were genuine and honest. Such was the case with Karl
Goldmark, the sumptuous Viennese composer, who was to music
what Makart was to art, and wrote the great opera *Die Königin
von Saba* (*The Queen of Sheba*), glowing with oriental tone-
colour and harmonies, the *Sakuntala* overture — neither of which
Brahms liked, any more than he did Goldmark's music in general — and the *Ländliche Hochzeit* (*Country Wedding*), which,
on the other hand, he esteemed very highly. The same was true
of Richard Heuberger, the composer of the *Opernball* and biographer of Schubert, and Robert Fuchs, the retiring, modest composer of so many delicate serenades for string orchestra, and
piano duets of an intimate character with a Viennese tinge. The
same applies to Ignaz Brüll, the composer of the charming grand
opera *Das goldene Kreuz* (*The Golden Cross*) and an exquisite
interpreter of Brahms, whose "most genuine musical talent,
wealth of enviably easy invention, and truly melodious ideas,"
besides his sound knowledge, Brahms ungrudgingly admired, but
for whom he would have desired "just a touch of the struggle
for existence," which would have had the "beneficial" effect of
"stirring him to more intensive energy" and enhanced the
smooth flow and invariable idyllic grace of his works by an
added depth of feeling. The same was true of the "Waltz King"
Johann Strauss, whose enchanting melodies and "neat operetta
scores, as clear as daylight," gave genuine gratification to Johannes
the first, and moved him to write on Frau Adele Strauss's fan,

beneath the opening bars of the " Blue Danube " waltz: " J. Brahms, who would like to have composed this." This artistic harmony was reflected in their personal relations, and every summer Johannes was a cherished guest of Johann in his beautiful villa at Ischl. In his early years he was united by a heart-felt friendship with Herbeck, who was the first to insist actively in Vienna upon the importance of the *Deutsches Requiem;* and he was on friendly terms with the two admirable piano-teachers and professors at the Vienna Akademie, Julius Epstein and Anton Door, and the professor of singing there, Dr. Joseph Gänsbacher. Among musical scholars and writers on music he was particularly intimate with Dr. Eusebius Mandyczewski, archivist to the Gesellschaft der Musikfreunde, and a prominent authority on contrapuntal theory, a " young, very capable man," whom he recommended as a teacher to his own pupil Gustav Jenner (a native of his own parts, and now professor of the musical sciences at the University of Marburg) and whose professional advice he liked to ask before publishing new works; besides these there were Gustav Nottebohm, the distinguished expert on Beethoven, who edited his note-books, C. F. Pohl, the biographer of Haydn, and Max Kalbeck, the writer on musical history and author of a biography of Brahms which is of fundamental importance for the sources. At the Tonkünstlerverein of Vienna, of which he was one of the founders and an honorary president, he came to esteem highly, among others, Dr. Ludwig Rottenberg, a pupil of Robert Fuchs, afterwards conductor of the Orchesterverein (Orchestral Club) of the Gesellschaft der Musikfreunde in Vienna, and now conductor at the Frankfurt opera-house. He was an intimate friend and cherished guest in the distinguished and art-loving Viennese families of Conrat, Faber, Fellinger, von Miller zu Aichholz, von Wittgenstein, and many others.

But his most intimate and confidential friendship in Vienna, after that with Hanslick, was that which sprang up between him and a leading representative of medical science, the famous surgeon Theodor Billroth. In the year 1867, as we have seen, this eminent surgeon was summoned from Zürich to the University of Vienna, and Brahms soon followed his friend for good. Billroth's pretty villa with its garden, in the suburb of Alsergrund, was soon the hospitable rendezvous of the leading Viennese musicians. As the great surgeon once said to Dr. Richard von Perger, Brahms's pupil, friend, and biographer, at that time president of the Viennese Tonkünstlerverein and conductor of the Singverein, his sole endeavour in his free time, which was exclusively devoted to art, was "to convert the lucre acquired through the sufferings of humanity into the purest joys." These pure joys consisted in cultivating chamber-music and singing in his intimate circle at home, and in performances by distinguished artists before a small and select musical public. Billroth, as Hanslick once said jestingly, had the *jus primæ noctis* over Brahms's new works and would not give up a jot of his rights. Many of the finest string quartets, piano duets, songs, and vocal duets were heard for the first time at his house, and the songs had the advantage of such splendid interpreters as Gustav Walter, the court singer, afterwards principal tenor at the Court Opera-house at Vienna, and the young Swede Philipp Forstén, afterwards professor of singing at the Conservatoire.

Billroth was a far greater anatomist in medicine than in music. In this sphere he was no more than an honestly enthusiastic, highly cultivated amateur and had an amateur's one-sided tendencies and attitude towards art. He was an out and out and exclusive "*Beethovener,*" as Schumann used to say, of whose antipathy for all that was modern, and chiefly for Wagner, even Brahms himself would at times make fun: "So friend Billroth is still determined not to become a Wagnerite? Why is he waiting so long? Sooner or later he will have to come to it." But there is one thing which gives a peculiarly high value and rare attraction to Billroth's letters, appreciations, analyses, and notes; they are the testimony of a highly sensitive and musical æsthetic nature, written under the fresh and immediate impression of Brahms's new creations. He was the author of a fragmentary treatise on the æsthetic of music, which was published by Hanslick, but cannot be taken at all seriously, *Wer ist musikalisch?*

(*Who is musical?*). Seven years before his death, "he rose again from his death-bed," to use Brahms's words to Kalbeck, after a severe inflammation of the lungs. "This Billroth," said Brahms, "was no longer his old self, my friend Billroth; he was hardly a shadow of his former self." Indeed, he had become deeply estranged from Brahms and wrote Hanslick constant complaints of Brahms's inconsiderate and insultingly abrupt manner towards his friends, which, he said, was, as with Beethoven, the consequence of a neglected bringing up. During Billroth's last years Brahms suffered severely and painfully from this misunderstanding on the part of his intimate friend, and it was not till after Billroth's death and the appearance of Hanslick's handsome memorial publication dedicated to their mutual friend that he recovered his old, unclouded affectionate feelings and memories of him.

In his native city of Hamburg, as in all the great German, Austrian, and Swiss musical centres, he also had a faithful little circle of intimate friends among the good families of the city (Otten, Avé Lallemant, Wagner, Hallier, Rösing, Brandt). In his earlier years, during his second Hamburg period, when he divided his time between Hamburg and Detmold, he was in particularly close artistic relations with Karl G. P. Grädener, a composer (as crabbed and reserved as Beethoven, but none the less remarkable) of chamber and piano works of merit, who occupies, as it were, an intermediate position between Beethoven and Schumann on the one hand, and Brahms on the other. In 1863 Grädener had moved to Vienna, as professor of singing and composition at the Conservatoire and conductor of the Evangelisches Chorverein, but in spite of the high reputation which he had won as an artist, chiefly by his octet, he had found it uncongenial to his harshly intellectual nature and at the end of three years had returned to Hamburg. During the eighties Brahms was also on terms of the most friendly personal intercourse with Julius Spengel, the distinguished director of the Cäcilienverein. Spengel was the most enthusiastic and musically competent pioneer and prophet in Hamburg of Brahms's later

choral works on a large scale. On April 6, 1883 he invited Brahms
to a great "Brahms evening" in his native city, at which the
Second Piano Concerto and the Rhapsodies for piano were performed with the composer at the piano, besides the motet *Warum
ist das Licht gegeben,* folk-songs and choral songs, and at the
close the *Akademische Festouvertüre,* conducted by the composer.
It wound up with an interesting little celebration at the Hamburger Hof, at which the leading musicians of Hamburg, the
Simrocks, and others were present. Brahms remained absolutely
faithful to this friend and fellow artist, who was his junior by
twenty years. On two other occasions, in 1884 and 1886, he
accepted the invitation of the Cäcilienverein, and it was by means
of the Cäcilienverein, with Spengel conducting, that his eight-
part *Fest- und Gedenksprüche* — his musical acknowledgment
(dedicated to His Magnificence the Burgomaster, Dr. Carl Petersen) of the freedom of the city of Hamburg which had been
conferred upon him — was presented to the world on the occasion
of the Hamburg Musical Festival arranged by Bülow. He was
also a devoted godfather and uncle to Spengel's third child, as
he was to those of the Dietrichs, Hegars, and Stockhausens and
to Robert Schumann's youngest son, Felix, who had a certain
poetic talent, but died in 1879 at Frankfurt am Main, at the age
of twenty-five.

Not only in the world of music, but also in that of literature
and the plastic arts Brahms was on good terms with all that was
truest and most significant in his day. He had many distinguished
friends among poets and painters. Of those who came from the
same parts as himself, he numbered among his familiar friends
Claus Groth, the author of *Quickborn* and the leading folk-poet
of Schleswig-Holstein. When we come to examine Brahms's
First Violin Sonata and his songs we shall see what rich artistic
fruit this friendship bore. In Switzerland, through his circle of
musical friends at Zürich, he formed a friendship with Gottfried
Keller, the greatest of Swiss poets and author of *Der grüne Heinrich,* whose acquaintance he had first made through Kirchner
at the time of the *Deutsches Requiem.* The crabbed, rugged,

and serious German-Swiss poet and the equally strong-minded, rugged, proud Low German were bound to be in sympathy. The friendship between these two great personalities, both of whom had slowly and steadily fought their way upwards out of the most modest and narrow circumstances by their own efforts, after a hard struggle with a perpetually antagonistic world, was determined, so far as external features are concerned, by the Low German, Alemannic element in them both, and inwardly by the affinity between their characters. Keller, though by his own admission he knew nothing of music, never missed a performance of a Brahms symphony, and felt " peculiarly stirred and attracted " by Brahms's music, " which really has something new and individual to say." Throughout his whole life Brahms remained an enthusiastic admirer of Keller's poetry and never wearied of enthusiastically thanking Professor J. Bächtold, his friend at Zürich, who afterwards wrote the biography of his " great, splendid fellow-countryman," for every new and particularly rare work of Keller's that he presented to him — as he was wont to do in the first instance in a manuscript copy. On one occasion it was *Therese* or the *Traum- und Tagebuch,* next the *Plauderwäsche,* or, again, some letters.

His actual circle of musical friends at Zürich was first grouped round Theodor Kirchner, at the time of the *Requiem;* and afterwards, during the eighties and nineties, round Friedrich Hegar, the then conductor of the subscription concerts and director of the Tonhalle orchestra, who reformed the style of German male choirs and was instrumental in the first place in making Brahms's art known in Switzerland. Among the musicians of Zürich, in addition to Hegar and his wife, Albertine, a discerning interpreter of his songs, he was on particularly intimate terms with Gustav Weber, the highly talented German-Swiss composer of chamber and piano music, who unfortunately died as early as 1887, and Robert Freund, the distinguished German-Hungarian pianist, a pupil of those great masters Tausig and Liszt.

In Bern, however, was settled the poet Josef Viktor Widmann, a native of German Moravia, and editor of the *Bund,* Brahms's

faithful companion on his Italian travels, whose reminiscences
of Brahms are among the most beautiful, poetical, and happy
of the sources for the composer's biography during the last twenty
years of his life, and whose libretto for Goetz's comic opera *Der
Widerspenstigen Zähmung* and *Francesca da Rimini* may have
added to the warm interest taken by Brahms in Ernst Frank's
completion of Goetz's opera *Francesca da Rimini,* which he carried out with pious and devoted care. For, as Brahms afterwards
wrote to Hanslick, he was " absolutely delighted with little
Frank," that splendid fellow and most estimable artist, and with
the fine seriousness and diligence with which he performed this
work. " It is to him alone that Goetz — his idol (*Götze*) — owes
his peaceful death, and his Francesca her life."

Among painters the first to whom he felt attracted was
Anselm Feuerbach. We may remember that it was the engraver
Allgeyer, Feuerbach's biographer, who paved the way for this
friendship, at Karlsruhe during the sixties. They remained firm
friends during his whole life, and Brahms touchingly crowned
this friendship, after Feuerbach's death (in Venice in 1880), by
dedicating his setting of Schiller's elegy *Nänie* to the painter's
mother, who published his fragmentary autobiography, written
in Rome in 1870 and known as his *Testament,* one of the most
interesting pieces of self-analysis in the nineteenth century. These
two great idealistic artists, too, were predestined to come together.
The pictures of this greatest of German neo-classic painters, who
was also highly musical, are pure music in their tranquil stateliness
and rugged beauty and the poetic magic of their atmosphere;
while the compositions of the greatest German neo-classic in
music show, partly, indeed, by their choice of words and their
titles — *Schicksalslied, Nänie, Gesang der Parzen, Rinaldo* — how
peculiarly at home and at ease the composer felt in the world
of antique or Italian beauty, which was that of the painter of
" Iphigenie " or " Plato's Symposium." Both masters transfigured,
revived, and renewed the antique spirit in poetic fashion and
with modern sentiment. Both were great imaginative and plastic
artists, who often worked slowly and painfully, and neither of

whom was spared a long struggle against the misunderstanding and indifference of the majority. Both were proud, aristocratic, and strong natures, well aware of their own worth. Feuerbach's last manner, again, in such " symphonies of form " as the " Battle of Amazons " and the " Fall of the Titans " approximates to the austere design and cartoon-like art of Cornelius — whose " Horsemen of the Apocalypse (*Apokalyptische Reiter*) " we shall find in Brahms's library — while Brahms's latest manner, in his E minor Symphony, approximates to the austerely polyphonic " cartoon-like " musical style of Bach's passacaglia forms. And, lastly, both these artists gave universality in the representation of human experience precedence over all technical considerations, as the determining force of character and atmosphere.

The last years of his life were enriched by his friendship with Max Klinger, the great Leipzig etcher, with his powerful imaginative and intellectual art. The glorification through painting of the leading art of the nineteenth century in Germany — that is, music — and of certain of its masters was no new thing even in Brahms's day. Gabriel Max had aimed at representing music, the transposition of musical impressions into painting, by purely colouristic means, thereby incurring the disapprobation of Brahms, who may be called the greatest of " black-and-white " artists in music. Klinger interpreted music in a more concrete fashion, by the pictorial art itself, and considered the monochrome effects of etching best suited to this. Through this medium, setting aside the old fables of visual colour effects and of the reproduction of sound as colour while listening to music, the primitive relations between painting and music could, he was convinced, develop with the most untroubled purity. Klinger's *Brahms-Phantasie*, published by Amsler and Ruthardt in Berlin (1891-4), caused the greatest delight to our composer, who received it as a present in the form of a particularly handsome presentation copy on Japanese paper, with Klinger's autograph dedication " to Herr Dr. Johannes Brahms. Dedicated by the author in all reverence, October 8, 1894." " They are simply magnificent pages," writes Brahms, " which might have been expressly intended to make one forget everything mean and transport one to the sunlit heights. You would not believe with what pleasure one gazes at them, constantly seeing more in them and finding deeper food for thought (*immer weiter und tiefer hinein sieht und denkt*)." Or later, to Hanslick: " Just to look at the latest *Brahmsphantasie* is a greater pleasure than to listen to the last ten [of my piano works]." And, indeed, these pages, pregnant with ideas, especially those devoted to Brahms's setting of Hölderlin's *Schicksalslied,* are, in their broad and artistic style of etching, and their inexhaustible power of imagination, the most wonderful thing that the draughtsman's art has found to say about Brahms's music. " These three " — the reference is to Feuerbach, Böcklin, and Klinger — " fill one's heart and house, and it is indeed no mean age in which one can enjoy such a trio; to them may be added, from your guild [the reference is to Widmann's Dichtergilde, or ' Poet's Guild '], say, Freytag, Keller, and Heyse — and since Menzel [the great Berlin etcher who revived the ideals of the age of Frederick the Great] just occurs to me, I remark how rich is our life and how transitory our judgments." But we shall soon test for ourselves whom and what Brahms read with the greatest pleasure, both in German and foreign literature, from an examination of his library at Vienna.

Brahms has often been censured for never doing for others what Schumann did for him: namely, introducing a great talent to the world unselfishly and ungrudgingly; but rather maintaining an exclusive and selfish attitude towards other creative artists of eminence. Nothing could be so foolish or unjust as this reproach. On the contrary, Brahms had an unerringly sharp eye for genuine youthful talent, and was ever ready to intervene on its behalf. Thus, as a member of the commission of musical experts, not only did he discover the splendid talent of the Czech Anton Dvořák in 1880, but by introducing him to his publisher Simrock he smoothed his young colleague's way from want and poverty to fame and comfort, from the narrow limits of Bohemia to greater Germany. He may have felt instinctively that the good genius of Dvořák, the composer of the chamber-music which has achieved the most notable success of modern times, after his own, had endowed him unstintingly in the cradle with the very quality which was to a certain degree denied to himself, its place being taken by the subtlest and most acute artistic insight: the gift of easy, flowing melody and musical inspiration with a national tinge. "I cannot understand you; I am beside myself with envy of the ideas that occur to the fellow quite casually," he would answer whenever anybody ventured to depreciate Dvořák before him. And when in 1881 he was playing over Dvořák's *Legenden* from the proofs, at Pressbaum with Door, he remarked to him: "It is extraordinary, ideas always come to the fellow." In Dvořák's String Sextet in A major, which he considered "marvellously beautiful," he admired the glorious invention, freshness, and lovely tonal effects, and next to this he was particularly fond of Dvořák's 'Cello Concerto. He never missed the first performances of Dvořák's works in Vienna, and when the Bohemian master, now famous, came to Vienna in February 1896 for the performance of his New World Symphony by the Philharmonic Orchestra, he gave him the following jesting introduction to Miller zu Aichholz: "Most honoured friend, In case Dworschak [Dvořák] were to come to the concert tomorrow and happened to be disengaged, would you have any objection to my bringing him to see you? I will let him eat out of my little plate and drink out of my little glass, and, so far as I know, he does not make speeches. Heartily yours, J. Brahms."

Brahms's friendship and esteem, which, moreover, he tried in vain to make Clara Schumann share, grew cooler in later days, owing to the unpleasant impression produced by the number and occasional superficiality of Dvořák's compositions, as well as by the fact of his defection to the neo-German program-music camp, which was so foreign to his naïve, spontaneous, bohemian artist's nature.

There was yet another Prague composer, the Czech Vitězslav Novák, whom he brought to the notice of Simrock, and in whose piano and chamber music he took special interest, owing to its

signs of remarkable ability, combining as it did something of
Brahms's style and manner of composition with the Slavonic folk-
music of his native Moravia.

But corresponding to this circle of Brahms's personal friends,
there was a "circle of enemies" inspired by non-personal, party
motives. They may be regarded as falling into three groups,
corresponding to three controversies: Brahms versus Wagner,
Brahms versus Bruckner, and Brahms versus Hugo Wolf. Of
these the first is by far the most important and fundamental;
the other two are to a certain extent secondary and arise out of it.

There are a number of authentic utterances and passages in
Brahms's letters which vouch for the undeniable fact that, even
though Brahms at first took up a cool, though not adverse, attitude towards Wagner — confessing, as late as March 1870, in a
letter to Clara Schumann: "I am not enthusiastic over this work
or for Wagner in general" — he became increasingly aware
of Wagner's outstanding greatness, and himself provides evidence
that he might with full justification call himself "the best of the
Wagnerites," a great, sincere, and deeply discriminating admirer
of Wagner's genius. Here is a small selection:

"Wagner: he is now the first of all," he says to Door.
"Nothing comes anywhere near him. Everything else disappears
in a moment before his importance, which nobody is so quick
to comprehend or appreciate as I am; the Wagnerites, certainly,
least of all." Or to Widmann: "If the Bayreuth Theatre were in
France, it would not require anything so great as Wagner's works
to make you and Wendt and everybody else go on pilgrimage
to it, and be full of enthusiasm for anything so ideally conceived
and executed." And again: "Wagner's works, so ideal both in
conception and execution." Or to Rudolf von der Leyen: "Indeed
I am a far older Wagnerite than all the rest of you put together."
"When Richard Wagner died, my first impulse was to send
a fine wreath to Bayreuth for his grave. Only think, even *that* was
misinterpreted as scorn, mockery, or what not. It is wonderful
to what lengths men's tactlessness and blindness are capable of
going." Or again: "Early yesterday morning I was walking alone

here by the Rhine, the mist lay deep and cold upon the waters, the stream flowed by dirty and turbid; then — suddenly — I heard from afar the song of a single nightingale — you see, everything is not necessarily by Wagner!" Or to Richard Specht: "Do you think me so narrow that I, too, cannot be enchanted by the gaiety and grandeur of *Die Meistersinger*? Or so dishonest as to conceal my opinion that I consider a few bars of this work worth more than all the operas that have been composed since?"

Thus he could justly call himself "the best Wagnerite," in speaking to Widmann, "insisting," as the latter tells us, "with a complacency which was indeed justifiable, though it seldom appeared in him, that his understanding of Wagner's scores was deeper than that of any of his contemporaries." But there is a sort of unintentional, though indeed entirely comprehensible, "sin of omission" to which it is certainly permissible to allude, and which seems to me to be no less important than Brahms's ad-miration of Wagner, though this cannot be too greatly emphasized: namely, the fact that his Low German nature, which avoided in dignified fashion all personal conflicts and party squabbles and was decidedly passive rather than active in such matters, took no effective or timely steps to impose silence upon the foolish, rabid attacks on Wagner by the literary and critical protagonists of his party, or at least to divert their personal vilification of the composer into the calmer channels of sober discussion. With Bruckner this was indeed more difficult, for here Brahms himself, in spite of his respect for Bruckner's honest work, threw all good-will, sense of justice, and discretion to the winds in his estimate of Bruckner's stately symphonies. But this time he was dealing with his own especial sphere — namely, the writing of symphonies. Let us hear his own words:

"With Bruckner it is quite a different matter," he writes to Richard Specht. "Here we are dealing, in the first place at least, not with the works, but with an imposture, which will be dead and forgotten in one or two years' time. Look at it as you will: Bruckner owes his fame to me alone, and but for me he would not have attracted the slightest attention; but this happened very much against my will. Nietzsche once alleged that I became famous only by accident: that the anti-Wagner party made use of me as the antipope whom they required. That is naturally nonsense, I am not at all a suitable person to place at the head of any party whatsoever, for I require to go my own way alone and in peace and have never got in anybody else's way. But in Bruckner's case it does apply. For since Wagner's death his party naturally requires a pope, and they could find nobody better than Bruckner. Do you think, then, that a single person in all these immature masses has the slightest understanding of these gigantic snakes of symphonies, and do you not think, too, that I am the musician of today with the best understanding of Wagner's works — better, at any rate, than any of his so-called partisans, who would like more than anything to poison me? . . . I am antipope! It is really too idiotic! And Bruckner's works immortal — or even symphonies at all! It is enough to make one laugh!"

We see the same thing in the Brahms-Bruckner controversy: Brahms took not the slightest steps to withdraw, while there was still time, from his equivocal position as antipope, created by his own over-zealous partisans. This would have been an easy matter for the "best of the Wagnerites," but in relation to Bruckner it ought to have been absolutely necessary. To Wagner, who was ignorant of Brahms's honest recognition of his art, he was naturally the head of the rival party, the "antipope," and Wagner's caustic sarcasm and antipathy for his work, which was in turn just as blind, unjust, and prejudiced as that of Brahms for Bruckner's, was his way of paying back the fanatical Wagner-hatred of the "Brahmins," as concentrated in Hanslick and his clique in Vienna.

The two other controversies — Brahms versus Bruckner, and Brahms versus Hugo Wolf — were of far less importance during Brahms's lifetime. Bruckner was still fighting hard for recognition as a composer of symphonies, and Hugo Wolf was far better known and more talked about as the savage critic of the *Salonblatt* and the champion of Wagner and Bruckner than as a song-writer of genius, in which capacity he was at that time quite unknown and obscure.

Nowadays these three opposing factors have been harmoniously resolved in an equation of three equal terms: Bruckner, Brahms, Hugo Wolf. How and why this has come about will be pointed out in our concluding remarks.

XVI

AT THE HEIGHT OF HIS FAME

With his triumph as a master of the great symphonic form, which, in spite of Bülow's advocacy, was only slowly and painfully achieved, Brahms stood at the summit of his outward fame. It made him neither proud nor careless in his artistic work, neither mercenary, nor arrogant towards others: he remained exactly what he had been before. Or, to quote his own words: "I have a sense of honour, but I am not vain enough to care for honours (*Ich besitze Ehrgefühl, aber weder Eitelkeit noch Ehrgeiz*)." The majority of his opponents either retired from the fray or became his adherents. The inveterate enemies of his art, as we have just seen, were not persons, but parties: the strictly orthodox Wagner party at Bayreuth, centring round Cosima Wagner, the Bruckner party, the Hugo Wolf party — in so far as it is possible to speak of such a party at that time. As an artist Brahms avoided all personal conflict with them, in accordance with his more passive Low German character. How he got on with them as a man we shall soon see.

The University of Cambridge, England, led the way in showing him outward honour and distinction by conferring upon him the honorary degree of Doctor of Music in 1877. It was followed in 1879 by the German University of Breslau, which honoured him with the degree of Doctor of Philosophy *honoris causa* in the following document, the original of which was in Latin:

"Under the exalted auspices of the Most Serene and Mighty Prince Wilhelm, German Emperor, King of Prussia, etc., our most just and gracious sovereign, and in virtue of his royal authority, under the rectorship of His Magnificence Otto Spiegelberg, Rector of the University of Breslau, Doctor of Medicine and Surgery, regularly appointed professor and director of the gynæcological clinic, medical privy councillor, Knight of the Order of the Red Eagle of the Fourth Class and of the Iron Cross, the name, title, and rights of an honorary Doctor of Philosophy are conferred upon the most illustrious Johannes Brahms of Holstein, now master of the stricter style of the art of music in Germany, in accordance with the resolution of the Faculty of Philosophy, by Peter Joseph Elvenich, Doctor of Philosophy, Master of the Humane Arts, duly appointed professor, privy councillor, and Knight of the Order of the Red Eagle of the Second Class, dean of the Faculty of Philosophy during the current year, licensed by statute to confer this degree; as publicly attested by this diploma, given this day, May 11, 1879."

In the year 1889 the freedom of his native city of Hamburg was conferred upon him — though, it is true, only at the direct instance of Bülow. Brahms's joy and gratitude were extreme. His first short telegram of acknowledgment refers to the distinction conferred upon him as " the finest which he could receive from human hands." His letter of thanks develops this idea in greater detail: " As an artist I am happy at such an exalted mark of recognition, but as a man I am more than happy at the glorious feeling that this native city is our beautiful, ancient, honourable Hamburg! . . . The precious gift of the freedom of the city . . . is all the more valuable and dear to me in that I can place beside it the letter (which is still in Low German) conferring it upon my father. In this splendid experience my first thought was for my father, and all that I wish is that he, too, might have shared in this joy. . . ."

Brahms received the presentation of the freedom of the city in person, in the presence of Bülow and Spengel, from the Burgomaster, Dr. Carl Petersen, at the latter's house in Hamburg, and, as Spengel tells us, he laid stress in his simple, heart-felt speech of thanks upon the happiness of a man " who can meditate with love and esteem upon his home and parents." In the same year the Austrian Emperor conferred the Order of Leopold on him, and in 1896 the golden decoration *Litteris et Artibus* as well, the highest mark of distinction for intellectual and artistic work in the Austrian Empire at that time. In 1886 Prussia made him a knight of the order *Pour le mérite,* Bavaria conferred on him the Order of Maximilian for arts and sciences, and the lesser courts followed suit. The Berlin Royal Academy of Arts elected him as a corresponding member. He was particularly pleased at receiving the same honour in the year 1896 from the French Academy, and would point out how very infrequently it was granted to Germans. On his sixtieth birthday, May 7, 1893, the Vienna Gesellschaft der Musikfreunde caused a gold medal to be struck in his honour by A. Scharff and presented it to him. This touched him deeply and drew from him the characteristically resigned words: " I feel abashed rather than glad at the great honour which has been done me; thirty years ago I should have been joyfully sensible of the duty of proving myself worthy of such a distinction. But now — it is too late." The Vienna Ton-künstlerverein had already chosen him as an honorary president before this.

All this pleased him and brought him deserved satisfaction after his silent but hard struggle for recognition as a composer. But just as he never plumed himself upon these titles and marks of distinction to his friends and colleagues, so he never regarded them in any other light than as obligations — encouraging though they might be — to produce artistic work of ever-increasing merit. For, he said, " when a nice melody comes into my head, it pleases me more than any Order of Leopold, and if it enables me to make a success of a symphony, I had rather that than the freedom of any city."

XVII

THE END

Brahms, the early riser, thickset and robust, who, like a true, hardy Hamburger, slept with his window open summer and winter alike, himself believed that he might live to a ripe old age. In 1892 he made light of Hanslick's warning to think about making his will in good time: " A will? Why, I am still quite hale and hearty." When his friend Billroth passed away, he said, again: " It seems to me a fine thing to die in the full consciousness of being well prepared for the end of things." But when Clara Schumann died, on May 20, 1896, he lamented more resignedly, like a lonely bachelor: " I often think I am to be envied because I have hardly anybody else left to die, whom I love from the depths of my heart; but this is really odious, and one ought not to think or say such things. . . . Is life worth living when one is so alone? . . . The only real immortality is in one's children."

Clara Schumann's death, indeed, indirectly hastened the onset of his own last illness. When she died, Brahms was taking the cure at Ischl. On the arrival of the news he hurried with his customary fidelity to her funeral at Frankfurt. But, as he described to Richard von Perger, a contretemps occurred on his journey: " In my hurry to arrive from Ischl in time for the funeral, I entered a train at Attnang bound for Vienna instead of Germany, out of short-sightedness or absent-mindedness, and only discovered my mishap after we had started. I naturally arrived late [at Frankfurt] for the funeral ceremony. [It was not till the funeral in the cemetery at Bonn, by the open grave, that Brahms was able to pay his last tribute to his noble friend.] This provoked an overflow of bile, as can still be seen from my face." He spoke jestingly; but he had no idea that the prospect for him was even more serious. At Ischl he was examined by his intimate friend,

the distinguished laryngologist and specialist on digestion, Dr.
Leopold von Schrötter, a member of the managing committee of
the Gesellschaft der Musikfreunde, who diagnosed a dangerous
morbid condition of the liver. Another Viennese doctor prescribed
a cure at Karlsbad for his "liver-complaint." On September 2,
already languid and exhausted, but still full of humour and spirits,
he arrived at the Bohemian watering-place and took a lodging
on the second story of the simple, pleasant inn "Zur Stadt Brüs-
sel" (since July 10, 1898, "Zum Johannes Brahms"), in the
Hirschensprunggasse. He was pleased with everything. "I am
grateful to my jaundice," he soon wrote to his friend Hanslick,
"for having at last brought me to famous Karlsbad. I was at
once greeted by glorious weather, such as we have not had all the
summer. What is more, I have an absolutely charming lodging,
with the nicest possible people, so that I am thoroughly contented."
Hanslick had brought him into touch with a few Karlsbad friends
to entertain him. "Hanslick's fat friends (*Kugeln*) here," he
wrote jestingly to Viktor von Miller, "revolve amiably round
me — though, recluse (*Abseiter*) that I am, I do not welcome
them very gratefully."

The report of the Karlsbad doctor who was attending him,
at the end of three weeks' treatment, is in alarming contrast with
this blissfully unsuspecting frame of mind: it notes that there is
"a serious swelling of the liver, with complete blockage of the
gall-ducts." On the master's return to Vienna, at the beginning
of October, this developed more and more rapidly into the same
disease as had caused his father's death: cancer of the liver. The
doctor in Vienna at once diagnosed the state of the case, but out
of consideration for the invalid refrained from "speaking the
hopeless word."

Brahms struggled against the rapid decline of his strength
with all the iron energy of his nature. He did not work any
longer, but continued his usual walks, though at the cost of
ever-increasing efforts; he took part, as before, in sociable gatherings at the midday meal, and drank beer with his friends in the
evening, attended all important concerts, and was even present

on several evenings in succession at a series of performances rendered necessary by a competition for a prize which the Tonkünstlerverein had offered for the best composition for wind instruments. His erect carriage relaxed as his body became thinner and more shrunken, his walk became unsteady, his complexion, which as early as 1895 had struck his friends at Zürich as ominous in its brownish tinge, denoting that a morbid change was taking place in the blood, turned a livid yellow; he was often to be seen, as Perger describes, huddled together upon his chair, with his drooping head falling limply forward on his breast in a slight doze, or else he would withdraw from table at meals, or from conversation, without taking leave. The public was aware of the danger threatening his life long before he was conscious of it himself. For their love and veneration for the mortally suffering composer seated in his box swelled higher and higher. On November 9 he heard his *Vier Ernste Gesänge* performed for the first time by Sistermans. He was present on January 2, 1897 when the Joachim Quartet scored a brilliant success with his G major String Quintet. On January 17 a few of his unaccompanied choruses aroused boundless enthusiasm at a concert of the Gesellschaft; the audience, with the splendid spontaneous fervour of the Austrian public, saluted the composer in his box with loud cheering and waving of handkerchiefs. Still more moving was the homage of the musical world of Vienna — and who is not musical there? — at the revival of the Fourth Symphony by the Philharmonic on March 7. Let us hear Hanslick's account: "They started with Brahms's Fourth Symphony, in E minor. Immediately after the first movement a storm of applause arose, so continuous that Brahms had at last to come forward from the back of the directors' box and bow his acknowledgment. This ovation was repeated at the end of all four movements, and after the finale it simply would not stop. A thrill of awe and painful sympathy ran through the whole assembly, a clear presentiment that they were greeting the suffering and beloved master for the last time in this hall." On March 13 he listened to part of his friend Strauss's new operetta, *Die Göttin*

der Vernunft (*The Goddess of Reason*) at the theatre, and on
March 24 was again dining with friends. He would still drag
himself into the open air, to the Volksgarten, hoping that the
soft, warm air of the early spring might bring about some improvement in his condition. Next, walking became impossible
for him, and his faithful friends, the Fabers, Millers, and Fel-
lingers, would take him for drives in the Prater in a comfortable
carriage, keeping everything from him, with touching and devoted affection, which might remind him of the alarming seriousness of his condition. Tended as he was with the utmost fidelity
and devotion by his housekeeper, Frau Celestine Truxa, he was
still unaware of its gravity. Only five days before his death he
wrote to his step-mother: " I have been lying up a little, for a
change, so writing is uncomfortable for me. But otherwise do not
be alarmed, my condition is unchanged, and, as usual, all I need
is patience." His hopes were deceptive. On April 2 he became
unconscious. He lay with his face turned to the wall, took no
more nourishment from that time onward, and never spoke
another word. On April 3, 1897 he turned over, as Door describes
it, " with a sudden jerk, his splendid blue eyes became glazed
with a film, and two great tears rolled softly and slowly down
his cheeks." At half past nine in the morning he sank, softly and
without pain, into everlasting rest.

*   *   *   *

All Germany mourned with Vienna and Austria, and the whole
world of music felt the irreparable loss of a great artist. The
municipal authorities of the city of Vienna gave him an honourable place of burial in the central cemetery, close beside the tombs
of Beethoven and Schubert and Mozart's funeral monument.
The funeral celebrations on April 6 assumed the proportions of
a deeply moving demonstration of mourning. The funeral procession — six carriages following the body and heavily laden
with flowers and wreaths, accompanied by funeral attendants
in the old Spanish costume customary in Vienna — started out
from the house where he died, through a vast crowd which lined

the route, to the premises of the Musikverein. Here the managing
body of the Gesellschaft der Musikfreunde and the Singverein
were awaiting the deceased master beneath a black canopy at
the entrance, in order to pay him the last tribute of respect at
his grave. The Singverein sang his own moving choral song
"*Fahr wohl*" in memory of him. In the Protestant Church
Pastor Zimmermann pronounced the benediction over the body
in the fine, carefully chosen scriptural words of the last movement
of the *Deutsches Requiem:* "Blessed are the dead which die in
the Lord, from henceforth. Yea, saith the Spirit, that they may
rest from their labours; and their works do follow them." Then
the great funeral procession moved off to the beautiful Wäh-
ringen central cemetery, outside the city. And here Brahms's
words to Widmann on the occasion of Billroth's funeral were once
more carried into effect: "I wish you could see, as I am doing,
what it means to be beloved here. We do not know it at home,
neither are we capable of it. We Germans do not wear our hearts
on our sleeve, our love is not displayed so beautifully and warmly
as here, especially among the best portion of the people (I mean:
among the people in the gallery!)." And again: "I could begin
all over again about our dear people of Vienna, for whom in any
case a 'lovely corpse' is a first-class attraction (*Haupthetz*). In
the whole of that countless multitude you would not have seen
a single merely curious or indifferent face, nothing was written
on any of them save the deepest sympathy and affection."

The coffin was lowered into the grave amid deep sorrow; a
choir sang the last farewell. The then president of the Tonkünstlerverein, afterwards director and trustee of the Gesellschaft
der Musikfreunde, Dr. Richard von Perger, pronounced the following feeling speech:

"This hallowed spot, this leafy mausoleum of German music,
is now about to receive into its chill, silent depths the mortal
remains of our revered contemporary. He who has so richly endowed and added to the happiness of the whole world, what has
he not been to us musicians above all! In the radiance shed by

his creative genius and acute artistic understanding we could indeed look up to his incomparable mastery, to his lofty, unflinching artistic principles; among the innumerable paths and devious ways which now traverse the realm of music in all directions, the torch which he held steadily on high as its high priest was our guide. Only today, indeed, has he found worthy brother-minds in proximity to him, here in his resting-place, but to his contemporaries and colleagues, in spite of the great distance at which he stood above them, he was always a simple, sympathetic friend and counsellor, the promoter of struggling talent, a sure and trusty help in need and affliction. It is our duty faithfully to guard the master's sacred heritage; let us pledge ourselves to work and strive towards the same end. His works, already the property of art-loving humanity, must through our agency be brought home more and more to men's ears and hearts. Here dost thou rest now, blest of God, in the great, solemn cosmic solitudes; the glowing clouds sail past above thee, and thine immortal essence floats blissfully with them through eternal space (*zieht selig mit durch ewige Räume*)!"

Next the funeral cortège approached the open grave. The charming Italian Alice Barbi, who was, with Hermine Spies, the interpreter *par excellence* of Brahms's songs during his lifetime and a valued friend of the composer's, was the first to cast a handful of earth into the grave of the departed master.

As we have seen, Brahms left no properly attested will. He had planned one with an intimate friend, but it never came to anything. A letter of the year 1891 to his Berlin publisher and trustee Fritz Simrock, making certain broad dispositions with regard to his considerable property, had to be recognized in lieu of a will. Unfortunately, serious complications and disputes ensued, as a result of claims set up by relations. A compromise was arrived at, by which the bulk of his property was assigned to his blood-relations, his library to the Gesellschaft der Musikfreunde, a legacy to his housekeeper, Frau Truxa, certain sums to a few musical societies (the Liszt-Pensionsverein, Czerny-

Verein, Gesellschaft der Musikfreunde) subject to the payment of
an income for life to Brahms's beloved step-brother, Fritz Schnack.

*   *   *   *

The first monument to be raised to the master in grateful
remembrance and veneration was that of the Duke of Meiningen
and his wife. On the day before the second great Meiningen
Musical Festival (September 7, 1899) a speech was made by
Joachim, followed by the unveiling of a beautiful monument
from the master hand of Adolf Hildebrand, in the form of a
portrait bust of the composer, more than life-size, set in the
middle of a great semicircular stone bench terminating at each
end in a cool fountain. Four years later, on the composer's seventieth birthday (May 7, 1903), the modern monument by Ilse Conrat in the Vienna central cemetery was solemnly dedicated. The
master is seen with his head resting on his hand, gazing thought-
fully at a score; on a relief behind him the musician's virginal muse
is seen handing back her lyre in silent mourning to the heavenly
powers who — in a somewhat artificial composition — are letting
the harmonious veil of music float downwards, while a youth,
representing grateful posterity, raises it to his lips with a reverent
kiss. Again, five years later, on May 8, 1908, Rudolf Weyr's fine,
decorative Vienna monument was unveiled in the Resselpark on
the Karlsplatz, near the composer's former residence. A full-
length figure of Brahms is seated, plunged in meditation, on a
pedestal, while the Muse strikes her lyre in ecstasy at his feet.
The most significant and remarkable of the monuments to
Brahms was raised by Max Klinger in 1909 at the entrance to
the new Musikhalle in the composer's native city of Hamburg —
a portrait bust, surrounded by the geniuses of music. There are
smaller Brahms monuments, in the form of portrait busts, erected
to his memory, one at Pressbaum, on June 4, 1905, in memory of
the summer of 1881 — a cast of the original at Meiningen — in
the garden of what was once the Heingartners' house, afterwards
belonging to the Ritter von Connevay, in the Brentenmaisstrasse;
and another at Mürzzuschlag, from the hand of Marie Fellinger,

in memory of the summers spent by the composer in this lovely
spot on the Semmering railway between 1884 and 1886.

Posterity has to thank the friendship and veneration of Viktor
von Miller zu Aichholz for a Brahms Museum. It is at Gmunden,
in a lovely situation high above the Traunsee, hidden away in
a great park in front of a little pool crossed by a pretty little
rustic bridge. It contains a faithful reproduction of the rooms
occupied by the composer at Ischl, with their furniture and
barred windows, now filled with the most precious autographs,
prints, pictures, busts, and personal souvenirs of every kind, and
bears on its outer wall, thickly overgrown with ivy, Ernst Hegen-
barth's marble medallion of Brahms.

XVIII

BRAHMS AS A MAN

In order to know Brahms as a man, we must pay a visit to him in his home. He is fairly sure to be at home during the morning. We cannot pluck up our courage to do it unannounced, and our hearts are beating violently; for his pupil Gustav Jenner once told us that a certain famous artist would only call on Brahms when he was quite sure not to be at home, for he had the reputation of being as uncouth a boor as Beethoven. He also told us candidly that Brahms was by no means polite to all his visitors, and that, in particular, during the visits of strange artists who were indifferent or unsympathetic to the composer he had witnessed some most painful scenes; and also, as is confirmed by Paul Kunz in his charming reminiscences of Brahms at Thun, written in collaboration with Ernst Isler, the composer understood extremely well the difficult art of dismissing inquisitive strangers, importunate autograph-hunters, and unwelcome visitors in the shortest possible time, having put them quite out of countenance by his rudeness and sarcasm.

From 1862 to 1865 and from 1867 to 1871 Brahms moved about a good deal in Vienna, always for preference to old houses: from the Deutsches Haus in the Singerstrasse he went to the " Goldspinnerin " in the Ungargasse, and from the Novaragasse and Czerningasse to the Postgasse, always within the first and second circle of suburbs. Then, after January 1872, he settled down in the Karlsgasse, No. 4, Auf der Wieden, on the third story, in the apartment of Fräulein Vogl and afterwards of her successor Frau Celestine, widow of the editor Dr. Truxa. We pause before the plain, three-storied old Viennese middle-class residence in the classical style of the late Empire, dating from about 1830. Crossing the vestibule, with its wooden floor and

closed French windows, with gaudily coloured glass, opening
on the garden, we stumble up the dark, worn, winding stone
staircase to the third story. There is no plate, no name, only a
No. 8 over the door, a little letter-box, and a peep-hole. Our
hearts beat more violently. We pull the old-fashioned iron bell-
pull. Frau Truxa opens the door. " Herr von Brahms is at home."
She leads us along a short passage lit by two windows on the
right, past the kitchen on the left, and in good old Viennese
fashion shows us straight into Brahms's bedroom unannounced.
Rohrbach's Johann Sebastian Bach over the bed, the bust of
Haydn in old Viennese biscuit china on the tiled stove, the simple
wooden music-stand which he used in conducting the concerts of
the Gesellschaft in the left-hand corner, at once show us who
lives here. As we are still hesitating in embarrassment to look
about us and wondering what the old Dutchman Van der Helst's
great historical daub of the " Conclusion of the Peace of Münster,"
hanging over the never-used old-fashioned upholstered sofa, has
to do with music, we hear within, behind the curtained glass
door, a heavy, hasty tread: it is Brahms hurrying into the library
in his slippers to put on a coat in honour of the lady who
accompanies us. For as a rule, like all men much absorbed in
their ideas, Brahms does not care much about dress and feels
most at home between his own four walls in slippers, a flannel
shirt with no tie, a detachable white collar, and trousers. On his
travels — we hastily recall the accounts given by Widmann and
Kunz while we are waiting — he had a profound dislike of all
table d'hôte or obligatory dressing. What he liked best was to
take his meals in a good, simple, cosy restaurant garden, and
he did not take it at all amiss — on the contrary, he would thank
them with delicate tact — if some modest band at Thun or elsewhere offered him a morning serenade by playing him his Hungarian Dances for the thousandth time. In Vienna, as in the
country, he preferred to carry his soft felt hat in his hand rather
than wear it, slung a convenient leather satchel round him,
and in bad weather wore round his shoulders a still more
old-fashioned bluish-green shawl, which he pinned together in

front with an enormous pin. For the rest, on his country holidays
he was quite content with a flannel shirt and light alpaca jacket.

But now he appears in person and insists on our passing
through the glass door into his music- and living-room, furnished
with the same simplicity. And since he intends to start for Italy
on the very next day and is therefore in high spirits, he first
shows us round his abode with an " amiably grumpy face." The
chief pieces of furniture in the music-room are the Streicher grand
piano, which had soon replaced that of Schumann, besides an
old square piano supposed to have belonged to Haydn, the
simple writing-table, with Calamatta's engraving of Leonardo's
mysteriously smiling Mona Lisa hanging over it, and an engraving
of Rietschel's medallion of Robert and Clara Schumann, with a
beautiful personal inscription, a simple breakfast- and reading-
table standing before the brown leather sofa, with Steinle's engraving of Raphael's Sistine Madonna hanging above it, and a
carved rocking-chair beside it. On the piano, which was always
open, a volume of the great collected edition of Bach's works
was usually standing open. The cover of the piano was used as
a show-table; here lay in exemplary order a pile of note-books,
writing-tablets, calendars, cigar cases, spectacles, purses, watches,
keys, souvenirs of his travels, portfolios, recent books, and musical
publications. The rest of the artistic adornment of the room consists of an engraving by Klinger, the portrait of Cherubini by
the French classical painter Ingres, with a Muse characteristically
shrouded in a veil crowning him with laurel — " I cannot stand
that female," Brahms had hinted to his landlady — an engraving
by Schütz of the Stefansdom at Vienna in 1792, Turner's mezzo-
tint of Hogarth's Handel, Rafael Morghen's engraving after
Guido Reni's Apollo in the chariot of the Sun, the young Mendelssohn at the piano, and, by way of sculpture, copies of the busts
of Beethoven by Klein and Zumbusch, and a bronze relief of
Bismarck, which was always crowned with laurels.

Brahms was a great patriot and an ardent admirer of the great
creator of German unity — " What *he* says to me is enough; that
is what I believe," as he once said to Rudolf von der Leyen. He

never forgot to put Bismarck's speeches or letters in his travelling-
bag. In speaking of the "absolutely passionate patriotism of this
earnest, virile soul," his Swiss friend Widmann coined the apt
phrase: "the faithful Eckart of the German people." True to this
character, he not only, like his great countryman Hebbel, took the
liveliest interest in the questions of the day and what went on
in political life, but kept a watchful and anxious eye on affairs,
which he took seriously to heart when they seemed to him
ominous and likely once again to imperil the German unity
created by Bismarck. He was capable of flying into a furious rage
at the ineradicable national political vice of Germany — namely,
jealousy, criticism, and dissension — when, as he once wrote to
Widmann, "the factions in Parliament begin bargaining and
chaffering over all the great achievements of the heroic days
which that very generation had experienced, but seemed so soon
to have forgotten"; and there was nothing he regretted so much
as not having done military service as a young man. When his
young fellow Holsteiner and pupil Gustav Jenner joined his regi-
ment at Schleswig, Brahms took leave of him at Hamburg with
the words: "I cannot say how I envy you. If I were only as
young as you are, I should go with you at once. But that too
I missed." We shall see below how eagerly he read books on
German history and the great German wars. In this respect, too,
Widmann has put a nice detail on record. Widmann having sent
him at Christmas 1895 a history of the Franco-German War for
older boys, for his housekeeper's two sons, he shortly afterwards
confessed that "I at once started reading the book on the year '70
as eagerly as if I had known absolutely nothing before about
Moltke and all that happened then."

Brahms too, like Bülow, revered the three "great B's" —
Bach, Beethoven, Bismarck — but with a better right. In his
eyes the *Triumphlied*, the *Fest- und Gedenksprüche*, were no
mere occasional pieces. It was with no self-seeking *arrière-pensée*
that he chose patriotic subjects for his compositions, as so many
German composers unfortunately did during the Great War; but
to him love of his country and people, his Emperor and army,

were an inward necessity, a matter of the heart. When he wrote
patriotic music, it was the immediate reflection of the patriotic
emotions and feelings, joys, forebodings, and alarms which were
always strongly alive in him. In one respect alone they are im-
mensely different from those of Hebbel: not only were they thoroughly conservative, monarchical, and imperialist, but they knew
no doubts or hesitations. He was mortally offended at any criticism of the German Emperor — whether the old Emperor or
the young one — even on the part of his best friends. His deep
friendship with Widmann was once threatened with a rupture
over quite a small matter. After violent arguments between them
as to the advantages and disadvantages of the monarchical and
republican forms of government respectively, Widmann appealed
to Gottfried Keller as arbiter. A slight undercurrent of irony can
be detected in his answer: " Only eighteen short years afterwards
this son of a free city [Brahms] now clings pathetically to the
Emperor and his house, as was scarcely ever the case in the great
old days [1870–1]." We see that Brahms's ideal of the State was
the conservative, Bismarckian one — namely, a united German
Empire, with Prussia as the North German predominant power.
In this too he represented the middle-class ideal of his day.

We must not forget that a finishing touch was given to the
appointments of the music- and living-room by two complete
coffee services. Opening off it at the side was the library, whose
array of books at once showed that this was the haunt of no
ordinary. " mere musician," with the usual deplorable lack of
culture, but of a highly educated great musician, exceptionally
well-read in the whole sphere of the arts and sciences and with
a commanding grasp of the vast field of literature from the re-
motest times onwards. For, though not very large, Brahms's
library — contained in a bookcase with five sections, which occupied the whole of one long wall of the room — was rich in
precious old books on music, autographs, curiosities, copper engravings, etchings, portfolios of pictures, etc.

What used Brahms to read? In order to ascertain this, let us
seat ourselves at his side for a while in one of the two upholstered

arm-chairs with the flowered covers which are already familiar
to us from the bedroom, and let our eyes wander up and down
the five long shelves while we chat with him comfortably. We
have already made the acquaintance of a few of his favourite
poets among his friends: Gustav Freytag, founder of the German
historical novel giving a picture of past ages, Paul Heyse, the delicate lyric poet of Munich, who enriched German literature with
short stories, often with an Italian atmosphere, and Gottfried
Keller, the great Swiss poet. He was attracted to Alexis and
Freytag by his historic sense and fervent love of German history
and middle-class German life, to Heyse by his love of Italy and
classic sense of form, to Keller by his deep, profound, and ruggedly
virile humanity and his feeling for popular humour. His patriotic
sentiments led him to subscribe for twenty-four years to his
favourite *Kladderadatsch,* with its satirical humour — the numbers lay in a pile in the wardrobe in the corner of the room —
and he was particularly fond of reading historical works on
Germany's wars and the doings of Parliament. As Widmann
informs us, Brahms was no friend of modern novelties; he preferred to read the good old books twice and three times over.
Here, too, he not only steeped himself constantly in the great
German and Austro-German poets, including Grillparzer, Kleist,
and Hebbel, for whom he had a special affection, but even as a
child he had marked preferences. On the one hand, as a good
Protestant, he was a great admirer of Luther's translation of
the Bible and his *Table-talk.* He also loved to make himself
thoroughly acquainted with the folk-poetry of all nations; Arnim-
Brentano's *Des Knaben Wunderhorn,* Grimm's German legends
and fairy-tales, German popular books, sagas, and folk-songs,
Herder's *Stimmen der Völker,* formed the most important nucleus
of his library and exercised a decisive influence on a large part
of his work. Among the older Romantics he was particularly
attracted by E. T. A. Hoffmann and Achim von Arnim; among
the later ones, by Berthold Auerbach, the poet of the Black
Forest and author of *Barfüssele.* Among his German national
treasures he also numbered such " solid " monuments of German

philological research as Grimm's great German dictionary. For recreation, and to stimulate his imagination, he was fond of reading the history of his native town of Hamburg, or interesting books of travel (North Polar exploration, Stanley's travels in Africa, etc.), and made no secret of the fact that Defoe's classic *Robinson Crusoe* was very near his heart, not only as a child, but as a man. But a closer inspection would also reveal many literary works of curious or special interest of the seventeenth and eighteenth centuries, such as Rollenhagen's *Froschmäusler,* Prätorius's *Weltbegebenheiten,* Le Sage's *Gil Blas,* Flemming's *Teutsche Poemata,* Klinger's *Sturm und Drang,* Printz's *Musicus vexatus,* and many others, in rare and beautiful old editions.

This is no more than a rapid "stock-taking"; but it is characteristic enough. We can see that in the sphere of literature, too, Brahms did not belie his nature, which was conservative and sound to the core. What he asked of all his books was that which is positive, intellectual, beautiful in form, clear, and plastic. Even in literature of a primarily entertaining and humorous order he demanded a strong, instructive, intellectual substratum. At the same time Brahms was thoroughly acquainted with the modern literature of his day — he was indeed one of the most zealous first-nighters at the Burgtheater, and when at Frankfurt would drag Clara Schumann round pitilessly to the latest Sudermann or Fitger. He approached it without prejudice, but with the most sincere desire for mental enrichment, interest, and stimulus to artistic creation. But he failed to find them, as was indeed inevitable in view of the austerely idealistic classicism of his art, and the noble reserve and intellectualism of his nature, which always impelled him towards harmony between form and content, a purified tranquillity and maturity of feeling, controlled passion, and resigned reticence — in short, towards a noble " moderation in all things," which could have found no nurture in the morbid hysteria and nervous unrest of certain modern literary tendencies. In spite of this, he prudently abstained from sharply subjective judgments, and with equal modesty and honesty excused his attitude of reserve towards what was modern by saying that in this sphere his criticism was only based on his own personal impressions and that he understood nothing about such matters. In a letter to Clara Schumann dating from his Detmold period he indulges in a regular "sermon on moral health," dictated by a touching friendly solicitude, on the subject of this noble " moderation in all things," on the grave harm which a persistently depressed mood may cause both physically and mentally, and how to fight against it and overcome it. The letter concludes with the following highly characteristic words: " Passions do not pertain to man as a natural thing. They are always exceptions or excrescences. . . . The fine, true man is calm in joy and calm in suffering and trouble. Passions must soon pass away, or else one must drive them away."

The simple furniture of the library is completed by the composer's reading-desk, Cornelius's " Horsemen of the Apocalypse " hanging between the two windows, and his travelling-trunk and valises, which always stood under the right-hand window packed ready for instant use. The windows of the music-room and library —which were always shut—looked out over the broad Karlsplatz and the copper-green dome of Fischer von Erlach's handsome baroque Karlskirche; his bedroom, whose windows were open night and day, looked out over the neglected gardens of the neighbouring houses and the " Technik " (technical school), above which towered a great walnut-tree, the higher branches of which almost rose as high as Brahms's rooms. It was only in the music-room that the old-fashioned floors of polished wood-blocks were covered by a few small rugs.

Even this hurried walk through his lodging gives us a few sidelights on this character. For the close connexion between the simple, practical style of his household appointments, entirely devoid of all easy, luxurious comforts, and the sound, robust lines on which his life was planned are evident at a glance. Nor is it possible entirely to ignore the analogy between his preference for black and white in the pictures adorning his rooms — engravings or etchings, insisting chiefly upon design or structure, rather than coloured copies or originals — and his neo-classic tendencies as a composer, with their corresponding preference for the architectonic or plastic.

And now that we are comfortably seated opposite each other — the guest always on the brown leather sofa or in the carved rocking-chair, the master facing him on a simple cane-chair — and the host in his irresistibly cordial, easy, and amiably " unbending (*aufgetaut* — i.e., thawed) " fashion is regaling us with freshly made coffee and Havana cigars, can we also answer the curious inquiry: " What was Brahms like to look at? "

According to Walter Hübbe, as a young piano-teacher at Hamburg before 1853 Brahms " had nothing in the least imposing about his exterior. There was something shy, awkward, and constrained about him." This " slight awkwardness " in his youth, which, no doubt, had its origin chiefly in his oppressive consciousness of his lack of ease in the forms of polite society and which he tried, as a rule, to conceal behind an apparently rough manner, is also confirmed by Eugenie Schumann. The young composer was a slender figure, walking the streets " with a somewhat uncertain gait, his body bowed a little forward, and with rather a wobbly tall hat," which at once led to his being christened " Brahmbessen " (besom) by the horrid little boys of Hamburg. Brahms's charming appearance, as drawn by Laurens, has been sketched for us in a few strokes by Ehrlich: " Who could have realized that in 1853 the portly gentleman of today [1893], with the strongly marked features and great full beard, the grave, self-contained, and occasionally discourteous bearing, and a way of speaking that is sometimes downright rude, was quite a slim youth, with a dreamy expression on his gentle, pale, beardless face, who spoke with a soft voice and used poetical expressions without the slightest affectation, signed himself Johannes Kreisler junior on his manuscripts, and quite bore out Joachim's description: ' Pure as a diamond, soft as snow.' " Franz Wüllner, who made his acquaintance in the summer of 1853 at the age of twenty, at Mehlem, near Bonn, describes him as a " slender youth with long, fair hair and a regular Johannine head, with energy and intelligence flashing from his eyes." Albert Dietrich adds the following picture of the " dear, splendid fellow ": " But now he [Schumann] brought a youthful musician to see me, with an appearance as interesting as it was characteristic, who produced a most attractive impression by his almost boyish appearance, his ringing voice, his long, fair hair, and his plain, grey summer coat. What was particularly fine about him was his vigorous, characteristic mouth and earnest, keen glance, in which the whole of his genius was expressed." And lastly Henry Schradieck of Hamburg completes it with reminiscences of merry travels and visits to watering-places, in which Brahms, that " extremely lively youth," was always ready to join him. Eugenie Schumann, with her brother and sister, who saw him at Düsseldorf performing " the most breakneck gymnastic exercises and feats of endurance," tells us that young Brahms was a good athlete and a sturdy young fellow, and Grimm, on returning to his old home at Hanover, after being forced to leave his " delightful Kreisler," longs to be back again with the " dear lad " and his " mad exuberances." Anton Door, who heard Brahms play with Clara Schumann and Joachim, also in the middle fifties, confirms this description. What chiefly impressed him in the slender young man with the long, fair hair, who had at that time only just arrived at the cigarette stage on his way to the long, strong cigars, was chiefly the proud, aloof way in which he kept pacing up and down at the back of the room without taking the slightest notice of his presence.

Young Brahms's head was of the characteristic Lower Saxon type: a longish head, with fair hair falling in soft waves, deep-set, candid eyes, of a childlike kindliness, a rapt, dreamy expression, and a clear, peculiarly radiant blue, a high, finely domed brow, a straight nose, full of character, delicate features, almost girlish in profile, a harsh, vigorously cut mouth and lips, which could form themselves to sharp, contemptuous words as well as jests, and rosy cheeks. Add to this, when he was a boy, a surprisingly clear and very beautiful soprano voice, which he spoilt by much singing while it was breaking, afterwards, by the force of an iron will, lowering it to such " manly depths," by talking in a gruff voice, that as a man he could sing only in an " absolutely broken, raucous voice," to quote Heuberger. The Rösings of Hamm have given a very fine description of young Brahms as he was about 1861 in Hamburg: " Of medium height, and delicately built, with a countenance beneath whose high, fine brow were set flashing blue eyes, with fair hair combed back and falling down behind, and an obstinate lower lip! An unconscious force would emanate from him as he stood apart in a gay company, with hands clasped behind his back, greeting those who arrived with a curt nod of his fine head."

His friend Widmann has given the best description of Brahms at the age of thirty: " Brahms, who was at that time in his thirty-third year, produced upon me the impression of a forceful individuality, not only by his powerful piano-playing, with which not even the most brilliant virtuosity could compare, but also by his personal appearance. Indeed, his short, squat figure, his almost flaxen hair, his protruding under lip, which gave a somewhat mocking expression to his beardless young face, were peculiarities which at once arrested attention and might easily be found displeasing; but his whole appearance was, so to speak, steeped in force. The broad, leonine breast, the Herculean shoulders, the powerful head, which he often tossed back with an energetic movement as he played, the thoughtful, fine brow, radiant as though with wondrous fire from between their lashes, revealed an artistic personality, which seemed to be charged to the very finger-tips with the magnetism of genius. There was also something confidently triumphant in this face, the radiant serenity of a mind happy in the exercise of his art, so that as I stood with my eyes fixed on the young master who was striking the keyboard with such power, the words in the *Iphigenie* about the gods of Olympus passed through my mind:

> *Sie aber, sie bleiben*
> *In ewigen Festen*
> *An goldenen Tischen.*
> *Sie schreiten von Bergen,*
> *Zu Bergen hinüber. . . .*

[But as for them, they remain at their eternal feasts, around their tables of gold. They stride from mountain to mountain. . . .]

The beardless Johannes of some thirty years, " a blond, lean figure of a decidedly professorial type," according to Richard Heuberger, astonished his friends at Zürich by his robust health. Like so many remarkably intellectual men, he was able to take a nap at any moment in the day-time, in the open air just as well as in his rooms, and even at night it did not upset him in the least if at times he was forced to camp out on the sofa in a friend's house, or even under the grand piano. The summer which he spent at Pörtschach in 1878 turned this beardless Brahms into a sturdy, mature man with luxuriant hair, which became silver with advancing years, and a voluminous beard and moustache. " With a shaven chin one is taken for an actor or a parson," he said to Widmann at Pressbaum in 1881. Brahms, who retained his delight in harmless jests and " boyish tricks " till an advanced age, took advantage of this " striking outward change " to play a delightful prank. He had himself announced to his friends at the café which he regularly frequented, by a friend who was in the secret, as " Kapellmeister Müller from Brunswick." And, indeed, he had become so unrecognizable, and succeeded in preserving his incognito so cleverly, by speaking in short, abrupt phrases, that Nottebohm, who was in the habit of talking to him every day, kept inquiring after affairs at Brunswick the whole evening! Portraits of him dating from the eighties show us the well-known imposing, fine, idealistic German artist's head, till the full beard, in contrast with the moustache — half-sandy, half-grey — took on a more and more silver hue, while a comfortable *embonpoint* gained upon him. Thus, at Leipzig in 1887 Brahms already appeared to Jenner as a "rotund little gentleman," and in 1894, to Clara Schumann's grandson Ferdinand, who was still quite young, as " a short, corpulent gentleman with a full beard, already rather grey." But his striking, noble, imposing head always caused everything else to be forgotten, and led the Italians to take him, sometimes for " a man of genius (*uomo di genio*) " — as on one occasion when he fell asleep in the train — sometimes, like the custodian at San Giovanni dégli Eremiti, Palermo, for their " venerable General Garibaldi." It was always his flashing blue eyes, which so easily filled with tears of emotion, either for happiness or at the pain of parting, and would rest so kindly and lovingly upon children — and Eugenie Schumann, who dwells upon his exceptionally " beautiful glance," confirms this.

As a boy and a young man Brahms was slightly built, but in later years he became squat and thickset. In the street he would trot about in an overcoat, with trousers that were " always too short, a black alpaca jacket, and bright-coloured shirts without any collar " (Eugenie Schumann), with a stiff, round black hat, or a soft, artist's broad-brimmed one, on his head or in his hand, with the inevitable great weed in his mouth, and pince-nez on his nose (he was extremely short-sighted) — taking short, brisk, light steps, always walking on his heels, his arms often crossed behind his back, while his eyes looked piercingly forward into the distance, and he breathed rather hard. From a distance his silhouette had a certain resemblance to that of Beethoven. Besides his long, terribly strong cigars, he was also fond of the strong, black Mocha coffee, which he prepared himself from " raw material," lavished upon him as a rule by admiring ladies; and so breakfast was his favourite and most important meal. He could drink this coffee at any hour of the day; indeed, he would maintain that he could sleep splendidly, no matter how heavy his supper had been, provided only that he washed it down with a cup of very strong coffee, his recipe for which was: as many coffee-beans as would ordinarily make ten cupfuls. He seldom composed in Vienna, and always standing at a desk, never at the piano; after his summer holidays he would bring home almost all he had composed in a fair copy.

The arrangement of his bachelor day was as simple and regular as could be imagined. He rose unusually early — during the summer holidays often as early as five o'clock — " You have no idea what you are missing if you don't go into the woods early, at

five o'clock," he once said to Eugenie Schumann. He then worked
without stopping till midday. At half past twelve he would go to
his luncheon at the " Roter Igel." He would take his coffee either
there or below in the Stadtpark and then go for a long walk,
usually in the Prater, but often out into the country or in the
Wiener Wald. He was particularly fond of the Prater as a focus
of Viennese life: " Nowhere else does one enjoy the amiable and
gay character of the Viennese so much as in one's strolls through
the Prater."

Like a man of the people and a true Low German, Brahms
faithfully preserved his deep and close relation with Nature, and
his reverent love and admiration for her beauties, till he was quite
an old man. Until his growing stoutness became an inconvenience
to him, he was, moreover, an enthusiastic tourist, " a fearsome
stayer (*ein gefürchteter Dauerläufer*)," as Door admits with a
sigh, who in his youth and middle age could walk all his friends
off their legs.

In the evening, often after a visit to a concert or opera, he
would go and take his evening drink at his regular table in the
little low-ceiled back room of the " Roter Igel " — which was, he
was firmly convinced, the best and cheapest of the old inns of
Vienna between Wildpretmarkt and Tuchlauben, and was, moreover, sacred in the eyes of musicians owing to a tradition that
Beethoven had visited it, and because of the hall on the first floor
which belonged to the Gesellschaft der Musikfreunde from 1831
to 1869. Here he would meet his few but carefully chosen intimates, Hanslick, Kalbeck, Door, Pohl, Brüll, Rottenberg, Nottebohm, and others. If he was not to be found at the " Roter Igel,"
he would be sitting — at least between 1875 and 1881 — at the
habitués' table at Gause's Pilsener Bierhalle in the Johannisgasse.
Though Brahms had a good appetite and stood his drink well, he
was moderate, simple, and frugal in both what he ate and what
he drank. As Jenner expressly tells us — thereby disarming in
advance all spiteful gossip — his midday meal, including a half
pint of red wine or a small glass of Pilsener beer, seldom cost
more than seventy or eighty kreutzer. This thoroughly middle-

class sobriety and frugality, which Dietrich was already touched to
observe in him as a young man of thirty at Oldenburg, and which
is confirmed by Marie Schumann to her sister Eugenie, was the
fine, simple heritage which came to him from his humble parents.
In society, and when travelling, he was the most cheerful and
grateful of table companions. But here, too, his healthy appetite
demanded no delicacies, only a good, solid, middle-class family
diet. At any rate, he thoroughly appreciated it, and so it was no
lie, but a simple and humorous " confession," when he once gave
little Marie Schumann, a clever little housekeeper and cook, a
Cookery-book for Good Housewives, nicely adorned with pictures
and little poems, and with the inscription: " For your kindly
use . . . in grateful memory of the summer of 1864, and in expectation of the next."

From childhood upwards Brahms was of a thoroughly virile
character. " I am not at all a sensitive person — absolutely without
nerves or sympathy," he confesses to Clara Schumann. While he
was still a young man, the rough exterior which grew on him
in later years was already to some extent noticeable; Dietrich has
briefly described it: " In the company of his equals he was lively,
at times even exuberant, rough, and full of mad whims. When
he came upstairs to see me, he would rush up with youthful
vehemence, bang on the door with both fists, and burst in without waiting for an answer." But he had already expressly insisted
that, with all his depth, young Brahms was " sound, fresh, and
gay, entirely untouched by the morbid modern spirit."

Brahms preserved throughout his whole life the physical and
mental health of a man of the people, the close inner identification
of himself with the people, the sympathy and noble practical desire
to help them, which he showed to all the needy and oppressed.
But with advancing years this developed more and more into a
masculine ruggedness and reserve. Physically, that is to say, for
it is precisely this outward impression that has given rise to most
of the talk about Brahms's " harshness " which has been so unduly
emphasized. We shall see in the second section of this book what
a thoroughly false and one-sided picture it gives of him as a

composer to ignore the gentler qualities of his art. And the reminiscences of his friends bear witness at every turn to how untrue it was of him as a man. In spite of all the ruggedness and abruptness, the roughness and intractability of his exterior, all his force and virility of character, Brahms was at heart a very gentle nature. We may cite a few examples: Widmann describes how, in the picture-gallery at Parma, a glorious Parmigiano — the " Betrothal of St. Catherine to the infant Saviour " — moved him to tears, while his brow glowed with emotion at the exquisite grace of all those fair girls' and children's faces pressed close against one another. At a consummately fine performance of his *Gesang der Parzen* at Krefeld, so von der Leyen tells us, tears of pure emotion and joy ran down his cheeks. Brahms once confessed to the same friend that when he saw or read Goethe's *Geschwister,* tears of emotion would rise to his eyes at every word. Widmann informs us that Brahms was unable to finish *Der Sonnenwirt,* that old Swabian classic, a romance of village life by the noble Hermann Kurz, because his heart was too deeply stirred by this gloomy tragedy of the destiny of a peasant's son, goodhearted and gifted by nature, who is gradually but inevitably driven into the arms of the gipsies and becomes a thief and murderer, owing to personal influences, starting with his weak father and wicked step-mother. When he said good-bye to his best friends, his eyes were always full of tears, and the same was the case when he thanked Hanslick, at the banquet given on his seventieth birthday, for the true friendship which he had shown him for years past. As Clara Schumann's coffin lay on the bier in the mortuary chapel, he stepped behind the laurels which formed the sombre decorations, fell sobbing on the neck of his friend von der Leyen, and wept till he could weep no more. While staying among his friends on the Lower Rhine after the funeral, so Ophüls tells us, he struggled in vain against his deep distress, which showed itself in the form of irritability, and so painful was his emotion that he was unable to reply to his host's words of welcome. As he sang the third of the *Ernste Gesänge* (*O Tod, wie bitter bist du*) to these friends for the first time, his voice was choked by bitter tears. During a performance of the slow movement of Schumann's A major String Quartet, when the memory of the death of Clara Schumann — " the only person whom I have ever really loved " — was still quite fresh, Brahms broke into sobbing. This soft side of his emotional nature and disposition, with its genuineness, depth, and noble aspiration, increased, as Door puts it, " to an almost alarming degree" during the helplessness and languor to which he was reduced by his last, mortal illness. He now followed his kind heart without reflection in giving presents to those surrounding him and was as grateful as a child for their slightest attentions.

As so often happens, the older Brahms grew, the more noticeable his innate Hamburg, Low German traits became, even in his way of speaking, curt, abrupt, vigorously rapping out his words, allusive rather than explanatory, with a sharp emphasis on the first syllables, and, in the persistent Low German fashion, still with a thoroughly North German Hamburg intonation, even after long years of residence in Vienna. He was utterly lacking in eloquence — another Low German trait — and spoke of his own works with the greatest difficulty, and in depreciatory and curt terms, rising to heights of positive rage at his own tongue-tiedness; and, unlike most great musicians, and in particular Schumann, he was apt to fall silent as soon as the conversation turned upon music or a piece of music. At large gatherings or in official society he was very reserved and a most attentive listener. But if a subject interested him, he would take part in the conversation with uncommon vivacity, using few words, but those well considered and to the point. Here, too, his gestures were always very quiet and deliberate. When among his intimate friends at table or in society, he was lively and witty; his exceptional intelligence only made itself felt when a deeper note was sounded in the conversation. Eugenie Schumann tells us how, the moment he began to speak about matters that interested him, " he would simply bubble over, which gave his personality something boyish and sunny, even in his later years." On such occasions — as his Swiss friends relate in connexion with the festivals at

the Zürich Tonhalle — he would lay aside all reserve, like Beethoven, showing himself jovial and unconstrained with the men,
gallant and amiable to beautiful women, and, temperate though
he was as a general rule, able to drink with the strongest-headed
topers. At such moments, as in Zürich, it might well happen that
the local brew, known as "Sauser," interested him far more than
his own Piano Quintet, which he had arranged to have performed
by Joachim and his friends, or that, as in Vienna, at the great
banquet of the Vienna Tonkünstlerverein in honour of Liszt and
Rubinstein, he deliberately chose for preference the lower end of
the gigantic table, among the "young folks," which he found
more congenial than the upper and more official end, in the immediate neighbourhood of the guests of the evening. Both these
instances were merely the expression of his deep-rooted antipathy
for putting on any sort of solemn, stand-offish airs as a great
man and artist, or giving himself out to be anything exceptional.
On the contrary, even on festive or state occasions like these, he
felt himself to be no more than a musician among his equals,
and, as Perger relates, expressed his disapproval of all Liszt's and
Rubinstein's pretensions to the dignity of "maestro" in the most
outspoken terms to the members of the committee who waited
upon him: "Come now, let us have no buffoonery and no
stickling for rank here, as if we were at a prince's table; we are
all musicians together, you are Herr X and you are Herr Y, and
I am Herr Brahms."

He cordially detested all the prying curiosity of professional
journalists and reporters, all autograph-hunters, all dedications,
and all painters and sculptors in quest of a commission, and often
gave somewhat violent expression to this in a way which did
him some harm. Brahms made thousands upon thousands of
enemies among critics and journalists; but he rightly set no value
at all upon the ephemeral glory of a newspaper reputation. "These
petty scribblers are nothing but skirmishers; they delay matters
a bit. Only a creative genius can be convincing in art," as he
once justly said to Clara Schumann. Autographs could only be
wrung from him by force or wheedled out of him by many wiles;
the best prospect was when he was travelling or when he hap-

pened to be in a cheerful holiday mood. But even then it was difficult — as difficult as to try to play him something on the piano
during his summers in the country "with a view to an introduction," unless he was willing. As Jenner and Widmann tell
us, he had become fully equal even to the most artful tricks of
passionate autograph-hunters. The most comical things sometimes happened in this connexion. Thus year after year an unknown lady at Kapstadt used to order from him "one of his
world-renowned, excellent Viennese pianos," or a firm of iron-
mongers at Solingen would threaten him with the arrival during
the next few days of ten dozen genuine Solingen knives which
he was supposed to have ordered — the money to be collected
through the post-office cash-on-delivery system. Brahms saw
through both attempts and made no reply. He was very chary
of dedications of his works. Out of his hundred and twenty-two
compositions with opus number, there are only twenty-nine with
dedications — that is to say, barely a quarter of them. It was even
harder to tempt him to sit for his portrait than to get an autograph from him. It is true that he was not altogether dissatisfied
with his outward appearance, and, as Steiner informs us, readily
related with laughing pride that his photograph with the full
beard had been used to illustrate the Caucasian type in one of
Velhagen and Klasing's school-books. But though he had himself
photographed fairly often, he rarely sat to painters or sculptors.
He did not do so until his later years, and in earlier days roundly
refused all such proposals even from his friend and master
Feuerbach; but he displayed the same wariness and presence of
mind when he noticed that anyone was attempting to sketch
him without his knowing it. On the other hand, amateur photographs, and especially impromptu snapshots, amused him greatly;
and here, like him, we shall gratefully recall the splendidly artistic snapshots taken in Vienna by Frau Maria Fellinger, in whose
house the composer became like one of the family as he grew
older. If we did not possess these photographs, we should be the
poorer by a treasure, for nowhere is the composer so lovable, so
intimate, and so truly human as in these pictures.

All these are but small things and characteristic trifles. But

they spring from the very depths of Brahms's native Low German
character, which hated nothing so much as false solemnity,
spurious pathos, and stilted theatrical pomposity, and show us
his simple, modest side. When Philipp Spitta speaks of Brahms's
" noble bashfulness (*edle Verschämtheit*)," he has hit upon the
right and apt expression. It is this very quality which has from
the outset most thoroughly misled those unacquainted with the
peculiarities of the Low German character in their estimate of
him. How often has his transparently sterling and noble character suffered from his offhand, thoroughly North German manner, often made so repellent and " prickly " by his solitary old
bachelorhood, his abrupt and rough manner — behind which a
" warm heart and a deeply passionate nature " tried in vain to
conceal themselves, and which was constantly " on the defensive
against supposed encroachments on his life and independence "
(Eugenie Schumann)! How it has suffered from his unsparing
candour, his abhorrence of all phrase-making, flattery, and sentimentality, his biting wit and sarcasm, which made him a thousand
enemies among musicians in particular, when he was faced with
strange and incompetent artistic work, which his unusually exacting demands in the sphere of technical ability in art were
bound to condemn! How often has it been injured by his rough
humour, which was often misunderstood, his telling irony, and
his honest hatred — we might almost say his honestly hearty
hatred — for his enemies! We may even say that, in very many
cases, his mockery and anger and humour were nothing but
a " lightning-conductor," a protection against his own soft-
heartedness, of which he was afraid. Widmann and his other
friends expressly insist how often, in his desperate efforts to
find a light, jesting expression, he failed to strike the right note
and said something sarcastic, pompous, harsh, or capable of mis-
interpretation instead, when he had not in the least intended
to be malicious. And this almost invariably happened when he
was forced against his will to say something about his own work.
Like Dickens's Weller senior in the *Pickwick Papers,* he was
far from being a " man of wrath," yet, especially in his relations

with his fellow artists, he was often far too prone to follow the impulse of the moment and say hasty, spiteful, disagreeable, and stinging things; indeed, he felt that he simply *must* say them, though nobody had less desire to be nasty, and nobody repented of them more sincerely, or tried harder to make amends for them, often in a touching way, by what Goldmark calls his " silent, almost secret tenderness " towards those whom he had wounded. But since not one person in a hundred is noble, intelligent, high-minded, or filled with a spirit of Christian forgiveness, Brahms did not always attain the desired result by his self-abasing remorse. Least of all among his " dear colleagues " of the little tribe of musicians, no small number of whom exude envy, ill will, vanity, ignorance, conceit, a thirst for glory, and greed of gain. Their incapacity for self-criticism, which is generally astonishing, simply could not bear such severe criticism of incompetent work as that of Brahms, founded upon the most inexorable self-criticism and commanding ability. In their mortally wounded vanity they requited his at times mocking, cutting, and contemptuous words with lifelong hatred. This ought certainly to be borne in mind when we recall the often amazingly absurd violence and persistence of the hostility to Brahms's art in the world of musicians, and not only in that of Vienna.

One of the inevitable consequences of this hostility and misunderstanding, both of himself and of his art, which was bound to be occasioned by his shy, harsh, reserved character, as it became more and more strongly confirmed in its abruptness and roughness with advancing years, was that Brahms suffered severely from his incapacity for " getting outside himself " and establishing direct and cordial relations with others. He once poured out his ardent longing for affection to Clara Schumann, at Easter 1872, in words which are as significant as they are deeply moving: " I always spent feast-days in a very lonely fashion, quite alone in my room with a few dear ones, and very quietly — for my own people are either dead or at a distance. How happy I am when I feel joyfully how love entirely satisfies the human heart! I am indeed dependent upon the outer world; the racket of existence —

I do not laugh at it, I do not join in its lies — but it is as though
the best in one could shut itself off, and only half oneself go
on its way dreaming." And two years later: " I am quite accustomed to bearing my own grief all by myself and within myself."
On reading Billroth's complaints of him to Hanslick he resignedly
admitted: " It is nothing new to me to be regarded even by old
acquaintances and friends as something quite different from what
I really am (or give myself out to be). I know how in earlier
days I used to maintain a scared and wounded silence at such
times, but for a long time past I have taken it quite quietly, as a
matter of course; this may seem hard and harsh to a good, kind-
hearted man like you — yet I hope I have not fallen too far short
of Goethe's saying: ' Blessed is he who without hatred shuts
himself off from the world.' " This is Brahms's milder mood of
resignation, which increased with his advancing years. But even
during his last years this same Brahms could say to Eugenie
Schumann, with alarming vehemence: " *I* have no friends! If
anyone says he is a friend of mine, don't believe it." How
many bitter experiences and disillusionments, how much spurned
or disregarded love and friendship, how much pain and sorrow breathe in these words, as human as they are purposely
exaggerated!

Among all those who came into close contact with him Brahms
had the reputation of being modest both personally and with
regard to his work. Just as he avoided all outward show, all
pretension and advertisement personally, so, as an artist, he was
from the outset fully and clearly conscious of his mission and
place in the development of his art. The fact that he insisted
over and over again to his friends and interpreters that concerts
entirely of his own works were not altogether to his liking, and
wished that at the end they would add " a proper piece by a
proper musician," and as much of " his colleagues Bach and
Beethoven " as possible, at least shows that it did not occur to
Brahms to set himself on the same level as Bach and the great
Viennese classical masters. On the contrary, in his excessive
modesty and self-depreciation, he would reckon himself among

the " poor composers of the lowest class," and was perfectly contented with the rank and position, say, of a modern Cherubini in the sphere of symphony and of larger choral works. Indeed, he carried this modesty so far as to be capable of saying to Clara Schumann on one occasion: " The fact that people in general do *not* understand and respect the best things of all — such as Mozart's concertos and Viotti — enables the likes of us to live and achieve fame." But Brahms's modest estimate of himself may well be recommended to the notice of those who nowadays, after Brahms has been underrated for decade upon decade, are indulging in an equally excessive estimate of him, placing him on the classical Parnassus of Vienna, on the same level as the great masters even intellectually!

In trying to pierce through Brahms's often rough shell and arrive at the golden core of deep kindliness, we need only lay our finger upon four things in particular: his love for his parents, step-family, and brothers and sisters, which found practical Christian expression, and his genuine religiousness, loyalty to his friends, and love for children and animals. Like a true Low German, he loved to do good and noble actions in secret. One after the other, many cases have come to light in which Brahms quietly offered a helping hand to fellow musicians who had fallen into want, or to his friends and their families, with that delicacy and tact which is only granted to good and noble men. Widmann and von der Leyen expressly praise his generous, benevolent heart, which occasionally moved him to send surprisingly large sums of money to persons entirely unknown to him, who perhaps abused his kindness. He was enabled to do this only by his own modest and unpretentious way of living. His purse lay open not only to those of whom he was fond — such as Clara Schumann, to the expense of educating whose children he contributed a small capital sum without hesitation in 1888 — but also to all who were in need, and above all to his parents, step-family, and brother and sister. And he always finds a hearty phrase, a kindly joke, in order to offer his practical help in as delicate and unobtrusive a way as possible. In almost every letter to Hamburg he asks whether they still have "enough money and to spare" and whether he may send any more, or whether they have any plans for the summer, " which may give pleasure to dear Mother, or be of advantage to her health." He is always encouraging his sickly step-brother, Fritz, to " waste some good money travelling." But most charming of all was the way in which he hinted to his father, with delightfully tender humour, that there was a rich hoard of bank-notes to be found between the pages of Handel's *Saul:* " Father dear, if at any time things go badly with you, music is always the best consolation. Only study my old *Saul* attentively; you will find something there that will be of use to you."

This is real, efficacious, practical Christianity. Brahms was a convinced and believing member of the Lutheran Protestant Church. Not as regards dogma, not in the letter, but in the spirit. We have frequently admired his uncommon knowledge of the Bible, most of all in connexion with the *Deutsches Requiem,* the *Triumphlied,* the *Fest- und Gedenksprüche,* and the *Vier ernste Gesänge.* It was the result of his education, his own inward craving, and his artist's delight in the incomparable Book of books. Love of religion and the Bible was early implanted in Brahms and constantly nurtured by his simple, God-fearing parents. Indeed, as in young Hebbel, it was early accompanied by a critical sense of justice. As a child Brahms felt no inducement to take part gratefully in the day of humiliation and prayer after the great fire of Hamburg, because the fanatical zeal of the clergy — which misinterpreted this disaster as a punishment visited by the Most High on Hamburg, which they represented as Sodom and Gomorrah — filled him with indignation, and he could not understand why God had not at least spared His own beautiful churches of St. Peter and St. Nicholas. The Christian teaching which he received from Pastor Geffcken, who prepared him for confirmation, laid the imperishable foundations of his love for old Protestant church music and its uncorrupted original melodies. This love of the Bible grew deeper and deeper in his mature years. " People do not even know," as he once said to his friend von der Leyen, in talking about Schumann's last days and his longing for the Bible, which was interpreted by the doctors as a fresh symptom of his mania, " that we North Germans long for the Bible *every* day and do not let a day go by without it. In my study I can lay my hand on my Bible even in the dark." The Bible — as the number of settings of scriptural words among his works bears witness — was not only a source of consolation to Brahms in sorrow (*Deutsches Requiem*), an expression of hope for a better life (*Begräbnisgesang*), of his own dire need (*Thirteenth Psalm,* motets), and thoughts of death (*Ernste Gesänge,* chorale-preludes), but also of the highest joy (motets), patriotic triumph in his country's victory (*Triumphlied*), and patriotic forebodings and anxieties (*Fest- und Gedenksprüche*). In addition to all this, it was a source and model of artistic beauty and of a noble, purified moderation. The fact that Brahms began his creative activity with the German folk-song (variation movement of the Piano Sonata op. 1) and closed it with the Bible (*Ernste Gesänge,* chorale-preludes) reveals better than anything else the true religious creed of this great man of the people.

Like all remarkable men and artists, to whom the beauty and purity of paradise is revealed in the eyes of childhood, Brahms was extraordinarily fond of children. He acknowledged this himself to Clara Schumann: " I cannot go out without rejoicing my heart, and feeling refreshed as by a cooling draught, if I have fondled a few darling children." With children he was, as Dietrich once said, "like a child himself, full of love and giving himself to them entirely." The reminiscences of his friends have handed down to us some charming little details. At Krefeld, relates von der Leyen, he would indulge in regular snowballing battles with the merry schoolgirls. It was a great amusement to him to tease children good-naturedly — for instance, on meeting a little girl who was trying to carry a jug of beer to her father, he would take the jug out of her hand and raise it to his mouth as if about to drink, just in order to see the child's startled and astonished eyes. At Bern he would set Widmann's five-year-old daughter on his shoulder and " ride " her through the busy street, regardless of the passers-by. To win the confidence of children

and give them pleasure by sweetmeats, merry pranks, and his
willingness to play with them — especially poor children, to
whom he felt particularly drawn by the recollection of his own
hard childhood — meant more to him than all the awestruck admiration of grown-up people. He regretted that the Swiss children, with their Alemannic dialect, did not quite understand his
North German and so would perhaps not chatter with him as
familiarly as he would have liked. In spite of this, Austrian, Swiss,
or Italian children instinctively felt in him a warm friend and
requited his affection by their fidelity and attachment. Long
years afterwards they would recognize him at Thun and follow
him in troops, as Widmann and Kunz describe, half shy, half
anxious to attract his notice. When he was in Italy and went out
from Rome to Nettuno and Porto d'Anzio to visit the scenes
painted by Feuerbach, the " *Signor Prussiano* " made a band of
lively brown children show off their feats of swimming and
diving before him, put them through an examination in what
they had learnt at school, and himself joined in their fun like a
child. One of them, a handsome lad with great dark eyes, divined
his love for children even more deeply than the others; he would
follow him, so Widmann tells us, " like a faithful little dog ";
he could hardly be separated from him, and even came to the
station to wave him good-bye. As in the Italians, Brahms may
have sought and found in the naïve egoism, the still pure and
unalloyed will, emotion, and imagination of children's lives, not
only his own faith in the goodness of mankind — which, as in
every man of any depth, had been severely shaken by so many
ugly disappointments, so much dishonesty and self-seeking vul-
garity — but also a necessary complement and compensation for
his own nature and art, which were complicated and lacking in
naïveté. At Ischl, too, as Ella Pancera tells us in her reminiscences,
he had " his pockets full of sweets for all the children." She has
described, in what is one of the most attractive accounts of the
composer's love of young people, how " the old man," sitting
" like a dwarf with a giant's head on the old wooden seat " under
the young pianist's window, with the apricots clustering round

it, was attracted by her playing of his Paganini Variations, stumbled up the old wooden steps, seated himself with a comfortably cantakerous growl in the great, deep arm-chair, and by all kinds of wiles — not to speak of sweetmeats — tempted the trembling little pianist to play the Paganini Variations again "just as nicely as you did before, as you alone play them," followed by the C major Sonata and the Handel Variations. It is further evidence of his Lower Saxon loyalty that he preserved till the end of his life his friendship and warm artistic sympathy for little Ella, who was often to play to him again at Ischl.

Brahms's love of children — and in this, too, he closely resembles Richard Wagner — was accompanied by a love of animals, in which he likewise admired " nature unalloyed," their wonderful fidelity and devotion, their touching obedience to the command: "Learn to suffer without complaining." He would roll on the grass with von der Leyen's savage great hounds like a boy, throw balls for them, and play with them. When Widmann's little red dog Argos, after wandering for days, found his way back, by a dog's mysterious instinct, from the Grindelwald Glacier to his master's house at Bern early in the morning, Brahms was the first to abandon his hands and face to the dog's ecstatic lickings, deeply touched and moved by such fidelity.

Brahms's way of hiding his deep feelings and strong emotions behind a jest or a sarcastic rebuff, out of fear of his own weakness, was a Low German trait. But this very fact has led to endless and deliberate misunderstanding, in those who approach the North or Low German nature from an unfamiliar or prejudiced point of view. Brahms's often pungent and malicious sarcasm is the last and hardest stage of his truly youthful exuberance, his delight in mad pranks as a boy and his irrepressible love of teasing as a young man. Least of all were the ladies spared by his teasing, which was, so to speak, a safety-valve for all budding sentimentality, emotion, and over-enthusiasm; and Clara Schumann, who took it all seriously because his face remained imperturbably grave, suffered particularly severely from it. In his later years it all became concentrated into sarcasm. " My heartiest

thanks; go on amusing yourself in the same way," was his standing remark when he had subjected somebody to drastic criticism
or a sharp rebuff.

Quite a little volume might be filled with delightful anecdotes
about Brahms. Many of them are concerned with his love of
teasing and can best be grouped under the category of boyish
practical jokes. He sometimes perpetrated these even as a man.
As, for example, when he mystified a young pianist, who was
to turn over one of his manuscripts at the piano for Clara Schumann, by secretly giving her all sorts of misleading directions,
resulting in a hopeless musical confusion. Or when he went into
the empty music-room in the house of some friends and there
murdered one of Czerny's scale studies so terribly, by intentionally breaking down and stumbling over it, that the indignant
mother rushed in from the next room, only to discover that
the sinner was not her Franzi, but the laughing composer. Or
when he skilfully and neatly took in Clara Schumann by having
a few extracts from his latest piano-pieces written out by another
hand on sheets of old note-paper bearing her name, and then
slyly attributing them to her as " youthful sins " of her own.
The letters from Brahms to Eugenie Schumann in her *Erinnerungen* should be read if we would join in the laughter over
the way in which the subtly contrived trick was deliberately
planned and carried out. Or when, at Venice, he incited Clara
Schumann's daughter to take Billroth, who was a passionate " nut-
cracker," a bag of nuts to his hotel on the pretence that it was
his birthday. Or when he tried to palm off a movement of a
symphony on Clara as a movement of a new piano concerto.
Or when, at Baden-Baden, he sent off a man whom he at once
recognized to be a professional interviewer, a voluble journalist
exuding flattery, along a path through the wood on the mountain
— where, he said, he might still hope to overtake " my brother
the composer." But most of them fall under the category of
sarcasm. As, for instance, in the case of the 'cellist at Vienna who
timidly grumbled and complained that, owing to Brahms's piano-
playing, which was always too loud, he could not hear himself

play — to which Brahms laconically replied: " Happy man! "
When some ladies were worrying him for a lock of his mane at
the banquet at Vienna, he fled in deep indignation at such " tom-
fooleries (*Alfanzereien*)," saying: " Bah! What silly nonsense! "
He publicly and successfully foisted a military march by Gungl
on to a conceited little Swiss musical director on the Lake of
Zürich, who assured him that he knew everything by Brahms,
as one of his own compositions. He assured a tiresome person
who commented on his short-sightedness that he naturally put
on his pince-nez at once when it was written in the score: " At
this place women go by." When a lady somewhat thoughtlessly
asked him whether he always thought for a long time before
composing, he promptly retorted caustically: " Do you always
think a long time before speaking? " When in Thun he would
direct unwelcome visitors who did not know him to the house,
and then, as Isler relates, " make himself scarce, with a chuckle."
At a party at Geheimrat Wach's house in Vienna, on discovering
some compositions of Reinecke's on the piano, he asked the
amiable old composer's wife, who was standing by, in a tone of
ironical surprise: "What, does your husband compose too? "
When Max Bruch had played him the whole of his *Odysseus* by
the sweat of his brow, all that Brahms remarked at the end was:
" Tell me, where do you get your beautiful manuscript paper? "
He abruptly asked the singer Gura (the elder) in Goldmark's
presence: " Do you not think it extraordinary that a Jew should
compose a setting of Martin Luther's words? " To Clara Schumann he gave the fatherly advice: " Take care of yourself and
do not quite wear yourself out with Hiller's music." And there
are numberless instances of such caustic pleasantries. They seem
to me to be for the most part the expression — often disagreeable
and wounding in form — of his strongly defensive attitude against
an intrusive and disingenuous world.

Was Brahms's celibacy voluntary or not? We are forced to
base our answer — which is in the negative — more upon his
own occasional remarks than upon clear and logical proofs. His
secret love for Clara Schumann as a young man developed into

the most tender, self-sacrificing friendship, which lasted till her
death. Scarcely anything in Brahms's life is more touching than
this friendship with Clara Schumann. She was his pattern and
ideal, not only as a woman — as we have already related, during
the early stages of his career — but also as an artist. If we read
Florence May's or Eugenie Schumann's reminiscences of Brahms,
we shall see that Clara Schumann is the final and supreme court
of appeal for him in everything concerning the piano. In consequence of the urgent representations of Clara Schumann and
Grimm, which he at first received with the deepest depression, he
had to allow his deep youthful passion for Agathe von Siebold,
the charming daughter of a professor at Göttingen, to die down,
because his future was not yet assured. When he was in his thirties
he remarked to Dietrich about a young girl at Oldenburg: "She
pleases me, I should like to marry her. And such a girl would
make me happy." But after that we hear nothing more directly.
From that time onwards, and especially in Vienna, Brahms re-
sisted all well-meant attempts to find him a wife. His reasons we
may learn from himself, through the mouth of Widmann: "I
have waited too long. At the time when I really felt inclined for
it, I should not have been justified in asking a woman to marry
me. . . . At the time when I should most like to have married,
my works were hissed in the concert-room, or at least received
with icy coldness. I was perfectly well able to bear this, for I knew
quite well what they were worth and how the tables would be
turned before long. And when I returned to my lonely bedroom
after such failures, I was not at all discouraged. On the contrary!
But if at such moments I had had to go back to a wife and see
her questioning eyes turned anxiously on mine and had had
to tell her: 'No success again' — I could not have borne that!
For, however much a woman may love an artist who is her
husband — or even 'believe in her husband,' as the saying goes —
she cannot have that full certainty of ultimate triumph that lies
in his own breast. And supposing that she had tried to console
me. . . . For a man to fail, and then be pitied by his own wife!
. . . Bah! I do not like to think what a hell that would have

been — feeling as I do, at least." Perhaps the words " his wife " may suggest the noble Elisabeth von Herzogenberg, Brahms's highly talented pupil; before her marriage — according to Kalbeck, early in the sixties — the composer had felt a silent, secret attraction towards her, but had suddenly broken off his lessons because he did not mean to marry. We see, then, that Brahms's celibacy was a sort of voluntary renunciation, due to the long delay in the recognition of his art; perhaps, so far as his unsuccessful offer of marriage to Clara Schumann's daughter Julie in later years was concerned, it was not altogether voluntary. In later years he became reconciled to it. For after a period of deep depression he bravely surmounted his failure even in the case of this serious and lasting — indeed, deeply sentimental — attachment to the enchanting, sunshiny Julie Schumann, who afterwards died in the bloom of her youth as the Countess Marenonito di Rodicati. But he did so only with difficulty. For he was unable to think of her " without a little sentimentality," as he said to Clara Schumann; and Eugenie Schumann informs us that he had had a secret tenderness for her even at the age of sixteen, which grew stronger with the years; and that at the end of the sixties she often saw " his eyes rest upon her [Julie] with a regular flash in them." Yet Julie's " charming, amiable indifference " prevented him from the first from approaching her at all seriously, and so, this time too, things went no further than an unrequited, deeply sentimental attachment. Thus when old Armbrust at Hamburg jestingly expressed the hope that next year he might see the composer of all those magnificent love-songs return with a wife at his side, Brahms replied, in the same sportive mood, with the closing words of the *Gesang der Parzen:* " He thinks of his children and grandchildren — and shakes his head! " And in response to the question of a pert young lady at Essen as to why the Herr Doktor was not married, he answered promptly: " None of them would have me; and if there had been one who would, I could not have stood her on account of her bad taste." He informed his friend Widmann that it was one of his good principles " never to attend another opera or another wedding "

— " yet," he added, " it used to be so good! " And if some noble woman tried to force him under the gentle yoke of matrimony, he was always ready with the same caustic remark: " Alas, madam, I am still unmarried! Thank God! " But on a few occasions he none the less betrayed how much he longed for the happiness of well-regulated family life. First, when he was barely thirty, in a letter to Clara Schumann: " And yet one would like to be in bonds and win what makes life worth living, and one dreads loneliness. Active intercourse with others in one's work, and in the relations of life, family happiness — who is so little human as not to feel a longing for these? " And again: " When I think how I hate the people who have prevented me from marrying! " And, lastly, after a performance of his C major Piano Trio he said to Frau Laura von Beckerath at Rüdesheim, in depreciation of her hearty congratulations: " After all, I am only a poor, unmarried man."

XIX

BRAHMS AS PIANIST, CONDUCTOR, AND TEACHER

Brahms the pianist and conductor must above all be judged as the interpreter of Brahms the composer. " Add to his other qualities," said Schumann of Brahms as a young pianist of twenty, " piano-playing of genius, which turned the piano into an orchestra of wailing and exultant voices." All musicians and friends of his, however contradictory may be their judgments of Brahms as a pianist, are in agreement on one thing — namely, that, *as a young man* he had a most individual and, as Schumann in particular insists, a thoroughly orchestral style of piano-playing. Walter Hübbe, who often heard him during the fifties in the houses of his Hamburg friends Avé Lallemant, Otten, Hallier, Wagner, and others, sums up the characteristic qualities of his playing as follows: " He does not play like a consummately trained, highly intelligent musician making other people's works his own (like, for instance, Hans von Bülow), but rather like one who is himself creating, who interprets the composer's works as an equal, not merely reproducing them, but rendering them as if they gushed forth directly and powerfully from his heart." Albert Dietrich confirms the " remarkable artistic impression which his always characteristic, powerful, and, when necessary, extraordinarily tender playing " made among the families of Düsseldorf at that time, and how even then he already had the habit, which was remarked even when he was old, of humming the melody softly while he played, trembling the while with inward excitement.

Brahms started with the usual routine of a young concert pianist, interpreting the great standard works of the pianist's repertoire, but after his inaugural concert at Vienna, as we have seen, he deliberately departed from it, and in future only appeared

as a pianist occasionally, mainly interpreting his own works. How
did he play them? If we collect all the personal accounts given
by his friends and by leading musicians, and place beside them
Willy von Beckerath's unusually characteristic page, "Brahms
at the Piano," we arrive at the following result: Brahms was a
robust and energetic player, with a lapidary sense of rhythm and a
broad conception of the works he played; but even in his youth
his technique was by no means of the highest finish, lucidity, or
commanding quality, though "bold and powerful" (Bernhard
Vogel). He was firmly rooted in the classical and romantic
soil of Bach, Beethoven, and Schumann, but astonished everybody by the intelligence, the irresistible fascination and wonderful spiritual inspiration and clarity of his playing. Let us listen
to an authentic judgment based upon constant personal observation of him — namely, that of his English pupil Florence May:
"At this time of his life" — early in the seventies of the
nineteenth century — "Brahms's playing was stimulating to an
extraordinary degree, and so *apart* as to be quite unforgettable.
It was not the playing of a virtuoso, though he had a large
amount of virtuosity (to put it moderately) at his command. He
never aimed at mere effect, but seemed to plunge into the inner-
most meaning of whatever music he happened to be interpreting,
exhibiting all its details, and expressing its very depths. Not
being in regular practice, he would sometimes strike wrong notes
— and there was already a hardness, arising from the same cause,
in his playing of chords; but he was fully aware of his failings,
and warned me not to imitate them." Beside this may be placed
the testimony of another pupil, Eugenie Schumann: "To hear
Brahms play his own works was, if not always satisfying, at any
rate in the highest degree interesting. He brought out the themes
very emphatically, with a tendency, which was characteristic of
his playing, towards slightly irregular accentuation; everything
in the nature of an accompaniment he merely sketched in, in such
a way as to give rise to remarkable effects of light and shade.
If he was playing an impassioned piece, it was as though a storm-
wind were driving through clouds, spreading devastation with

heedless recklessness. On such occasions one felt how inadequate the instrument was for him. From the point of view of piano technique his playing could never be satisfactory; in general he confined himself in later years to playing his own things, and in these he did not trouble about technical perfection." Hermann Kretzschmar, in the middle eighties, stated emphatically that he had never " received stronger or warmer impressions from the piano " than from Brahms's performance of his great piano and chamber-music works when he was in good form, and confirms Schumann's impression that Brahms had " a gift all his own for drawing orchestral or organ effects out of the instrument." Ophüls and von der Leyen remark on the orchestral massiveness and strength of his playing — though on occasion it could be tender, full of deep feeling and poetic dreaminess — and say that he never demanded more of the instrument than it was capable of giving without overstepping the bounds of artistic beauty. Julius Spengel admits that he never " felt so completely absorbed in the music at a public performance " as when working with " the fiery master "; and the features of Brahms's pianoplaying to which he gives particular praise are its great freedom and elasticity of attack, the remarkable precision of the left hand in taking wide leaps, and the independence of both hands and fingers; in his interpretation he praises the blend of unconstrained, impetuous freedom and great restraint of feeling. Another Hamburg colleague and friend, Richard Barth, likewise notes young Brahms's unique mastery of his instrument and his consummate piano-playing, astonishing in its technique even in his later years, when he would sit down to the piano in private among his intimate circle of friends and musicians and perform in his incomparable and moving way Bach organ preludes, fugues, and toccatas, Beethoven sonatas, Schumann fantasias and sonatas, and his own piano and chamber works. On one great point, at least, all judges are agreed: the remarkable way in which he played Bach. He would go on playing half Bach's *Wohltemperirtes Klavier* to Florence May after her lesson, with a rendering which she says to have been unforgettable, as poetically

emotional as it was modern; he would have none of the colourless convention and traditional theory of the old puristic manner
of playing Bach. Heinrich Reimann praises Brahms as a pianist
for his clear thematic exposition of the polyphonic structure of
a piece of music, recalling Bülow, and the indescribable impression of his enthralling performance of old Schubert waltzes or
Strauss's modern Viennese ones. When he was playing in public,
before a large audience or to critical ears, his calm and self-
command often deserted him, as well as that absolute and irre-
proachable technical precision which only comes of daily technical
practice and the habit of playing in public, which was entirely
lacking in his case even in his later adolescence. Eugenie Schumann clearly describes his playing of broken chord passages of
every kind in contrary motion, starting with " enormous energy "
in the highest and lowest register. He had, however, at times, to
quote Perger, his " sulky days," and when he had first to overcome his inward dislike of playing, he did not in the least care
whether he " thumped " or " smashed " to any extent whatever,
or held the pedal down remorselessly. It was for this reason that
his excellent landlady at Thun could describe his trying over on
the piano of what he had previously written as " these anything
but beautiful rehearsals "; or Eugenie Schumann could speak of
a " wholly unenjoyable performance " of Schumann's E flat major
Quartet; or Paul Kunz observe that, " in his shyness of inquisitive
visitors," Brahms only very seldom let this ability as a pianist be
heard. He regularly turned a deaf ear to all well-intentioned, and
by no means unjustifiable, requests, even from Clara Schumann,
that he would let some leading professional pianist introduce the
piano part of his works to the public; there is no doubt that by
so doing he often did more harm than good to their effect at the
first performance. To strike the balance between these opinions,
we may say that Brahms's piano-playing should be judged as an
interpretation of his own works and not solely from the pianistic,
technical point of view; and this became more and more so as
time went on. As such, it was, to use Kretzschmar's words,
" highly individual and remarkable."

Our information with regard to Brahms as a conductor is not quite so plentiful. Materially, his extreme short-sightedness was a very severe handicap to him. Even with strong glasses he could only make out the notes roughly; but for him this was enough, for he carried it all in his head. As a conductor he was altogether himself, with his short, quiet gestures, indicating the entries pleasantly, with a grave expression. Geheimrat Wichgraf, a relative of Billroth at Essen, has left us the following graphic sketch of him: " His manner of conducting is extremely vigorous and full of go. When he wants a *pianissimo,* he bends right forward, while for a *fortissimo* he draws himself up erect, but always with a perfectly natural movement, without any theatrical striving for effect. One can see from the expression of his face, from his every movement, how he throws himself into every note. The passion which emanates from him communicates itself automatically to the members of his choir and orchestra." Bernhard Vogel, who got to know him from frequently hearing him conduct his own works at the Leipzig Gewandhaus, praises, here too, the commanding intelligence and energetic will with which he conducted, and his terse, definite, and clear directions, which were uttered in a clear, powerful voice. He was no mere mechanical, routine conductor, but a strongly marked personality. We may best sum up in the words of Clara Schumann, who is our best witness to these characteristics of Brahms as a conductor: " You really have nothing to fear; you have many a time given brilliant proof of how you can conduct; add to this your quick eye, which takes in everything at a glance, as none can do like you."

As a teacher — a function to which he would only lend himself in exceptional circumstances in his later years — Brahms has been best characterized by his personal pupils, Gustav Jenner, Eugenie Schumann, and Florence May. The curious thing is that these accounts are absolutely contradictory. Florence May sees everything through rose-coloured spectacles. Brahms may have made a special effort for a lady. In any case, this English biographer of Brahms cannot praise him highly enough as a piano-teacher; she mentions in particular his splendid method of

producing suppleness of the wrist, the delight he took in praising
and encouraging, his readiness to play to her, his attention to
playing with feeling and expression. The same is true of Eugenie Schumann; and indeed her *Erinnerungen* supplement
Florence May's sketch of Brahms as a piano-teacher in the happiest way, in that they assign the greatest importance to his
method and technique. Eugenie Schumann likewise confirms the
importance attached by him to producing suppleness of the wrist,
which he supplemented by special exercises for the thumb, throw-
ing it down on to the key " with a sharp attack, the other fingers
being curved, so that even in the strongest *forte* the touch remained soft and full." For the rest, his method in elementary
technical exercises was the traditional one of rhythmical accentuation. And here, in the playing of scale and arpeggio exercises
with the most varied accentuation, Brahms created a regular little
system of elementary piano method, the most valuable part of
which eventuated in his *Einundfünfzig Übungen für das Pianoforte,* which was not published till early in the nineties. To Brahms
rhythm was everything, and the formation of a living and subtle
feeling for rhythm was his main care. The rest of his pupil's
information about her year's lessons with Brahms bears witness to
his strictly classical training: a thorough study of Bach and Beethoven, an esteem for Clementi's *Gradus ad Parnassum.* In these
the " Brahmsian " element consists perhaps only in the exhaustive
special treatment lovingly devoted to syncopations and suspensions. Finally, his pupil draws what is undoubtedly the right
conclusion: namely, that while her mother's teaching stimulated
imagination and feeling above all, that of Brahms taught her to
use her intelligence.

Jenner's notes perhaps lay a too one-sided emphasis upon
this purely mental and intellectual side. For in them, we are
bound to say, Brahms appears as a pedagogue and disciplinarian
of the severest and harshest kind, to whom correctness in a pupil's
composition, and solid contrapuntal knowledge, which was best
acquired, he would say, " among old village cantors," were everything, while mind, imagination, and heart counted for practically

nothing. A few years of rigid contrapuntal study seemed to him absolutely necessary to start with, as " the spectacles through which one must look out on the world for a good long time." A second principle was: " One must not spoil young people "; out of which arose the third: never to encourage the pupil with words of praise, and to pass over comparatively successful work and passages in silence. If the pupil could not bear this, then what he had in him was only fit to perish. As a beginner, exercises in short strophic form or variations seemed to him the most suitable; later he added sonata form.

More significant is his advice to young Richard Strauss at Meiningen after he had composed the F minor Symphony: " Young man look at Schubert's dances, and practise inventing simple, eight-bar melodies." This respect for the " workmanship " of inventing simple eight-bar melodies (yes, melodies!) as the necessary preliminary and basis of true talent and the means of revealing it, this refusal to be dazzled by contrapuntal displays and " the piling up of a number of themes, merely contrasted in rhythm, upon a triad " once more bring Brahms into relation with the great German classics.

Even during his lifetime Brahms's achievements as a composer by far overshadowed his activity as pianist, conductor, and teacher. Our examination of him in this capacity now brings us to the second and more important section of this book.

PART TWO

BRAHMS'S WORKS

XX

PRELIMINARY SURVEY

What has Brahms produced? If we wish subsequently to grasp the true relation of his individual works to his creative work as a whole, we must divide up this whole into its several parts, into particular periods of production distinguished by some essential quality. And this although in the case of Brahms it is impossible to speak of a strong and progressive inward development in the sense in which this was true of the German classical masters. On the contrary, throughout all the changes and variations of his purely musical life, of the purely musical development and output in each separate period, one thing is clear from beginning to end, and it is perhaps the most typical feature of Brahms's character: namely, the comparatively clear-cut quality of his nature as a man, its unvarying consistency as regards psychological factors. In this respect, then, the divisions and transitions between one period and another can hardly be treated in too imperceptible and elastic a fashion.

Always bearing this in mind, we may divide Brahms's total output into four periods. The first includes the youthful works and extends up to about 1856, as far as the piano Ballades, op. 10. It is the direct expression and record of the poetical, romantic tendencies referred to in Schumann's article " *Neue Bahnen*," and the places at which these works were produced were Hamburg, Hanover, and Düsseldorf. The second extends up to about 1867, including the Detmold period, the second Hamburg period, the first period of residence in Vienna, and the first in Switzerland, up to the last works written before the *Deutsches Requiem*. The third period, which extends from his residence in Switzerland to his final settlement in Vienna, includes the years from 1868 to about 1884, from the *Deutsches Requiem* to the Third

Symphony, in F major. The fourth and last extends from this point to the composer's death, in 1897, from the Third Symphony to the last and posthumous works, the *Vier ernste Gesänge* (*Four Serious Songs*) and the chorale-preludes for organ.

The first period is chiefly occupied with piano music, the second mainly with chamber-music; the third is predominantly that of the great choral and orchestral works; the fourth, again, like the second, is principally characterized by chamber-music.

Let us now take a rapid survey of the several periods. The first, which is mainly occupied by the piano music of his ten early years, has as its principal works the three piano sonatas, op. 1 in C major, op. 2 in F sharp minor, op. 5 in F minor; the piano Scherzo, op. 4, in E flat minor; the Piano Trio, op. 8, in B major (first version); the Variations for piano, op. 9, in F sharp minor, on a theme from Robert Schumann's *Bunte Blätter,* dedi-cated, like the Sonata op. 2, to Clara Schumann; and the four Ballades for piano, op. 10. To this may be added six songs for soprano or tenor, op. 3 (including the well-known *Liebestreu*), op. 6, and op. 7 (including among others *Treue Liebe* and *Heimkehr*), the *Volks-Kinderlieder* (*Children's Folk-songs*) (including *Sandmännchen*), which appeared in 1858 anony-mously and without opus number and were dedicated to Robert and Clara Schumann's children, and the setting of Eichendorff's *Mondnacht* (previously set by Schumann), which appeared in the collection called *Albumblätter*. The musical basis of the in-strumental works of this period, which only includes a portion of his youthful production characterized by a "storm and stress" quality full of a wild and exalted imagination, is to be found in Beethoven (especially the later works), Schumann, and German folk-song; the psychological basis may be sought in the Nordic character of his country of origin, which, looked at from the broadest point of view, may be regarded as extending geograph-ically as far north as Scotland. This Nordic character consists in a peculiar tendency towards the gloomily fantastic, the ghostly, dæmonic, uncanny, and grisly (cf. the *Edward-Ballade* and the E flat Piano Scherzo). If we care to speak of Hebbelian traits in

Brahms's music, and if it is possible to do so — and they are undoubtedly present in it, in a form which may legitimately be explained by the fact that both were natives of Ditmarsh, since Brahms's family had its origin in western Holstein — they will occasionally be found in these youthful works, and most clearly so in the individual stamp of imagination and romance which they bear. And this youthful imagination and romance also determine the style of these youthful works: Brahms already displays both the qualities of Hebbel and the entirely contrasting ones of Theodor Storm and Claus Groth in abrupt juxtaposition, the gloom and austerity of the former side by side with the clarity and gentle elegiac spirit of the latter, their sentiment and tenderness with his powerful genius and fierce defiance. He is still struggling vigorously with a plethora of subjects, images, and figures, drawn mainly from ballad sources: his work is accordingly characterized by the sharpest contrasts within the separate themes, movements, and collections of songs, firmly held together, as in a framework, by the prevailing mood, which is consistently and uniformly sustained with the most definite intention throughout every section of the great cyclic works. The often lightning changes in the character of the themes are quite in the manner of Beethoven; Beethovenesque, too, is the large extent to which he used the piano sonata, which was not at all typical of that period; and, finally, the formal and intellectual basis of these youthful works is also in general Beethovenesque. They were conceived, almost without exception, beneath the melancholy, rainy northern skies of Hamburg, with their gloomily fantastic cloud-formations — which belong to the North Sea — their often astonishingly rapid changes from brightness to gloom, from sun to rain-squalls, their silvery mists which sometimes collect as rapidly as these, and their wonderful wealth of colour, which, though subdued, has a delicate and many-hued opalescence. It is not unimportant to recall this if we wish to arrive at an understanding, not only of the character and style, but also of the colour of these ten youthful works. If we are to award the palm for outstanding merit to any particular works of this first period, it will certainly fall to the Third Piano Sonata, op. 5 (F minor), the Schumann Variations, op. 9, and the Ballades, op. 10.

The second period, which tends mainly towards chamber-music, is exceptionally rich in important works of every kind and form. Chamber-music welcomes a new recruit in the young composer of the two piano quartets (G minor, op. 25; A major, op. 26), the two string sextets (B flat major, op. 18; G major, op. 36), the Piano Quintet (F minor, op. 34), the Trio for piano, violin, and French horn (E flat major, op. 40), and the First 'Cello Sonata (E minor, op. 38). The piano music turns with surprising abruptness from sonata form to that of variations (Variations for piano duet on Schumann's " Last Theme," op. 23; Variations for piano solo on an Original Theme and on a Hungarian Song, op. 21; the well-known great Variations on a Theme from Handel's *Leçons,* in B flat major, op. 24; the so-called Studies in the form of Variations on a Theme by Paganini, op. 35). The studies of the Paganini Variations are supplemented by the *Studien für das Pianoforte* (*Studies for the Pianoforte*), without opus number. The first two books contain a study based on Chopin's *Étude* in F minor (with the melody in sixths), and the finale from C. M. von Weber's C major Sonata arranged as a *moto perpetuo,* in which a very extensive use is made of the left hand; the last two books, which appeared ten years later, contain two arrangements of a *Presto* by J. S. Bach, the Bach *Chaconne* (D minor) for left hand only, and Gluck's *Gavotte* in A major arranged for concert performance — a fascinating piece of old ballet music, which was promptly reintroduced to the public by Clara Schumann. The music for piano duet is likewise distinguished by two supremely successful productions: the first two books of *Ungarische Tänze* (*Hungarian Dances*), without opus number, the last two books of which appeared seven years later, and the *Wiener Walzer* (*Viennese Waltzes*), op. 39. The Hungarian Dances, arranged with an astonishing capacity for entering into the characteristic qualities and art of a foreign people, represent the first stage on the stony path of Brahms's excursions into national folk-music. The chief examples of Brahms's songs in this period preceding the *Deutsches Requiem* are the Fifteen Romances from Tieck's *Magelone*, op. 33. To these may also be added a few volumes of solos, which may already be reckoned among the finest examples of Brahms's song-writing: op. 14, containing, among others, *Ein Sonett;* op. 19, with *Scheiden und Meiden, In der Ferne, Der Schmied, An eine Äolsharfe;* op. 32, with *Wie bist du, meine Königin;* and op. 43, with *Von ewiger Liebe, Die Mainacht,* and *Das Lied vom Herrn von Falkenstein.* To the period of the *Requiem* belong the following collections of songs: op. 46, with *An die Nachtigall, Magyarisch, Die Schale der Vergessenheit, Die Kränze;* op. 47, with *O liebliche Wangen, Botschaft,* and *Sonntag;* op. 48, with *Herbstgefühl;* op. 49, with *Wiegenlied, An ein Veilchen,* and *Abenddämmerung.* During this period, too, Brahms triumphantly entered the new spheres of orchestral and choral composition. The former is represented by his first exercises and studies in orchestral writing, the two Serenades for orchestra in D major (op. 11) and A major (op. 16); the latter by a whole series of works, mostly composed at Detmold, which should likewise for the most part be regarded as studies in older styles and forms: the *Ave Maria* (op. 12), for female chorus, with accompaniment for orchestra or organ; the *Begräbnisgesang (Funeral Ode)* for chorus and wind instruments (op. 13); the *Marienlieder* (op. 22), for mixed choir; the *Gesänge fur Frauenchor (Songs for Female Chorus)* (op. 17), with accompaniment for two horns and harp; the *Thirteenth Psalm* ("*Herr, wie lange willst du mein so gar vergessen?*")(op. 27), for three-part female choir, with accompaniment for organ or piano; the two motets (op. 29) for mixed five-part choir unaccompanied, "*Es ist das Heil uns kommen her*" and "*Schaffe in mir, Gott, ein rein' Herz*"; Flemming's *Geistliches Lied (Sacred Song)* (op. 30), "*Lass dich nur nichts nicht dauren,*" for four-part choir, with accompaniment for organ or piano; *Drei Geistliche Chöre (Three Sacred Choruses)* with Latin words (op. 37), for female voices unaccompanied; *Fünf Gesänge (Five Songs)* (op. 41), for four-part male-voice choir;

Drei Gesänge (*Three Songs*) (op. 42), for six-part choir un-accompanied; twelve *Lieder und Romanzen* (op. 44), for female choir, unaccompanied or with piano accompaniment *ad libitum*. Brahms's earliest and most faithful love — the German folk-song — matured its second precious fruit during this period: the *Deutsche Volkslieder* (*German Folk-songs*), including *In stiller Nacht, Ich fahr dahin,* and *Schnitter Tod*), dedicated to his Vienna Singakademie, arranged for mixed choir after the fashion of the early masters, and published without opus number. There was a further contribution in the way of compositions for one or more solo voices: the duets, op. 21 and op. 28, and the three vocal quartets with piano accompaniment, op. 31 (including *Wechsellied zum Tanze*). In the way of organ works, which Brahms cultivated only very infrequently, all that we have to record in this period is the A minor Fugue published in 1864 as a supplement to the *Allgemeine Musik-Zeitung*.

As regards the musical basis and development of the works of this period, the influence of Beethoven decidedly begins to recede before that of the older classical composers of Vienna, Haydn and Mozart, those masters of the idyllic instrumental serenade. The classical masters of Vienna are now supplemented by the so-called " *Altklassiker* " or early classical composers — that is, those of the purely contrapuntal unaccompanied choral style of the sixteenth and seventeenth centuries, the great old masters of Germany, Rome, and Venice. Brahms's early love for German folk-song receives new and powerful reinforcements. The psy-chological basis undergoes a change from–the wild dæmonic character of the First Piano Concerto, in D minor, op. 15, sketched as early as the first period, which is in the direct succession from Beethoven's Ninth Symphony and Bach's D minor Piano Con-certo; it begins to give way, on the one hand, to the mournful, subdued melancholy of the two idyllic orchestral serenades, and, on the other hand, to the progressively ripening maturity of this first great group of chamber works, in which the vagrant imagi-nation and dreamy romanticism of the youthful works is in-creasingly superseded by a more austerely formal and concentrated classical style. In this second period Brahms's individuality reaches its complete development. Everything in his music that we associate with the name of Brahms, the broad sweep of his melodies, resembling those of Beethoven in their superb breadth and amplitude, his subtle processes of musical thought, worked out with an incomparable natural logic — the first movements of his larger instrumental works being apt to develop out of quite a short motif, or even out of a few notes — the noble resignation of his nature, and its characteristically subdued and indeterminate moods, summed up by some German writers in the term "*Moll-Dur*" (i.e., "minor-major"), his individual harmonic technique, with its often fascinating tinge of archaism, drawing fresh strength from the early masters, the variety and character of his rhythms, again suggestive of Beethoven, his grave, deep vein of emotion, whether spiritual, poetic, or intellectual — all this is already present to the fullest extent in the works of this second period, or is at least quite clearly foreshadowed in them.

The third, and ostensibly the most decisive and important period of Brahms's production, is that of the great choral and orchestral works. It was now that Schumann's prophetic words were fulfilled: "If he will only point his magic wand to where the might of mass, whether in chorus or orchestra, lends him its strength, even more marvellous glimpses into the secrets of the spirit world await us." The composer of the *Deutsches Requiem* now further appears as a composer of symphonies. Around the *Deutsches Requiem* — which, as we saw from Brahms's biography, once and for all established the greatness and importance of his name in the world of music, for future generations as well, and will be primarily and indissolubly connected with his name as a supreme monument of choral composition in the grand style belonging to the nineteenth century, yet set up in the temple of classic art — are grouped the remaining great choral works with orchestra of this period.

In comparatively close and intimate relation with it, as great laments over the transitoriness of human destiny, tinged with a grand, tragic resignation, and with words inspired by the spirit

of antique poetry, are his settings of Hölderlin's *Schicksalslied,*
op. 54, for four-part chorus; the *Gesang der Parzen,* op. 89, from
Goethe's *Iphigenie;* and his elegy on the death of Anselm Feuerbach, a setting of Schiller's *Nänie,* op. 82, for four-part chorus
and orchestra, with harp *ad libitum;* besides the grandiose
Triumphlied, op. 55, for eight-part chorus with orchestra, and
organ *ad libitum,* in the manner of Handel's festival odes; and
two works for male-voice choir with orchestra, the *Alto Rhapsody,* from Goethe's *Harzreise im Winter,* op. 53, for alto solo,
male-voice choir, and orchestra, and the setting of Goethe's
Rinaldo, op. 50, a cantata for tenor solo, male choir, and orchestra.

Slowly and systematically he passed through the preparatory
stages leading to symphony. The two essays in the form of orchestral serenades were followed at an interval of fourteen years
by the Variations on a Theme by Joseph Haydn, op. 56, for
orchestra, which are, as it were, the direct prelude to his symphonic works. Then, after another interval of three years, came
the First Symphony, op. 68, in C Minor, followed in turn, four
years later, by the Second, op. 73, in D major, and the third, op. 90,
in F major. This period is marked by other novelties besides
Brahms's symphonies: namely, the pair of overtures, the *Akademische,* op. 80, and the *Tragische,* op. 81, and a pair of concertos
(the Second Piano Concerto, op. 83, in B flat major, and the
Violin Concerto, op. 77, in D major). Among his new achievements in the field of chamber-music must be reckoned the three
string quartets dating from the seventies: op. 51, in C minor and
A minor; op. 67, in B flat major; the first of the three violin
sonatas, op. 78, in G major; and the First String Quintet, op. 88,
in F major, dating from the early eighties. The first youthful
Piano Trio, op. 8, in B major, has as its pendant the Second Piano
Trio, op. 87, in C major, dating from the early eighties, and the
first two piano quartets have as theirs the Third, op. 60, in C
minor, dating from the middle seventies. In this third period,
piano music falls decidedly into the background. The appearance of a third and fourth book forming a continuation of the
Hungarian Dances for piano duet in 1880 scores another marked

success in national folk-music; and equally great was that of
the enchanting *Liebeslieder-Walzer,* for piano duet, with quartet
for solo voices *ad libitum,* op. 52, followed eight years later by the
Neue Liebeslieder-Walzer, op. 65, arranged in the same way. And
so the precious cycle of Brahms's works for piano duet, whether
arrangements or original compositions, is complete: Waltzes,
Hungarian Dances, *Liebeslieder-Walzer, Neue Liebeslieder-
Walzer.* The orginal compositions for piano solo include only
one important work on a large scale, but it is a correspondingly
important one: the two Rhapsodies, op. 79, in B minor and G
minor, and a work of minor importance which inaugurates the
later series of *Lyrische Stücke* for piano — the two volumes of
Klavierstücke, op. 76. As regards songs, too, this third period of
Brahms's production may be called the great vocal period. The
rich output of songs during the second period appears to be considerably increased during the third. Among the collections containing songs for solo voice we may mention op. 57, the *Daumer-
Liederkreis* (song-cycle written to Daumer's words); op. 58,
containing *Serenade* and *Schwermut;* op. 59, with *Auf dem See,
Regenlied, Nachklang;* op. 63, with the *Heimweh-Lieder, An die
Tauben,* etc.; op. 69, with *Des Liebsten Schwur* and *Tambour-
liedchen;* op. 70, with *Abendregen* and *Lerchengesang;* op. 71,
with *Minnelied;* op. 72, with *Alte Liebe* — all dating from the
seventies — and op. 84, with *Vergebliches Ständchen;* op. 85, with
In Waldeinsamkeit, Sommerabend, and *Mondenschein;* op. 86,
with *Feldeinsamkeit* and *Therese;* op. 94, for low voice, with
Sapphische Ode; op. 95 and op. 96, with *Wir wandelten, Der Tod,
das ist die kühle Nacht;* op. 97, with *Nachtigall, Dort in den
Weiden* — dating from the eighties. To these may be added the
duets, op. 61, op. 66, and op. 75 (*Balladen und Romanzen*),
dating from the seventies, and the vocal quartets, op. 64, dating
from the seventies, and op. 92, from the eighties.

From the musical point of view the novelty of the works of
this third period lies not so much in their fundamental character
and content as in their form. In them we see Brahms as the slowly
but steadily maturing composer of the great symphonic and

choral forms, handled strictly and logically, but at the same time freely and progressively. But besides this his works display a more and more conscious mastery; there appears in them an entirely distinctive technique of composition, perfected by him quite independently, and having as its essential basis an extraordinary concentration, not so much psychological as concerned with form.

The fourth and last period, extending roughly from the Third Symphony to the master's death, is devoted not so much to mastering fresh ground as regards the form and category of his compositions, as to developing the forms and categories which he had already practised in the three previous periods, accompanied by an ever-increasing subtilization of his technical processes and concentration of form. The series of his symphonies came to a close in the mid-eighties with the Fourth, op. 98, in E minor. His choral compositions on a large scale approximate once more to those of the second period in the preference shown for unaccompanied settings, and in the archaistic harmonizing, reminiscent of the early masters; among them are the eight-part *Fest-und Gedenksprüche* (*Festival and Commemorative Pieces*), op. 109, with which Brahms acknowledged the conferment upon him of the freedom of the city of Hamburg; and the three motets for four- and eight-part chorus, op. 110, both of these works dating from the year 1890. The extraordinary amount of attention devoted to chamber-music also constitutes to a certain extent a fresh parallel between the fourth period and the second. A novel feature of it is the powerful stimulus given to Brahms's use of the clarinet, that noble, mellow wood-wind instrument, by his friendship with Richard Mühlfeld, the famous clarinettist in the Meiningen court orchestra: witness the Clarinet Quintet, op. 115; two Clarinet Sonatas, op. 120, in F minor and C major respectively; the Piano Trio with clarinet, op. 114, in A minor — all from the early or middle nineties. With the Clarinet Quintet is grouped the Second String Quintet, op. 111, in G major. The First Violin Sonata is followed by the Second, op. 100, in A major, the so-called "Thun Sonata," and the Third, op. 108, in D minor, dedicated to Bülow; the First 'Cello Sonata, in E minor, by the

Second, op. 99, in F major. The piano music of the last period carries on the impulse started by op. 76, by once again intensively cultivating the slighter forms of short, lyric piece (*Lyrische Stücke*) in forms which are for the most part entirely peculiar to Brahms, the intermezzi, fantasias, capricci, romances, ballades, and rhapsodies of op. 116 to op. 119. Among works on pianoforte technique may be enumerated the *Einundfünzig Übungen für das Pianoforte* (*Fifty-one Exercises for Pianoforte*), without opus number, dated 1895, a continuation of the studies of the years 1869 and 1879. In contrast with previous periods, songs for solo voice are somewhat scanty in the fourth period, but they are of outstanding excellence as regards quality. The few volumes of songs of the last period — op. 105, with *Immer leiser wird mein Schlummer, Wie Melodien zieht es, Auf dem Kirchhofe,* and *Verrat;* op. 106, with *Ständchen* and *Auf dem See;* op. 107, with *Salamander* and *Mädchenlied* — contain some of the most imperishable pearls among Brahms's songs, and the most frequently sung. But they are all surpassed by the peculiar merit of two collections, one of which was written by the composer of the *Deutsches Requiem* under the overwhelming impression of Clara Schumann's last fatal illness as a sacred tribute to her and in some sort in preparation for his own passing, and dedicated to Max Klinger: the *Vier ernste Gesänge* (*Four Serious Songs*), op. 121, for solo bass voice, to scriptural words. With the other the composer of the *Deutsche Volkslieder,* arranged for four-part chorus, and of the early *Volks-Kinderlieder* crowned his precious contribution to folk-music: namely, the *Deutsche Volkslieder,* for solo voice, with piano — the last volume for solo voices and small choir, of which seven books in all appeared in 1894, without opus number. We may venture to say today that the Brahms of the *Deutsches Requiem,* the *Deutsche Volkslieder,* the *Ungarische Tänze,* the *Zigeunerlieder* (*Gipsy Songs*), and perhaps the *Liebeslieder-Walzer* as well, is the popular Brahms. We have just mentioned the well-known sister-work to the *Liebeslieder-Walzer* in the last period, which is perhaps equally popular, the *Zigeunerlieder,* op. 103, in the form of a vocal quartet with piano accompaniment, and Nos. 3–6 of op. 112. We may also mention the eleven posthumous chorale-preludes for organ as a surprising and wonderful contribution to Brahms's very limited number of organ works — the A minor Fugue of 1864, and a Chorale-Prelude with Fugue, dating from 1881, on the chorale " *O Traurigkeit, O Herzeleid,*" thus concluding the cycle of Brahms's works of the fourth and last period, and with it that of his whole production.

Both as a man and as a musician the Brahms of the " last " or " late " manner, as seen in this fourth period, is the fulfilment and consummation of what he was in the third period, sub-tilized to the highest degree. The already strongly introspective nature of the virile, heroically vigorous fighter of the Third Symphony deepened in his mature years into a resignation which, though still virile, attempts in vain with infinite melancholy to stave off a sense of isolation. As regards both things temporal and things eternal, Brahms trod to the very end the path which is that of every profound and spiritually minded man and artist. First as regards things temporal: starting from the conscious, and for that very reason rather unconvincing, tragedy, the con-scious pathos of his Beethovenesque manner in the First Sym-phony, he reached in his Fourth Symphony an incomparably spiritual, self-forgetting, serene, manly resignation, the ultimate experience of a deeply spiritual human life. And secondly, as regards things eternal, starting from the earnest faith in the bliss and peace of the future life expressed in the *Deutsches Requiem,* in which both music and words breathe a gentle spirit of con-solation to those who are left behind, he reached the equally firm faith of a man of advancing years, expressed in a form rendered incomparably more melancholy and grave by its modern *Weltschmerz* and Schopenhauerian pessimism, in his heart-rending swan-song, the *Vier ernste Gesänge.*

XXI

THE PIANOFORTE MUSIC

Johannes Brahms started his creative career as a composer of piano works, and he gave proofs of his love for the piano right up to the closing years of his life. His first published piano-piece, the C major Sonata, op. 1, appeared in the year 1853; his last, the *Klavierstücke,* op. 119, in 1893. Between these came a long series of piano works, which we propose first to classify according to their various categories, by way of a rapid preliminary survey.

As regards sonatas, we have the three great youthful works: op. 1, in C major; op. 2, in F sharp minor; and op. 5, in F minor. As regards variations, we have the Variations for piano solo on a Theme from Robert Schumann's *Bunte Blätter,* op. 9, in F sharp minor; the Variations for piano duet on a theme by the same composer, his *Letzter Gedanke,* op. 23, in E flat major; the pair of variations which appeared simultaneously, on an Original Theme, and on a Hungarian Song, op. 21, in D major; the great Variations and Fugue on a theme from Handel's *Leçons,* op. 24, in B flat major; the Variations on a Theme by Paganini, op. 35, in A minor, written as studies in piano technique.

The piano works on a large scale of the first period — that is, of Brahms's youth — are completed by the E flat minor Scherzo, op. 4, and the four Ballades, op. 10, belonging to the early period. To these we may add, in the way of detached works of some size, the two later Rhapsodies, op. 79, in B minor and G minor, belonging to the middle period. In the way of works for piano solo, we have, moreover, from this middle period, to which belongs op. 76 (capricci, intermezzi), but even more from the later period, in the nineties, the collections of short pieces of a lyric character: op. 116 (*Fantasien*), op. 117 (*Three Intermezzi*), op. 118 and op. 119 (*Klavierstücke: Intermezzi, Balladen, Romanzen, Rhapsodien*). Besides the Schumann Variations (op. 23), mentioned above, we have also a noble profusion of lighter music: *Walzer*, op. 39; *Liebeslieder-Walzer*, op. 52, with vocal parts *ad libitum;* their continuation, the *Neue Liebeslieder-Walzer,* op. 65, with vocal quartet; and, lastly, the four books of *Ungarische Tänze (Hungarian Dances)*. Finally, there is a separate group of Brahms's piano music formed by the technical studies, to which belong, besides the Paganini Variations, op. 35, mentioned above, the *Studien für das Pianoforte,* in the form of five arrangements: the *Étude* in F minor after Chopin, the *Rondo* in C major after Weber, two arrangements of a *Presto* of J. S. Bach's, Bach's D minor *Chaconne* for left hand only, besides the transcription of Gluck's *Gavotte* in A major, dedicated to Clara Schumann (without opus number, like all these works); and lastly the *Einundfünfzig Übungen für Pianoforte,* which appeared during the last ten years of his life, and two cadenzas for Beethoven's G major Piano Concerto. The last category of Brahms's piano music of the concerto type consists of the two piano concertos, op. 15, in D minor, and op. 83, in B flat major, of which a detailed appreciation is given below in the chapter on the concertos. The technical difficulty progressively increases, rising in an ascending scale from the collections of *Lyrische Stücke* through the ballades, rhapsodies, variations, and sonatas, to the concertos.

Technique, pianistic idiom, and pianistic style are inextricably bound up with one another. Brahms's mode of pianoforte composition, like that of Beethoven, Schubert, Mendelssohn, Schumann, Chopin, or Liszt, bore from the outset the most strongly individual stamp. It cannot be said that he enjoys any particular popularity among pianists even in Germany. On the contrary, it is only the growing fame of Brahms's name that has positively forced them to master his music, in spite of their antipathy for its pianistic idiom and style. Certain peculiarities of Brahms's writing for the piano, which, as in Schumann and Chopin, are completely foreshadowed even in his first work, have been characterized by epithets which were not originally intended to be at all flattering, such as " crabbed," " dry," " harsh," " with awkwardly long stretches," and " offering difficulties out of all proportion to the effect obtained." Even his pianistic idiom demands an effort. He rejects on principle all the well-known hackneyed effects of brilliant virtuosity and superficial " tunyness." Brahms makes no concessions either to popular taste, to the virtuoso's craving for " effectiveness," or to sensuous melodiousness for its own sake and not as the expression of an intellectual conception. He will never allow scope for *bravura* as an end in itself. Everything, down to the most apparently subordinate musical figures, can be seen to be worked into the close, fine tissue formed by the development of his motifs, as a direct outcome of it. Yet in spite of his lofty renunciation of all the tricks of virtuosity, of all that tickles the ear, of all soft, sensuous luxuriating in beauty of tone, what a wealth of entirely novel and original tone effects is his!

They will never be found, it is true, to arise out of technical display. Technical *bravura* as such is given no opening for showing itself off in all its glory, and, even in the piano concertos, is never resorted to for its own sake. The technical and tonal phenomena of Brahms's piano music are merely the expression of the intellectual and poetical ideas of a vigorous and strongly marked personality. The fact that, in his composition too, we are not on the look-out for technical problems, but are accustomed to consider even the most complicated technical devices as subordinate to his intellectual conception and musical characterization, bears witness to the harmonious union of personality, expression, and style in Brahms. And so it is quite impossible to think of a single one of Brahms's piano works which is a mere piece of elaborate virtuosity, with a dazzling embellishment of scales and arpeggios — whether with or without a solid melodic idea underlying them — or decked out with massive or crashing chords; so intimate is the connexion between his personality, his intellectual conceptions, and his pianistic style, which, however intractable, has its roots deep down in his personality. *" Der*

Dichter spricht (The poet speaks)," to quote the title of one of
Schumann's piano-pieces — and in Brahms the virtuoso has
to be silent, or else, as the Paganini Variations show, to learn
from what are avowedly pianoforte studies that the poet can
speak to us even in the most difficult pianistic exercises, free and
unhampered by all the material difficulties of technique.

On the other hand, even in its outward features, there is
scarcely any other pianistic style which displays such sharply
defined idiosyncrasies as that of Brahms. The progressions of
thirds, sixths, and octaves, their redoubling, with its orchestral
effects, the preference shown for wide intervals and for a sombre,
sonorous effect of depth, the wayward rhythms, with their tendency to dissolve into a perfect filigree-work of subordinate figures,
and their inclination towards all sorts of syncopated effects and
triplet figures, the rugged, proud force of his strongly accented
Beethovenesque chords, are all clear to view. The "Gothic"
quality of Brahms's manner of composition for the piano, too,
seems less easy to grasp, with its elaborately fretted workmanship
and strictly formal thematic development, which had already
been foreshadowed in all its features in Beethoven's later manner
especially, and most plainly in the Bagatelles. Brahms gave it
an added depth and enriched it with fresh stylistic elements
through his loving study of the early masters, particularly those
of the Netherlands in the sixteenth century. The antiquarian,
archaizing element in Brahms's art, and the unique beauty and
harmony with which he fuses it with his own thoroughly modern
and personal feeling, produce the most radical and all-pervading
effect upon his manner of composition; to it are due not only
his contrapuntal mastery, but also the wholly novel and often
elemental and magical tones and tonal effects which arise from
the importation of the peculiarities of the old polyphonic vocal
style into the " Gothic " instrumental style of his writing for the
piano.

As with all great creative artists, Brahms's piano style bears
evident traces of an imagination which readily responded to the
stimulus of improvisation at the instrument. We may note the

same thing in all piano composers. Brahms's arabesque and arpeggio passages — I am thinking, for instance, of the fantastic close of the F sharp minor Sonata — are the direct outcome of a genius for improvisation, which arises from clearly defined intellectual ideas and imaginative conceptions and therefore exacts from the player a quite exceptional elasticity of mind, technical boldness, and precision of execution in enormous leaps, passages and scales in double notes and octaves, and crossing of the hands.

We shall understand these intellectual ideas and imaginative conceptions aright only if we extend our field of vision far beyond technical and artistic considerations and penetrate behind Brahms the piano composer to Brahms the man. A short psychological analysis of this kind is particularly desirable, and even necessary, as a prelude to the first chapter of the section devoted to the master's works. In spite of the fact that Vienna became his second home, as a piano composer Brahms always remained a North German, displaying, indeed, both sides of the Nordic nature: on the one hand, that of the meditative Holsteiner, inclined to imaginings, now of a fantastic, dæmonic order, now romantically idyllic; and, on the other hand, that of the robust, materialistic, reserved Hamburger. His piano music, too, on the whole recalls the spirit of Theodor Storm rather than that of Hebbel. In the sonatas, the First Piano Concerto, and the ballades, rhapsodies, and capricci the accents of Hebbel may often be heard; but in the intermezzi, romances, and fantasias we hear those of Storm; and in the last analysis this side of Brahms seems on the whole the most genuine and permanent, and this not to us alone. In these pieces Brahms is all that is artistically most characteristic of the Holsteiner: epic, and permeated with the ballad spirit, rhapsodic, idyllic, elegiac, and dreamy, with moods of noble resignation and veiled melancholy. One of the unpleasant results of narrow, sentimental, bourgeois German artistic parochialism is that people nowadays smile at any insistence upon the Low German note in Brahms. All the same, in the last analysis it is the man who makes the art, and no artist can with impunity deny his nature, which is fundamentally conditioned precisely by his

race and origin. Hence those characteristic qualities which have
been recognized in the music of Brahms point back through the
medium of his artistic personality to his homeland and people.
Emphasis has quite rightly been laid on the preponderance of
the architectural and plastic element in it over that of colour, on
the harsh and reserved elements in Brahms's art, its self-willed,
dogmatic quality, cross-grained, irascible, or sullen, its dæmonic,
fantastic side, its asperity and sombreness, which are sometimes
almost repellent. Its deeply pessimistic and for this very reason
quite modern element was very soon recognized. People have
found much that seemed to them peculiar in his scherzos, and
have been arrested in amazement by an idiom full of sombre
passion, transcendental mysticism, or wild elemental daring —
by forms, images, and moods of which the young composer first
struck the note as early as his First Sonata. His music has even
been referred to as morose and bitter, as " old bachelor's " music,
which has waited in vain for deliverance through love; but such
a view of it overlooks the fact that the motive of sensuousness and
love took strong hold upon Brahms — witness his settings of
Daumer's sombre, deeply passionate love-songs.

All these qualities are not only Low German, but German
through and through, in the reserved reticence with which they
are expressed. Though it often costs us a severe struggle to penetrate to the heart of this Holsteiner, this Hamburger, yet he repays
it with unqualified confidence and truth. But though Brahms
demands this struggle, this co-operation, on our part, the reward
promised by his art, and by his piano music, is commensurate
with it. Vienna lent it her brighter sunshine and greater warmth,
Hungary her fiery rhythms, but it remained North German in
character up to the very last volume. The three sonatas, the Edward Ballade from op. 10, could as little have been written by a
central German — more mobile and supple, but with less strength
of character — as by a South German — lively and warm-hearted,
but easy-going and optimistic; but it is no different with the
last book of fantasias, intermezzi, romances, capricci, and rhapsodies. In their moods of intimate dreaminess or contemplative

charm, in their tendency towards a naïve folk-tone, the various German types can, in certain circumstances, find points of contact, but in the harsh, proud force of the ballade, the rhapsody, or the epic they are mutually exclusive, and even the note of lamentation or elegy in music differs as completely between one German stock and another as does the note of caprice. It was, moreover, quite in keeping with the proud sense of liberty and independence of the Low German character that Brahms should have thrown down a challenge to prevailing taste in his very first work, and, struggling obstinately against the current, sent three sonatas out into a world which had for long past shown no interest whatever in sonatas. And what sonatas! For all their reminiscences of Beethoven, for all the affinity between their fantasy and that of Schumann, they are original from the very first bar.

And upon this we enter the mighty portals leading to Brahms's piano music. His three piano sonatas are masterpieces of Nordic romanticism in a classic form. The Nordic element lies in their general character, which tends towards the wildly fantastic, towards the ballad and rhapsody, the heroic epic, and the folk element in saga, myth, and folk-tunes. The themes of these sonatas are " character themes," their development represents the struggle with man's own inner nature and with the outer world. In them Brahms strove like a young hero who knows no fear. But in his struggle with the world and with himself alike, he is fighting against elements and qualities implanted in him by nature, which, however, he to a certain extent fails to surmount in spite of all his efforts. Brahms's still comparatively restricted range of feeling and emotion is already evident in the first piano sonatas. In them he had not yet found himself completely, nor indeed could he have done so.

The slow movements of these three sonatas are filled with a young lover's sentiment and dreams. In the First (op. 1, in C major), dedicated to his dearest friend and colleague, Joseph Joachim, there are some variations of a Schumann-like tenderness on a soft love-song for solo voices and chorus popular in Berg

and on the lower Rhine, the words of which are written under
his music:

> *Verstohlen geht der Mond auf,*
> *Blau, blau Blümelein,*
> *Durch Silberwölkchen führt sein Lauf;*
> *Blau, blau Blümelein.*
> *Rosen im Tal,*
> *Mädel im Saal,*
> *O schönste Rosa.*

> (The furtive moon is rising,
>   Blossom, blossom blue,
> 'Mid silver cloudlets riding,
>   Blossom, blossom blue.
> Rosebuds in the valley,
> Maidens in the hall,
>   Rosa, loveliest rose of all.)

The four variations corresponding to the four stanzas of the
poem are no more than perfectly simple, neat pianistic variations.
The young composer gives the theme for preference to the bass;
and at every turn hints of the varied tones of the orchestra,
whether of wind, wood-wind, or strings, already greet our ears.
The middle parts in one section of them are characterized by a
triplet figure in semiquavers quite Bach-like in its firm *legato;*
these are the most " North German " among the variations. The
B minor theme of the *andante con espressione* in the Second
Piano Sonata (op. 2, in F sharp minor) is not embellished by
any verses. But in the style of its variations it is very closely akin
to that of the First, and so, according to Albert Dietrich, it is
founded upon another Old German love-song: " *Mir ist leide,
dass der Winter beide, Wald und auch die Heide, hat gemacht
kahl* (It makes me sad that winter has bared both wood and
heath) " (Graf Toggenburg). Dietrich tells us, moreover, that
during the middle section in A minor (in 6/8 time) of the finale
of the First Piano Sonata the young composer was haunted by

the words of the Scottish ballad " My Heart's in the Highlands."
This heart-felt love for folk-poetry and song, to which we shall
return in greater detail in the chapter on Brahms's songs, is one
of the most winning and beautiful traits in the character of
Johannes Brahms, as a young man of the people. In the Third
Piano Sonata (op. 5, in F minor) the glorious, great love-scenes
of the *andante* in F minor, deeply intimate and German in their
sentiment, at the head of which are written the following verses
by Sternau:

> *Der Abend dämmert, das Mondlicht scheint,*
> *Da sind zwei Herzen in Liebe vereint*
> *Und halten sich selig umfangen*

> (The twilight falls, the moonlight gleams,
> Two heads are united in lovers' dreams,
> And embrace one another in rapture),

are full of the fair young composer's dreams. It is due by no
means least to this wonderful movement, so grand, clear, and
simply articulated, and flooded with all the young German's
tender love-dreams, that the Third Piano Sonata ranks, both in
general estimation and in the practice of artists, as *the* Brahms
sonata *par excellence*. The way in which the principal theme
is accompanied by more and more animated figures in the middle
parts at each of its three repetitions, the way in which the second
section of the first subject, in A flat major, makes use of the
ethereally high treble register of the piano, the way in which
the bell of the village church chimes in on a high note with
the tender sighs of the young lovers in the subordinate subject
(*poco più lento,* in D flat major), the way in which passion
awakes in the short middle section (*con passione e molto espressivo*), and finally, after a repetition of the principal subject,
it all dies away into the silence and dusk of the summer evening,
while the dreamy, insistent murmur of the semiquaver figure
in the bass, on G – A flat, heralds the great nocturne of the coda

in D flat major — all this is so peerlessly lovely, so tender and romantic in feeling, that mere words fail one. But we may venture to affirm that the most glorious part of these magnificent slow movements is found in their concluding sections. In the First Piano Sonata everything resolves itself in the end into the smooth, devotional tolling of the evening church-bells in the bass, in the Third into the celestially lovely and tenderly subdued D flat section of the *andante molto,* which, with its soft, meditative reminiscences of the old folk-tune *" Steh' ich in finst'rer Mitternacht* (When I stand in midnight's gloom)," seems in its serene peace to draw down the brightly glittering stars from heaven and strew them upon the pair of lovers wandering slow and silent through the still night. I believe that it is through their slow movements that one can most easily find one's way into the world of romantic poetry contained in these three piano sonatas, especially as they reveal it partly in words. Moreover, the slow movements of the First and Third Piano Sonatas came into being *before* the other movements.

From them we may go on to the scherzos. In these the poetical element on which the three sonatas are based appears to be contained in its most concentrated form — a form rich in contrasts, audacities, novelties, and subleties of detail full of genius and originality, and hence most easy to grasp. The theme of the scherzo of the Second Sonata in F sharp minor (which is really the first) is formed from that of the *andante* by a transformation of rhythm (*rhythmische Umbildung*); the principal subjects of the other scherzos are quite independent creations. Here, in the very first sonata, the typically Brahmsian quality finds full expression even in the ruggedness of the composition, with its orchestral feeling for combinations of the third and sixth, doubled in the bass, suggesting wood-wind. The most Schumannesque touch is naturally still found in the astonishingly terse and concentrated principal subject of the scherzo of the F sharp minor Sonata; the most Brahmsian in that of the F minor Sonata, with its spirited attack, consisting of a dashing run up the piano. Like the slow movements, the trios of these scherzos, with their lyrical

quality, are full of a young man's dreams. In the C major Sonata
he already displays the wonderfully broad, amply-traced melodic
line, the sustained inspiration and noble passion of Beethoven.
In these trios, even more consistently than in the principal subjects of these scherzos, Brahms strikes the note of folk-song.
The D major trio of the Second Sonata (really the first), in
F sharp minor, with the simple folk-melody of the " doubled
wood-wind," develops, as it becomes more closely packed and
amplified, into the nucleus and principal section of the whole
scherzo. The trios of the scherzos of the First (really second)
and Third Sonatas, which are also in two parts, are conceived
on essentially broader lines. That of the First, as we said just now,
is in a mood of noble, sombre passion; that of the Third, with
its full, glowing theme in simple chords, in D flat major, is in a
mood of overflowing and heart-felt happiness and thanksgiving.

The principal or key movements (*Ecksätze* — that is, first
and last movements) of the three piano sonatas are highly interesting records of an originality which is personal and artistic
rather than musical in character. If it is permissible to use the
expression " storm and stress " at all — in the sense of the post-
Goethean period — in speaking of Brahms, we may apply it
to the great principal movements of the piano sonatas, and possibly, too, of the First Piano Trio, in B major, in which the wealth
of images, characters, and apparitions from the world of Nordic
fairy-tale and saga sometimes threatens to burst the bonds of
sonata form. These great first and last movements of the three
Brahms piano sonatas are conceived in a thoroughly ballad spirit
of romantic fantasy, full of the pictorial, visual element characteristic of the Nordic style. Their principal and subsidiary themes
are characters, forms, and apparitions, at times exquisitely dreamy
and contemplative, at times of a wildly awe-inspiring, fearful,
and harshly defiant nature. They are of a ballad type, because
their subject and character seem to be drawn straight from Nordic
ballad sources — Brahms's true ballades (op. 10) are unthinkable
without the three piano sonatas. They are romantically fantastic
in the Nordic sense of the word and in the fact that they are

characterized by the sharpest contrasts, by a typically indeterminate Brahmsian quality, hovering between the major and the minor (*Moll-Dur*), and by a trick of echoing a major motif in the minor, which is absolutely Schubertian.

This fantastic, romantic spirit impels him to the use of orchestral effects and to a powerful display of volume and sonority; while his pictorial, plastic genius induces a dramatic, operatic style. Thus at every turn in these movements we are haunted by ghostly kettledrums; or again, in the development section (in D major) of the first movement of the First Sonata we detect horns and violins; while the second subject (in F major) of the finale of the Third Sonata almost foreshadows Mascagni and the Italian *Veristi*. But in spite of all the youthfully tempestuous spirit still to be found in them, in spite of the vigour of development, rich in abrupt changes of mood and phrases full of terror, in spite of all the strained overcharging, the looseness and audacious liberties of form, there is nothing disjointed or formless in them; but here, too, we find an unerring sureness, of both form and content, which at such an early age could only have been won in the classical school, in that of Beethoven.

In the first movements of all three sonatas alike the principal subject is informed by a spirit of exuberant, virile power. They are true "character themes" with an architectonic plasticity of outline and a monumental weightiness of modelling. That of the first movement of the First Sonata (in C major) has for too long suffered from the undue stress laid upon its rhythmical similarity to the principal subject of Beethoven's Hammerklavier Sonata or Schubert's *Wandererphantasie*. The most overpowering and typical of them is perhaps the terrific principal subject of the first movement of the Second Sonata, in F sharp minor, which extends its fearful, threatening length over a whole page. Hermann Kretzschmar has compared it, by a happy stroke of fancy, to the terrible dragon in the early mediæval saga of *Beowulf*. But since this saga represents the most ancient traditions of Schleswig-Holstein, coming down from the darkest antiquity, this verdict once again confirms the striking Nordic character which predominates in these three piano sonatas. Lastly, the principal subject of the first movement of the Third Sonata is also thoroughly Nordic and typically Brahmsian in the double nature expressed by its extremely abrupt and sharp contrasts between hard and soft, *forte* and *piano*.

It is significant that the greatest freedom of form is to be found in the last movement of the F sharp minor Sonata — that is to say, in what is really the earliest of them. The principal subject (*allegro non troppo e rubato*) grows out of the wonderful, free, and informal improvisation forming the introduction (*Introduzione — sostenuto*), with its Schumannesque manner of expressing a tense and mysterious suspense; the opening of the development section melts fantastically into a prelude-like figure in long sustained chords; but the coda, which corresponds to the introduction, breaks up and dissolves into lyrical dialogues, rushing harplike passages, soft, flowery garlands of trills, and light whispering runs up and down the piano; this poetic cast forms the most conclusive of dedications to Clara Schumann, the godmother of this, the softest and most romantic of all Brahms's piano sonatas.

The principal subject of the *allegro* movement of this F sharp minor Sonata — "which has never had its like (*so gab es noch nie einen*)," as Robert Schumann justly remarked — is thematically derived from that of the slow introduction; that of the scherzo, by transformation of rhythm, from that of the *andante*. And now that our attention is aroused, if we examine the other two sonatas, we soon notice to our astonishment that both of them likewise make use of this system of "rhythmical transformation." The principal subject of the finale of the C major Sonata arises out of that of the first movement by this process, and the opening of the scherzo out of the final cadence (*adagio*) of the slow movement. The intermezzo (*Rückblick*) of the F minor Sonata adapts the principal subject of the *andante espressivo,* transposed into B minor, to the style of a sombre funeral march, and the coda, in F major, of this sonata (*più mosso*), which leads into a grandly worked up and strictly constructed

stretto, is formed from the fine joyous theme of the middle
section in D flat major, with simultaneous diminution into
quavers in the bass.

This system of "rhythmical transformation" is that of Liszt.
Its adoption by Brahms was at once noticed in the neo-German
camp, and conclusions were somewhat prematurely drawn as to
the young Hamburg composer's neo-German creed. But Brahms's
use of this external architectonic device — made, moreover, with
extreme discretion — is quite a different matter, for it takes place
within the frame of classical sonata form and is for the most
part confined to the principal themes. By the time we reach the
lovely lyrical episode, the very ghost of this constructional method
has vanished. Not only this quite restricted adoption of Liszt's
principle of replacing the classical development of themes by
rhythmical transformation of the same root theme, but, still more
so, the character and content of the three Brahms piano sonatas
might have proclaimed to the neo-German party that in him
it had found a glorious new offshoot. For these sonatas, which
are the most important testimony to the fundamentally romantic
and fantastic tendency of the art of " Johannes Kreisler junior,"
are strikingly indicative of his future development.

We know that, especially after becoming acquainted with the
great Scherzo in E flat minor, op. 4, dedicated to Brahms's friend
Ernst Ferdinand Wenzel, Liszt believed himself to be justified
in hailing this young visitor from North Germany as an adher-
ent of the neo-German artistic ideals of Weimar. This Scherzo
was produced before the sonatas and directly approximates to
them in its manner and character. We should be more justified
in speaking of the Schumann Variations, op. 9 and op. 23, than
of the F sharp minor Sonata, op. 2, as a direct outgrowth of
Schumannesque romanticism. It is a broadly conceived characteristic piece (*Charakterstück*), which, in spite of Liszt's first impression and the slight rhythmical affinity of its principal subject with Chopin's B flat minor Scherzo, is far removed from
all scherzos on Chopin's model. Not only on grounds of form —
in that, after Schumann's fashion, it includes two trios — but

because the thoroughly poetical, romantically fantastic character, the North German humour, of its principal section, which, like that of Schumann, is often clumsy, arrogant, and abrupt — a quality which already finds expression in the principal theme, pressing breathlessly onwards, as it were, and checked by pauses — at once suggests the young composer of the *Davidsbündler,* the *Papillons,* the *Kreisleriana,* and the *Faschingschwank aus Wien,* and also, in the principal section, E. T. A. Hoffmann. In the two trios we hear the voice of Jean Paul; in the first trio (B flat major) we hear it in the dialogue, now roguish, now (as in the second part) exaltedly lyrical; in the second trio (B for C flat major) we hear it in the youthful boisterousness of the syncopated rhythms, which afterwards leads into a broad melody full of feeling. But in both, for all their Schumannesque echoes, their Schumannesque rhythms and idiom, he is already speaking the genuine Brahmsian language: the mellow suggestion of the sixths, the combinations of the third, sixth, and octave and their doubling — these are already present in them all. And if any proof be needed that the real Brahms had come into being in this piece, even before the sonatas, the principal section of the Scherzo would provide it. For the brazen hammering of this crotchet rhythm, which seems to take us straight into Vulcan's smithy, the strict thematic uniformity, which subjects even the melodious theme of the episode to the same predominant rhythm, is not Chopin, nor is it Schumann; it is wholly and solely Brahms.

A true pendant to this specimen of Brahms's humour is provided by the Third Ballade ("*Intermezzo*" in B minor) from the *Vier Balladen,* op. 10. In this piece of romantic fantasy, which seems to be leaping breathlessly onwards before a pursuer and is full of uncanny, ghostly elements, the later type of Brahms's intermezzi and capricci alike is already adumbrated. All the fantasy of the E flat minor Scherzo appears here in its most concentrated form, crowded into four pages. But this First Intermezzo of the Brahmsian type in ballade form is quite as Nordic as the other numbers in this incomparable collection of ballades. The Nordic element is plain to view in the very form of the first and most important number. The Scottish ballad *Edward,* from Herder's *Stimmen der Völker,* already known to us through Carl Loewe, has inspired the young composer with a tone-poem thrilling in its gloomy grandeur and pitiless, steely harshness. It relates the drama of Edward in no more than three pages, in the old dæmonic key of D minor, as it were in three acts: in the first and the third, which corresponds to it, it describes the country, place, and time; in the second — with its middle section working up in hammering triplets to a passion which strikes terror — it describes his parricide. It does this with such economy and absence of ornament, within the limits of the ternary *Lied* form, with such concentrated fantasy and powerful plastic force, as to produce on the whole a tragic effect, in Lessing's sense of the word, purging the passions through pity and terror. The Second Ballade, in D major, with its sharp contrast between the blissfully serene, celestial peace and tranquil profundity of its wonderfully melodious principal theme, soaring slowly upwards, as it were, on angels' wings, and the gloomy mood of the central section (B minor), reminiscent of *Edward,* betrays its origin more particularly in the fantastic episode in B major (*molto staccato e leggiero*): namely, Schumann's *Nacht-* and *Phantasiestücke.* In the Fourth and last Ballade (B major), on the other hand, a similar contrast between brightness and gloom, peace and passion, is softened, lulled, and subdued into a restrained and deeply intensified absorption in the ego. The wonderful wide sweep of the principal subject in the first section, the weary, contemplative meditation, longing, and reverie in the sombre-coloured harmonies of the central section in B major (*più lento*) with its Schumannesque *cantabile* "inner melody," are as Brahmsian and Nordic as the other numbers.

The two Rhapsodies, dedicated to Frau Elisabeth von Herzogenberg, op. 79, in B minor and G minor, which appeared twenty-four years later, approximate very closely to these ballades in their true ballad spirit, as Billroth has already justly observed: "In these two pieces there lingers more of the titanic young Brahms than in the last works of his maturity." The

Rhapsodies form a sort of sequel in the minor to op. 10, not only because the episode of the second one, in D and B minor, is a direct reminiscence of Loewe's ballad *Archibald Douglas,* but because its prevailing tone of virility and defiance, its great, clear, plastic form, and its harshly passionate character are thoroughly in the ballad spirit. The second is the more important, as well as the more effective outwardly. Together with the finale of the First Piano Trio, the Third Piano Quartet, and the Daumer song-cycle, it forms in its tone of intense passion, its quivering modulations, and its great leaps of a tenth in the bass, which can "best be studied," as Hans von Bülow jocosely remarked, " in any of the noble beasts in the zoological gardens," it throws an important light upon the subject of Brahms's sensuous life. The First Rhapsody—which is, of course, not a rhapsody at all in the sense of those of Liszt, which are rhapsodical in form as well—conceals within itself elements which are more lyrical, and, in so far as such an expression is permissible, in view of the character of these two pieces and of their minor key, more pleasing. Side by side with the aggressive, harsh strength of the principal theme, a youthful, innocent pensiveness and a gentle yearning (in the tender D minor episode), as well as an idyllic, pastoral sentiment and serene delight in nature, come into their own in the B major trio, in the style of the old musettes, accompanied by a drone (*liegende Stimme*), this time in the treble, and, to use Bülow's words, " gleaming in a mild twilight." We may say that the first Brahms rhapsody is epic and idyllic, the second full of heroic pathos.

Like a true composer of a North German school, Brahms was extraordinarily fond of variations. We know from Jenner's *Erinnerungen* how highly he esteemed this artistic form. Variations and songs in strophic form (*Strophenlieder*) were his first and most important test for rising young composers, and Beethoven's variations were the unsurpassed model for all others. There are also a few remarks of his on record which indicate his own views, such as: " The fewer the variations, the better; but they must say all that is to be said." Or: " Few themes are suitable."

Or: "They must always keep their aim firmly in view, and this is only possible if the bass is firmly established; otherwise they are left hanging in the air. Then straight ahead towards the goal, without beating about the bush." In other words, "The bass is more important than the melody." There is hardly any other musical form which admits of combining the spiritual with the intellectual, sheer wealth of emotion and fancy with the organizing, plastic intelligence, depth of feeling with technical skill, in such intimate and organic fusion. Brahms had practical experience of this form even in his early years: it is very characteristic that his first work, the Piano Sonata in C major, already contained his first simple variations.

Brahms's work in the form of variations can only be profitably elucidated if viewed as a coherent whole. We may distinguish four groups. The first of these consists of a pair of Schumann variations: the Variations for piano solo, op. 9, in F sharp minor, and for piano duet, op. 23, in E flat major, respectively, on themes by Robert Schumann. The second again consists of a pair: Variations on an Original Theme and on a Hungarian Theme, op. 21, in D major. The third consists of the great Handel Variations ending in a fugue, op. 24, in B flat major. The fourth, of the Variations on a Theme by Paganini, op. 35, in A minor (2 books), written as technical studies. The first of the Schumann variations (op. 9) is half unconsciously Nordic, half consciously Schumannesque. The languorous theme — a true Schumann theme from the year 1841, weary, resigned, and noble — is taken from the *Bunte Blätter,* op. 99, No. 4 (*Albumblatt* No. 1). Brahms wrote sixteen variations on it, which he dedicated to Clara Schumann, thereby intimating that he intended it to be understood as a memorial gift, a funeral- and thank-offering to the beloved master. Schumann's very accents are to be heard over and over again, not only in the theme, but also in the ninth variation (in B minor), with its quotation from *Albumblatt* No. 5, and in the closing bars of the following variation, in D major, with its almost note for note reminiscence of Clara Wieck's theme from Robert Schumann's Impromptu, op. 5, treated by diminution and introduced into the middle part. From the technical point of view, these variations reveal an extraordinary advance on the piano sonatas both in form and in contrapuntal elaboration. Brahms handles the upper and lower parts each as an independent theme. The second and tenth variations, but especially the sixteenth, in which the higher part consists merely of sobbing syncopations sighed out against a bass which drags itself along, weary and broken, are definitely "bass variations." The tenth variation is, in addition to this, a little tour de force in the style of the old masters of the Netherlands: the higher part repeats the bass in inversion, and the bass the higher part. The Nordic element is chiefly noticeable in the more agitated variations; the final cadence of the fourth variation might be by Grieg.

Far simpler in content and composition are the Schumann Variations for piano duet, op. 23, which are really free variations. The theme is that of the dead composer's *Letzter Gedanke,* which the composer's clouded intelligence imagined to have been communicated to him by Schubert and Mendelssohn on the night of February 17, 1854. Nobody will be able to forget this heart-rending story as he studies the Brahms variations. This master of resignation in music was just the man to illuminate the theme from a fresh point of view in each variation, entering into it anew every time with an uplifted exaltation of grief; and he does so in the most arresting fashion when, in the last variation, he associates it with a funeral march. The theme certainly has not the slightest Schubertian character; but it is all the more reminiscent of Mendelssohn, and, in its tender, noble resignation, of Schumann himself. Brahms has preserved this dual character with great subtlety in his variations—and yet from the first onwards they are pure Brahms; most of all, perhaps, in the closely woven contrapuntal tissue of the second and fourth, which, again, differ from each other as firm, concentrated energy does from the premonitions of autumnal decline and death. For all the uniform consistency of the prevailing mood, it is again the very diversity and finely discriminated contrasts of atmosphere and character between the several variations that proclaim the born master of this artistic form. They are all free "character variations," and the whole is written round and for the beloved master. Powerful, aggressively truculent numbers are not lacking — witness the sixth and ninth — but, on the whole, the tender note prevails, and the ones which go most straight to our hearts are precisely those which offer the tenderest and most loving tribute to the dead master: for instance, the third, with its dreamy, gliding thirds and sixths; or the fifth, in which the melody, with its sylvan horn-like echoes, seems to pour forth as from an over-flowing heart; or the seventh, which is already thoroughly Brahmsian in its accents, for all the Beethovenesque and softly romantic colour of its second section. The funeral-march vari-ation which closes the series soars up in joyful hope in the second section, poetically introduces Schumann's theme once more under a different aspect and with different harmonization, and ends with a soft, resigned lament which seems to say: " He is no more: may he rest in peace."

The two sets of Variations in D major, op. 21, have fallen almost entirely into the background, so far as the public is con-cerned, even in these days when the cult of Brahms has reached such a high pitch. One would be inclined to attribute the blame for their neglect to the regrettable lack of initiative among our pianists, the great majority of whom unfortunately confine them-selves for life to performing the few important stock pieces which they learnt at their college of music. But on closer examination we must indeed admit that another cause suggests itself: these two sets of variations are not only among the harshest of Brahms's creations, but also among those in which the constructive and analytical intelligence says the last word. This is already revealed even in the unusual scheme of the periods forming the themes. That of the "original theme" consists of nine, instead of eight bars, and that of the Hungarian theme is a combination of 3/4 and 4/4 time, of four- and five-bar periods. Both of these must have attracted such a mind as that of Brahms, as points lending themselves to treatment in variations. In the Variations on an

Original Theme, which are so interesting harmonically, gentle, pensive reminiscences of Schumann still linger at every turn. Thus in the first variation, in which the left hand opens both periods by itself, we are reminded of the deceased composer's Romance in F sharp major; and in the finale, with its fervent emotion and soft "dying fall," of his wonderful love-song *Du meine Seele, du mein Herz*. For the rest, from the middle of the series onwards the head rather than the heart predominates. That old Netherlandish tour de force, the tenth variation in op. 9, has its counterpart in the canon *in motu contrario* in the fifth: the melody in the lower part is the reversed reflection (*Spiegelbild*), the inversion, of that of the higher part. Brahms's youthful manner can be detected in the agitated variations, many of which have a tone of vehement and discontented revolt, in the peaceful third one with its syncopated figure, and in the *legato* fourth one, reminiscent of church music and especially of Bach; but most obviously of all in the minute, masterly finish with which the themes and motives are dissected and fused. The Hungarian variations, to a greater extent even than the sister variations, are an intellectual feat, fascinating above all in their lilt and rhythm; but they are even more of the nature of technical studies than those, and therefore incomparably harsher and more ungrateful. Many features in them arrest the attention as clearly foreshadowing Brahms's later development. The art with which the emotion is heightened by the use of "rhythmical diminution" ("*rhythmische Verkürzung*"; i.e., diminution of time-values) in the figuration — first triplets, then semiquavers, then demisemiquavers — in the variations from the tenth to the thirteenth, can be found, employed in an exactly similar way, in the central, D major section of the Romance in F major from op. 118; while the finale in csárdás form which leads up to the exultant repetition of the orginal theme, with its steely rhythm, and the more tranquil second section in B flat major, with its attractive ruggedness, already prepare us for the composer of the Hungarian Dances.

The third group, the great Handel Variations with fugue in B flat major, op. 24, forms the radiant crown of all Brahms's

variations. The theme is taken from Handel's *Leçons* (the concluding theme of the *Petite Suite,* B flat major). The older composer
wrote only five modest variations on it; the younger wrote twenty-
five, and, to crown all, a great fugue, quite in Handel's manner
and spirit. But in other respects, too, his work is Handelian in its
power, fire, brilliance, freshness, and mighty entrain and swing.
It is a thorough concert-piece, of great and unfailing effectiveness.
It is true that the performance of these Variations calls not only
for unusual intelligence, but for physical strength as well. Clara
Schumann had to admit to her friends in London: " I cannot
say how sorry I am that the Variations, about which I am so
enthusiastic, are beyond my strength." Perhaps Carl Reinecke
may have been right, after all, if, in spite of all his admiration,
he found them, as Clara relates, " a little too long," if only —
yes, if only one could spare a single variation! As in every true
work in the form of variations, the theme, with its clearly defined character and fundamentally cheerful mood, which conceals all the elegantly intricate arabesque ornament of its age
behind the power and naïveté of the great master of the idyllic
pastoral, is illuminated from every point of view, both psychologically and musically, by " character variations." The novel
and individual musical element is most clearly to be found in
the " orchestral suggestion " of the piano effects. It really is not
difficult to hear a suggestion of wood-wind in the charmingly
animated and *legato* second variation (in triplets), or a resound-
ing horn quartet in the seventh, or trumpets in the fanfares of
the insistent bass part of the eighth, or a soft clarinet solo in
the dreamy pensiveness of the eleventh, a flute solo in the twelfth,
stringed instruments in the lower register in the thirteenth, with
heavy *pizzicato* double-stopping on the double-basses, or the
united wood-wind in the naïve Siciliano of the nineteenth, the
full string orchestra in the deeply plaintive and chromatic twentieth, the bell-notes which ring out through the middle part of
the twenty-second, which resembles the Siciliano in its naïvely
pastoral colour, or the Hungarian strains of the pathetic *Lassan*
in the thirteenth (in B flat minor). It is only in the strongly and

robustly accentuated first variation that a Handelian note is struck; from the second onwards it is the voice of Brahms alone that is heard. In the working-out of the variations we may justly admire the unobtrusive, but very delicate and well-calculated contrasts in form and feeling as reflected in the various *tempi,* keys, and schemes of construction. The few variations in a minor key (Nos. 5, 6, 13 in B flat minor, 21 in G minor) are skilfully and evenly distributed through the whole. As regards piano technique, these variations are typical of Brahms's more youthful style. The erudite element is concentrated in one alone — No. 6, in B flat minor, with its canon. From the twenty-third onwards there begins on the dominant, hovering vaguely between minor and major, that mighty approach, working up more and more breathlessly and stormily, both in rhythm and force, to the great final fugue, the subject of which embellishes the first four notes of Handel's theme, B, C, D, E flat, with passing notes in semi-quavers. The striking contrapuntal skill, which brings up its biggest guns — inversion, augmentation of the theme, and a combination of the two — and the natural inevitability and logical consistency of development, are worthy of Bach, while the character and construction are typically Brahmsian. Just as in the twenty-five variations we have to marvel at the art with which the contrast of both form and feeling are handled, so in this imposing, masterly fugue perhaps the most wonderful thing is the art with which, while slowly working up to the climax, Brahms manages to keep the theme constantly in the listener's mind up to the very last note, stamping it upon the memory at once in all its lapidary brevity and plastic power, and to defer till the third bar from the end the cadence which is long imminent upon the dominant (F major) with an effect that is thereby rendered all the more unexpected.

Brahms's Handel Variations have suffered for a long time from the fruitless comparison with Beethoven's piano variations and fugue on the concluding theme of the Eroica Symphony, or else with the character of Handel, at which he had no intention whatever of aiming; and, incredible as it may seem nowadays, they only achieved fame and success very slowly. Today they unquestionably represent for us the Brahms piano variations *par excellence*.

The fourth group includes the technical studies comprised in the thirty Variations on a twelve-bar theme in A minor by Paganini, op. 35 (two books), which is itself, in turn, a variation on a short one-bar theme in 2/4 time. Their character and style are indicated by the word " Paganini," and by realizing the technical nature of the work; both have been more influenced by considerations of pure virtuosity and of solving the technical problems of the keyboard than of purely musical content and spiritual import. Each variation exhausts a technical problem: one chord-passages in sixths and thirds for both hands simultaneously, another crossing of the hands, another a sucession of trills, another unusual stretches; another offers hard nuts to crack as regards rhythm by its combination of 2/4 and 6/8 time, another presents octave and *glissando* passages, and so on indefinitely. In short, the capricious little Paganini of Schumann's *Carneval* has now grown into a monstrous " devil of a fellow (*höllischer Kerl*)," and Clara Schumann is quite right when she speaks of them as " witch variations (*Hexen-Variationen*)." Op. 35 is still more exclusively an " intellectual feat (*Spiel des Geistes*) " than op. 21. But it is not altogether devoid of heart or feeling. A deeper and more heart-felt tone is perceptible at least in the more sustained numbers, in spite of their roughness of tone; and most surprisingly so in II, 4, where the enchanting slow waltz in A major, "*Es gibt nur a Kaiserstadt, es gibt nur a Wien*," seems to sing to us. As a whole, the effect of this work in the concert-room under the hands of a virtuoso of the first rank — nobody else has a sufficient technical equipment for it — is somewhat the same as that of Beethoven's Studies in the form of thirty-three variations on a waltz by Diabelli: dazzling us and commanding our admiration by their consistently clever and unexpected treatment of technical " fireworks," rather than glowing with genuine fire. Clara Schumann was certainly right in desiring to banish the " witch variations" from the concert-hall to the study. " The combinations," she says, "are too startling, and unpalatable to the uninitiated on a first hearing," and she recommended her friend to abridge them into a single book, with the Schumannesque title of *Études en forme de variations*. Brahms did not do so in the new edition, but secretly he approved of her advice. For when little Ella Pancera played them to him, he remarked: "All of them are too much," crossed out "the bad ones" for the young pianist with a growl of satisfaction, and undertook to rearrange the order — in which, too, Clara Schumann made the most precise recommendations — and, again by her advice, recast the final pages of both books in a more concentrated form.

In the collections of *Lyrische Stücke* (short, lyrical pieces) for piano solo (intermezzi, fantasias, capricci, ballades, rhapsodies, romances), op. 76 (two books), op. 116 (two books), op. 117, op. 118, and op. 119, Brahms has conceived the minor forms of piano-piece far less in the mood of Hebbel than in that of Theodor Storm. Hanslick has applied the term "monologue" to his contribution to the genre of "characteristic pieces (*Characterstücke*)" for the piano, of which only those of op. 76 belong to the late seventies, all the other books dating from the early nineties; by this term he indicates, on the one hand, their thoroughly personal and subjective character, and, on the other, their intimate, contemplative quality and preponderating preference for the pensive, graceful, dreamy, resigned, and elegiac note. The later these pieces are, the more intimate and introspective they become. In form they are a late efflorescence of the minor, poetical forms of piano-piece as written by Mendelssohn, Schumann, Kirchner, Jensen, or Heller; but in their feeling, and their tendency towards a gloomy, serious view of life, they seem to have gained vastly in spiritual depth and intellectual intensity.

It is impossible to attempt any rigid classification. In the first place, even their titles are of no assistance. The intermezzi are in no sense of the word interludes between other pieces; the capricci in every phrase dissociate themselves from the gracefully sportive capriccio style of the Romantics, from Mendelssohn onwards; the only Rhapsody, that in E flat major from op. 119, has nothing whatever in common with the truly rhapsodical Lisztian type; and it is only the one Ballade and the one Romance from op. 118 which entirely answer to our ordinary conception of these categories. This much alone can be said: that all the seething passion, all the North German morosity, ill humour, and vehemence, all that quality expressed in the *Liebeslieder-Walzer* in the words " *Nein! es ist nicht auszukommen mit den Leuten* (No, there is no getting on with people!) " roars and rages in the capricci; that the intermezzi are in the main characterized by pensiveness, grace, and resignation; that the fantasias (op. 116) merely serve as a collective title for two books of intermezzi and capricci; that the Rhapsody and the Ballade from op. 118 are tinged with a heroic pathos; and that the Romance out of the same book is lyric and idyllic in cast. The class of intermezzi and capricci is entirely peculiar to Brahms. In the intermezzi he loses himself in inward contemplation and dreams, in the capricci he passionately comes to grips with the outer world. Brahms's intermezzi are magnificent pieces, descending to the secret springs of the emotional life, and inspired by a wonderfully tranquillizing depth and intensity of feeling, which reveals itself more and more the deeper one enters into them; by the soft melodiousness of their music they give the lie to the legend of Brahms's harshness and reserve in the finest possible way. The Ballade in G minor, from op. 118, with the violent agitation of its principal subject, and the massive and proudly vigorous Rhapsody in E flat major, from op. 119, are the only contributions to this gallery of gentle, graceful, or sorrowing feminine figures that are characterized by epic pathos and combative virility, and may be classed with the ballades and rhapsodies of op. 10 and op. 79. All these pieces are of a thoroughly intimate nature, and hence ideal music for a small circle in the first place. We look in vain in them for poetical " program-music." The first of the three intermezzi of op. 117, in E flat major, has a quotation at the head of it from *Lady Anne Bothwell's Lament,* a Scottish ballad translated by Herder:

Balow, my babe, lie still and sleep!
It grieves me sore to see thee weep.
(*Schlaf sanft, mein Kind, schlaf sanft und schön!*
Mich dauert's sehr, dich weinen sehn.)

It is significant that once, in speaking to his friend Rudolf von
der Leyen, Brahms alluded to these three deeply resigned and
sombrely subdued pieces as "three lullabies of his grief." Yet
they, again, differ as much among themselves as the many other
pieces. All these *Lyrische Stücke* of Brahms's are true " characteristic pieces " in that each of them represents a perfectly definite
character, a separate individuality.

I will now take certain separate characteristics and group
them according to these. Let us first turn to the comparatively
few numbers in these collections which recall the spirit of Hebbel
rather than that of Storm. In the first place, they are nearly all
capricci. They are, properly speaking, Brahms's *Nachtstücke*
(night-pieces), of a romantic, Schumannesque type. A wailing
autumn wind sweeps through the uncanny, restlessly agitated
Capriccio in F sharp minor (op. 76, No. 1) — " horribly difficult," as even Clara Schumann admits — as though through a
lonely, moonlit graveyard in one of Hebbel's poems. No. 5 o!.
the same collection, in C sharp minor, with the indication "*Sehr
aufgeregt, doch nicht zu schnell* (very agitated, but not too fast),"
typifies, if only in its rhythmic scheme, which produces a syncopated effect by a combination of 3/4 and 6/8 time simultaneously,
the stubborn obstacles that oppose its despondent, striving hero
in the battle of life, both from within and from without; but
that in C major (No. 8 in the same book), with its wonderful
conclusion (*adagio*) swelling, as it were, with a fervent emotion
of happiness and thanksgiving — a splendid great piece which
Brahms actually intended at first to omit — turns away from
Hebbel to warmer and more joyous spheres, and forms a transition to the most popular and frequently performed capriccio of
op. 76, No. 2, in B minor, with its poignant Hungarian colour —
though this is not true, of course, of its closely woven and

intricately knit structure, based on arpeggio forms and broken
chords. The same emotional, elegiac tone of passionate excitement and indignant discontent which characterizes Brahms's
capricci is also to be found in the three capricci among the
Fantasien forming op. 116: No. 1, in D minor, defiant and unruly,
with its hard *sforzati* on the final unaccented beat, the third
quaver in a 3/8 bar; No. 3, in G minor, with its extreme agitation
and the broad chord-effects and powerful sweep of its middle
section in E flat major (*un poco meno allegro*); and, closely akin
to this in character, No. 7, in D minor, with its tender, fantastic,
Schumannesque, syncopated middle section.

The eighteen Brahms intermezzi all belong to the gentle
world of Theodor Storm's poetry, with its prevailingly elegiac
mood. They are the most typical, genuine, and, thanks to their
number, strongest emotional nucleus of all Brahms's numerous
lesser characteristic pieces on a small scale. First we have a group
full of pensive charm and miniature-like daintiness, to which
belong the Intermezzi in A flat major and B flat major, Nos. 3
and 4 from the first book of op. 76 — "two little pearls," as Clara
Schumann called them — and No. 6, in A major, from the second
book. No. 3, with its bright, light melody in the upper register,
is an enchanting serenade to the lute; the left hand provides an
accompaniment of arpeggios, as though plucking strings; the
right has a dreamy, languishing syncopated rhythm. The fourth,
with its repeated, even syncopations in the alto part on middle E
flat, and its second section in thirds hovering between major and
minor, is strongly tinged with melancholy and unrest. The sixth
is all soft, ecstatic reverie, calm happiness, and tender, ardent
longing, and even the F sharp minor of the middle section —
which Clara Schumann, strangely enough, considers "very Cho-
pinesque," the whole number being, in her opinion, "too slight"
for Brahms — fails to cast a serious cloud over its mood. The
conclusion, gradually fading away in soft, sweet tranquillity, with
its elusive subdominant effect, is enchanting in its beauty; nobody
but Brahms has written such tender, romantic codas since Schumann. Next comes a second, incomparably larger group in a

quiet elegiac tone, with a soft, pensive, resigned grace which
seems to be smiling through tears; to this belong all the rest of
the intermezzi. It is in this group that the sharp distinction of
feeling between the first book of *Lyrische Stücke,* op. 76, and
op. 116 to op. 119, which appeared almost twenty years later, at
once becomes clear to every eye. These late works of Brahms have
been appropriately described as " children of autumn, golden,
juicy fruit, full of ripe, strong sweetness," in allusion, above all,
to their prevailing mood, which is for the most part deeply resigned, weary, and full of a pessimistic *Weltschmerz.* This is most
subtly and movingly perceptible in the intermezzi. Quiet " autumn pictures" predominate. With these I also class the Intermezzo in A minor (No. 2), greeted by Clara Schumann with
particular enthusiasm, from the fantasias, op. 116, with the
sweet, soft lament in the high register in its middle section, like
the plaint of a nightingale; No. 4, in E major, with its peculiarly
loose thematic scheme, growing out of a triplet motive almost
like an improvisation, and its smooth, suavely soothing second
theme; No. 5, in E minor, the scheme of which, constantly
broken by rests, with overlapping of the hands (" one is positively
rocked by it, as in a cradle," says Clara Schumann), is merely
the outward expression in notes of its sobbing, sighing melancholy; and finally No. 6, in E major, quite a slow piece in
the style of a minuet, whose gently subdued pensive grace seems
to be lifted at once into an atmosphere of sweet sorrow by its
strongly chromatic middle part. The three intermezzi of op. 117
belong entirely to the category of tranquil autumn pictures. The
" Scottish Lullaby " (No. 1), one of the most popular and frequently played piano pieces by our composer, seems to breathe
the purest maternal happiness in its suave principal section, with
its melody hidden away in the alto part; it is only its frequent
meditative little catches of the breath, and, above all, the uneasy
dialogue of its sombre, subdued middle section (*più adagio*), in
E flat minor, which betray the secret, yearning grief of the soul.
The second number of this collection, in B flat minor, seems in
its middle section, in D flat major, to portray man as he stands

with the bleak, gusty autumn wind eddying round him. This
principal section, full of an inward unrest and uneasiness, which
expresses itself in wide-spreading arpeggio forms, is thematically
highly elusive; it is not till the coda (*più adagio*) that this ghostly,
shadowy piece comes to earth, on the repetition of the second
subject, in one of those deeply, intensely inspired, arresting
laments over life in which Brahms's art is so rich. No. 3, in
C sharp minor, advances in stark grief in a funeral-march rhythm,
and even the central section, in A major (*più moto ed espressivo*),
with its syncopated, dotted rhythms, and its yearning, oppressive
unrest, brings no ray of brightness into this gloomy picture. Of
the intermezzi of op. 118, No. 2, in A major, and No. 6, in
E flat minor, belong to this group. The Intermezzo in A major,
with the noble, tranquil, melodious beauty of its principal section, and its tenderly plaintive middle section, in F sharp minor,
which passes in the second part into the fervent, dreamy canon
in F sharp in crotchets — a section which may be compared with
that of op. 76, No. 6, an exactly similar section in the same
key — is one of the most glorious masterpieces among Brahms's
piano-pieces in the lighter forms. No. 6 might be entitled
" Roman Elegy "; it is charged with premonitions of death and
of the transiency of life, full of an autumnal atmosphere, and
accordingly to be classed with the Intermezzi No. 2, in B flat
minor, and No. 3, in C sharp minor, from op. 117. It has the
uncanny, rushing arpeggio passages of the former, suggesting the
cold wind as it sighs through the trees when the autumn leaves
are falling; and it has the sad, graveyard atmosphere of the
principal section of the latter, suggesting the refrain " *Gewesen* "
in Detlev von Liliencron's *Am Kirchhofe*. How heart-rending is
the opening solo for the right hand, which might have been
written for a clarinet or oboe! With what an inexhaustible
eloquence of grief do the poignant thirds rise one above the other,
pressing closely upon one another! Yet in the middle section, in
G flat major, the proud, heroic past in all its tragic greatness rises
before the eyes of the painfully agitated wanderer. This inward
tendency to sorrowful resignation is carried on by the intermezzi

of op. 119 in two pieces, the first of which (*adagio,* in B minor)
resolves into an overwhelming triad, broken up into a moonlit
web of infinite tenderness; and in the second of which, in E
minor, we hear a throbbing, agitated urgency as of a restlessly
beating heart, with the fascinating Viennese waltz idyll of its
middle section, in E major (*andantino grazioso*), at the end,
formed by rhythmical transformation from the principal subject.
This "wonderful piece in B minor, so sadly sweet in spite of
all its dissonances" — to quote Clara Schumann — is unusually
typical of Brahms. He himself gives the best indication as to
how it should rightly be performed when he says: "The little
piece is unwontedly melancholy, and it is not enough to have
indicated '*sehr langsam spielen* (to be played very slowly).'
Every bar and every note must sound as if played *ritardando,* as
though one were trying to draw melancholy out of every single
one, luxuriating in and enjoying the dissonances that you mentioned." There remains in these later books a small residuum of
passionately agitated intermezzi, or of those with a ballad character or in a lively mood. Here we have the rebellious Intermezzo
in A minor (op. 118, No. 1) with its atmosphere of autumnal
storm, suggesting at the same time those of the senses; here, too,
is op. 118, No. 4, in F minor, a breathlessly rushing, intricate,
and closely interlocked dialogue; and here, in op. 119, No. 3, in
C major, we have a pleasant walk in a park round a sparkling
fountain in play, pensive, but with a sprightly note expressed
in the little jet-like figures ("*Spritzer*"). But once only has Brahms
struck the note of a folk ballad or saga, and that is in op. 76,
No. 7, at first sight quite inconspicuous in its low-toned colour.

The treasury of Brahms's *Lyrische Stücke* is completed by yet
another ballade (op. 118, No. 3, in G minor), romance (op. 118,
No. 5, in F major), and rhapsody (op. 119, No. 4, in E flat major).
The strongly virile and vigorously marked ballade, with its subdued, tenderly dreamy middle section, in B major, full of romantically broken colour, is a sort of miniature edition of the
four ballades, op. 10. In this ballade the ageing composer once
more reverts to the Nordic spirit of his youth. The lovely romance,

the theme of which is presented in double counterpoint, while
the middle section is built up over the lulling D major triad,
which forms a pedal-point in the bass, is one of the composer's
most exquisite and pleasing pastoral idylls. The way in which
the four-bar theme of this middle section is diversified by different figures, and, so to speak, disintegrated into a more and
more animated rhythmical movement, is conceived with such
charming naïveté, and so delightfully carried out, that one is
tempted to seek the original inspiration of this romance in the
pastoral life of sunny Italy! The rhapsody is quite a worthy mate
to the two rhapsodies of op. 79, alike in the significance of its
content, the weightiness of its diction, and the grandeur and
breadth of its form. Like them it is a greeting from the heroic
era of northern Europe: rebellious, triumphant, delighting in
action, fantastic and mysterious in its middle section, and romantic through and through! In the transition passages leading
up to the reprise the drooping semiquavers surprise us by "a
striking analogy, mainly rhythmical" (Ludwig), with the third
theme of the finale in Grimm's D minor Symphony. The conclusion rears itself up to threatening heights, then dies away
sombrely in E flat minor. There is no room for miniature-
painting and finished detail in this broadly conceived piece; the
Brahms of the last period can be felt only in the rhythmical " disintegration (*Auflösung*) " of the principal subject when it re-
enters *pianissimo*. For the rest, this splendid piece in Brahms's
grandly pathetic piano style is eloquent of eternal youth, glowing,
insubordinate, and hot-blooded.

There is but little to be said about the subsidiary group of
Fünf Studien after J. S. Bach, Weber, and Chopin, and the
Einundfünfzig Übungen (two books) for pianoforte, which may
be grouped with the Paganini Variations. The *Übungen,* which
were not printed till many years later, were suggested by his
revision of Czerny's *Klavierschule* (*School of Pianoforte Playing*)
for Clara Schumann. Brahms rightly recommends "caution in
dealing with them," for they might "do all sorts of harm and
damage to a delicate hand" if too energetically practised. But

it is only another sign of the poverty of ideas of our pianists, and their ignorance of the range of music available for performance, that, unlike the Paganini Variations, the *Studien* have been to all intents and purposes ignored in the concert-hall and the instruction room. Yet, as Brahms himself says, they are indeed "very jolly (*lustig*) to practise, and difficult, too,"; moreover, such originals, when thus rendered more difficult by a meticulous virtuosity, are sure of a success of sheer astonishment and stupefaction when the musical amateur hears what can be made of them by an adornment of thirds and sixths (as in the case of Chopin's F minor *Étude*), by inversion (as in the case of J. S. Bach's *Presto*), by transcription for the left hand only (as in the case of Bach's *Chaconne* for violin solo), or by a newly-invented counterpoint for the right hand (Weber's *Rondo*), etc. The idea underlying these ingenious studies, arranged in five books, is the same throughout: deliberate heightening of technical difficulty, with the development of virtuosity as its special object. And it is carried out so brilliantly that we are really forced to wonder why, in the "*da capo* section" of modern concerts, in which the artist displays his virtuosity with a view to encores, it is always Tausig, Schulz-Evler, and Godowsky's concert paraphrases that figure in the program, and hardly ever these paraphrases of Brahms's in the form of technical studies. Brahms's remarks upon Bach's *Chaconne,* and his justification to Clara Schumann of his transcription of it for the left hand alone, are of particular interest in this connexion: "To me the *Chaconne* is one of the most wonderful, inconceivable pieces of music. On a single stave, for a single instrument, the man writes a whole world of the profoundest ideas and mightiest emotions. If I were to have tried to imagine that I had been able to write this piece, or conceive it, I am sure that excess of excitement and violent emotion would have driven me distracted. If one has not a violinist of the greatest eminence at hand, quite the finest enjoyment one can have is simply to let it sound in one's mind. But the piece stimulates one to busy oneself with it in every way . . . but whatever I take — the orchestra or the piano — the enjoyment

is always spoilt for me. Only in one way do I find that I can
procure a much diminished, but approximate and entirely pure,
enjoyment of the work — if I play it with the left hand alone!
. . . The similar kind of difficulty, the sort of technique, the
arpeggio-work, all combine to make me — feel like a violinist! "

With these larger studies we may also group two valuable
posthumously published cadenzas for Beethoven's Piano Concerto
in G major, and a fascinating trifle of old ballet-music, the
arrangement of a lovely gavotte in A major from Gluck's *Paris
and Helen,* made in 1871 for Frau Clara Schumann, which rapidly
became a favourite concert-piece, thanks to its classical piano
technique; both the principal section and the trio have gained
in softness and tenderness, the former by the characteristically
Brahmsian use of thirds, sixths, and octaves, and the latter by its
exquisite, filigree-like elaboration. The artist to whom it is dedicated was certainly right in saying: "Nobody can do it like
you. . . ."

The great popular successes among Brahms's piano music
are to be found in the piano duets of a more intimate character:
the *Walzer,* op. 39, and the *Ungarische Tänze* (Hungarian
Dances). The waltzes, dating from the middle sixties, were a
great surprise to the musical world of the time; Brahms the
"harsh," the "austere and earnest" — and waltzes! The two
ideas seemed incompatible. They are the first strong reaction of
Vienna and the Viennese atmosphere upon our composer's creative work, and the immediate harbingers of the *Liebeslieder-
Walzer* and the *Neue Liebeslieder-Walzer* for piano duet with
vocal parts. Their Viennese origin is confirmed by Brahms himself: he calls them "two books of innocent little waltzes in
Schubertian form." The waltzes had an enormous success:
arrangement upon arrangement of them proved necessary.
Hanslick, to whom they were dedicated, found the following
charming and apt words to describe them:

"What bewitching, lovely strains! Naturally, nobody would
look for real dance-music, but for waltz melodies and rhythms
handled in free artistic forms and, as it were, ennobled by their

dignified expression. In spite of this, no artificial affectation jars on us in them, no over-refined detail to blur the impression of the whole — a simple ingenuousness informs them all, to an extent which we should hardly have expected. The waltzes, sixteen in number, make no sort of pretensions to size; they are all short and have neither introduction nor finale. The character of the individual dances sometimes approximates to the lilting Viennese waltz, but oftener to the easy swaying *Ländler,* and through them we hear, as it were, a distant echo of Schubert or Schumann.

" Towards the end of the book we hear, as it were, the clank of spurs, first softly, and as though tentatively, then with growing fire and resolution — without question, we are now on Hungarian soil. In the last waltz but one this Maygar temperament breaks forth with vehement energy; the accompaniment is no longer the peaceful ground-bass of Strauss's orchestra, but the passionate clang of cymbals. This number would undoubtedly have formed the most effective finale, but it is quite characteristic of Brahms to prefer a delicate and profound impression to a more exuberant one. Reverting to the mood of the Austrian *Ländler,* he closes with a short and enchantingly seductive piece; a gracefully lulling air above an expressive middle part, which appears without modification in the second section as the higher part, while what was before the principal melody becomes the inner part. The whole composition, with its limpid clarity, is one of those genuine works of art which startle nobody and enchant everybody."

We may further add that Brahms has included every style and type of waltz in his collection. The festively exuberant type (Nos. 1 and 13), the easy, swaying type, recalling Johann Strauss (No. 2), the Schubertian *Ländler* (No. 15), the pensive type (Nos. 5, 10), the agitated, fluttering type (No. 9), the passionately vehement (No. 4), the light-hearted and playful (No. 6), the elegiac (Nos. 3, 7, 12, 16), and those with a Hungarian tinge in melody and rhythm (Nos. 11, 14). But perhaps the earnest North German speaks in the loveliest and most characteristic

accents in those of an elegiac type, and, next to these, in the
gently and pensively dreamy numbers. These are also the most
lovingly and delicately elaborated from the point of view of
workmanship. Such numbers as the second, the fifth, and the
last but one are sure to be found in the work of such a master
of the noble folk-dance in a more sophisticated arrangement.
There is perhaps no other work of Brahms in which his pensive
side, his quiet, deep delight in simple, domestic joys, is revealed
so frankly and simply as in these waltzes for piano duet, which
have made their way all over the world in arrangements of every
possible kind. By their aid one quickly comes into personal and
affectionate touch with him Hanslick is right: this volume is
a secret tribute to the city of Schubert, Lanner, and Strauss. Many
a suggestion is hidden away in it of the *Ländler,* or of Hungarian
melodies; but all the same, what is best and most popular in it
is truly Brahmsian and once again reminds us directly of the
composer's childhood and youth.

But the Hungarian Dances for piano duet (without opus
number), the first two books of which appeared in 1869, and
the last two in 1880, met with an immeasurably greater success —
indeed it is significant of public taste that they had the greatest
success which ever fell to the lot of Brahms's art. Even nowadays
they are the only work of Brahms's that many unmusical people
really know and like. The original melodies of these dances are
the ownerless property of gipsy orchestras; the names of their
composers are long since forgotten, but their melodies have become immortal through Brahms's setting — he has honourably
laid stress on the word " arranged " on the title-page. It was
Brahms's ennobling art which helped towards the rediscovery of
the composers. Among his predecessors were Haydn, Beethoven,
Schubert — the *Divertissement à la hongroise* for piano duet —
Liszt, in his Hungarian rhapsodies and paraphrase of the *Rákóczy
March.* None of them has brought the genuine, essential, individual quality of gipsy music so close to us by a faithful rendering and reproduction as Brahms. The enormous, apparently in-
surmountable difficulty of such transcriptions can only be rightly

appreciated by those who have heard Hungarian melodies of this kind performed by genuine Hungarian orchestras. They are pure nature-music, full of an unfettered, vagrant, roving spirit and a chaotic ferment, drawn straight from the deepest well-springs of music by children of nature. It seems impossible to imprison them in the bonds of measure, time, and rhythm, to convert their enchantingly refreshing, uncivilized character, their wild freedom, their audacious contempt for all order, into a civilized moderation and order. Brahms has succeeded in doing so to the most amazing extent. His powerful auxiliaries were: rhythm and harmony. With the sound and inspired instinct of a born musician he brought out the individual character of the melody sharply in every case, and this is infinitely more important than literal, philological fidelity. It is still more amazing to hear how he has maintained and preserved the essential, individual, genuine features of gipsy music in his musical idiom: these dances sound like original Hungarian folk-music and demand to be played in this spirit. And for this reason they delight and enchant everybody: the amateur by their natural quality, the specialist by their art.

Their success was enormous, and arrangements of them were legion. Even envy and ill will unintentionally helped to advertise them: Hungarian composers, chief among them Reményi, accused the composer of plagiarism, of unjustifiably appropriating the spiritual heritage of others to the detriment of its owners. They were only able to make these accusations by considering nothing but appearances, for very few of the melodies of these Hungarian Dances originated with Brahms himself; most of them are of truly Hungarian origin. But apart from the fact that all great composers have been in the habit of taking other people's melodies and giving them a fresh and entirely independent existence by their arrangement of them, Brahms himself obviated all possible misunderstanding by two means: the absence of opus number, and the words: "*arranged (gesetzt)* for the piano." And so these charges, refuted in a telling pamphlet published by the house of Simrock: *A Defence (Zum Abwehr)*.

Johannes Brahms and the Hungarian Dances (Berlin, 1897) — directed against Otto Neitzel and the *Kölnische Zeitung* — recoiled upon those who had originated them; Brahms himself kept silence and quietly went on his way, regardless of Reményi and his associates.

XXII

THE ORGAN MUSIC

With the exception of that uniquely lovely and valuable post-humous work the eleven chorale-preludes, Brahms's organ works are a side issue, of subordinate interest among the composer's works. Brahms never sounded the real depths of organ composition. His organ works — as indeed goes without saying in the case of this, the classic instrument of strict polyphony — are, throughout, studies in the high contrapuntal manner, patterns of organ style of an intimate kind, characterized by delicate subtlety and finish. This character of technical studies is most strongly present in the two small separate works of his earlier years: the Fugue in A flat minor (supplement to No. 29 of the Leipzig *Allgemeine Musikalische Zeitung* for 1864), and the Chorale-Prelude and Fugue in A minor, to the words: *" O Traurigkeit, O Herzeleid "* by the old Hamburg poet Johann Rist (supplement to the *Musikalische Wochenblatt* for 1882). Both of these date from the time when Brahms, having been pronounced master of his art by Marxsen and Schumann, continued for years on end, partly by himself, partly in correspondence with Joachim, to pursue the most exacting contrapuntal studies. Of all his many exercises these two occasional pieces are all that Brahms's inexorably severe self-criticism considered worthy of publication. Of the two the Fugue in A flat minor is by far the more important and valuable work. The rising young organist of twenty-two had written it as early as 1856, while staying with Schumann at Düsseldorf. Even in this first contrapuntal work from his prentice hand — apart from student's exercises, including " canons in every conceivable ingenious form," such as he reports to Clara Schumann as early as February 1855 — there is something peculiarly erudite and out of the common: the

"comes," the answer to the subject of the fugue, is at once
repeated in inversion. The strict working-out of the fugue is
interspersed with tender, pensive episodes. The second piece
touches its greatest spiritual depths at the point where the transition to the fugue is effected, the theme of the latter being derived
from the *canto fermo* of the pedal, and being in turn immediately answered by its inversion.

It is not improbable that for the eleven chorale-preludes,
written in 1896 and only published after his death, in 1902,
Brahms took up some of these studies from his early years and
perhaps worked over them again. Or perhaps in these eleven
chorale-preludes Brahms only intended to make a first experi-
mental selection from the treasury of his miniature instrumental
works. When the chorale-preludes are described as Brahms's
" little organ book (*Orgelbüchlein*)," this at once correctly points
to their pattern and prototype: Johann Sebastian Bach's *Orgelbüchlein*. The scheme and style of these chorale-preludes of
Brahms's is exactly similar to those of Bach, but the way in which
they are written is as unmistakably Brahmsian. Their minute
contrapuntal finish, as unobtrusive as it is masterly, recalls Bach;
while the ripe and clarified experience of life, the deep seriousness expressed in them, is Brahmsian. Even from the ideas upon
which they are based it can at once be observed that they were
written on the threshold of death, partly under the influence
of a premonition of death, and may be classed with the *Vier
ernste Gesänge;* no less than eight of them deal with the " last
things " — death, the Passion and death of Jesus Christ, bidding
farewell to this world, and eternal life in the next. Two of them,
" *O Welt, ich muss dich lassen* " and " *Herzlich tut mich verlangen,*" both occur in two arrangements, and one chorale-
prelude alone — the eighth, a setting of old Michael Praetorius's
immortal chorale " *Es ist ein' Ros' entsprungen* " — is steeped in
the peaceful joy of the German Christmas. Lastly, the varied
fashion in which Brahms places the *canto fermo* of the chorale
now in the lower part as a pedal, now in the higher part, in the
soprano, the skilful way in which he makes the other parts

imitate the melody of the chorale — often, in these pieces, in the
form of a canon or in contrary motion — the poetical use which
he makes of the echo, as in old music, and the way in which
each fresh variation adds another little piece of characterization
and atmosphere, different in rhythm and measure as well — all
these points again recall Bach.

But such a great and discriminating expert in old music as
Brahms would not have stopped at Bach. He must also — as we
know from his Detmold and second Hamburg period — have
studied the great masters of the organ chorale and chorale variations and fantasias before Bach, such as Samuel Scheidt of Halle,
author of the *Tabulatura Nova* (1624), or the Nuremburg composer Johann Pachelbel of St. Sebald's, or the Thuringian composer Johann Gottfried Walther of St. Thomas's, Erfurt, and
been acquainted with the works of the great North German
school of organists in the seventeenth century, most of whom
were trained by the celebrated Dutch "organist-maker" Sweelinck and practised their art for the most part in Brahms's native
city of Hamburg — Scheidemann, Reinken, Lübeck, Weckmann,
Jacobus Praetorius. We may indeed say without exaggeration
that the typically Protestant instrumental art of organ arrangements of chorales, which sprang from the polyphonic, vocal art
of the Netherlands in the sixteenth century, can hail Brahms's
eleven chorale-preludes as a last belated modern offshoot. This
artistic form must have been highly sympathetic to such a strongly
logical mind as Brahms, who produced chamber-music of such
delicate and elaborate finish. The words and character of the
chorale on which each is based determined in advance the character and atmosphere of the music. The widest scope is afforded
for polyphonic contrapuntal finish and delicacy by the most
varied combinations of the chorale motif with the other parts
in augmentation, diminution, and inversion, imitating one another as in a canon or treated fugally. The *canto fermo* of the
chorale might be placed either in the bass, the middle parts, or
the treble or else divided up among the several parts.

Brahms availed himself of these countless possibilities to the utmost of his power. Words fail us more than ever when we try to analyse these chorale-preludes. In order really to appreciate the infinitely subtle musicianship displayed by these precious gems of the most intimate and subtle polyphonic and contrapuntal art, one must study and analyse them down to their minutest details. For of what use is it for me to call in the aid of Dryasdust, and record the arid facts that in this or that prelude the chorale is placed in the bass or in the soprano, that No. 5 (*" Schmücke dich, O liebe Seele "*) is written in three parts, that Nos. 5 and 6 (*" O wie selig seid ihr doch "*) and No. 9 are the least imposing even in scope, and that No. 4 alone (*" Herzlich tut mich erfreuen "*) is infused with a lighter, brighter mood; that No. 3 (*" O Welt, ich muss dich lassen "*) is in five parts, with a concluding section in six parts, and that the sixth flows on in a perfectly simple, tranquilly contemplative vein, with the *canto fermo* entirely in the soprano? Or of what use is it to assure the reader that the musical " workmanship " is naturally of admirable subtlety and maturity in every prelude? It seems to me both more important and more profitable to call attention to the actually novel and " modern " elements in these chorale-preludes: namely, their subtlety and diversity of mood. It is consistently serious, for we have Kalbeck's assurance that Brahms wrote these organ pieces with his dearest and most faithful friend, Clara Schumann, in mind, and in memory of her. They are a retrospect and an epilogue, a salutation to youth and its musical ideals, and a farewell to this world, which is, in spite of all, so fair. And over all this — both retrospect and prospect — Brahms throws that fine, tender veil of resignation which is all his own. It is from this personal point of view that we shall most readily learn, not only to understand and deeply love these chorale-preludes, but also to feel for ourselves what it is that distinguishes them essentially from the organ chorales of Bach and his predecessors: namely, the whole subjective modern art of atmosphere and resigned *Weltschmerz*. Anyone who examines them in detail — and sees how, for instance, in No. 2 (*" Herzliebster Jesu, was hast du verbrochen "*) Brahms makes use of the faltering, diminished fifths in the delicately fretted accompaniment as a subtle allusion to the sufferings of Christ; or how in No. 3 (" *O Welt, ich muss dich lassen,*" I) he sends a motif in quavers sighing through the piece, simultaneously introducing it in inversion; or in the last number (" *O Welt, ich muss dich lassen,*" II), he makes the concluding bars float past and fade away into nothingness in a gradually dying rhythm — will feel clearly and with deep emotion how much Brahms has enriched these chorale-preludes with new and modern atmosphere through the subjective, pessimistic resignation of his deep, rich North German emotional nature.

XXIII

THE CHAMBER–MUSIC

As we learnt from our preliminary survey, Brahms's chamber-music is almost entirely confined to his second and fourth periods: that is, to the sixties in the first place, and afterwards to the eighties and nineties. The sole exceptions are the string quartets and the Third Piano Quartet, which fall within the seventies.

Our preliminary review of Brahms's works as a whole shall now be followed by a special survey of his chamber-music, which will always form a crucial and more than ordinarily important section of his work. The duets published by Brahms were as follows: three violin sonatas (op. 78, in G major; op. 100, in A major; and op. 108, in D minor), dating from the eighties; two violincello sonatas (the first, op. 38, in E minor, dating from the middle sixties; the second, op. 99, in F major, from the end of the eighties); and two clarinet sonatas (op. 120, in F minor and E flat major), from the nineties. His trios include: three piano trios (op. 8, in B major, dating from the late fifties, and, in its second version, from the early nineties; op. 87, in C major, and op. 101, in C minor, from the eighties); a trio with French horn (op. 40, in E flat major, from the sixties), and one with clarinet (op. 114, in A minor, from the early nineties). The quartets include: three string quartets (op. 51, in C minor and A minor, and op. 67, in B flat major, from the seventies), three piano quartets (op. 25, in G minor, and op. 26, in A major, from the sixties, and op. 60, in C minor, from the seventies). The quintets include: two string quintets (op. 88, in F major, from the eighties, and op. 111, in G major, from the early nineties); one with piano (op. 34, in F minor, from the middle sixties); and one with clarinet (op. 115, in B minor, from the early nineties). The sextets include: two string sextets (op. 18, in B flat major, and op. 36, in G major), dating from the sixties. Here, too, we see that the works appeared for the most part in pairs or threes of the same denomination at a time.

This is a pretty considerable list, and in order that it may live, we must bring out the distinct and independent personality of each separate category, and of each of the twenty-two works.

Of the three violin sonatas the first two (op. 78, in G major, and op. 100, in A major) are related to each other by a close inward affinity. The First Sonata, the so-called "Rain Sonata (*Regen-Sonate*)" is a tender instrumental idyll, thoroughly intimate both in style and in writing, with an elegiac and tenderly melancholy tinge and a prevailing atmosphere of still contemplation and pensive cheerfulness; a "retrospect (*Rückblick*)" such as we first meet with in Brahms's works in the Piano Sonata in F minor: grave, but the mild and serene offspring of yearning grief and sorrow, and with a softly veiled quality even in its happy moods. The "three D's," echoes of which form a recurrent motif in both the first and the second movements, finally become more frequent in the third movement, with its *rondo* character, where the full, suavely elegiac G minor theme for the violin, of which Clara Schumann "was so enthusiastically fond," and the monotonous, incessant, running semiquaver figure of the piano part, combine to suggest a gentle downpour of rain.

Walle, Regen walle nieder,
Wecke meine alten Lieder,
Die wir in der Türe sangen
Wenn die Tropfen draussen klangen!
Möchte ihnen wieder lauschen
Ihrem süssen, feuchten Rauschen,
Meine Seele sanft betauen
Mit dem frommen Kindergrauen —

CLAUS GROTH AND JOHANNES BRAHMS
(*Regenlied,* from op. 59)

(Stream down, rain; awaken my old songs, which we used to sing at the door when the drops were pattering outside. Would that I could listen to you again, hear your sweet plashing, and steep my soul softly in the holy awe of childhood.)

The *adagio,* too, is in harmony with this restrained retrospect over his childhood and youth. It is tender, with a folk-simplicity in the theme and the occasional two-part melody of the violin; while the conclusion breathes the atmosphere of the woods and resounds with soft horn-like tones. In the middle section, however (*più andante*), the rhythm of the rain motif is adapted to a funeral march in the manner of Beethoven; is it the thought of the Rhine, and of Schumann's tragic death, which at this point casts its shadow over this movement, with its Schumann-esque depth of feeling and simplicity? In any case, its principal theme is a favourite and leading poetical idea of the composer's, for it makes its appearance again in the concluding section of the last movement. The extraordinarily intimate plan of this sonata, in both style and composition, is supplemented by a great and unobtrusively concealed art in the treatment of detail, and a quite unusual concentration and terseness of form. Thematically everything, even down to the figures and runs in the piano part, is closely interrelated in this filigree-like part-writing, traced with the most limpid clarity, as though in silver-point. All the more sombre passion of the minor key is concentrated in the working-out of the first movement; in all the rest its voice is not heard at all. The finest passage comes quite at the end of the last movement: as it dies away in a blissful ecstasy of sweetly sad resignation, it directly recalls the end of the Third Symphony in its echoes of the sounds of nature, rippling springs and murmuring brooks. In such broad codas as this, dying softly away, Brahms is incomparable. It is this conclusion in particular, and the tender contemplativeness and graceful charm which pervade all three movements of this First Violin Sonata, that mainly contributed towards its great success at the time. Owing mainly to the agency of Joachim, it found its way to men's hearts perhaps

even more than any of Brahms's previous works, and its first
effect upon Clara Schumann at once confirmed this. She wrote
to a friend that she " simply had to have a good cry for delight
at it."

Nowadays it is the Second, or " Thun " Sonata (*Thuner-
Sonate*), op. 100, in A major, that is fairly generally accepted
as the finest of the composer's violin sonatas. It is, at any rate, the
most grateful and effective in outward form, the most convincing
and the easiest to grasp as regards feeling, and the most enchanting and intense in its tonal effects. In the composer's life
we described the happy, sunshiny summer spent on the Lake
of Thun in 1886, which saw its genesis. His friend Widmann,
in whose house at Bern it was first heard, together with the
'Cello Sonata, op. 99, and the Piano Trio, op. 101, has celebrated
the Thun Sonata in a pleasant little fairy ballad, the first stanza
of which reflects very prettily the place and time which gave birth
to it.

> *Dort, wo die Aare sanft dem See entgleitet*
> *Zur kleinen Stadt hinab, die sie bespült,*
> *Und Schatten mancher gute Baum verbreitet,*
> *Hatt' ich mich tief ins hohe Gras gewühlt*
> *Und schlief und träumt' am hellen Sommertag*
> *So köstlich, wie ich kaum es künden mag.*

(There, where the Aar glides softly from the lake down to
the little town which it washes, and many a noble tree spreads
its shadow, I rolled deep in the long grass and slept, and dreamed
through the bright summer day, dreams so delicious that I could
hardly describe them.)

The homogeneity of the filigree-like writing of the First Violin
Sonata, full of such intimate feeling, has as its counterpart the
unity of mood in the Second, which is one of happy and intense
contentment in all three movements. When it first appeared, a
chance similarity was noticed, and insisted upon with unnecessary
acrimony, between the first three notes of the enchanting principal subject of the first movement and those of Walther's

Preislied in Wagner's *Meistersinger*. It may be taken as symbolic
of the springlike spirit of the work, which both breathes happiness
and inspires it in the hearer. The slow second movement, in
D major, almost suggesting church music in its *legato* quality,
is a glorious great vesper hymn, with the sounds of the angelus-
bell floating across the lake. But just as the composer seems to
be losing himself in blissful dreams and meditation, he suddenly
rallies vigorously and once again, in the alternating theme (*vivace,
alternativo*) in D minor, which recurs in all twice more after the
repetition of the principal subject, casts a rapid glance in the
direction of Hungary; and lo! a spirit of *joie de vivre* is restored
in an instant. The most delicious passage comes in the final movement, an *andante grazioso quasi allegretto*. This broad, deliberately flowing cantilena for the violin, with its easy spaciousness
and happy ecstasy, produces an effect like that of a golden sunset
glow; in its sombre, saturated intensity and heart-stirring fervour
it is such that, to adapt Billroth's remark about the *Regenlied,*
if it were played as we hear it with our inward ear, we should
be unable to restrain our tears. "*Meine Liebe ist grün wie der
Fliederbusch* (My love is fresh as the elder-bush) ": such is the
burden of its melody, as we think we are justified in concluding
from many slight echoes of that song which are to be discerned
in this movement.

The Third Violin Sonata, in D minor, op. 108, dedicated to
his friend Hans von Bülow, and only given to the world by
the composer with some reluctance, somewhat departs from
the three-movement plan of the Thun Sonata, being composed
of four movements; it is, moreover, conceived in an ampler form
and on an ampler plan, with its principal or " key " movements
(*Ecksätze*) in the grand style, and its prevailing spirit of passion
and pathos. In its "*appassionata*" character it stands in somewhat
the same relation to the Thun Sonata as the Second 'Cello Sonata,
in F major, does to the First, in E minor. Its crowning movement is the second (*adagio*), with its superb, grandly conceived
cantilena for the violin on the G string, extending over twenty-
four bars. The first movement, an *allegro alla breve,* forms a

pendant to the third: in the latter we find passion in repose; in the former, passion in agitation. As in the Third Symphony, it is not till the finale (*presto agitato*) that the dramatic conflict reaches its climax; all that precedes this merely serves to foreshadow it, now with calm solemnity, now with passionate emphasis — as in the first movement — now with sublime self-forgetfulness — as in the second movement — now wearing the form of a typically Brahmsian intermezzo (F sharp minor in 2/4 time) darkly revolving within the narrow limits of a very few motifs, full of subdued mystery and cold in colour — as in the third movement, the scherzo. Alike in content, style, and writing this sonata reveals to us the real Brahms of the later period far more than the A major Sonata: there is more reflection than spontaneity in its invention; the form is terse and concentrated; it has a rugged virility, a powerful, massive weightiness, and a rich treatment of the piano part, which at times rises to positive virtuosity. And so we arrive at our verdict: the first two sonatas may possess a greater psychological subtlety, a more tenderly intimate quality of style and composition, but the greater effectiveness and power of gripping an audience belong to the Third. But those who have recognized that it is the tender, ecstatically happy, pensively contemplative, and mournfully resigned side of Brahms, rather than his alleged " harshness," that is perhaps far more typical and precious after all, will not be long in doubt to which of the three violin sonatas they will give the palm.

Nor will there be any hesitation in the case of the two 'cello sonatas. Of these the First, op. 38, in E minor, dating from the middle sixties, might be called the Elegiac and Pastoral Sonata; the Second, op. 99, in F major, from the middle eighties, the Appassionata and Pathetic. Even the first, it is true, is far from maintaining the elegiac, pastoral atmosphere so uniformly as the first two violin sonatas. The finale, at any rate, somewhat departs from it: it is a fugue, worked out with consummate mastery, with three rugged, virile themes, rather rough in their effect, full of trenchant, abrupt rhythms and robust, restlessly urgent strength, dating from the same time as the fugue which concludes the great Piano Variations on a theme by Handel, op. 24. But the first two movements preserve this atmosphere all the more faithfully. Hardly ever again did Brahms write such a movement as the first, so rich and fervent in its inspiration, both human and spiritual, or such an unalloyed record of intimate emotion. But we must give particularly high praise to the wise insight with which Brahms has treated the 'cello, as a noble, *cantabile,* singing instrument, both in the principal theme, with its epic, ballad quality and peaceful, narrative tone, and in the more agitated and insistent beautiful second subject, suggesting the lovely Sulima of the *Magelone-Lieder;* and with what a world of passion and fire he has endowed it in the highly interesting development section! Between the first and third movements stands the typically subdued Brahmsian intermezzo of the middle movement, in the manner of a minuet, with its reserved and pensive cheerfulness; this tribute of the composer's to the period of the *Liebeslieder-Walzer* for piano duet possesses a peculiar thematic unity, in that the theme of the trio is derived from the opening notes of the principal subject of the minuet, diversified by decorative figures.

The Second 'Cello Sonata, op. 99, in F major, preserves its atmosphere of passion and pathos as far as the deeply poignant lament of the *adagio affettuoso.* The fact that it consists of four movements places it in somewhat the same relation to the First 'Cello Sonata as that of the Third Violin Sonata, in D minor, to the first two. The two principal movements are full of the storm and stress of all the passions, as is also the scherzo, a stormy *allegro passionato,* with its restless ferment and will-o'-the-wisp character. They are palpable even in the dramatic melodic outline, notably in the wild agitation of the " outcries " and " appeals " of the 'cello, above the distractedly seething and heaving tremolo of the piano, in the principal subject of the first movement. For the slow movement he has chosen the apparently remote key of F sharp minor. We say " apparently," for F sharp by enharmonic change corresponds to G flat, the subdominant

of D flat, which is in turn the submediant of F. This movement
certainly had in view the idiosyncrasies of the great 'cellist Hausmann; it is of the utmost richness of tone and grandeur of style.
As always where Brahms speaks to us in accents of suffering
passion rather than of soft lamentation, the Second 'Cello Sonata
does not on the whole quite come up to the level of the first.
Hence it has not found such a wide and faithful circle of admirers up to the present.

The two sonatas for clarinet and piano, op. 120, in E flat
major and F minor, like the Clarinet Trio, op. 114, in A minor,
and the Clarinet Quintet, op. 115, in B minor, are the golden
fruits of the composer's late maturity, inspired by his artistic
association with Richard Mühlfeld at Meiningen, "absolutely
the best wind-instrument player" that Brahms knew. Brahms's
belated love for the clarinet was a very deep one. Ferdinand
Schumann tells us that Brahms considered the timbre of the
clarinet better suited to that of the piano than that of stringed
instruments, the quality of whose tone is of quite a different
order, and that he advocated a far more extensive use of it as a
solo instrument and in chamber-music than had previously been
made. Nowadays we have to accustom our ear slowly at first
to the oboe-like timbre of the clarinet, as agreeable and mellow
as it is " open " and incisive when used as a solo instrument. Once
we have succeeded in this — and it is by no means easy, for in
the case of the clarinet, as of the horn, Brahms's first love among
the wind instruments, we always think of it in the first place
as an orchestral instrument and as played by an orchestra player
— we shall better appreciate all the peculiar and intimate charm
of the two clarinet sonatas. In the E flat major Sonata it is found
in the sweetly ecstatic and tender first movement and the attractive variations of the second movement; and in the F minor
Sonata, in the enchanting, pensively contemplative, and naïvely
bucolic pastoral style of the *allegretto grazioso*. Perhaps, indeed,
on the whole, this infinitely lovely and graceful movement forms
the crown of the two sonatas. The *andante* of this F minor
Sonata reminds us, in its suave resignation and melancholy, of

the slow movement of the Clarinet Quintet. With wise discrimination the atmosphere of suffering passion is introduced with marked economy, as being less compatible with the bucolic, idyllic, and lyrical character of the clarinet. In the E flat major Sonata it only makes a brief appearance in the E flat minor scherzo (with trio), the *allegro appassionato,* which, in its imposing and pretentious bearing, rather stands apart from the general spirit of the whole; and, in the F minor Sonata, in the deeply impassioned and complicated *allegro appassionato* of the first movement. I far prefer the concluding movements to these, especially that of the F minor Sonata, with its rondo-like character, the fresh, sprightly rhythms in which it plays upon the "three F's" of its principal theme (in minims), and the free variations of the last movement of the E flat major Sonata.

Of the three piano trios the First, op. 8, in B major, occupies a peculiar position. It is a youthful work, a young man's confession of faith, with all the beauties and merits of youth, which can never be recaptured, and all its weaknesses of form. In his mature years Brahms was more deeply conscious of the latter than of the former. It was this, together with Hanslick's censure of it as "immature workmanship," that induced him to produce a new and thoroughly revised and modified version of the 1859 trio as late as 1891. In the first place, the new version leaves the peculiar and characteristic sequence of keys of the separate movements untouched. Only the first and third (*adagio*) movements are in B major; the second and last are in B minor. This gives it a decidedly sombre, bleak, autumnal tinge. Further, the new version leaves the scherzo and its trio untouched, with the exception of a new, concise, and wonderfully individual conclusion. In the first movement it at once suppresses the former second subject, and does away with the noticeable *longueurs* and imitations in the old fugal development section. It replaces them by a new and extraordinarily skilful working-out, which, with its thematic and rhythmical intricacy and finished polyphonic workmanship, characteristic of Brahms's later, mature manner, is, to an expert observer, in strange and palpable contrast with the broad, limpid emotional current of his more homophonic youthful vein, as seen in the old first movement. The three themes of the older movement are reduced to two, and the two development sections are replaced by one; their fugal treatment has disappeared, and the transition to the recapitulation of the principal theme is effected imperceptibly and unexpectedly, with the extraordinary skill which Brahms did not possess till his later years. And so Heinrich von Herzogenberg was quite right when he said to Brahms: "The facility with which the older Brahms adapts himself to the younger in the second, third, and fourth movements of the trio is simply astonishing; in the first I cannot get over the impression that it is a joint composition of two masters, who are inwardly no longer quite in harmony. This is a personal impression of mine, for I still shed a parting tear over the lovely little section in E major." The slow movement (*adagio*) has been thoroughly worked over, and its citation of Schubert's "*Das Meer erglänzte weit hinaus*" and its magnificent coda eliminated. The middle section, with its gloomier colour, its uneasy questionings, for ever checking itself only to press forward on its course, was given a due measure of noble reserve; and a new and melodious truly Brahmsian theme in G sharp minor, entrusted to the 'cello, was introduced to lead up to it, which is almost Slavonic in its soft melancholy. The *doppio movimento* of the earlier edition is expunged. The movement most drastically dealt with is the finale, the dramatic climax of the work: the wonderful, broadly flowing cantilena in F sharp major for the 'cello is eliminated, and a new, robust second subject in D major substituted for it, which starts off in a strong, tramping measure and has little of the characteristically Brahmsian ring. In the present state of musical taste this late, new version is invariably preferred for public performance; and, however little we may feel able to accept all the reasons for this custom as sufficient, it must naturally serve as the basis of our observations.

As in the great piano sonatas of the early period, the young composer of the B major Trio takes Beethoven as his point of departure half unconsciously, yet to a certain extent quite intentionally and deliberately. The broad sweep of the many glorious melodies forming all the principal themes of this work, which pour forth thrillingly from the fullness of a rich nature stirred to its depths — witness the enchantingly lovely principal subject of the first movement, given out so beautifully by the 'cello at the very beginning, which at once goes straight to our hearts — is quite Beethovenesque; as are also the noble, broad lines on which the work is planned, and the vigorous energy of the development and detailed working-out. So also is the rapt melancholy of the *adagio* closely akin, both in form and content, to the corresponding movement in Beethoven's G major Piano Concerto; here, as there, we hear in the dialogue between piano and strings the tender, still lament of a noble soul, heightened in the middle movement to a deep agitation. And, lastly, so is the furtive, ghostly way in which the B minor scherzo steals in, like the corresponding movement in Beethoven's C minor Symphony. We may add the touching, almost symbolical citation from Beethoven's song-cycle *An die ferne Geliebte* ("*Nimm' sie hin denn, diese Lieder*") in the second theme, in F sharp major, given to the 'cello, in the last movement of the first and older version. On the other hand, there is also a Schumannesque, romantic element which occasionally finds strong expression, being most noticeably present in the scherzo, and in the restlessly seething and surging last movement, which, as in the other youthful works, is unmistakably Nordic, and wildly fantastic in colour; there is also a simple folk-element, which is most deliciously expressed in the trio of the scherzo, with its bright, pleasing colour and singing melody. Brahms's perfectly simple trio themes of this kind, clothed in soft sixths and thirds and written in the style of folk-tunes, are directly akin to the middle movements of the first piano sonatas and are derived straight from Schubert. But the concluding sections of all the movements are already noticeably Brahmsian in character. And I am thinking in particular of that of the scherzo. The way in which the whole, as it were, disintegrates into its atoms and original elements under our hands and evaporates into nothingness; the way in which the bare, sustained chords of the piano part place all these northern, elfin elements in a spectral, unreal light; the way in which the whole grows gradually fainter and more impalpable; all this is thoroughly Brahmsian, thoroughly novel and individual. Other Brahmsian features are the well-known tender chords of the third, sixth, and octave, which already appear in the piano theme of the *adagio,* and, above all, the ample and sweeping melodies. Brahmsian, too, is the predilection for syncopation and syncopated and triplet figures of every kind. And, lastly, the temperamental storms of the finale are true Brahms. The atmosphere of passion without peace or respite, held in check and subdued by an effort, in the inexorable onward drive of the chord figures in the piano part, is still quite Mendelssohnian. The hidden theme, the variations upon which were supplied in the biography of the composer, is a Brahmsian one, and its name is: the young Brahms. And so, as a record and confession of human experience, this piano trio will be directly associated with the Third Piano Quartet, op. 60, in C minor, the sketch for which, at least, surely dates from the fifties. Those who know how to read between the lines and notes might already find, hidden in this seething, simmering finale of the First Piano Trio, with its deep stirring of emotion, the whole story of Brahms's love and suffering. In it he has not surmounted his hopeless love: the end — the great coda — is all furious rage and sheer despair. Whatever youthful deficiencies and dross may be left in this trio — and we gladly excuse them a thousand times over in return for the merits of youthful freshness — our objections are in the main concerned with its form: the long-windedness of the first and last movements, which in the original version both came into the world with three themes, the two long-drawn-out fugal development sections in the first movement, the somewhat disjointed scheme and development of the finale. Yet, in spite of this, in its wealth of melodic invention and fresh directness of effect this youthful trio was never surpassed, nor, indeed, equalled, by the later piano trios of the mature composer.

The two later piano trios, the Second, op. 87, in C major, and the Third, op. 101, in C minor, date from the middle period of his production — namely, the eighties. In them the composer stands before us as a past-master of his art. Of the two, I should give the preference to the former. In it, indeed, the key of C major produced an extraordinarily vivifying influence upon Brahms's indeterminate "*Moll-Dur*" nature. Ideas expressed in this key call for a peculiar freshness and naturalness, for it is this very fresh and natural quality which has contributed in the course of centuries, from Bach's C major Prelude and Fugue in *Das Wohltemperirte Klavier* onwards, towards determining its peculiar character, as a key with a steely flash in it, a bright, healthy, vigorous, and vital key; so that this suggestion has become inseparable from it. This can be seen in the C major Piano Trio, notably in the first movement. Brahms has seldom written a piece of chamber-music so grandly and boldly planned and so imposingly built up as regards form, or which sets to work so graphically and energetically in the statement and development of the typically C major themes. This movement is informed with the spirit of Beethoven, most of all in the development of its ideas; in the first, transition passage, with its aggressive *stretti,* it puts on its heavy contrapuntal armour, and the typically Brahmsian way in which the piano part of this work is written — full, weighty, and rich in syncopated rhythms — is in harmony with this, finding, as it does, a sharply diversified rhythmical formula as a basis for each of its great, broad, amply planned separate periods. The distinction between it and the B major Trio is obvious enough; here too the current of invention still flows richly, but in both form and feeling it already requires all sorts of powerful restraints ("*Hemmungen*") in order to develop aright and no longer reflects so many romantic images and figures, producing such an immediate reaction or such a tender, emotional, or imaginative exaltation as in the B major Trio. The romantic element in this first movement of the C major Trio is confined, rather, to the episodical, subordinate parts — as, for example, the episode in G major, reminiscent of the spirit of the *Magelone-Lieder,* or the second section of the great final theme-group derived from it, with the mysterious chord of the sixth on E flat major; or, like the glorious great episode in D flat major in the development section, derived by augmentation from the principal theme, which leaps out in unison from the two stringed instruments at the very beginning. The predominant note of the whole is one of keen intelligence and fiery will and energy, which in the mighty lines of the coda (*animato*), again formed by augmentation from the principal subject, rises to a pitch of pathos and triumph worthy of Beethoven. The Nordic tone which prevails in the whole work is established by the slow movement in the form of variations, which emphasizes the old Scottish abrupt rhythm ♩, known to us moderns, for example, from the American Edward MacDowell's piano sonatas, but also from Hungarian folk-music; and further by a progressive, inward clouding, which increases with every variation, of the simple folk-spirit of the ideas in the ballad-like theme (*andante con moto*); and again by the scherzo and finale, with their half passionately agitated, half ghostly and uncanny character. The crown of the work is the scherzo, which might be called a northern night-piece (*Nachtstück*). It is fantastic to the core, gloomy in its conception and bleak in colour, muffled, ghostly, and illuminated by sudden lightning-flashes. In movements such as this, which seem elusive from beginning to end, Brahms has certainly created a tradition: the ghostly gropings, titterings, and goblin pranks in the impish scherzos of Max Reger's chamber-music are a direct development from them. Unfortunately he has found hardly any followers in the typically Brahmsian C major trio, forming a sharp and brilliant contrast with it in its sunshiny brightness — which, curiously enough, struck Clara Schumann as "not imposing enough" after the scherzo; broad in its lines and plastic in its simplicity, it has a folk-colour in the duet between the two strings, which seems to pour forth in a blissful mood, as from a full heart and breast,

with exquisite progressions towards the end and a Beethovenesque
sustained flow of melody. The finale has a certain inward kin-
ship with that of the Second Symphony: Cherubini's restrained
and subdued festal mood, so to speak, translated into the idom
of Brahms — a true example of his *"Moll-Dur"* quality. As
regards tonal effect, it is written in Brahms's more reticent
manner, the thematic invention and development being characterized by reflection and elaboration rather than by spontaneity.
Even here, however, a fine human warmth and romantic atmosphere break through it at last in the coda, which opens broadly
in F major and finally works up to that vitality and combative
spirit that characterize the key of C major.

The Third Piano Trio, op. 101, in C minor, is the most important of the three, thanks to its extreme concentration, terseness,
and closely packed quality. It is pure, genuine Brahms in his
C minor mood, just as the previous trio is in his C major mood —
lowering, defiant, wild, and forceful to the verge of asperity.
This is most clearly perceptible in the two principal movements,
the first of which practically amounts to a translation of the
corresponding movement of the C major Trio into a minor
atmosphere. But here everything is still more passionate and
full-blooded. This can be seen even in the second theme (in
E flat major), a melody of wonderful intensity, both of feeling
and of tone, which flows forth in a broad, full stream of melody
from the two stringed instruments in unison. The C minor
scherzo (*presto non assai*) represents, so to speak, a fusion of
the moods of the scherzo and finale of the C major Trio. It
mingles the fantastic, spectral elements of the unadorned flowing
principal theme with the passionately restrained *"Moll-Dur"*
mood of the second subject; it subdues the " sportive (*scherz-
haft*) " element and smooths away the uncanny, uneasy something that one feels, as it were, glowing and sparkling fitfully
beneath the ashes in both these movements. The slow movement
(*andante grazioso*) of the C minor Trio corresponds to a certain
extent with the trio of the scherzo in the C major Trio; the way
in which the time varies freely between 3/4 and 2/4 in this late

but faithful reminiscence of similar movements in the earliest
piano sonatas betrays at once their folk-origin. The whole movement produces the effect of a folk-song in a more sophisticated
arrangement. Naturally though the melody flows, there is a strong
element of rhythmical correspondence: just as the principal
theme of this movement mingles two 3/4 bars with four 2/4
ones, so the melancholy, agitated second subject varies between
9/8 and 6/8 time from bar to bar. The finale (*allegro molto*),
with its sprightly 6/8 time, has a decided scherzo character. In the
second theme, too, which is essentially of an uncertain, prelude-
like nature rather than clear-cut and unambiguous in cast, the
interest of the typically Brahmsian intricacy of the writing is
greater than its inspiration. It is not till the coda, which, as in all
the piano trios, is constructed on uncommonly broad and powerful lines, that the somewhat scanty flow of invention is turned
into the broad, splendid channel of C major and gives the whole
a grandiose conclusion, with a sense of release, achieved by the
same means as in the C major Trio — namely, thematic augmentations with a melodious effect.

There are two other piano trios which are all too rarely performed in public, owing to the fact that they are written for
an uncommon combination of instruments — though one which
is entirely in keeping with Brahms's manner. These are the Trio
for piano, violin, and French horn, op. 40, in E flat major; and
the Trio for piano, clarinet, and violincello, op. 114, in A minor.
Both the horn and the clarinet are romantic instruments, and,
accordingly, both works are romantic chamber-music. The extremely beautiful Horn Trio was written when Brahms was about
thirty. As we have seen in his biography, it came into being as
early as the beginning of the sixties, among the dark fir-woods
of the Black Forest at Baden-Baden, and Dietrich tells us how, in
later days, Brahms once showed him the spot " on the wooded
heights among the fir-trees " where the theme of the first movement of this composition first came to him. The horn was the
first love of Brahms's youth: he had practical experience of it
as early as his Hamburg days, and it was a favourite instrument

of his. In his great choral works with orchestra (chief among them the *Deutsches Requiem*), in the First Orchestral Serenade, in D major, in the Second Symphony, in D major, in the finale of the First Symphony, in C minor (at the point where the key of C major makes its radiant entry), in the Second Piano Concerto, in B flat major, the horn has the decisive if not the first word to say. The combination of the horn with other string and wind instruments was a general favourite in the palmy days of that classical and post-classical music which was in part intended definitely for performance in the open air with wind instruments, and has come down to us in the vast mass of *divertimenti, cassazioni,* and *notturni*. But from the first the combination of horn and piano was extremely unusual and rare. In the early years of the nineteenth century we have a Horn Sonata with piano by Beethoven, op. 17, in F major, a Piano Quartet with horn by Lessel, and that is about all. Among the horn sonatas with piano inspired partly by Brahms, partly by Beethoven, may perhaps be mentioned Josef Rheinberger's, op. 178, in E flat major, and Max Zenger's, op. 90, in F major. Brahms had had one isolated predecessor, inspired by Beethoven, in the Horn Sonata in F major, which appeared in the middle fifties, by the Leipzig critic Eduard Bernsdorf, the head of the conservative group then gathered round the *Signale*. The Brahms Horn Trio, one of the loveliest and most individual of all the composer's chamber-music works, still reveals its old associations with all the horn music of the classical and post-classical period as regards form. This is true even in the first movement, which is otherwise constructed in the grand sonata form. For, after the manner of the old *divertimenti,* it is made up of several sections; it combines a frequently recurring lovely, melodious, tranquilly flowing principal subject (*andante*) with a restlessly passionate, insistent second subject (*poco più animato*) in both major and minor, which is likewise repeated, but it abstains from any development section. And the same is true of the content as of the form. Even this first movement goes far beyond the long since vanished society music of the *divertimenti,* which was, for the most part, light and charmingly entertaining. With the tender, rapt exaltation of the principal movement it at once mingles the gloomy, poignant elements of the second subject. Even the scherzo, rapped out in curt quavers, is already, in spite of all its supple lightness, pervaded by a strong undercurrent of morosity and defiant strength. Its trio, in A flat minor (*molto meno allegro*), has a glorious broad cantilena with a tenderly elegiac and folk character; both the style and the formula of the piano accompaniment are strikingly reminiscent of the trio of the scherzo in the First Piano Sonata, in C major. And now comes the slow movement, in E flat minor, an *adagio mesto* full of profound resignation and hopeless, oppressive dejection, full of faint, anguished questionings of fate, brooding fugal passages, and passionate movements of revolt; here the very last link with the old chamber-music for wind instruments is completely severed, so far as feeling is concerned. The finale, which is in harmony with the scherzo both in spirit and in the character of its motifs, is far more than a hunting piece in the old romantic spirit, lively in form and uncommonly effective and graceful; it enhances these qualities by its powerful rhythmic vigour and lends a distinctive depth to the harmony — for instance, in the second theme-group — by means of mysterious, fantastic, romantic or elegiac elements. Thus Brahms's Horn Trio ennobles and elevates the character of such incidental music for wind instruments, idealizing it, just as he does his chamber-music works with a clarinet part, by the deep humanity of its content and by a mastery of musical workmanship which was quite unknown to those modest woodland and field flowers the old *divertimenti*.

The Clarinet Trio, op. 114, in A minor, appeared in the same year (1892) as the Clarinet Quintet; and up to the present it has always been outshone by the superior radiance of that magnificent work. The romantic element in the Clarinet Trio, as in the two clarinet sonatas and the Clarinet Quintet, lies in the tone-colour. Brahms has learnt the secret of drawing quite individual and highly romantic effects from the characteristic, dreamy beauty of the deep notes of the clarinet, notably in the central section of the slow movement, with its Bach-like intensity of feeling in the wonderful duet passages between clarinet and 'cello; while in the finale he has drawn the last ounce of passion from this tender, pastoral instrument by the use of the high register and of agitated figures. As in the Second Clarinet Sonata, it is the pensive, agreeable intermezzo of the *andantino grazioso,* in A major, that has made most friends, though it is of no great weight, so far as ideas are concerned, and is written in a style and character reminiscent of an old-world minuet from the happy, Philistine days of Waldmüller and Spitzweg. How mischievously is the "sensibility" of those days emphasized by its languishing pauses, how delicately patterned is the writing, how delightfully the concerted element is turned to account in the graceful garlands of quavers in the trio, and how poetically the conclusion dies away (*un poco sostenuto*)! In the truly Brahmsian way, the principal movements establish the character of the key, A minor. The first movement establishes its elegiac, fantastic character, the last its passion. The first movement is one of those "narrative" movements which are apparently so unpretentious in their thematic material and reveal their whole secret only after long study. Both the theme-groups are simply derived from triads. The second theme, as so often occurs in Brahms's later period, at once makes its appearance with an equipment of subtly disguised contrapuntal devices: the 'cello gives it out; the piano accompanies it with shortened time-values; the clarinet at once repeats it, the 'cello simultaneously playing it in inversion. The last movement is of an even harsher and more reserved aspect than the first, mingling 2/4 and 6/8 time with a true Brahmsian delight in complication, the principal subject, introduced by the 'cello, being immediately taken up by the clarinet and diversified by light figures. The tender, resigned elements of this closing movement are to be found only in the uneasily questioning, faltering second 'cello theme, in 9/8 time, which, in accordance with Brahms's latest manner, is contrapuntally worked out with its own inversion immediately upon the entry of the clarinet. For the rest, here, too, the delicately finished workmanship, of both

the rhythm and the treatment of the motifs, and the intricate
writing, have to conceal a certain slight deficiency of spontaneous
and freshly flowing thematic invention. Indeed, both the style
and the composition of this work unmistakably reveal Brahms's
later manner. Both of them might be provided with some such
"identification" marks as the following: extreme concentration
and terseness, clarity, plainness and simplicity of the formal
scheme, a lace-like intricacy of writing, a complete renunciation
of atmosphere and colour as an end in themselves, a combination
of elements, often of the most diverse and opposing character,
by a consummate contrapuntal finesse and virtuosity which are,
as far as possible, slyly concealed, even from the expert and initiated, a stronger and deeper admixture of the intellectual and
subjectively individual element; accompanied, on the other hand,
by a slight relaxation of unity, a slackening of the naturally welling stream of invention, and of the immediate, purely musical
and tonal effect.

All Brahms's string quartets date from the seventies, which
were otherwise unproductive of chamber-music. Like every serious composer, Brahms had a tough struggle to master this the
most difficult of musical forms and, as he used to relate himself,
sketched out at least twenty string quartets before he considered
a single one worthy of performance and publication. The first
two Brahms string quartets, in C minor and A minor, appeared
together in the year 1873 as op. 51; the Third, in B flat major,
came out three years later as op. 67. This separation in time
seems to be borne out by their content as well. The first two
quartets should be grouped together here as typical Brahms
"minor-quartets (*Moll-Quartetten*)." The First String Quartet,
op. 51, No. 1, in C minor, is one of the most reserved and
least inviting of Brahms's chamber works and is typical of his
C minor mood: harsh to the verge of asperity, crushing down
and repelling all more tender stirrings of lament and mourning
with an iron energy and gloomy defiance which surge up
tempestuously in the principal theme. This is most plainly
perceptible in the two principal movements, which make no

concession to the public — no, not even the slightest — and are
developed homogeneously, down to the smallest motif of the
accompaniment, out of quite a small and simple nucleus of
musical ideas. Their cold, steely intellectualism is also echoed in
the A flat major romance, with its unadorned, simple reticence,
informed by a Beethovenesque spirit, and noble, unsensuous
emotion; the F minor intermezzzo alone (*allegro molto moderato
e comodo*), revolving, as it were, irresolute and full of turbid
agitation, within the narrow limits of the 4/8 bar and the brief
periods founded on it, with its rueful and reserved cheerfulness
and its melody hidden away in the viola part, brightens up for a
fleeting moment, at least, as though smiling through tears, in
the rustically naïve idyll of the trio (*un poco più animato,* in
F major), with its instrumentation as deliberately primitive as
it is original, and its bagpipe drone. In moods like these Brahms
is incomparable, and so, for all its terseness, this movement certainly forms the crown of the work. What little emotional warmth
there is in this C minor Quartet is confined to these two central
movements.

The second and more inviting Second String Quartet, op. 51,
No. 2, in A minor, bears quite another stamp, being in Brahms's
typical A minor mood. In conformity with the key, passion, pain,
lamentation, and mourning appear under a more tender, subdued,
and elegiac veil of resignation. The old defiant, proud energy
of the First Quartet reappears only in the finale, but there it is
to be seen in the inexhaustible rhythmical transformation of the
csárdás-like, fiery, vigorously syncopated principal theme with its
rebellious strength. It is the quieter parts which will be listened
to with particular attention, especially in the last section, before
the beginning of the coda, where the first violin and 'cello in
canon ecstatically and dreamily give out the principal theme, now
transformed into a lyrical, singing form, in the brighter key
of A major; and again, immediately afterwards, where the first
notes of this theme, augmented to minims, seem to die away
pianissimo into nothingness, in visionary, mysterious strains which
are almost Wagnerian. In this quartet, indeed, the visionary,

mysterious element plays a not unimportant part. We are most surprisingly conscious of this in the curious, subdued part-writing of the slow third movement, in the style of a minuet (*quasi-minuetto*), with its most happy tonal effects and slightly Slavonic tinge—the strings playing *piano, mezza voce* above a rustic-sounding montonous bass with its fifths or sixths. The thoroughly *cantabile* quality which predominates in the first movement, its principal theme, based on the Joachim-Brahms motto F A E ("*Frei aber einsam*"), which unfolds itself with such an ample, mournfully elegiac, and imploring sweep, its softly veiled *mezza voce* second subject, in C major, with its ecstatic yearning, floating above a *pizzicato* bass, and the piquant, rapid alternating section (*allegretto vivace*) of the minuet, which flits past twice in a light, filigree-like guise, give us at least a distant inkling of the approach of the gay *Liebeslieder-Walzer*. On the other hand, the noble, gloomy resignation of the almost too ample and protracted slow movement, which passes solemnly by in nearly inflexible repose, still appears to have a certain affinity in style and character with the more Beethovenesque elements in the First Quartet.

While the few parts of the two "minor-quartets" which are written in the style of dances remain the only elements with a more pleasing Viennese local colour, the Third and most pleasing of the string quartets, op. 67, in B flat major, still more clearly suggests the splendid, luxurious city of the Wiener Wald and the lovely blue Danube. Haydn adds his benediction, but still more so does Beethoven—the Beethoven of the Pastoral Symphony. This B flat major Quartet is Brahms's "Pastoral Quartet," as everything proclaims: in the first place, the character of the thematic content. It prefers brief nature-motifs of a pastorally idyllic, naïve, and comically humorous kind, as, for instance, in the lively "horn-calls in triplets" of the principal subject in the first movement, exultantly repeated each time in fragmentary fashion by the whole "chorus" of instruments. In keeping with this is the highly subtle rhythmical resource, frequently recalling the Beethoven of the Pastoral Symphony; the free, vivacious changes of time — the first movement, for instance, mingles 6/8 and 2/4 time, the second 4/4 and 5/4, the last, again, 2/4 and 6/8 — and, lastly, the dynamic scheme, rich, delicate, intimate, and often changing from bar to bar. Thus the merry subject-matter creates itself a merry, loosely constructed form. Among the most fascinating passages in the work is that where, in the *doppio movimento,* after the composer has lavished his whole wealth of variations on the previous movement, the jovial horn-calls of the first movement ring out once again, only at last to die away deeper and deeper in the forest in the dusk of the evening, exquisitely interlaced with the graceful lilting theme of the variations in 2/4 time in endless combinations. And Beethoven is reinforced by Schumann: the glorious *andante* is a romance filled with Schumannesquely romantic dreaminess and delicate intricacy of writing. All that is left of Brahms himself is the movement in the style of a minuet: a typically Brahmsian intermezzo in D minor, full of painfully controlled discontent, suppressed passion, and ill humour, the tone of the three instruments grouped about the sombre viola part, to which the melody is entrusted, being damped by the mutes, until at last, in the coda, it grows brighter by passing into the more pleasing key of D major.

Of the three piano quartets — op. 25, in G minor; op. 26, in A major; and op. 60, in C minor — the first two, composed at Hamburg in 1863, also appeared together. The First, in G minor, is one of the most beautiful, grateful, and widely known of all the chamber works dating from the composer's early years, and one of the few compositions of Brahms's which are capable of firing an audience even at popular concerts, thanks to its extraordinary wealth of glorious, thrilling musical inspiration, accompanied by an equally extraordinary simplicity and plasticity of form. But at the same time it is unusually interesting for the light which it throws upon Brahms's manner of inventing and developing themes, and in particular the first movement. In the works of the classical masters a " character theme " — to take, for instance, that of Mozart's G minor Symphony — in spite of all the modifications and complications which its character may undergo during the working-out, remains essentially unchanged; whereas Brahms's themes, in passing through a series of swiftly changing moods of fluctuating emotion, often end by becoming something completely different. The principal theme of this movement consists of but a few notes; it is purely a "theme of emotion (*Gefühlsthema*)," passing by in rapt absorption, handled in a way which would be inconceivable in the classical masters. The second theme, too, strongly chromatic and melodious, in the most closely related major key, is ecstatically soft and tender in its exquisite, yearning urgency. If these were character-themes in the classical sense, they would have combined to form a gentle, dreamy movement. But not so with Brahms. He immediately heightens the mood of the principal theme into one of heroism and virile strength by the use of *stretto* and by calling in the aid of a figure with a most vigorously marked rhythm in the piano part. It is as astonishing as it is wonderful to see what a totally new and varied world he succeeds in drawing out of a simple, short theme by this means. In other respects, too, Brahms's indeterminate "*Moll-Dur*" nature is radically distinct from that of the classical masters. A classical composer would never have introduced the second subject first in the minor, and started it in its true major nature only on its second entry. Nor would a classical master have worked up to the mighty conclusion, only to make it evaporate into nothingness just before the end, by a typically Brahmsian, northern stroke of fancy, in an almost spectral, phantom fashion. And, lastly, never would a classic master have replaced the true scherzo by what is once more a typically Brahmsian intermezzo, full of that same subdued northern chiaroscuro, and, in the trio, of that visionary, nocturnal character, which are distinctive of these works of the early Hamburg period. This second movement is one of the composer's most characteristic ones, full of troubled excitement, throbbing as though with the incessant beating of an agonized heart, at the same time capricious and bleak. And then, in the third and fourth movements, comes the romantic part of this piano quartet.

The slow movement presents it like a German hymn, with all the grave, joyfully uplifted solemnity of a glorious Sunday morning in the forest, and, in the magnificent, martial-sounding middle section, like a landscape full of romantic memories of the glorious days of chivalry and courts of love. Detmold and Hamburg had carried Brahms back to the classics. Here, in this movement, the spirit of the Rhine and of Schumann speaks once more. The last movement goes for its romance to Hungary, like that arch-Romantic Berlioz. We know how Brahms loved Hungarian folk-music. Its unfettered freedom, its naïve quality, free from all trammels or restraint, were as necessary to balance and complete his austere nature, which lacked naïveté, as were Italy, or the society of children. This *rondo à la Zingarese* not only is the fieriest of his Hungarian gipsy pieces, but is constructed with the rarest artistic skill. Everything in it, even the effects of timbre, down to the astonishing imitation of the dulcimer, is enchantingly genuine in its folk-character, but it is all ennobled by an art and skill such as have never been displayed in combination by the Hungarian people, in spite of their extraordinary musical ability; for their only great composer of lasting importance, Franz Liszt, was not a pure-blooded Hungarian.

In the quartet which forms a pendant to this — op. 26, in A major — Brahms has repeated this " Hungarian movement " without any express indication of its character and with less national colour, but still unmistakably as regards both time and rhythm. The outward effectiveness of this Second Piano Quartet falls short of that of the First, just as, on the whole — as is always the way with Brahms in such cases — the Second is inferior to the First in spontaneous freshness and directness of conception and execution; while in concentration of form and delicacy of technical workmanship, in finish and musical significance, it is superior to it. The first movement, and, most of all, the scherzo, perhaps suffer a little from a certain dryness and timidity of thematic invention. To Clara Schumann, indeed, the close of the trio of the scherzo appeared " harsh and languid." But it is astonishing what Brahms develops out of this material. This remark applies notably to the grandly planned first movement, the first theme of which, in triplets, with its interesting rhythm, contains certain harsh, archaistic elements, while the second theme combines pleasingly anacreontic elements with others full of intensity and urgency; this theme is introduced by the strings, as the composer was particularly fond of doing in his chamber-music compositions with piano; then and not till then does he make the piano take it up *grazioso;* in the development section these themes are worked up to an intensity of pathos which also inspires the powerful two-part canon in D minor between piano and strings in the trio of the scherzo. But the crown of the work is the *adagio.* Once again, as in the corresponding slow movement of the First Piano Quartet, the romantic Schumann speaks to us through the mouth of Brahms, this time in the form of a marvellous moonlight scene or night-piece in the vein of Eichendorff or Storm. It combines the tenderest abandonment and sentiment in the softly subdued principal subject, which seems to sob with ecstasy, with great arpeggios on the piano, in which a whole world of supernatural forces seems to be stirring and surging up, spectral and threatening, beneath the motionless surface of the deep lake, lying dreaming in the sultry atmosphere of a summer night. We are reminded of the slow movements of the D minor Piano Concerto, the B major Piano Trio, the Horn Trio, and the violin sonatas, movements in which the soul of nature and of man seems to be harmonized in a supersensuous unity of ravishing tenderness and depth. From the purely tonal point of view, too, this *adagio* is novel and thoroughly romantic in colour: the two stringed instruments play with muted strings, but the piano *a tre corde,* without the soft pedal. Romantic, moreover, is the noble melodic line of the principal subject, hovering softly in a dim, vague atmosphere. The piano introduces it clearly and decidedly in tranquil crotchets; the violin plays it in unison, veiling it in soft floating trails of quavers — just as Schumann makes it do in the romance of his D minor Symphony.

The Third Piano Quartet, op. 60, which is played very much

less frequently, is in C minor. That is the key of the First Symphony, the First String Quartet and the last piano trio. We already know what this key, like that of D minor, means to Brahms: hard, pitiless struggle, dæmonic, supernatural shapes, sinister defiance, steely energy, dramatic intensity of passion, darkly fantastic, grisly humour. All these are to be found in this piano quartet, which may be reckoned among the master's most important achievements in the nobility of its plan, the ideality of its aim, and the power of its execution. It is the immediate outcome of personal moods and hard inward experience. When Brahms showed his friend Deiters the first movement of this quartet at Bonn in 1868, he added: "Imagine a man who is just about to shoot himself, and to whom no other course is left." And in sending the finished work to Billroth six years later he again added: "I am showing you the quartet purely as a curiosity! An illustration, as it were, to the last chapter of the man in a blue swallow-tail coat and yellow waistcoat." By these words he has quite clearly lifted the veil which in other cases he always managed to draw over the internal and external factors which prompted the creation of his works. We know now that the rough draft of this quartet was sketched as early as the middle fifties at Düsseldorf, at a time when, as Kalbeck intimates, the young Brahms was forced to crush down with iron force of will "violent upheavals of feeling, going beyond the bounds of friendly affection and faithful devotion," for the bereaved wife of the ill-fated master who was already declining into mental and physical extinction in the lunatic asylum at Endenich; and was manfully fighting his way through his own Werther period.

And so Brahms's Third Piano Quartet is the direct record of his spiritual experience and, like his other compositions in C minor, is no mere work intended to please, but one of the most complicated and difficult of all his chamber-music compositions. The first movement, beginning with the bleak double octave twice sounded in the piano part, and an uneasy, sighing motif on the strings — sketched in the first draft in the gloomy key of C sharp minor and considered by Clara Schumann not to be on

a level with the other, but to lack freshness of inspiration — is
practically a new edition of the similar movement in the First,
D minor, Piano Concerto, even down to the dæmonic trills: now
surging with passion and full of wild, unearthly agitation, now
dark, dejected, and full of lamentation, with only a few fitful
gleams of brightness here and there — for instance in the beautiful second subject, in E flat major. Its second part breaks up into
a series of variations on the theme established by the piano. The
second movement, the scherzo, which is emotionally the real
dramatic climax of the work, is still sinister, wild, vehement, and
abrupt in its rhythms and modulations, and ghostly and uncanny
throughout. One immediately thinks of the dark, ghostly doings
in the scherzo of Beethoven's C minor Symphony, and, in the
more pleasing parts, of the hunting-calls in Brahms's Horn Trio.
In the middle is placed a little dialogue between strings and
piano, like a holy vision (suggesting Beethoven's " *In questa
tomba oscura* "). Both the first and the second movements produce the effect of an etching, in the almost impalpable and unreal
hues of night, intentionally avoiding all colour. It is not till the
slow third movement, the crown and climax of this quartet, that
colour is added. Just as the scene of the first, second, and fourth
movement is laid by night upon earth, so that of the third is laid
in heaven. It is Brahms's avowal of love, tender and romantic
through and through. For the first and only time in this repellent, gloomy piano quartet, the drearily surging passion is
softened into emotions that are gentle and amiable, with a fine
warmth of tone, in the sunlit key of E major, far removed from
the predominant key of the work. This movement is broadly
planned, extraordinarily strict and skilful in the treatment of its
themes, and of the greatest beauty, notably in all the graceful
adornment of arabesques and garlands woven by the other instruments about the principal theme on the 'cello, with its soft,
fervent avowal of unspoken love. The finale once more takes
up the predominant key of C minor, in the same spirit as the
two first movements. It is a piece of contrapuntal music, such
as Brahms is fond of in his last movements; not in fugal style,

it is true, as in the E minor 'Cello Sonata, but in regular form all the same, at once associating with the theme an aggressive, ceaselessly throbbing counterpoint in quavers, which throws the second theme quite into the background. The movement is by no means pleasing, but it is, on the whole, less eloquent of strife than of assuagement and release. The great calm, bright, and more pleasing middle section, which is essentially constructed out of two notes of the principal subject, is marvellously beautiful. In its austere and powerful plan, in the ideal and intimate relation between the movements, in the unity and consistency of its mood and form, this Third Piano Quartet, though esteemed and admired rather than beloved and popular, owing to the exceptional intellectual demands which it makes upon both player and listener, stands in the forefront of Brahms's larger chamber-music works. As regards character, it occupies a peculiar and essentially a quite distinct position among its sister quartets: with its prevailing note of dramatic passion and dæmonic gloom, which once more recall the vehemence of the youthful works, it takes its stand among the works of the third period immediately beside the C minor Symphony and those works which subsequently cost Brahms long years of intensive revision and modification — for example, the Piano Quintet, in F minor. It may surprise us in this connexion that these works (among which may also be classed the B major Piano Trio, op. 8, and the new version of it published some decades later) were all of a thoroughly personal, dramatically passionate and explosive character. It really looks as though, in these revisions and modifications, which usually take the form of toning them down and retouching them, Brahms had felt ashamed of the first naked and undisguised exhibition of his passions and was now trying to soften it down and veil it as much as possible subsequently.

Brahms's two string quintets date from his middle and later periods — that is, from the eighties and nineties. The First, op. 88, in F major — the so-called "Spring Quintet (*Frühlings-Quintett*)" — may be reckoned among the composer's masterpieces. Like the First String Sextet, the First Piano Quartet, the

Second Violin Sonata, and the First Piano Trio, it has already won as great popularity with the public as is possible where Brahms is concerned, and this is due to the clarity and compactness of its structure and form, and the beautiful warmth of its ideas, which are easily grasped by all. Both of these bring it into relation with Beethoven. We can see this at once from the two themes of the first movement. How simply they are harmonized, how melodious they are, and how thoroughly winning and attractive! The first, which makes its entry at once on the first violin, without any sort of introduction, might almost be taken for a more sophisticated arrangement of a folk-song. The second, in A major, given out by the viola, interwreathed by the two violins with soft quaver and triplet motifs, while the 'cello accompanies it with a glowing counter-melody in crotchets, already displays a more Brahmsian reticence and intimacy. The second movement (*grave ed appassionato*) combines the qualities of a second and third movement, an *adagio* and a scherzo, within the limits of a single movement, in something the same way as the corresponding movement of the A major Violin Sonata. But here two attractively animated episodes in A major are interpolated between repetitions of the nobly resigned *grave* theme, in C sharp major, with its Beethovenesque character; one charming and pastoral, in dotted 6/8 time with a Siciliano rhythm (*allegretto vivace*), and the other a mocking and elusive *presto,* which flits hurrying by in a rush of *pianissimo* quavers. The crown of this work is its finale: a magnificent masterpiece in the contrapuntal, fugal style, joyous, wildly excited, and full of Dionysiac ecstasy. The way in which this movement opens in a tumultuous, powerful fugal style, works up to a wild transport of exultation — while still allowing its place to the enchanting, pleasantly musing and melodious second theme — and then at the close gradually leads us back to a peaceful evening mood — all this is so irresistible and natural that one can understand the love and admiration aroused by this work above all others in the concert-room, as is, indeed, only its due, forming as it does in some sort the counterpart in chamber-music of the master's Second and Third Symphonies.

Of all the composer's works, the Second String Quintet, in G major, op. III, is the one which most revels in tonal effect, the most passionate, the freshest, and the most deeply inspired by nature. We are at once plunged into the heart of nature by the tremolos on the violins and violas at the opening of the first movement, from beneath which, as from behind a veil of shimmering water, the principal subject, given out by the 'cello, soars on high, free, proud, and bold, like the very spirit of nature itself. The second subject, in D major, first given out by the violas and then taken up by the violins, forms a splendid contrast with this in its Schubertian fervour. The development section rises to unprecedented heights of power and grand Beethovenesque pathos. The short romance, the *adagio,* in D minor, is introduced in the minor, suggesting that mood of typically Brahmsian resignation which informs the whole of the G minor intermezzo of the third movement (*un poco allegretto*). But through both the elegiac middle movements a strong undertone of restrained passion makes itself felt. In the *adagio* it betrays its presence in the abrupt, sudden *forte* outburst of the middle section, in the *allegretto* in those touches of shadow which linger on even in the delicious duet between the two violas and violins in the G major trio, with its folk simplicity. The last movement, with its striking modulation from B minor into G major, is of the same Hungarian folk-character as the finales of the first two piano quartets, with the brief, choppy periods of its principal subject in 2/4 time, the precision and fire of its rhythm, restless and eager, with a profusion of sharply contrasting themes, culminating at the end in a *Frisca* full of wild Bacchanalian exultation. We may note its proximity in date to the *Zigeunerlieder,* which were composed three years before; but both in its style and in its composition, which knows so well how to combine and weld together such diverse and heterogeneous elements, with the maturest mastery and self-control, into a whole which produces an effect of homogeneity, we admire the later Brahms, the Brahms of the " last manner." In harmony with this are the delicacy and richness with which the viola, a favourite instrument of Brahms's, is treated. With Brahms, the later the work, the more sombre the colour; and accordingly the noble instrument of melancholy resignation is exactly what he requires. The viola gives out the second subject of the first movement and the theme of the *adagio;* it takes the lead in the dialogue with the violins in the trio of the *allegretto,* and, lastly, it introduces the first theme of the finale. The subtly balanced coda, in G major, of the *allegretto* is of enchanting delicacy. It harks back once again to the trio; but here the first violin opens the duet with an inversion of the theme of the trio, and the viola responds with the second half of the theme in its original form.

The solitary Piano Quintet, op. 34, in F minor, is among the composer's most famous chamber-music works. Together with the First 'Cello Sonata, the Horn Trio, the first two piano quartets, and the two string sextets, it forms one of the series of concerted works written by the young composer when he was about thirty. It is one of the works most typical of his early style, but at the same time it is, comparatively speaking, one of the most difficult to understand. This explains the extremely slow and gradual process by which it has won recognition. Like the above-mentioned works of this decade, which was so extraordinarily productive of chamber-music, the Piano Quintet, notably in the first movement, bears witness to the fact that in the mean time Brahms had gone over from Schumann to the strict, classical school of Beethoven — even, indeed, to that of Haydn, who was decidedly underrated by Schumann the Romantic as rather an antiquated "old fogy (*alter Papa*)." For its style and character are not, as usual, in Brahms's own typical manner, or like that of Schumann, in whose grand sonata form the principal movements are as a rule developed as far as possible out of two independent themes or motifs, but rather of the Haydn type — namely, an idealized and sparkling "conversation (*Unterhaltung*)," enhanced by consummate art, which is in any case a rarity among the great chamber-music works of the nineteenth century. It calls for an almost prodigal and quite exceptional profusion of thematic ideas. It is possible that the original plan of this work, in the form of a string quintet with two 'cellos, remodelled as a sonata for two pianos, and the fact that it was recast three times, have contributed towards this peculiar style, which renders its analysis considerably more difficult. In the very first movement we can distinguish four great independent theme-groups, in the scherzo three themes, differing fundamentally, even in rhythm, together with a shorter fugal development section. The general character and undercurrent of the Piano Quintet are thoroughly Beethovenesque: full of pathos, grand and monumental, rebellious, harsh, and audacious to the verge of asperity, defiant in its strength and powerful in its sonority. But it has generally escaped attention that the Brahmsian spirit of gentleness and resignation is striving against this defiant and passionate spirit. This appears in the first movement, often in a quite surprising manner, in a variety of mournful, touching passages, which are worked into the organic structure; among these are the second theme-group, in F minor, with its thoroughly elegiac feeling, and the mysteriously subdued third theme-group, in C sharp minor. But it is quite patent in the slow movement, with its luxuriant profusion of tender, dreamy, Schubertian melodies, the setting of which shows a truly Brahmsian preference for the use of thirds and sixths. And, finally, it is illustrated in the last movement, with its Beethovenesque, unrestrained humour, now jovial and boisterous, now full of ironically mocking laughter. It is the first and last movements, powerfully planned and full of ingeniously variegated developments, which offer the greatest difficulties to the understanding, in their attempt to fuse into a single whole the most heterogeneous elements, jest and earnest, asperity and tenderness, profundity and exuberance, native humour and the most fervent, still absorption. And it is in this that we may find the reason why the typically Brahmsian features in this Piano Quintet have hitherto escaped attention as compared with the Beethovenesque elements, strongly represented though these undoubtedly are. I find it above all in the struggle alluded to above between asperity and tenderness, defiance and lamentation, passion and dream. It is most clearly prominent in the first movement, which is also the most important in its scope. The scene is at first dominated by the virile pathos of the principal subject, but the tender lamentation of the second theme-group already creates a diversion from the sinister defiance of the first, and the third and fourth groups also play quite an independent and mitigating role. Brahms does not abandon his gentler mood again; on the contrary, he claims considerable space for it in the development section too; it is only at the end, in the coda, that there is a powerful revulsion towards the first theme. The slow second movement, with its luxuriant, sensuous combinations of the third and sixth, is essentially even more languorous, like much of Schumann's music in a similar mood. In the scherzo all the tender elements are concentrated in the glorious trio. The theme, in C major, given to the piano, which seems to sing its whole soul out in its fullness of blissful joy, is one of those soft melodies, with the simplicity of folk-music, in which Brahms is so rich from the piano sonatas onwards. It is surely because of the glorious, singing melody of the trio that it appears to Clara Schumann to have turned out "rather too short." The last movement places all the gravely meditative and dejectedly subdued elements in the slow introduction (*poco sostenuto*) which rises mysteriously out of the depths to a high pitch of intensity in a *stretto* canon passage in minims and semibreves, as Schumann was fond of doing in his last movements. It breaks off abruptly *pianissimo,* on the dominant; and now, to our great surprise, the finale shows its tone aspect in the *allegro non troppo:* in spite of the minor key, with its short-phrased rhythm in 2/4 time, it is thoroughly contented and jovial, inclined for all sorts of amusing little rhythmical tricks, and altogether sportively disposed. The coda, with its ample lines (*presto non troppo*), compresses and squeezes the principal subject by rhythmical transformation into a breathless C sharp minor scherzo in 6/8 time, which goes laughing by till it is finally concentrated still more drastically by means of syncopations. Yet all this does not succeed in checking its joyful mood; and in the concluding bars it takes its leave by breaking off abruptly as though with bright, ringing laughter.

The end of the Piano Quintet is as spacious and serene as its opening is grave and full of pathos — though still in accord with the character of its key, F minor. And here, to conclude, we again have cause to recall Clara Schumann, Brahms's "artistic conscience," with especial gratitude. For it was *she* who brought the threefold recasting of this work to a happy issue; and, though she greeted its first version, as a string quintet, with enthusiasm, by a true instinct she rejected out of hand the second version, as a sonata for two pianos, as a mere "arrangement," so that during that same summer at Baden Brahms set to work again energetically on the third and happiest version of it, as a piano quintet.

The series of quintets is closed by the Clarinet Quintet, in B minor, op. 114, heard for the first time on November 24, 1891 at the court of Meiningen, with Joachim, Wirth, Hausmann, and Mühlfeld as performers. This wonderful, mature work, belonging to Brahms's autumnal years, is a confession of resignation; as Deiters puts it, "we enter into Brahms's feelings as he looks back musingly over a life rich in powerful creative work, artistic successes, devotion, and love and steers his ship of life on its further course not without a feeling of grief at all that is no more." The tender clarinet is eminently suited to such a confession of quiet or painfully agitated resignation. As in the Clarinet Trio and the two clarinet sonatas, this classic wood-wind instrument is turned to account with consummate art to express all the noble, intense emotions of love, yearning, and grief, now leading, now accompanying, now forming the melody, now sinking into the depths, now breaking off into a free cadenza or improvisation, now used to fill in an inner part, the fullest use being made of all its different registers, with their varying tone-colour, whether in upper, middle, or lower parts. All four movements are characterized by a soft, peculiarly tender melodiousness, and we often ask in amazement: how could the legend have arisen of a Brahms who was harsh and nothing else, and that on the very grounds of his best-known concerted work? It is the first and last movements (the latter in the form of variations) that are most profoundly steeped in resignation. The quite peculiar freedom and diversity of this work, and its occasional looseness of construction, almost suggesting an improvisation, are most surprisingly displayed in the *adagio,* which is bound together into a coherent whole by its great ternary *Lied* form, into which is interpolated a middle section (*più lento*), with a slightly Hungarian tinge, quite freely constructed and rhapsodical in character, and interwoven with a fantastic riot of arabesques and *fioriture* on the clarinet. The only touch of humour, of the subdued and veiled Brahmsian type, is to be found in the *presto non assai ma con sentimento,* in B minor, which is interpolated into the third movement, and again has a slightly Hungarian suggestion, notably in its rhythm.

The tenderness of tone, the character of noble resignation, the freedom and diversity of form, the occasional soft touches of Hungarian local colour, such as are typical of Brahms's chamber-music of the last decade — that of the *Zigeunerlieder* — were further supplemented by another characteristic quality of Brahms in his last period: namely, a growing simplification and outward " unobtrusiveness (*Unscheinbarkeit*) " of the thematic content, which has a preference for the elegiac mood. All these themes are such that one has to play them over and over again in order to taste to the full the intellectual and emotional content which is concealed in their depths. In this connexion it can not, of course, be entirely disputed that the musical invention, as such, in Brahms's later works is undoubtedly less spontaneous and intuitive, tending, rather, to reflect the most subtle artistic insight. It is undeniable that many of these themes, which often approximate closely to one another in their character of tender, plaintive resignation, have an extraordinary musical similarity. For example, we may compare the theme of the third movement (*andantino*) with the theme of the variations in the fourth movement (*con moto*); they have an intimate resemblance, which extends even to the two-quaver figure. Or, again, a comparatively slight difference of feeling exists between the noble principal subject, in B minor, ushered in with that air of quiet grief with which we are familiar, especially in the *Deutsches Requiem,* and the second subject, in D major, of the first movement, with its Beethovenesque intensity of colour, which remains plaintive in character even in those passages which are overflowing with happiness (*forte espressivo!*). This is undoubtedly a slight inward weakness; for chamber-music, like all other music, cannot dispense with the necessity for contrast. Yet, on the other hand, this inward monotony and lack of contrast heighten the unity of the work, and, with his marked subtlety of insight, Brahms manages to counteract them by means of a powerfully efficacious antidote — namely, a relaxation of the form by introducing elements of a rhapsodical character, savouring of improvisation. In the principal subject of the first movement the two violins enter with a passage in which they seem to be improvising in thirds and sixths, and then, as it were tentatively, run through their whole compass from the lowest to the highest register, all this occupying a good dozen bars; the middle section (*più lento*) of the *adagio* is an incomparable great plaintive improvisation, as it were beneath the wide heavens of the Hungarian *puszta,* and the last variation in the concluding movement (*un poco meno mosso*) leads back to the principal subject of the first movement in an equally free and less strict form, thus completing the cycle on a pensive note. And when, in the last variation but one, the clarinet leads up to this by taking up the semiquaver motif again as a counterpoint to the theme played on the viola (with a change of rhythm from 2/4 to 3/8), we realize that here again Brahms is playing an unexpected card, just as he does in the finale of the Third String Quartet, in B flat major.

And now, after this review of the quintet as a whole, we will take a quiet look at the special features of the four movements in turn. The first movement maintains a predominant character of quiet, resigned surrender, even in the development section. In the sharply staccato quavers of the transition passage leading to the second theme, it is true, we find arrogant defiance, and in the close of the principal section a fiery surge of emotion; the quieter and resigned elements, however, prevail, and that even in the development section, which accordingly prolongs the

dotted rhythms of the introductory bar of this transition passage
into a sustained and weighty one. Thus the conclusion of this
movement determines the character of the whole work and produces an almost symbolic effect: it closes in the deep register
on the sighing principal theme, with growing tranquillity and
resignation. The second movement maintains this mood, accompanied by one of dreamy intensity and yearning. Like the slow
movement of the Third Piano Quartet (C minor), it is a great
love-song. But its peculiar tone-colour — the melody being given
to the clarinet in its loveliest register, while the muted strings
accompany it with gently murmuring triplet figures — throws
a subdued atmosphere of tender resignation over even this movement, as is subtly and plainly enough announced in the very first
bar, with its bitter-sweet quality suggested by the G (instead of
G sharp) of the accompanying first violin. The middle section
(*più lento*) — the character of which has been indicated above —
is a piece of gipsy music from the Hungarian *puszta*. Here the
clarinet is treated as a solo instrument, above the floating, waver-
ing tremolo of the strings, and even amid all its apparently
rhapsodical and fantastic freedom and waywardness it is firmly
based upon the steady foundation of thematic unity characterizing
the work as a whole: the first three notes of the theme of this
middle section for the clarinet, obtained by diminution and
adorned with dainty runs, in the style of the early masters, are
an exact reproduction in the minor of the first bar of the principal
theme. The concluding section of this movement is of wonderful,
gently serene beauty, with its tender dialogue between the clarinet
and the first violin; it is due by no means least to this section that
this movement is reckoned among the finest and most poetic of
the whole Clarinet Quintet, and one of the most magnificent and
moving slow movements that Brahms ever wrote. The third and
fourth movements may be grouped together, owing to the lyrical
character of their principal themes, with their folk simplicity. In
the third the thematic homogeneity within each separate movement of this work is once more clearly emphasized, for again, as
in the second movement, the first bar of the theme of the middle

section (*presto non assai*), which here, too, has a Hungarian tinge, is an exact reproduction in the minor key of the candid, clear-cut principal theme. The delicate filigree-like writing of this middle section is heightened, in the five variations on the simple, plain theme of the last movement, with its narrative character, to that astounding subtlety which is peculiarly characteristic of Brahms in his " last manner." It starts at once in the pensive and tenderly plaintive principal subject, given out in conjunction by the first violin and clarinet, which seem, as it were, to snatch the words out of each other's mouth. In the first variation the lead is given to the 'cello solo, the other instruments only, as it were, supplying a running commentary upon it. The second opens on a note of agitation, whose fevered throbbings find outward expression in the syncopated accompaniment. In the third the theme breaks up into a fleeting rush of semiquavers. The fourth leads the gloomy B minor into the soft brightness of B major and introduces a dialogue between the clarinet and the first violin, full of tenderly exalted serenity. But the fifth — which we have already examined above in greater detail — gently and imperceptibly leads us back, by a "rhythmical transformation" of the theme into 3/4 instead of 2/4 time and by an echo of the semiquaver figure from the beginning of the first movement, still more freely modified as a counterpoint in the clarinet part, to the peaceful, broadly protracted closing section (*un poco meno mosso*). And, even if our own feeling did not tell us so, at this point not only have the form and the theme of this Clarinet Quintet completed their full process of development, but also its character and atmosphere. The great coda of the concluding movement, an expansion of the short coda of the first movement, finally dies out and fades away after a last short solo cadenza of the clarinet, with a deep poignancy which goes to our inmost hearts, amid sighs and laments of still resignation which seems to say: "Once upon a time — "

The two string sextets, for two violins, two violas, and two 'cellos, complete the series of Brahms's chamber-music works dating from the sixties. The First String Sextet, op. 18, in B flat major, came into being during his happiest hours. In it Brahms's grave face wears an almost Apollo-like brightness and breathes a strong, healthy spirit of almost exuberant vitality. It is of extreme importance in Brahms's development. It is the beautiful and absolutely fresh fruit of the " self-communion (*Selbstbesinnung*) " of his Detmold period. The romantic Brahms of the first great piano sonatas, the E flat minor Piano Scherzo, the B major Piano Trio, the Schumann Variations, and the piano ballades comes to the conclusion in fullness of time, during his silent ponderings, that the eternal well-springs of musical art are not to be found in the romantic land of Schumann, however enticing it may be, but on the classic soil of Beethoven, Haydn, and Mozart. And so, during his time at Düsseldorf, he once more takes up the almost severed thread of classicism, dating from his Hamburg days, and goes back to the severe school of the classical masters of Vienna. In character, style, and composition the first Brahms string sextet is very closely related to the Beethoven septet. These are the two works which first made the name of their respective composers really popular. Brahms's First String Sextet in particular, with the *Magelone-Lieder,* which came later, were his first great success up to the time of the *Deutsches Requiem.*

The classical influence in this sextet is obvious. As regards form, it is seen in the beautiful symmetry of its clear and amply planned architecture, which, as, for instance, at the close of the exposition section of the theme-groups of the first movement, loves to build upon the broad, firmly laid foundations of a great pedal-point (in this case on C). It is further displayed in the manner of the development, and the illumination of the themes from quite new points of view, and the wonderful art, belonging to Brahms alone, with which the recapitulation of the principal subject is prepared and led up to in a way as logical as it is surprising; how splendid is its re-entry in this first movement; how triumphant is the radiance and brilliance of the principal subject, played *forte* in two octaves by the two violas and the first 'cello! Classical influence is further perceptible in the art of the simply figured variations in the second movement (*andante, ma*

moderato), an adaptation of some piano variations. We are reminded of Haydn, Mozart, and the young Beethoven, and even
of Handel, long before them. The vigorously and simply harmonized theme — which is full of the spirit of Beethoven —
dissolves into flowing semiquavers in the first variation; this
movement works up in the second variation into a jolly triplet
figure in semiquavers, in the third into ominously thunderous
demisemiquavers on the two 'cellos, with jagged flashes, as of
lightning, on the other instruments. So far, the variations on the
theme have proceeded solely by means of a figuration based
simply upon a resolution, or disintegration, of time-values. But now
begin the melodic devices. The fourth variation for the first time
shows us the theme as flexible, flowing inner parts on the first
violin and viola, in a pleasing major aspect. The fifth sports and
dallies with it on the first viola over a bass in fifths suggestive
of a rustic musette on the second viola, to the accompaniment
of gallant little dips on the two violins, while not till the second
section do the two violoncellos enter trippingly, in the softest
pizzicato, into this daintily fascinating piece of rococo atmosphere.
The sixth and last variation again repeats the D minor theme
note for note, but this time mournfully on the first 'cello, *piano,*
accompanied by soft mocking *pizzicato* imitations on the two
violins, while the two violas throw in grave admonitions to
dignity, concluding, in the coda, with a sombre dialogue carried on
confidentially and mysteriously between the two violins in thirds
and the violas at the same interval. Classical influence is again
revealed in the choice of the old rondo form for the last movement (*poco allegretto e grazioso*), with its comfortable, cheerful
Haydnesque spirit, rising to positive jubilation in the final coda.
As regards the style and technique of composition in this first
sextet, the constant doubling, at an interval of an octave, of the
parts to which the melody is given, or even of those which merely
form the accompaniment, reminds us of a favourite device of
Haydn's. But in its character it reveals the influence of the classic
masters of Vienna, by its lovely warmth of feeling, its overflowing liveliness, and its wealth of glorious melodic invention:

the very first movement has as many as three themes. But here the reminiscences of Beethoven's septet are reinforced by those of yet another classic-romantic chamber-music composition — namely, Schubert's Trout Quintet. Indeed, the softly sensuous tone of the two Brahms string sextets is quite Schubertian. And so, in both the first movement and the last, Brahms chooses to give prominence to the 'cello, with its noble warmth and intensity of tone, which gives out the melody of the principal subject and does not allow the first violin to repeat and enhance the melody till the 'cello has said its say to the very end. This was Joachim's excellent advice, which was gloriously justified by the result. And when, in the very first movement, the theme of the transition passage — which enters, by a touch of genius, so unexpectedly in A major — and the second theme in F major, which seems to pour itself out in song, lull us with the agreeable delights of the Viennese *Ländler,* we at once divine that this, too, is the voice of Schubert. But it is Beethoven who has exercised an immeasurably stronger influence upon Brahms's string sextet than Schubert, Haydn, and Mozart. This influence is palpable in the F major scherzo (*allegro molto*). Its rough, rustic humour is absolutely that of the corresponding movements in Beethoven's Sixth Symphony (the Pastoral) — and perhaps even in the Seventh (in A major) — down to the very treatment of themes and key. Both character and technique are the same in them both: jolly *stretto* passages, verging upon the boisterous, in the second section, the trio, and the coda derived from it, and a popular humour, pushed to lengths quite astonishing in the reserved and aristocratic Brahms. Yet, in spite of all its outward roughness, there is much neatly dissimulated subtlety; who, for instance, would look for the opening of the principal subject, in a slightly varied form, in the bass of the trio and coda? The minute and delicate art, too, with which all the thematic material is broken up into a loose, yet firm and subtly knit web, is quite Beethovenesque; Beethovenesque, too, though Haydnesque at the same time, is the organic and easy combination of the two pensive, graceful, *allegro* principal themes, Mozart-like in their *cantabile,* with the separate episodes, one of them pleasing, the other — namely, the G minor section — powerfully and vigorously rhythmical, in the finale in rondo form, with its easy amplitude. In this movement, indeed, the skill with which the transitions and reprises are handled, the idea of deriving the coda, leading up to a jubilant *stretto* (*animato poco a poco più*), from the " energetic" episode in G minor, are so classical and Viennese that one might say of this delicious movement, so full of concentrated *joie de vivre:* if it were not by Brahms, it must have been by Haydn or Beethoven!

By comparison with the Second String Sextet, the First is planned on practically homophonic lines; which is a reason the more for the comparative speed with which it won popularity. The themes, with their easy melodiousness and their great harmonic and rhythmic simplicity, are nobly planned, with a view to as broad a " general effect" as possible; and when, as we saw, each of the principal subjects of the chief movements enters twice — first on the 'cello, and then on the first violin — or when the theme of the variations movement, entrusted to the first viola, is repeated each time, in both sections, by the ensemble of the other instruments, led by the first violin, all this contributes towards increasing the ease with which we can grasp these leading ideas, the more so by reason of the pregnant and impressive form of their exposition. Even the working-out of the first movement, which is often so intricate in Brahms's other works, is on the same lines as the whole work, with its delightfully youthful freshness and its rich swelling flow of melody. It is as simple as possible; and in contrast with the exceptionally amply planned exposition group, with its three themes, it is comparatively tersely conceived and simply treated.

The First String Sextet is the simpler and more popular, the more powerful and comprehensible, and the greater favourite. Psychologically, the " composite (*zusammengesetzt*) " Second Sextet, op. 36, in G major, is not so simply " compounded (*unzusammengesetzt*) " as the first. It is decidedly the finer of the two, being of superior artistry and more personal. At the same time it is eminently a work inspired by nature. In its deep, romantically idyllic feeling for nature, it already foreshadows clearly the Second, D major, Symphony. It reveals its nature quite plainly, as regards both character and composition, in the passage where the two violins, after first giving out the principal subject, in turn take up the quaver figure of the first viola on D, C sharp, forming a transition to the second statement of the theme by the 'cello. This thoroughly romantic string sextet is naturally far from offering the same scope as the First for the classical element, for a Haydnesque, Mozartian, or Beethovenesque quality. All that it contains of a classic, Beethovenesque nature actually lies solely in the last variation of the slow movement (*poco adagio*), in E minor, full of noble resignation and quiet grief — a variation which dies away in E major in a soft farewell mood of wondrous beauty. Into this fifth variation Brahms has packed all the warmth, depth of feeling, and magic of tone which were to a certain extent held in check by the reserved and not very tersely rounded-off theme — based essentially upon two intervals of a fourth, with an accompaniment of plaintive, chromatically descending quavers on the second violin, by the bleak, autumnal key of E minor, and the strict *legato* of the preceding variations.

In the remaining three movements, on the other hand, the Brahmsian character is present to a preponderating degree. In the first movement in the form of suave, tender, elegiac sentiment; in the second, the scherzo in G minor, as a dance-idyll with a slightly Slavonic tinge, heralding all the later Brahms intermezzi by its subdued, veiled mood, intentionally confined within narrow limits, as though tired and depressed, half monotonous, half wayward and capricious; in vain does the robust, lively waltz of the G major trio (*presto giocoso*) try to infuse a more cheerful life into its sullen dreariness. Musically, too, this character is reinforced by all kinds of delicate little touches: the stressing of the unaccented beat of the bar, the second crotchet in the opening theme, by a plaintive mordant; the triplets in the second subject in D minor, stealing sullenly past like a grey mist; the comfortable Hamburg atmosphere suggested by the moderate *tempo* (*allegro non troppo*). We need only compare this scherzo of the Second String Sextet with that of the First. What a difference! How much gloomier is this conception of the scherzo, the trio being kept as the sole representative of rustic jollity in both scherzos! The Brahmsian quality of the last movement (*poco allegro*) is found in the broad, tender, singing melody given out by the first violin and first 'cello, with rich, deep tone-colour, and in lightly gliding 9/8 time.

The first movement (*allegro non troppo*) stands quite apart, forming a pendant to the last in its pleasing character, just as the second does to the third in its sullenness. The softly veiled, "sultry (*schwül*)" sensuousness of tone in which it is written, brilliant with softly prismatic yet luxuriant colour, the sustained inspiration and ample development of its principal theme, striving repeatedly upwards in Neapolitan sixths as though intoxicated with bliss and rapture, the truly German romance of the woodland with its murmuring springs and wafts of fragrance, which echoes and sings at every turn of this wonderful movement, bring it into direct rapprochement with the first great vocal production of Brahms in the days of his young love: the *Magelone-Lieder*. We know now what secret the young composer confided to this sextet — in the notes A, G, A (T), H, E, in the second theme-group of the first movement: a fervent farewell to his first and last serious love, Agathe, the charming young daughter of Professor von Siebold of Göttingen. This first movement of the Second String Sextet is one of the most wonderful things which Brahms ever wrote in the way of chamber-music. Only take the principal theme: with what tender mystery is it stated (*p mezza voce*), hovering between the major and the minor in romantic rainbow hues; how hesitating and pensive is its development, in short bar-by-bar imitations, how remote from the world and mystically visionary is the tranquil *pianissimo* passage in peaceful crotchets which forms an appendage to it! How sharp is the contrast between the broad lyrical amplitude of this principal theme and the transition section, with its angular rhythm and harsh *stretti*! It is not till the second theme, with its broad, warm, singing melody for the 'cello, with the first violin coming in an octave higher, that its relationship to the First Sextet is re-established. Here again we have quite a Beethovenesque tone, which is at once struck by the two principal themes of the first movement of the later sextet. But one of the most superb features of this movement — as of all the principal movements of Brahms's instrumental works in grand sonata form — is the hesitating passages in which, with infinite delicacy, the way is prepared for the recapitulation of the principal subject before and after the development section — which in this work, as Clara Schumann already observed, is worked up with peculiarly loving care " to the warmest and most heart-felt expression." Just as Brahms takes the fifth from the beginning of the principal subject and uses it as material for a *stretto* in the passages leading up to the reprise, so here he leads us back gently and unexpectedly through a chromatic, drooping bridge passage on the first violin, with a slight minor suggestion of gloom, to the secret woodland spring which seems to murmur in the viola part. These are extraordinarily subtle touches, such as we are accustomed to expect only in the later Brahms of the last period.

XXIV

THE SERENADES

The two serenades for orchestra, op. 11, in D major (the "Bonn Serenade"), and op. 16, in A major, form, as it were, the romantic, flower-wreathed portal leading to the second period of the master's production, which opened at Detmold. In them we hear the voice of the young Brahms of the *Magelone-Lieder,* of Brahms at the age of twenty-six.

If we consider these two serenades in the light of Brahms's work as a whole, we must characterize them as essentially essays and studies in orchestral composition. The first struggle to achieve a symphony had been a failure and had ended resignedly in the Piano Concerto in D minor. And now, with his austere and shrewd self-criticism, he at once began to master the predecessors of Beethoven, with their simpler content and technique. His Detmold period (1857–60) was, in the sphere of instrumental, symphonic composition, a period of quiet, dogged study of Haydn and Mozart. Brahms laid aside his projects for a symphony for the time being and wrote two serenades. And, as always happened with this extremely acute self-critic, this loyal, conscientious, artistic craftsman, the Second Serenade endeavoured to perfect by the most far-reaching subtlety and minuteness of workmanship whatever he did not feel to have been fully achieved in the First.

What position did Brahms originally adopt towards the serenade? With the death of art as the "handmaid of aristocracy" the whole range of serenades, *cassazioni,* nocturnes, and *divertimenti,* all the varied "night- and garden-music" of the eighteenth and early nineteenth centuries, disappeared from street and market-place, though a few isolated specimens migrated to the modern concert-room. Even in Vienna the taste for such productions as

Robert Fuchs's intimate *Serenade* for string orchestra, with their local Viennese ring, has unfortunately become lost. Volkmann's, Brahms's, and Draeseke's serenades are practically the only representatives — and very rare ones at that — of a class of music which was originally the gayest form of good " occasional " music (*Gelegenheitsmusik*), in the best acceptation of the word. Of Brahms's two serenades, now well over half a century old, it is the Second, in A major, in particular, which shows us most clearly how dreary and grave the serenade has become in these days of excessively laborious art, with its exacting demands for new creative ideas and treatment in a new spirit. It does so not only by the fact that it excludes the violins, and so gives the preference to the characteristic quality and tone-colour of the violas, which do, indeed, produce in the long run a great effect of weariness, evening gloom, melancholy, and mystery, but, most strongly of all, by the very character of its five movements. This is no south German Spitzweg, but a north German one, who is offering his lady-love a serenade. Even the scherzo, with its original character, the best movement in this serenade, and the minuet, which is already genuinely Brahmsian in the subtle intricacy of its constantly broken rhythm and measure, remain full of subdued humour. The delicate and wonderful *adagio*, of which Clara Schumann was so enthusiastically fond, with its subtle and complicated design, its insistent bass in the form of a *chaconne,* which enters softly with a Bach-like dignity, and its prevailingly religious spirit, recalling church music, which was so finely appreciated by Clara Schumann, assumes a positively melancholy and poignant character; the first movement, indeed, allows a little scope for a softly restrained, tranquil cheerfulness, but only in its second theme, with its tender thirds; and it is not till the fresh, light finale, in rondo form, with the sprightly triplets of its epilogue on the oboe, that we at last arrive at the true spirit of the old serenades of the classical masters. It is this movement — after it had once more passed through Brahms's " mint " and been " melted down again " — which first gave rise to the astonishment, loudly expressed on all sides with such joyful satisfaction, at the fact that the earnest Johannes of Hamburg was actually capable on occasion of relaxing almost into boisterous light-heartedness, in the manner of Beethoven, and that even in a serenade. But he might excuse himself by saying: "What can I do? My night sky is not clear and voluptuous like that of Vienna or Munich, but the heavy, cloudy sky of Hamburg; and my lady-love, to whom I am offering this serenade, is not a fiery Viennese Josephine, but a prudent, domestically minded Dorothea of Hamburg."

The concluding rondo of this Second Serenade shows, however, by its sharp, abrupt contrasts, that the young Brahms is well aware of his too exclusively gloomy and melancholy emotional life and of the necessity for something enlivening and cheerful to counterbalance his inborn qualities. From this point of view — that is, of holding the balance between brightness and gloom, light and shadow, of repressing the darker and more melancholy emotional impulses as much as possible in the loosely knit form of the bright serenade — the First, in D major, is decidedly by far the more successful and has more style, in the classical sense of the word. But this applies to its character, not to its scoring: instead of the small chamber-orchestra suited to a serenade, and chosen for the Second, it prefers the "bulk" of the "full orchestra," which, it absolutely requires (as Clara Schumann remarks), though with only four wood-wind instruments and doubled horns, it is true, omitting the trombones and reinstating the violins. In technical finish both of form and of composition, in delicacy and intimacy of detail, it is surpassed by the Second Serenade, as is, indeed, the case with every form of composition of which Brahms produced a pair; but in its incomparably fresher thematic inspiration, as well as its pleasingly sentimental pastoral note of tranquil happiness and youthful merriment, and in the broad — almost too broad — plan of its principal movements it displays a truly Viennese and classical character. The naïvely merry principal subject of the first movement — assigned to the horn, Brahms's favourite orchestral instrument — with its short crotchet progression and its primitive bagpipe-like harmonic scheme, with its almost jerky alternations, is in itself a compliment to " Father Haydn," and the minuet in G major, as original as it is simple, with its theme given out by the two clarinets, above a rustically clumsy bass in broken octaves, is a piece of genuine *ancien régime*. In this serenade the dreary, gloomy sentiment is to be found in the two middle movements: the scherzo, which even by its dæmonic key (D minor) foreshadows the themes of the corresponding movement of the Second Piano Concerto, and the B flat major *adagio,* the principal subject of which at once strikes a melancholy, meditative, and timidly faltering note, after which, for the rest, it is worked out perhaps too broadly and with too little coherence. In this movement the general pastoral tone of this serenade is intensified into a tender nature-music of woodland peace and murmuring brooks.

In conclusion: Brahms's serenades, which were at once greeted by Clara Schumann with rapture and rated by her above all other serenades for wind instruments, which in the long run appeared to her far too monotonous in tone, are, on the whole, characterized by human interest and character rather than by artistry. The First is more classical, Viennese, and fresh in its effect; the Second is more Brahmsian, North German, and personal, precisely in virtue of its sombre tone-colour, its subdued, restrained emotion, atmosphere, and sentiment, moving in a world of evening shades and heavy night skies. Both of them are rare visitors to our concert-halls, and the Second is the rarer of the two. In its scoring (for a small orchestra) and in the concentration of the first movement — though the working-out is, indeed, of considerable length — we shall find the old genuinely classical type of serenade preserved in a purer form in the Second; but as regards thematic content, invention, and character, in the First. The First is the more naïve, fresh, diverting, and recreative; the Second shows a more thorough artistic mastery and is the more clarified and mature in form and composition. If it were not that the mysterious colour of the violas, chosen with such conscious subtlety for its suggestion of night, produces in the long run too wearisome and monotonous an effect after five whole movements, we should

be bound to give the palm to the Second, on account of its
handling of the wood-wind, which discourses so engagingly,
though its outward effectiveness is inferior to that of the First.
The First Serenade stands at the opening of Brahms's second
period of production, and by its weaknesses of form — the excessive breadth with which its principal movements are planned
and worked out, the variegated colour of its many subordinate
and episodical passages, though they form such a fascinating
mosaic — in short, the predominance of creative imagination
over systematic technical skill — still plainly reveals its affinity
with the first or youthful period of production. The Second
Serenade, which is far more typically Brahmsian, and characteristic of his Detmold period in its use of archaic elements of style,
melody, rhythm, and measure, is a direct preparation for the
third period of supreme achievement, as is most evident in the
maturity and concentration of its form. In mere time the interval
separating the Piano Variations, op. 9, and the piano ballades,
op. 10, from the First Serenade is not very great — six and four
years respectively — though inwardly it is of great importance.
But the interval separating the two serenades from the great
chamber-music compositions of the third period is incomparably
shorter, as regards both time and inward development. And the
fact that a good twenty years separate the second orchestral serenade from the next orchestral work proves better than anything
else how anxious Brahms was that his two serenades should be
regarded as a mere transition work, of the nature of essays and
studies, a "preliminary canter" in the process of mastering
orchestral style and composition in the classical manner, which,
by the breadth and eloquence of their movements, tend in the
direction of the *sinfonietta* rather than of the serenade.

XXV

THE OVERTURES

As in the case of the serenades for orchestra, the piano concertos, the string quintets, and the string sextets, Brahms produced a pair of overtures at the same time, one with a laughing
and the other with a weeping aspect: the *Akademische Festouvertüre,* op. 80, and the *Tragische Ouvertüre,* op. 81. Both of them
fall within the period between the Second and Third Symphonies
and were published simultaneously in the year 1881. We saw in
the biographical section that the *Akademische Festouvertüre*
represents his musical acknowledgment to the University of
Breslau for conferring upon him the honorary degree of Doctor
of Philosophy. We know from Heuberger that he wrote two
"academic festival overtures," so that he must have destroyed
the second. This "thesis" of Brahms's for his musical doctorate
has become one of the most popular of his larger instrumental
works and, owing to the free use which it makes of well-known
students' songs, is within the grasp even of those to whom
Brahms's artistic work, and his orchestral works in particular,
remain, as a rule, a sealed book. Severe professional criticism has
often underrated it in a carping and unjust spirit for its sacrile-
gious attempt to be jolly and humorous even in ponderous
academic robes. For in it, as in all Brahms's works, the point is
not so much the matter as the manner, the fashion and form in
which the student songs have been turned to account. And on
closer examination it is soon evident that Brahms remains himself,
true to his own nature, even in the guise of a jovial Doctor of
Philosophy *honoris causa,* and of a hearty friend to all genuine
student jollity: the *Akademische Festouvertüre* is the half-sad,
half-solemn restrospect of a mature man looking back over his
own vanished youth and the fun of his glorious student days,

rather than an exuberant, boisterous piece of student life in the present. This is at once evident from the significant stress laid upon its meditative parts, which, in the whole of the first third of it, seem, as it were, to force themselves to take a humorous turn by an effort. It is in this blend of past and present, of serious-ness and jollity, sadness and exuberance, that the peculiar beauty of this overture consists, as well as the human and poetic charm which are all its own. It does not, indeed, advance matters much to know which German student songs have been freely made use of: *" Wir hatten gebauet ein stattliches Haus"* (*" Ich hab' mich ergeben,"*), the *Landesvater* (*" Hört, ich sing' das Lied der Lieder "*), the *Fuchslied* or Freshmen's song (*" Was kommt dort von der Höh' "*) and *Gaudeamus*. For all the simplicity and fidelity to the originals of their setting, the artistic form imparted to them by means of tone-colour is so subtle that we only notice, as it were, half consciously how, in their very choice, the comical humour of the descent of the young foxes seems to be fully counterbalanced, if not outweighed, by the solemn, chivalrous pride of the *Landesvater,* the stately and restrained rejoicing of the hymnlike *Gaudeamus,* and the earnest, patriotic devotion of *" Ich hab' mich ergeben."* The overture begins *pianissimo,* in a mysteriously subdued fashion, in C minor, in the lower register of the strings and bassoons, and ends, like Weber's *Jubel-Ouver-türe,* with the brilliance and fire of rushing scale-passages in demi-semiquavers on the strings, and with the mighty sonority of the full orchestra on a scale rare with Brahms, including double bassoon, two trumpets, three trombones, bass tuba, three kettle-drums, bass drum, cymbals, and triangle.

So far the popularity of the *Akademische Festouvertüre* has been equalled by the unpopularity of the *Tragische Ouvertüre*. Before Brahms's art emerged from what may be called its " Saul " period into its " Paul " period, Hans von Bülow alluded to " the striving of a Brahms, tragic in its aspiration (*Prätension*) as that of a Tantalus." And in Brahms's *Tragic Overture* it is the note of effort on which we would lay particular stress. For Brahms was not a tragic composer in the sense that Hebbel was a tragic

poet. Grand though the *Tragic Overture* sets out to be, vigorously
though it reverts to the rigid, stony, dæmonic power of the
Edward Ballade for piano, from op. 10, it certainly cannot be
reckoned among Brahms's strong or fresh works. Those of them
which are most genuinely and thoroughly tragic are rather the
ones which are not expressly labelled tragic or titanic. Brahms
is not convincing when consciously tragic. Just as in Ovid we
would give all the battles of Lapiths and centaurs for Echo and
Narcissus, so in Brahms we would give up the *Tragic Overture*
in exchange for the first movement of the First Piano Concerto,
in D minor, not to mention either of the four symphonies.

But though it is not truly — that is to say, unconsciously —
tragic, its harshness and asperity are none the less tragic in character. Indeed, they exceed those of any other of Brahms's instrumental works and in this respect go far beyond those great
" character " overtures which have a genuine right to be called
tragic: Handel's *Agrippina*, Beethoven's *Coriolan*, Cherubini's
Medea, Schumann's *Manfred*, and Volkmann's *Richard III* overtures. No throbbing vein of more pleasing or tender emotions
runs through the cold, classic marble of Brahms's overtures. Even
the second theme, in F, remains austere and palely conventional,
and its yearning is, as it were, frozen into a sort of rigidity. The
minor predominates throughout, and the few major themes and
episodes are for the most part, according to Brahms's wont, at
once mingled harmonically with the minor; they are, moreover,
purely rhythmical rather than melodic in quality; forcibly insisting upon power and strength rather than confidently and
unreservedly conscious of them. The really tragic quality, the
fleeting touches of thrilling, individual emotion in this overture,
are not to be found in conflict and storm, but in the crushing
loneliness of terrifying and unearthly silences, in what have been
called " dead places." Thus, at the very beginning of the development section, where the principal theme steals downwards *pianissimo* note by note, amid long-sustained, bleak harmonies on the
wind instruments, and in its final cadence, on A, E, sighed out
by the wind after the strings, we almost think we can see the

phantom of the blood-stained Edward flitting spectrally through the mist on the moors of the Scottish highlands; or again, at the *tempo primo* at the close of the development section, where all is silence and emptiness after the funeral march derived from the principal subject has died away; or lastly, at the close of the whole work, where the curtain rapidly falls on the gloomy funeral cortège to the rhythm of the funeral march.

XXVI

THE CONCERTOS

Brahms started his career as a composer of instrumental concertos with orchestra with a great fiasco. We saw in his biography that his First Piano Concerto, op. 15, in D minor, was a failure when he conducted it at the Leipzig Gewandhaus in 1859, with kettledrums and trumpets. But this reverse did not deter him from continuing to cultivate this field of composition. On the contrary, he wrote yet another Piano Concerto, in B flat major, op. 83, a Violin Concerto, in D major, op. 77, and a Double Concerto for violin and 'cello with orchestra, op. 102.

It is the custom to allude to Brahms's instrumental concertos as symphonies with obbligato solo instrument and to dispute their title to the academic rank of solo concertos with orchestra. In support of this, evidence based upon grounds of form is adduced — namely, the fact that the First Piano Concerto was almost certainly planned originally as a symphony. The decisive proof is provided by Brahms himself. In 1855 he writes to Schumann: " For the rest, during the past summer [1854] I have been experimenting in a symphony, having even scored the first movement and composed the second and third (in D minor — 6/4 time — slow)." But in the same year he describes to Clara Schumann a dream in which " I had used my luckless symphony to make a piano concerto and was playing this. Made up of the first movement and the scherzo, with a finale, terribly difficult and grand. I was quite carried away."

The first movement has a peculiarly sad history. It is now established, thanks to a communication made by Joachim to Kalbeck, that this heart-rending musical representation of mighty spiritual suffering and conflict was sketched out under the direct impression of Schumann's tragic attempt at suicide, and that the

motto which originally stood at the head of the slow movement —
"*Benedictus qui venit in nomine Domini* (Blessed is he who
cometh in the name of the Lord) " — was intended to be interpreted in the sense: " Blessed be he who returns in the name of
the dear lord (Schumann) to the deserted *Domina* (Clara
Schumann) and the children bereft of their father." Like the
Piano Quintet, the Third Piano Quartet, etc., this First Piano
Concerto is one of those great works with which the composer
strove and battled for long years. On this occasion it was impossible to satisfy Joachim — with the rondo, at least — or even Clara
Schumann, with the first movement: " Strangely enough, I understand why the first movement of the concerto still troubles you;
it is so wonderful in detail, and yet the whole is not yet vivifying,
though it inspires enthusiasm. But what is the reason of this? I
really can not make it out." Of the three movements referred
to by Brahms above he had taken over the first two into the
concerto. In 1862 Albert Dietrich describes how he had previously
seen the beginning of the D minor Piano Concerto as a sonata
for two pianos and says that a " slow scherzo" from it was afterwards used as the second movement in the *Deutsches Requiem*
(*langsam, mässig* 3/4, " *Denn alles Fleisch, es ist wie Gras* ").
That makes three movements. It was probably the fourth over
which the symphony came to grief. Brahms's faculty for self-
criticism, which was already strongly developed when he was
young, must have told him that it was not yet adequate as a
symphony, and so, passing through the transition stage of a
sonata for two pianos, the symphony became a piano concerto
with orchestra.

The mere name " symphony" is immaterial. What is more
important is the intrinsic evidence of Brahms's concerto style,
with its new and reforming tendencies. Three points are decisive
in this connexion: in the first place, the suppression of all display
of technical virtuosity by the soloist as an end in itself; next, the
equal footing maintained by the soloist and orchestra, solo and
tutti; and, lastly, the approximation of the concerto to the symphony in intellectual content.

In Brahms's concertos technical virtuosity as an end in itself
is entirely suppressed. All the themes and motifs, down to the
figure-work, runs, chord passages, and scales, develop organically
out of the whole. Thus Brahms's manner of writing a piano
concerto is the Brahmsian pianistic idiom raised to its highest
power; it is displayed with by far the greatest diversity in the
First Piano Concerto, but with an incomparably more Brahmsian
character in the Second — that is to say, directly reducible, in a
far more exclusive and stereotyped fashion, to a few basic technical formulas. The equal footing established between soloist and
orchestra, on the model of the old concertos of Corelli and
Handel, for instance, and of Liszt's new reformed type (*Reform-
konzert*), enables the soloist to become organically incorporated
outright in the orchestra, as an equal member of it. The rapid,
intimate reciprocal exchange of ideas is complete; there is no
mere juxtaposition of the two elements, or subordination of one
to the other, but a harmonious association and fusion of them;
the orchestra, the individual range of whose tone-colour was not
uninfluenced by his friend Grimm's advice on the instrumentation, no longer acts more or less as an accompaniment to the
soloist, but soloist and orchestra play harmoniously " in concert "
in a firmly and finely knit psychological and musical connexion.
But the conscious approximation of the Brahmsian type of instrumental concerto to the symphony is vouched for, not so much
by the symphonic four-movement plan of the Second Concerto,
as by the extraordinarily enhanced demands which it makes on
us as regards intellectual content. In this respect Brahms's instrumental concertos hark back to the old concertos of the eighteenth
century, which far surpassed the symphony of that period in
seriousness of content and austere solidity of workmanship.

It is no wonder that the public of the Leipzig Gewandhaus,
accustomed to the easy, agreeable, brilliant society or recreative
music of the superficial piano concertos fashionable at that time,
was necessarily completely nonplussed by a piano concerto opening with such alarmingly dæmonic passion as the first Brahms
concerto, in D minor, and even showed hostility to it, in spite of

Beethoven, Chopin, Schumann, Mendelssohn, and Liszt. For this concerto is directly derived from Beethoven's Ninth Symphony, in D minor — and in particular from the titanic conflicts, rebellious outbursts, and passion of its first movement — and from Bach's D minor Piano Concerto. Like these two works, it is in the old dæmonic key of D minor. Its outward form also bears witness to a close affinity in feeling with Beethoven's Ninth Symphony, which Brahms had heard for the first time at Cologne in 1854, at the age of twenty-one, conducted by Ferdinand Hiller, and the impression of which had naturally been an elemental one which revolutionized his inner life. The decisive influence, both spiritual and musical, of the first movement of Beethoven's Ninth Symphony is most clearly manifest in the equally dæmonic and highly affecting first movement of Brahms's D minor Piano Concerto, down to the individual themes and motifs. We may indicate, in particular, both the principal subject, which breaks forth with elemental force, and the first subsidiary theme, in D minor. In this, incomparably the greatest and most important movement of the concerto, Ovid's battle of centaurs and Lapiths, of which we spoke in connexion with the *Tragic Overture,* flames up anew. Never before, not even in Beethoven, has any instrumental concerto struck such a wild note of passion and revolt, indeed of dæmonic terror, as this first movement. The principal theme in particular, in which all the passions rage, is entirely novel and original, as is also its scheme, which develops five great theme-groups and postpones the really lyrical theme in F major to the very end of the second half of the theme-group. This principal theme consists of furious declamations on the violins and 'cellos, vehemently hurled out into the world, above the D sustained throughout with inexorable rigidity by the double basses and rolling kettledrums. All idea of the piano is silenced before this elemental outburst of the most terrible despair and the most open revolt. Thus the piano is left as the exponent of the somewhat scanty elements in this movement which are musing, agreeable, dreamily lyrical, or fervently imploring, crystallizing in the main round the magnificent theme in F major.

In comparison with this grandiose battle of giants any subsequent movement, however greatly conceived, must naturally mark a falling off. This is chiefly so with the final rondo, a movement which starts off with a rhythmically firm, joyous impetus, virile and full of rugged character, but, fundamentally, still containing an element of strife. It is least so with the *adagio,* one of the most wonderful slow movements in a religious, devotional, chorale-like strain that Brahms ever wrote: here for the first time we have before us the Brahms of the *Deutsches Requiem.* The first movement, for all its grand scheme and working-out, none the less merely gives us Beethoven's grand pathos in Brahms's rendering, based, after all, more perhaps upon study and acquired knowledge than upon deep-rooted inward experience of his own. In the second and third movements Brahms gives us himself. In the second we find his gentle side, in the third his pensive, reserved, but cheerful side. Themes such as the devout principal subject of the *adagio,* given to the strings and accompanied by suave passages in thirds on the bassoons, are among the tenderest and most saturated with feeling that Brahms, whom some would have to be so "harsh," has ever written; and we shall again become familiar with such themes, expressive of blissful peace, later on, in the *Nänie,* the *Schicksalslied,* and the *Gesang der Parzen.* But even from the purely pianistic point of view, this Piano Concerto in D minor must rank immeasurably higher than the Second, in B flat major. In the First Piano Concerto Brahms's later treatment of the piano part in his concertos, dense and slow-moving, with its constant preference for working with massive chord effects and broken chords with an awkwardly wide stretch, is as yet not fully developed. The handling of the piano part is more varied, more naïve, more naturally sensuous in tone, and happier in its avoidance of any intentional stressing of his peculiar "harshness."

The Second Piano Concerto, in B flat major — first jestingly announced by the composer in the summer of 1881, to Clara Schumann and Elisabeth von Herzogenberg simultaneously, as "quite a little piano concerto, with quite a little scherzo" — is incomparably more pleasing, but also elaborated with immeasurably more pains, and, from the point of view of piano composition, more one-sided. The fact that it consists of four movements may induce us to regard it erroneously as a symphony with a solo instrument; but one can only do so — and this is still more so than with the First Piano Concerto — on grounds of its purely external formal scheme. By putting forth the whole of his exceptional will-power, Brahms endeavoured in this work to write a piano concerto and a symphony at once. He can hardly be said to have succeeded. He came to grief on the extraordinary difficulties involved in the combination of piano and orchestra, which a Mozart managed to vanquish in pure sport, a Beethoven by the might of his intellect. This can be seen above all in the first two movements. From the intellectual point of view, this B flat major Concerto ought never to be characterized as merely a "piano symphony." Brahms was made of essentially different stuff from our really great masters of the musical art. The wide, free intellectual horizon which is absolutely demanded by all symphony — not only the classical type — is narrowed down, precisely in this Second Concerto, to a German tone of assured and articulate middle-class Philistinism. Thus this work remains a peculiarly significant example of one side of Brahms, the manifestations of which constantly recur more or less strongly in his works. His B flat major Piano Concerto is one of his laborious artistic feats, one of those works in which the sweat and toil which they cost him are to a certain extent apparent; and it stands in absolutely immense contrast with the piano concertos of Mozart, created with a godlike facility and producing, for all their noble content, a divinely light effect — works which our composer wisely and modestly held in extraordinarily high veneration and love, as peerless models for all true concerto-writing.

In spite of all our reverence and admiration for the formal and technical workmanship lavished upon the first movement in particular, with that conscientiousness and solid thoroughness which are so characteristic of Brahms, enabling him to weld to-

gether a superabundance of ideas into a united whole, it is
necessary to make this preliminary reservation, and at the same
time to show by this example that it is not right to place Brahms
on the same level as our great classical masters — as, for instance,
in Bülow's senseless paradox of the "three B's": Bach, Beethoven, Brahms. This can be seen most clearly in the slow movement. Such music as this, full of pure and unadulterated emotion,
blissfully absorbed in it, saturated with it — almost revelling in
it — music of a nobly sentimental character such as we hear
from the very outset in the 'cello solo, could never have been
written by a Bach, a Haydn, a Mozart, or a Beethoven! And
this voluptuous suavity of the 'cello tone proves once again that
Brahms was not a hard, rugged nature, but at heart a thoroughly
tender one, who has, moreover, written much that is tender. Even
at that period the legend of the harsh, reticent Brahms ought
surely to have melted into thin air before this movement! The
second movement is the only one which does not maintain the
general spirit of the concerto as a whole — a tone which we must
boldly declare to be bourgeois to an almost Philistine and prosaic
extent. This second movement is a scherzo, recalling the Piano
Scherzo in E minor, op. 4, and the later piano capricci, by its
morose, uncouth, and Nordic tone. Its principal subject (*allegro
appassionato,* in 3/4 time) deliberately borrows its first four notes
from the scherzo of the First Serenade, in D major. The dæmonic
key of D minor preserves it from the outset from too great a
mood of contentment or idyllic bliss, which might have been
suggested by the key of B flat major, in using which it is necessary
to be equipped with Beethoven's intellectual power and Schumann's rush of passionate emotion if, in the long run, one is to
avoid a too cheerful impression. In this movement there still
lingers a touch of Brahms's D minor Concerto, of the spirit of
his rhapsodies and ballades. Its other features may best be discerned by comparison with the corresponding movement of the
First Piano Concerto. Here again the first movement decides
in favour of a multiplicity of themes and theme-groups. But
here what was dæmonic and charged with pathos in the First

Concerto becomes idyllic, pleasing, and meditative, with a slight dramatic undercurrent of silent conflict — the germ of which is already contained in the principal subject — between delight in nature and the country, with its forests and plains (expressed by the horn), gentle lamentation (wood-wind), and fiercely excited declamation (piano). The slow movements of both the piano concertos revert to a devoutly religious, serenely uplifted tone of faith and prayer. Indeed, the prayerful tone of the F sharp major theme (*più adagio*), given out in a singing melody by the clarinet in the slow movement of the B flat major Concerto, acquires a deeply poetic significance from the fact that Brahms used it again in the last number, *Todessehnen,* of the book of songs, op. 86, which appeared at the same time, a setting of Schenkendorf's words: *"Hor' es, Vater in der Höhe, aus der Fremde fleht dein Kind."* And yet the element of prayer and pleading, of uplifted devotional feeling, in the slow movement of the D minor Concerto becomes merely emotional in the B flat major Concerto. Again, the last movements of both concertos adopt the rondo form. But what was virile defiance and rugged character in the First Concerto is here translated into Brahms's "free and easy (*aufgeknöpfte*)" mood, of a slightly reserved grace and a charmingly tranquil contentment, and softly subdued, pensive cheerfulness, which fortunately states no deep problems, but simply pours itself out in fresh, unconstrained music. Not only in the broadly elegiac A minor intermezzo of its episode, but in other passages as well, he does homage to the style of the Hungarian Dances, which had their origin in the same year. Both the piano concertos close with a last burst of exultant *joie de vivre;* in both it is the first movement which determines their value and effect. But the Second Piano Concerto departs still further from the classical type in its treatment of the piano part, and in the relation between piano and orchestra, than it does in its intellectual content. In the First Piano Concerto the treatment of the piano part still varied in character; but in the B flat major one it is already quite exclusively and narrowly Brahmsian: slow-moving, robust, inelastic, with wide stretches, arising out of purely intellectual rather than musical considerations, inordinately difficult and impracticable from the point of view of beauty of tone — and not only piano tone, but the concerted effect — which is, after all, the object aimed at. The pianist who plays this B flat major Concerto must to a great extent renounce his position as a virtuoso and become a mere journeyman at the piano, executing the pianistic toil imposed upon him by the composer with groans — and by the sweat of his brow. The piano concerto as conceived by Mozart and Beethoven is a display of touch (*Anschlagskonzert*), that of Brahms is — at least to a very large extent — a display of sheer dynamics (*Schlagkonzert*)! This B flat major Concerto, in particular, is one which calls for blood and sweat. "It is decidedly not for little girls," as the composer once remarked jocularly to young Ella Pancera, when she played it at Vienna with the Philharmonic Orchestra under Hans Richter. But the difficulties which it involves are out of all proportion to the result achieved. One sees and hears the pianist striving and battling with things that are as extraordinarily difficult and unmanageable as they are exacting and fatiguing. But the effect is poor. Unfortunately, with the organic and "unselfish" incorporation of the piano in the orchestra, which was the goal of Brahms's endeavours, one entirely legitimate and beautiful adornment of the piano concerto disappears: its brilliant individual character as a solo instrument, combined with the orchestra, with its effects of true and noble virtuosity, expressed, as occasion serves, in the sparkle and limpidity of the runs and figures for which it is used. The piano concerto of the Chopin type, in which the orchestra is used practically as an obbligato accompaniment, that of the Schumann type, in which what the orchestra has to say is of almost equal import, become in Brahms's hands — at least in this Second Concerto — a concerto for orchestra and piano in the fullest sense of the word. But is that the real significance and aim of the concerto?

Brahms's Violin Concerto, in D major, like that of Mendelssohn in E minor and Max Bruch's First Concerto, in G minor, is now established as a decidedly romantic work, but already

touched with a breadth of classicism. And yet, on account of
the "inexorable and imposing gravity" (Emil Krause) with
which it is filled, and by reason of its technical difficulties, which
made it appear to the same biographer of Brahms, as late as the
early nineties, "clumsy and almost devoid of flexibility," it has
made its way into favour only very slowly and with difficulty.
Its key — which is that of the Second Symphony — and the fact
that it came into being at almost the same time, give it a place
among Brahms's great idyllic instrumental pieces with a serious
tinge. This is most evident in the *adagio* (F major). The naïve
melody of the principal subject on the oboe, framed, as it were, by
the wind instruments, has a North German open-air atmosphere,
at once serious and charming. The first movement opens with its
simple principal subject, ascending and descending within the
compass of the D major triad, in an uplifted, joyful tone which
is not lacking in a certain brightly festive spirit. It works up to
a pitch of powerful energy, then changes into a lyrical mood,
and quickly loses itself in rapt, twilight dreams, out of which
Brahms rouses himself, so to speak, with the sharp, staccato
rhythm of the D minor second subject, and impetuously rallies
his forces for fresh action. The virile struggle of this so-called
"harsh" composer against his tender North German emotional
nature, his conflict with self, follows almost the same course as
in the first movement of the Second Symphony. Thus the entry
of the solo violin, after the rush of the great, broad *tutti* of the
orchestra which precedes it, produces a truly regal effect, as it
improvises freely on the principal theme, and works it up from
the idyllic to the heroic mood. The mighty, amply planned theme-
group forms the crown of this movement, but the working-out is
conspicuous for workmanship — though, it is true, of a masterly
order — rather than for inspiration, thus forming an exception to
Brahms's general practice. The last movement, which is once
again cast in rondo form, and has a slightly Hungarian tinge, is
to a certain extent a pendant in the major key to the corresponding movement of the Second Piano Concerto. But it intensifies
the charming, restrained grace of the latter into a merry mood,

marked by a decided rhythm, an abrupt, strongly vigorous energy, and a robust, serenely sunny humour. Its nature is at once revealed in the single bar leading up to the repetition of the theme; the violins and violas having rushed up the scale in an impetuous onset, the solo violin on its next entry glides down it with a droll slide. The concluding movement (*poco più presto*), with its humorous *gruppetti* on the wood-wind, leads up to the delightful revels of a rustic dance-idyll, with the rhythm of the rondo theme made smoother by the conversion of the semiquaver figure into triplets. We are reminded here, in a way, of the march-like or-chestral introduction (*alla marcia — allegro assai vivace*) at the words "*Froh, wie seine Sonnen fliegen*" in the last movement of Beethoven's Ninth Symphony; indeed it is impossible not to recognize a certain affinity of feeling between the Brahms Violin Concerto and that work of Beethoven's, quite apart from the fact that they are in the same key. This much we may say: even though it neither is nor could have been in the style of Beethoven, yet of all modern violin concertos it certainly stands nearest to Beethoven both in the charm and significance of its content, which is as earnest as it is attractive, and in its genuine, powerful virility. Just as Spohr, Mendelssohn, and Bruch may be said to have composed the feminine romantic German violin concertos, so Brahms may be said to have written the masculine one. So masculine, in spite of the emotional tenderness and rapt absorp-tion of its lyrical parts, that it has had almost exclusively men as its first and most important interpreters: Joachim, Halir, Heermann, Brodsky. And for similar reasons we should be glad to see the same masculine interpretation extended to Brahms's piano concertos.

Brahms's last concerto is an experiment in the revival of the old Italian form of the "orchestral concerto," the "*concerto grosso*," of the seventeenth and eighteenth centuries, in which the orchestral *tutti* of the *concerto grosso* are contrasted with a *concertino* for several soloists. And it is this form which Brahms has adopted — obviously in its modern form, as developed in the Beethoven Triple Concerto, in C major, for piano, violin and 'cello with orchestra. The result is very much the same; we are bound to give up Brahms's Double Concerto almost for lost both at present and in the future, for it is so seldom heard. This is because it demands two players of consummate technique and sure mastery, so thoroughly accustomed to playing together as can hardly happen except with members of the same family. In spite of its pleasing effect upon a wide public, the Double Concerto is among Brahms's weaker works, and on the whole, notwithstanding the happy days at Thun (1887) when it was conceived, it must be reckoned as one of the works elaborated by strictly polyphonic methods, rather than as the record of an intense experience. This is what Hanslick had in mind when he said that this concerto is the product of a great constructive mind, rather than an irresistible inspiration of creative imagination and invention. And even the composer, who plumes himself not a little to Clara upon the " jolly idea " of having written " a concerto for violin *and 'cello,*" admits that he did not feel quite at ease with it as to either form or feeling, for the following reasons: "Indeed, it is not at all the same thing to write for instruments whose nature and timbre one has in one's head, as it were, only from time to time, and hears only with one's intelligence, as it is to write for an instrument which one knows through and through, as I do the piano, in which case I know thoroughly what I am writing, and why I write in this way or that." But this certainly does not apply to the most lovely slow second movement in D major (*andante,* in 3/4 time). It is a great ballade, steeped in the rich, mysterious tone of a northern evening atmosphere. But in other respects too — though this assurance is hardly necessary — in spite of its classical form, this Double Concerto of Brahms's gives us music which is entirely modern and Brahmsian — music which we ought to learn in time to view not only from a positive, but perhaps also, to some extent, from a negative point of view. But there can surely be no mistaking what a world separates this modern "*concerto grosso,*" not only from Bach, Haydn, Mozart, and Beethoven, but also from the early, pre-classical *concerto grosso.*

XXVII

THE SYMPHONIES

AND THEIR PRELUDE, THE VARIATIONS ON A THEME BY HAYDN

It was not till late in life that Brahms embarked upon symphony, at the age of forty-four. His extremely severe self-criticism and conscientiousness caused classical symphony in the manner of Beethoven to oppress him with a fearful, crushing weight. To quote his own words, it was " no laughing matter " to write a symphony after Beethoven. And again, after finishing the first movement of the First Symphony, he admitted to his friend Levi: " I shall never compose a symphony! You have no conception of how the likes of us feel when we hear the tramp of a giant like him [Beethoven] behind us." And ten years after the completion of the " Fourth " he alluded to his own symphony before Hermann Kretzschmar as " mediocre (*halbschürig*)."

Nowadays we know that Brahms *had* the right to compose symphonies after Beethoven. Indeed, he has created a new and entirely individual modern type of symphony, new both in content and in form, which gives the lie in the happiest fashion to Richard Wagner's premature assertion that this, the highest category of instrumental music on a large scale, had exhausted its possibilities, as regards both content and form, with Beethoven's Ninth Symphony.

Brahms's symphonies only won recognition in his own day by a hard struggle. The blame for this was chiefly due to external circumstances. Immediately upon the appearance of any important new musical composition in the greater forms it was the custom to drag them into the most violent party controversies, on the part of either the neo-German progressive wing or the reactionary classical one, and to play off Brahms against Wagner and Liszt. It is quite certain that this was foreign to Brahms's own mind and taste, for he stood aside in dignified aloofness from all musical cliques and parties, and all controversies based on narrow personal grounds. But it was certainly no more to his liking that his enthusiastic friend and admirer Hans von Bülow should, in his own personal over-estimation of Brahms's art, have coined the witty but meaningless and dangerous paradox about " Bach, Beethoven, Brahms," on the strength of the symphonies. Brahms himself knew perfectly well exactly why he was content with a niche among the great writers of symphonies in the temple of fame on the level, say, of Cherubini and not of Beethoven. But Bülow's *mot* has done Brahms endless harm and has been a serious obstacle to a just estimate of his symphonies in particular. It was unfortunate that this happened during Brahms's own lifetime, because it unnecessarily embittered the quite justifiable protests that were made then, even more than today, when we have at last accustomed ourselves to do justice to Wagner *and* Brahms or to Brahms *and* Liszt alike.

The two serenades, with their character of exercises and essays, mark the pleasingly diffident debut in orchestral style and composition made by Brahms at Detmold in his twenty-sixth year. Next came a pause of nearly fourteen years. The Variations on a theme by Joseph Haydn (the so-called *Antonius-Chorale*), op. 56, in B flat major, written during the summer of 1873 at his beloved Tutzing on the Starnberger See, mark the only intermediate stage in his progress from the serenades to the First Symphony. To an infinitely greater degree than the two serenades they may claim to be the first truly symphonic work of Brahms. For this reason they should not be classed with the serenades, but as intermediate between them and the symphonies, of which they are the immediate precursors. Moreover, the orchestra for which they are written is already the full symphony orchestra; besides the usual quintet of strings and wood-wind (with piccolo) it requires to be reinforced by the double bassoon, two horns in low B flat, two horns in E flat, two trumpets in B flat, two kettledrums, and triangle.

The theme known as the " Chorale of St. Antonius," with

its simple folk-character, half grave and solemn, with a certain
suggestion of an old Catholic pilgrims' song, but with a rugged
charm and pleasing quality, is derived from the second movement of an unpublished *divertimento* for wind instruments by
Haydn; its first phrase of ten bars, ending on the tonic, B flat
major, is divided into two five-bar periods, producing a measure
as interesting as it is uncommon; the soft middle section, which
leads back to the recapitulation of the theme, consists, on the
other hand, of an eight-bar phrase (two periods of four bars
each); while the powerful concluding section (with the recapitulation of the theme and *smorzando* close) consists of twelve
bars (three periods of four bars each), through which can be
heard at the end a booming note as of bells — the B flat minims
on the wood-wind and brass. Brahms has displayed all the
subtlety of which he was capable in the choice of the characteristically incisive, sombre, and restrained tone-colour in which
the theme is given out: the wood-wind and brass (with double
bassoon and two horns in low B flat) are supported by nothing
but the *pizzicato* basses. The variations — as can but rarely be
said of modern works in this form — are a thoroughly organic
whole. These Haydn Variations, like the Handel Variations for
piano, are among not only the most erudite, but also the most
brilliant, effective, and varied of the composer's works. As regards
invention, they are among Brahms's freshest and richest productions. In spite of the obvious reminiscences of Bach and
Handel in the polyphonic variations, they are absolutely genuine
Brahms, even in their quite individual effects of timbre, which
are completely novel and wonderfully lovely. But they are also
quite genuine Brahms in that they are the first work in the form
of variations for orchestra which is independent and complete
in itself, thus bearing important testimony to his high esteem
for this form. Great variation movements were frequent and
long familiar in both old and more modern symphonies, and so
were independent works in the form of variations for piano solo
or piano duet, and to a certain extent for chamber-music too
(Stozzi, Hofmeister, Hellmesberger, Jansa). But Brahms was

breaking fresh ground in writing variations as a separate work for orchestra, and he was followed by many others (e.g., Rudorff, Heuberger, Knorr, Noren, Reger). But he did not fail to publish them (op. 56b) in a version for two pianos also, in part slightly rewritten.

The variations are eight in number and, in accordance with Haydn's manner and spirit, end not in a fugue, but a finale. The piquant five-bar measure of the first period of the theme is preserved throughout all the variations, in homogeneous and close connexion with it. The same is true of the key, B flat major. It is only in the second, fourth, and eighth variations that it changes to the more sombre key of B flat minor. Like the Handel Variations for piano, the Haydn Variations are also " character " variations, sharply contrasted and varied in movement, rhythm, style, colour, and atmosphere. As always in Brahms's work, we marvel at the rich diversity of life which he can extract in such abundance from the simple theme in the different variations.

The first variation, pensive and softly animated (with triplets against quavers), is directly connected with the close of the theme by its soft bell-like echoes. The second, with its Brahmsian dotted progressions in sixths on the clarinets and bassoons, above the *pizzicato* basses and the ringing " challenge (*Anruf*) " of the *tutti*, is more animated, but still subdued, as is indicated by the key of B flat minor. The third, pensive and full of warm inspiration in its perfectly tranquil flowing movement, introduces a melodious duet between the two oboes in its first section, accompanied an octave lower by the two bassoons, and in the second part, where it is taken up by the first violin and viola, weaves round it an enchantingly delicate and transparent lace-work on the wood-wind. The fourth, with its solo on the oboes and horns in unison, steals by in semiquavers, as sad and grey as a melancholy mist, again in B flat minor. The fifth goes tittering, laughing, and romping merrily off, in light passages in thirds in a 6/8 rhythm on the wood-wind (with piccolo) against the 3/4 rhythm of the strings, which starts at the seventh bar. The sixth, with its staccato rhythm, is given a strong, confident colour by the fan-

fares on the horns and trumpets. The seventh is a Siciliano, breath-
ing a fervent and tender emotion, with the melody given to the
flute and viola, in 6/8 time, Bach-like in character, yet every
note of it pure Brahms. Here at last he speaks to our hearts as
well. The eighth, in B flat minor, hurries past, shadowy and
phantom-like, with muted strings and soft wood-wind, in a
thoroughly ghostly and uncanny fashion — a preliminary study
on a small scale for the finale in F minor of the F major Symphony. The finale opens, very calm, austere, and sustained, as a
further series of variations on a *basso ostinato* of five bars:

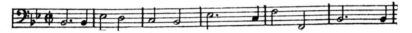

It is developed with extraordinary ingenuity, works up through
constant repetitions of the chorale theme, each time in a clearer
form and with cumulative intensity, to a brilliant close, with,
as it were, a dazzling apotheosis of the wind instruments, thrown
into relief against mighty rushing scale-passages, as in the concluding section of the *Akademische Festouvertüre*. We may, if we
like, see in this *basso ostinato* the first germ of the mighty final
chaconne on a *basso ostinato* of the Fourth Symphony.

*   *   *   *

This intellectual tour de force of the Haydn Variations, characterized by a cold sparkle and brilliance, rather than by any
warmth and pleasing quality, led up to the spirit warfare of the
First Symphony, op. 68, in C minor, four years later, in 1876.

None of his symphonies bears witness so clearly as the First
to how far people then were in Germany — and still are today —
from a true and generally prevalent understanding of Brahms,
and how it was precisely the novel element in them, which was,
and is, typically North German and Low German, that formed
the same obstacle to judging Brahms aright as it did in the case of
Hebbel. Our first business is to clarify our ideas, and first to make
it clear once for all that the undeniably sharp local, North German
stamp which Brahms's art bears — for which very reason it is

unpleasing to central and South German susceptibilities — is a
matter of secondary importance in comparison with the peculiar
greatness and richness of its musical and, what is more, its spiritual
content. Brahms, like Hebbel, is still generally alluded to in Germany as hard and harsh, dull and dreary in tone. As if we could
not point to musicians of Low German stock as soft and sensitive as
Jensen and Götz, or as sparkling with humour as Nicolai! But the
great musical centres in Germany from the fifties to the seventies,
and particularly Leipzig, had become accustomed to the more tender and pleasing musical idiom of Schumann, a central German,
and Mendelssohn, who speedily became sleeker than the sleekest
of central Germans. Then appeared for the first time a composer
of great importance whose works were the spiritual and musical
expression of the North German element; from the outset, in his
very first symphony, he showed not the slightest indulgence for the
taste of the great public, so that people were merely taken aback
and astonished, and inveighed chiefly against Brahms's asperity
and harshness, which were no more than the ordinary North
German melancholy, grave, mournful, or dreamy quality. But
they were also startled and astonished at Brahms's " mannerisms
(*Manier*) " in instrumentation. It gives a wide berth to all dense,
massive, and compact effects, to the unrelieved tone of wind
instruments scored in close position, to all Wagnerian tremolos of
the strings in the upper registers, all pretensions to predominance
on the part of individual instruments in solo parts, and all brilliance for its own sake. Density is replaced by open writing, not
closely crowded together, but broadly spaced out. The glowing
tapestry of Wagner or Richard Strauss's orchestra, with its great
" purple patches " of tone, becomes a most open-meshed tissue
with the subtlest possible design running through it. One has
only to look at the general appearance of an orchestral score of
Brahms's to see this: there are often a surprisingly large number
of blank bars and pauses; as a rule the instruments and their
different groups do not so much play together as succeed to and
help one another. The bass in particular is handled in a most
individual way: only very rarely does it make its entry altogether

with the full weight of its sonority; as a rule it does so severally and, what is more, divided according to the two leading groups — trombones and tuba on the one hand, horns and trumpets on the other — and in widely separated registers. As Widmann tells us in his Italian reminiscences, what Brahms praised in the old masters was " a trait which was so highly developed in himself too: namely, their conscientious finish, even in detail, the devoted industry which may be noticed, for example, in every one of three thousand or so statues, even in the most neglected corner of the roof of Milan Cathedral." And this marvel of Italian architecture brings us to Hugo Riemann's illuminating remark about the " Gothic " element in Brahms's composition. In the wondrous lightness and transparency of their " Gothic tracery," Brahms's symphonies are just like a Gothic cathedral, soaring heavenwards with its columns, its buttresses, its arches and pinnacles, its noble carving and finials.

It was the First Symphony which naturally had to suffer most from this general ignorance, and Bülow's witty but daring *mot* alluding to it as the " tenth symphony " — the heir and successor of Beethoven's Ninth — was another serious obstacle to a just estimate of it. On the other hand, we may venture to say that the exclusive and fanatical over-estimation and veneration of it by the narrower Brahms clique at the outset led in course of time to a gradual cooling, slight but unmistakable, even in the general estimate of this symphony's spiritual qualities. Unprejudiced and impartial persons, in spite of all their honest admiration for its musical glories and peculiar beauties, both intellectual and spiritual, slowly came to recognize what it is that distinguishes Brahms's symphony from those of Beethoven. We may cite one striking example: Hermann Kretzschmar, one of the first and most enthusiastic of the distinguished and learned musical champions of Brahms's cause, speaks of the First Symphony eight years after its appearance — in his essay on Brahms in the *Grenzboten* — as " the most important of the composer's instrumental compositions," and, in general, " the mightiest symphonic creation written since Beethoven's Ninth Symphony," going on to express the opinion that "in this sense it had been called, not altogether inappropriately, the tenth symphony" and would still live "when every trace of our names, our controversies, and our writings has been forgotten." But about fifteen years later he speaks of it in a criticism of a Leipzig Gewandhaus concert as "an imposing and highly notable" work: he describes its first movement as a mighty experiment in the pathetic style, classing it among mere imitations, and will only grant to its representation of spiritual processes the value of "studies" rather than of "real experience."

The First Symphony is Brahms's "Pathetic Symphony." Movement by movement, third by third, it struggles upwards, in a titanic striving against the most grievous tribulation, to a triumphant pæan of confident vitality. The first movement is in C minor, the second in E major, the third in A flat major, the fourth in C minor and C major. The comparison with Beethoven's "Pathetic" Symphony is obvious and well-founded both on spiritual and on musical grounds. In both respects Brahms manifestly takes Beethoven as his point of departure in his First Symphony. Its "grand style," its earnest, elevated spirit, its rugged pathos, "purging the emotions through pity and terror" (to quote Lessing), all suggest Beethoven; as do also the virile, concentrated, defiant energy and rugged passion of his musical idiom, which stirs us to our depths, glosses over nothing, spares us nothing, and even in its moments of exultation and joy maintains a certain restrained and remote quality. Beethovenesque, too, is the monumental pathos and dæmonic character of the first movement — Beethovenesque the grandiose musical conception, which, exactly as in the first movement of Beethoven's Fifth Symphony, forms a whole first movement out of a few notes, out of a short motif — for example, in the introduction to the dæmonic first movement of the first Brahms symphony, out of a "Fate motif" on the violins, striving painfully upwards in a chromatic progression against thirds, which are likewise chromatic. And, finally, the scheme of the work, too, is Beethovenesque in its homogeneous and closely knit form and poetic and significant feeling, and in the extraordinary concentration of both. If it is legitimate to speak of any of Brahms's symphonies as in the manner of Hebbel, it is so of the first. A gruesome atmosphere, recalling Hebbel in its suggestion of gravestones in a churchyard, lying phantom-like by night in the moonlight under the wild, storm-tossed winter sky, broods and lurks in the chromatic "Fate motif" in the introduction to the first movement (*un poco sostenuto*) and in the last movement (*adagio*). It is everywhere, in every movement, in places where we least expect it; even in the slow movement (*adagio*) it struggles upwards in the fifth and sixth bars, like the statue appearing uncannily at the feast, while even in the third movement there is no lack at any rate of echoes of it. A dæmonic passion, a wild energy, a harsh defiance, and a hard, cold, stony grandeur like those of Hebbel make themselves felt in the two principal movements of this C minor Symphony. In the still, tranquil passages of the first movement — and here I am thinking, for instance, of the transition passage leading up in more and more yearning and moving accents to the second theme, given out by the oboe in a melody of such intense lamentation, and the subsequent dialogue between horn and clarinet in the exposition section; or of the two great *piano* passages in the development section — we are oppressed by a ghostly, supernatural, visionary suggestion, as of Hebbel's peaceful graves, rendered doubly so by contrast with all the agitated striving which preceded it. But when in the finale, at the moment of most imminent crisis and wild upheaval in the orchestra, in which the kettledrums now join, the horn raises its mildly assuaging voice in the *più andante,* and, immediately afterwards, the gloriously broad and grandly projected C major melody, with its folk simplicity, makes its entry on the strings, working up to a high pitch of dithyrambic and triumphant jubilation, we recognize a voice like that of Beethoven in the great Hymn of Joy in the Ninth Symphony, with its message of international harmony. The denouement is to a certain extent forced, producing an almost jerky effect in the music. It suggests deliverance and release, but does not stir us so profoundly as the far more Brahmsian and typical passage in the finale of the Third Symphony. In the finale of the First Symphony Brahms assumes the mask of Beethoven and works himself up with great, vigorous gestures to a joy which is occasionally rather forced; in the finale of the Third it is his very self who submits to fate in a mood of the most manly and serene resignation. The orchestration of the symphony is in keeping with this: it is thoroughly Brahmsian in its preference for sombre, subdued colour, in the glorious use which it makes of oboe and clarinet, viola, horn, and trombone; but it scores the great heavy mass of the strings and the brilliant mass of the brass in a far more open and "undisguised (*ungedeckt*)" way than in the later symphonies. The instrumentation of the First Symphony is in all essentials still in the manner of Beethoven; that of the later ones becomes progressively more Brahmsian.

But after Hebbel, Theodor Storm must always be associated with Brahms. It is with him that we shall connect the truly Brahmsian intermezzo of the third movement, which takes the place of the customary scherzo, with its softly elegiac, veiled mood and its only transitory moods of subdued cheerfulness. This very rejection of the merry scherzo of classical symphony, which seems in this case to be a concession to the necessity of bringing the movement into line with the deeply serious poetic idea on which the work is based, and the highly pathetic character of its first movement, are inspired by an eminently modern, subtle idea, entirely in Storm's manner. But at the same time this shows, as early as the First Symphony, that from the outset Brahms takes up a thoroughly individual and independent standpoint with regard to symphonic form.

In the *adagio,* with its grand and sublime conception, though it is undoubtedly a little loosely knit and proceeds by abrupt, violent contrasts, we can first see that the purely Beethovenesque scheme and development of the First Symphony are not really in inward harmony with Brahms's nature. This *adagio* has a tinge of resignation and weariness after the terrible passions and conflicts and the fearsome apparitions of the first movement; the tragic, chromatic "Fate motif" of that movement is echoed in it as early as the fifth bar. It is, however, not so much a chance effect as a genuinely Brahmsian touch that in this movement, which is somewhat disjointed both in form and in thematic treatment, we are most deeply thrilled by the accents of grief, piteous entreaty, sweetly sorrowful remembrance, and consolation — especially in the coda. It is not for nothing that in this Hebbelian symphony, with its asperity and concentrated power, it is the horn, oboe, and clarinet, with their idyllic suggestion, which speak to us with the most moving, soothing accents even in the dæmonic pathos of the principal movements.

Even the first Brahms symphony already exacts from the listener that strenuous intellectual co-operation which is demanded by the strictly logical working-out of its musical ideas, the genesis and development of which owe more to formal than to spiritual concentration, by the rugged skill of the design, and by the delicate touch of archaism in the treatment of measure, rhythm, and harmony. The First Symphony already displays the composer's firm, clear sense of tonality, which unfortunately becomes gradually obscured in proportion as he progresses in a modern direction. Like the Fourth, it is as decidedly a " minor-symphony (*Moll-Symphonie*) " as the Second and Third are, to all appearances, purely " major-symphonies (*Dur-Symphonien*) " (though they are in reality a typically Brahmsian blend of the two, which may be called "*Moll-Dur-Syphonien* "). But while genuinely minor in feeling, it is also genuinely Brahmsian even in those passages where, starting from Beethoven's latest quartets, he tries to rise to a pathos and spirit like those of the great master. It is only when we are not content merely to hear Brahms's First Symphony played, but, as it were, live with it and into it, that Bülow's *mot* about the tenth symphony becomes comprehensible and finds some solid basis. It is only then that it awakens in us the consciousness of a deeply stirring and even shattering inward experience. It is only when, for instance, an Arthur Nikisch succeeds by his magic spells in converting the reserved, low-spirited Low German, intellectual rather than sensuous, into a southerner with intense, passionate emotions, and fanning the latent ardour of feeling and passion glimmering beneath the ashes into a devouring fire which has something at once terrifying and ravishing about it, that this grandiose symphonic cartoon in the style of a Cornelius becomes an oil-painting, full of glowing colour, like that of a Böcklin. Such power is only granted to a very few of the elect and great among conductors. On the whole we may accept the following conclusion as final: Brahms's First Symphony aspires towards the lofty heights of Beethoven. It is not, however, this symphony of Brahms's, but his Third that is really comparable to Beethoven's Fifth. Brahms's First is rather his "Pathetic" Symphony and takes its rise most obviously from Beethoven's pathetic and dithyrambic side. Musically it is second to none of Brahms's symphonies, or, at any rate, to the Third alone, but spiritually it is inferior to all the later ones, owing to its Beethovenesque character, which is not really in harmony with Brahms's inmost nature; though, on the other hand, it surpasses all the rest, and even the Third, in the impressiveness and mighty, monumental effect of its rugged, grandly conceived pathos.

The Second Symphony, op. 73, in D major, which followed the First three years later, may be called Brahms's Pastoral Symphony. Just as the First Symphony, with its sombre pathos, struggled upwards in thirds from movement to movement out of darkness into the sun, to a godlike serenity and freedom, so the Second, with its loftily anacreontic mood, descends in a peaceful cycle of descending thirds in its three movements, the first being in D, the second in B, the third in G major. Even today Brahms's Second Symphony is still undeservedly a little overshadowed by the First and Third. Like Beethoven's Pastoral Symphony, on its appearance it was dismissed, far too curtly and prematurely, as marking a "little rest" on the part of the composer — perhaps due to fatigue after the deeply impassioned heroics of the First Symphony — and as being throughout a harmless, pleasing, agreeable, cheerfully "sunlit" idyll. Nothing could be further from the truth! The period between the sixties and eighties of the last century, which, in spite of all Germany's victorious wars, was so peculiarly languid, inert, and full of bourgeois sensibility in art, as well as in politics and human relations, had, none the less, as its artistic ideal a heart-rending pathos and monumental grandeur. Nowadays, regarding things from a freer and less prejudiced point of view, we are fortunately able to detect far more clearly the often oppressive spiritual limitations, moodiness, and atmosphere of resignation in such pleasant, apparently cheerful and anacreontic works as Brahms's Second Symphony. Like its sister-symphony in the major — namely, the Third — the Second, though nominally in the major, has the veiled, indeterminate Brahmsian " *Moll-Dur* " character, hovering between the two modes.

Indeed, this undercurrent of tragedy in the second Brahms symphony, quiet and slight though it may be, is perceptible to a fine ear in every movement. It is audible in the first movement, with its almost excessive wealth of themes and the unusually broad plan of its exposition section, which amalgamates so many diverse elements into a united whole — in the two A major themes of the concluding section, one with its aggressive upward leaps in a dotted rhythm, the other unified by strongly imitative devices and full of passionate insistence; but it can also be perceived in the fragments of the theme worked into an ominous *stretto* on the wind in the development section. The second movement, the *adagio non troppo,* also reveals the tragic undercurrent of this symphony in its suffering, melancholy, and deeply serious spirit. How dejected and tremulous in mood is the noble principal theme on the 'cellos, to what a pitch of deep, passionate agitation does the development section work up, how musing and sorrowful is the close! It is only the F sharp major second subject, floating softly by in Schumannesque syncopations, that brings a touch of brightness into the melancholy scene of this *adagio* by the brief glance which it casts back into the lost paradise of childhood and youth. The serious undercurrent also makes itself felt within quite small limits in what is perhaps the most typical and individual movement, the Brahmsian " *intermezzo pastorale* " of its *allegretto grazioso.* Less, perhaps, in the trio which forms the middle section (*presto* in 2/4 time) — with the slight Hungarian tinge in both its rhythm and its theme, formed by diminution from the principal subject of the first section — than in the enchanting, half-elegiac, half-mischievous principal section of the G major *allegretto.* The way in which the naïvely pastoral oboe sings forth the perfectly simple, simply harmonized theme in accents of sweet, suave melancholy once again recalls the young composer of the D major Serenade. But it is perhaps in the finale that the quiet, tragic undercurrent of this ostensibly cheerful symphony is most plainly apparent: in the frequent energetic attempts to shake off the all too peaceful and idyllic reverie, in the fantastic, romantic, and ghostly elements which can be seen glimmering beneath the ashes in a supernatural, uncanny way throughout the whole development section. For all its apparent vivacity of movement and the apparently unclouded brightness of the D major key, the finale hides within it many sombre features, and even spectral and supernatural visions.

Thus Brahms's Second Symphony, as a great idyll with a slightly tragic tinge, which we may compare with that great, ruthlessly tragic poet Hebbel's fine epic *Mutter und Kind,* was at the same time, as a "tragic idyll," a piece of the most genuine and typical local Holstein and Low German art. Its quiet, unconscious tragedy, hidden beneath the blossoms of a soft idyll of man and nature, with a subdued evening tinge and a prevailing pastoral spirit, carries direct conviction to a discriminating and unprejudiced listener — far more so, in any case, than the conscious and almost forced and deliberate tragedy of the First Symphony or the *Tragic Overture.* Here again, perhaps, there has been no conductor save Arthur Nikisch, the one and only great Brahms conductor of our day, who has simply ignored the traditional legend as to the innocent, idyllic character of the second Brahms symphony and interpreted it as what it really is: a great, wonderful tragic idyll, as rich in sombre and subdued colour as it is in brightness. If one knew nothing but the finale, one might rather call it an "anacreontic" symphony. For the

subdued shimmer of festal joyousness in its principal subject
(*allegro con spirito*) reminds us of Cherubini's *Anacreon* Overture, and the broad, jovial singing quality of its second theme, in
A major, breathes pure *joie de vivre*. What is more, the transition
passages and development sparkle with a Haydnesque spirit.
Yet, in spite of its predominant character, now pungent and
sparkling, now dreamy and romantic, even this movement,
though apparently so full of unclouded cheerfulness, is rich in
mysterious Wagnerian visions, suggestive of the Wanderer, in a
mystic, woodland, faery, nature atmosphere recalling the *Rheingold* and in many sombre and even ghostly passages.

The Third Symphony, op. 90, in F major, is Brahms's
" Eroica ": heroic, that is to say, in the Brahmsian spirit. In spite
of its truly heroic and virile strenuousness and conflicts, its last,
supreme word of wisdom is a serene resignation. This is, moreover, expressed with such wonderful truth and moving effect
in the musical form in which it is clothed that we may venture
to say that in its purely human qualities the Third Symphony
is Brahms's most typical, personal, and important symphonic
work. In no other symphony has Brahms unveiled his own individual nature so wonderfully, in no other has his whole
personality found such marvellously pure and undisguised expression, in no other symphony has he displayed such spiritual independence as in this. Moreover, it is not Brahms's First, but his
Third Symphony which was his " Fifth " in the Beethovenesque
sense of the word; it, too, takes Beethoven as its point of departure, but in contrast with the First Symphony, in which he
tries, as it were, to solve the problem in a purely Beethovenesque
manner, which is therefore not fully in harmony with his own
nature, it states and solves the problem of symphony entirely on
the basis of his own individuality.

No other symphony of Brahms's bears, to the same extent
as the Third, a healthy, heroic stamp, serenely conscious of
strength born of the fusion of vigorous energy and tenderness, in
the manner of the corresponding movement of Beethoven's
Eroica; especially in its first movement, which, like the third, is

full of a spirit of combat. The proud spirit of Horace's " *Odi profanum vulgus et arceo,*" and the resignation of Byron's Childe Harold, are both present in it. And once again we hear the accents of Harold, when he said:

> " I live not in myself, but I become
> Portion of that around me; and to me
> High mountains are a feeling, but the hum
> Of human cities torture."

For no other symphony of Brahms's is so instinct with the spirit of nature, and, significantly enough, it is precisely these parts which remind us of the great musical nature-painter of the *Rheingold* — Richard Wagner: the transition to the A major second theme of the first movement, with the glorious diminished chord recalling that of " *Naht euch dem Strande,*" or the stately close of the meditative *andante,* with its reminiscence of the Valhalla music, or the light, subdued murmur of rippling semi-quavers in the coda of the finale, like the sound of a bubbling spring. And so we may call Brahms's Third Symphony a North German heroic epic, the finale of which conjures up the heroic landscape of the old Beowulf saga, with its procession of driving, heavy clouds, ending in a wan, tempered gleam of sunshine such as one sees in Schleswig-Holstein. It is not till the impassioned principal section of the finale that the composer, whose mood had become more and more overcast during the middle movements, with their elegiac colour in the manner of Theodor Storm, is once more rapt away into the " tumult of humanity," so that he " must needs lament."

These passionate conflicts and laments in the finale display a feature which is novel and peculiar to the third Brahms symphony. In order to lay our finger upon it unerringly, let us once more glance at the sequence of keys in the separate movements. The first movement is naturally in the key of the tonic, F major. Brahms lays the second, slow movement in the key of the dominant, but in the major (C major), only to exchange this for

C minor in the third, reverting to F minor for long portions of the finale. This is extraordinarily characteristic of Brahms, as of all modern composers in general. The humour of Dickens, Raabe, and all the great, genuine, and eternally modern humorists springs from a soil steeped in suffering and conquered by their own hard experience. Brahms's positive vital energy is limited by strongly negative factors, by melancholy and pessimism. His temple of mirth often stands on a stony, thorny rock; one has constantly to rally one's strength and fight one's way onward or else sink downwards step by step. It is these severe inward limitations, which have their source in Brahms's peculiarly indeterminate "*Moll-Dur*" nature, that have determined the course of the "psychological scheme (*innere Handlung*)" of this symphony: the actual denouement of the drama, the conflict, is postponed till the last movement; the three which precede it — now spirited and full of energy, as in the first movement, now absorbed in heavy brooding thoughts and forebodings, as in the second and third — are accumulating the fuel for the dramatic conflagration.

This is quite an innovation. And another novelty is the truly regal architecture of the symphony, in the first place as regards its form, which is of consummate finish and conciseness. The theme or exposition sections of the principal movements are of quite exceptional breadth, as a set-off against which the working-out is correspondingly brief. For example, there are only nine pages of working-out in the score of the first movement as against fourteen pages of exposition. These theme sections contain a melodic power which is almost unprecedented even for Brahms. But the most novel and individual feature is the stylistic principle which Brahms introduces into the symphony in the shape of a "leitmotiv": F, a flat, F. According to Kalbeck's ingenious explanation, F-a-F stands for the motto "*Frei, aber froh* (Free, but cheerful)," adopted by Brahms as a young man in opposition to the motif F-a-e, standing for young Joachim's motto, "*Frei, aber einsam* (Free, but alone)." This motto of Brahms's recurs in a whole series of his works, from the Second

Piano Ballade, of op. 10, to this first movement of the Third
Symphony, and after. Here Brahms has used it as a structural
principle, first as the poetic "motto" which ushers in the horns,
trumpets, and wood-wind, afterwards as a bass or a counter-
theme in the middle and higher registers. Here too, in his Third
Symphony, Brahms has acted with the greatest spiritual freedom and independence, by rounding off the form of this movement and knitting together the great separate periods in this
homogeneous and uniform fashion by means of this "inner link
of the motif (*Motiv-Band*)."

The end reverts to the principal subject of the first movement,
in a tone of nobly subdued and purified resignation. This is truly
Brahmsian. But in view of the deeper, symbolic significance of
the F-a flat-F motto, it is also the most affecting and wonderful
thing that Brahms ever wrote. For what he means by it is that, in
spite of all our manly and heroic conflicts and efforts, we cannot
dispense with an equally manly but restrained and purified
resignation. And this honest confession is touching in the case
of any true man, but most deeply and doubly so in that of
Brahms. No other symphony of Brahms contains so much that
is intimately related to his nature as a man, both as a whole or
in detail. But when we ask the question: Where has the composer said, as it were between the lines, what he intended to
express in this symphony, which opens with such a tumultuous
outburst of high spirits; or on what intellectual ideas, both human
and musical, is it based? — we would indicate in particular the
whole of the conclusion, the coda of the first movement, which
once again opens with the principal subject above the six-four
chord, and the "motto" (c, e flat, c), and in so doing establishes
itself with a mighty swoop in the original key; the elegiac pastoral idyll of the *andante,* rich in mystically dreamy and tenderly
dissonant tone effects, due to his characteristic suspensions, with
the singing melody of its simple folk-song-like principal theme,
given out by the clarinets and bassoons, which appears again in
the reprise in an amplified form, wonderfully interwoven with
syncopated triplets on the violin; or again in the hovering and

veiled third movement (*poco allegretto*), a truly Brahmsian
C minor intermezzo, interpreted in a very slow sense, with its
subdued elegiac and sombre tones and its meditative second
section, in A flat major, to which the syncopated rhythm of the
'cellos lends a dance-like lilt; and, lastly, the whole of the fourth
movement.

We have already laid stress above on the fact that Brahms
has postponed the real " dramatic denouement " of the symphony
to the last movement. His mode of doing so is so to charge the
three preceding movements with inward drama that in each of
them we plainly feel that something oppressive is latent, an
inward conflict which has got to come to a head. Thus it is only
in appearance that this third Brahms symphony is a " major
symphony "; even at the beginning of the fourth movement for
ten whole pages of the score we are in the key of F minor, in
its most sombre and passionately agitated mood. Such an entirely
novel and individual solution of the problem of the symphony
could have been discovered by none but Brahms, with his severe
inward limitations, the first and only master of the " *Dur-Moll* "
mode, the master of resignation. Hence this concluding movement of the Third Symphony is passionate, " dramatic," and
sombre through and through, up to the entry of the second
theme. It is rich in uncanny, dæmonic, and ghostly elements in
the F minor principal theme, which fleets by in the lower register
on the strings and bassoons in unison, unquiet, restless, and dis-
traught, and immediately afterwards rears itself up threateningly.
It is also rich in sombre solemnity in the " Fate theme," with
its broad triplets given out *pianissimo* on the trombones, and in
wild, unruly outcries in the F minor transition passage (*tutti,
forte*) to the second theme, the repetition of which works up
to the open conflict. It is not till the second theme, in triplets,
given out by the wood-wind and violins in the bright key of
C major, and the broad concluding passage in C minor, that the
mighty theme-groups are brought to a confident conclusion. The
end of this movement, and of the symphony, belongs, however, to
the mood of resignation: a broader concluding section, which is

also in a more moderate *tempo* (*un poco sostenuto*), frames the
wonderful ending of the whole work in a great nature setting,
by means of the semiquaver figure which enters for the first
time on the strings in this section, with its suggestion of the
ebb and flow of waters; while by its repeated reminiscences of
the heroic introductory motif of the first movement, now transformed into a much softer mood, it suggests an atmosphere of
serene, tranquil submission.

The Fourth Symphony, op. 98, in E minor, may be called
Brahms's "Elegiac" symphony. The virile, energetic hero of
the Third, with his conflicts and strivings, has become transformed
in the Fourth into a resigned philosopher, withdrawing by de-
grees into inward solitude with advancing years. In this lies
the deeply moving and genuine quality of this Fourth Symphony,
which may truly be called a "character symphony." The tone
of defiant, concentrated, and superior strength, such as is found
in the first movement of the Third Symphony, is intensified in
the Fourth, with his growing maturity, into the most concise
and monumental symphonic style. In this it recalls Hebbel, but
even in the great *chaconne* with variations of the finale he is
in no wise titanic or tragic. The inward tragedy of the Fourth
Symphony — the resignation of solitary old age — is revealed,
indeed, in quite a different way: in the weary, veiled tone,
curiously objective and reminiscent of epic or ballad, which predominates in it. The Fourth Symphony bears the beautiful stamp
of that "*Lengen* (longing)," that unappeasable yearning for their
lost home, the lost paradise of childhood, which is innate in the
Low German, and particularly in the Holsteiner. In its harsh,
subdued, and faded autumnal colouring, in its quiet command
of the more sombre passions, which in the first three movements,
including the scherzo, with its almost forced and thoroughly uncanny joviality, can be felt everywhere glimmering in ghostly
fashion beneath the ashes and held in check by an effort, the deep
resignation of Theodor Storm makes itself felt. In the archaistic
tinge of its broadly projected themes is displayed the overmastering Low German fondness for the ballad (witness Liliencron,

Frenssen, and Seeliger). Their prevailing tone, working up to a pitch of virile defiance, and even haughty, morose aloofness and furious revolt, is nothing but the deeply moving reaction upon us of Brahms's own tragic recognition of the fact that, as a tragic composer, his place is not at the side of Beethoven, but perhaps of Cherubini or Volkmann.

In the Fourth Symphony, again, let us first consider the sequence of keys. To an even higher degree than the First, the fourth Brahms symphony is purely and decidedly a "minor-symphony." The first movement, which cannot be taken at too quiet and sustained a *tempo* (*allegro ma non troppo*), is naturally in the key of the tonic, the wan, faded, autumnal E minor. This is not a favourite key for symphonies. Haydn's "*Trauer-Symphonie*," in E minor (1772), remains almost symbolic: it is a key for serious matters, for "old unhappy, far-off things," for long-past storms of passion. So it is not at random that, in his Fifth Symphony, in E minor, Tschaikowsky has chosen precisely this same key for the pallid phantoms of the lovers Paolo Malatesta and Francesca da Rimini, agonizing in the inferno of Dante. The E major of the second movement (*andante moderato*), with its touch of archaic flavour and ballad suggestion, produces an extraordinarily individual effect in contrast with the E minor of the first: it is wonderfully mysterious, entirely lacking in the usual brightness and radiant brilliance of this sunshiny key, veiled, elegiac, subdued, and hence almost elfin, and far more moving than in any "major symphony." The sub-mediant key (C major) of the third movement too, a scherzo full of dæmonic excitement (*allegro giocoso*), which is, as it were, a sort of Edward Ballade in symphonic form, full of wild and uncanny merriment, expressed as a scherzo of a wayward and defiant character, produces, with its steely, hard aggressiveness, a more unalloyed major effect, and, what is more, a C major effect, than in any out and out "major-symphony." Contrary to his custom, Brahms has not been sparing in his instrumentation of effects suggesting dæmonic mirth: neither the double bassoon, the kettle-drum, nor even the triangle is lacking. Moreover, by obvious thematic reminiscences of the first movement he has left us in no doubt of the essentially somewhat forced and serious character of this merriment: the continuation of the principal subject *fortissimo* recalls the aggressive " contradiction motif (*Widerspruchsmotiv*)," in F sharp major, given out in unison by the horns and wood-wind in the first movement, and in another passage the principal subject of the first movement is even subtly introduced again in the inner part, in a short staccato form. The finale naturally returns to the original key of E minor. Thus the sequence of keys in the fourth Brahms symphony is immeasurably simpler, more rigid, and more established than in the three preceding symphonies; it does not go beyond the short interval of the sub-mediant. The prevailing character of the symphony, which is deeply earnest, elegiac, or resigned, is in keeping with the somewhat shadowy and blurred dimness of the key of E minor, and so it is most strongly marked in the two principal movements, which are in the minor. Here it is combined with a wonderfully delicate intricacy of writing to produce that characteristically filigree-like effect of Brahms's composition, which is maintained through all the movements in a consummate and consistent fashion, as in none other of his symphonies. For example, the principal subject of the first movement is already marked by this open yet intricate workmanship characteristic of Brahms's later compositions, its melodic line extends itself as though in hesitation and plaintive appeal, on a rhythm consisting of two-note groups eloquently punctuated by crotchet rests, recalling the sighing " hoketus " of mediæval music; the 'cellos and violas accompany it in alternation with an arpeggio motif, for ever striving upwards as though in urgent appeal, and the wood-wind (clarinets, bassoons, and flutes) interjects the notes of the theme mezzo-staccato and *piano*. This delicately interwoven tissue of the first movement becomes still more subtle at the repetition of the principal subject: the melody is played in octaves broken into quavers, and given to the first and second violins, with the same arrangement of rests, the interposition of the theme on the wood-wind is replaced by a similar setting of

broken octaves for the 'cellos and basses, while the arpeggio
motifs on the 'cellos and violas dissolve into smoothly flowing
scale-passages in quavers for the violas and wood-wind, entering
every time on a syncopated crotchet.

These are the external devices of form by which Brahms
achieves an intenser but at the same time subtler expression of
the mood of deep and elegiac resignation which dominates the
symphony. This resignation naturally finds still more profound
and moving expression in the character of the music itself. It is
plainly to be detected in all four movements by those who are
accustomed not only to hear with their ears, but to feel the music
in their hearts and souls. There are in the Fourth Symphony a
series of what have been called "dæmonic" passages, which, in
accordance with Brahms's later manner, seek their dæmonic
effects not so much in a somewhat forced joviality (as in the
scherzo) as in a ghostly, uncanny stillness, a shadowy desolation
and mystically supernatural atmosphere. Such a passage occurs
in the very first theme section of the concluding group, where the
violins flutter uneasily up and down like a whirl of sparks above
the grey, ashen effect of the chord of the diminished seventh
— G sharp, B, F (E sharp) — in a phantom-like *pianissimo,* while
the kettledrum mutters *pianissimo* in the depths, for the first time
in the whole movement, and the trumpets give out a sombre,
solemn warning *pianissimo* in the deep register.

Finally, to the resigned, elegiac character of the Fourth Symphony, its note of quiet tragedy and uncanny merriment, and its
epic, ballad quality, may be added a strong tendency to archaism.
There is no other symphony of Brahms's which has so individual,
strong, or consciously archaistic a character both in harmony and
in form. As regards the harmony, this is chiefly the case in the
slow movement. It begins on the dominant, A minor, with the
two horns and a few of the wood-wind in unison, in a curiously
still, weary, and dispassionately narrative tone; then, after four
bars, the principal subject enters in E major and is immediately
placed in an old-world and ballad-like light — though at the
same time thoroughly romantic — by a *"Moll-Dur"* device —

that is to say, by reference to the minor chord on the subdominant of E major in the inner part, suggesting the Phrygian mode by using E, D, C, B instead of E, D sharp, C sharp, B. There are also occasional harmonic archaisms in the scherzo; but in the finale there are archaisms both of harmonizing and of form. This concluding movement (*allegro energico e passionato*), powerful in both its content and its scope, chooses and masters with supreme art the strict form, associated with Bach, of the old *ciaconna* or *chaconne* — that is to say, variations upon the theme:

maintained as a *basso ostinato* throughout all the thirty-two variations. It is at once introduced in the upper part at the opening of the movement over the heavy chord given out by the wind (wood-wind, double bassoon, horns, trumpets, and trombones, with kettledrum), with rigid, archaic stateliness and sombrely menacing pomp. Next follow the variations, the theme being heard now in the bass, now in the upper part, now in the inner parts. Out of this theme Brahms creates a whole enchanted garden of new formations, infinite in their variety, especially as regards harmony. The chromatic step of a semitone (A, A sharp), in particular, and the leap to a lower octave (b, B) tempt him to an inexhaustible series of variants, counter-melodies, and counterpoints. Variations on the whole or half scale, the " hexachord," had been no rarity since the days of Sweelinck and his great North German school of organists (Samuel Scheidt, etc.). But the rigid consistency, the iron strictness, the length, the immense contrapuntal resources, with which in this concluding movement of his Fourth Symphony Brahms has solved this problem, which in itself appears academic, dry, and cold, towers far above all that had previously been done in this connexion in the sphere of symphony. Indeed, he has succeeded in so wrapping up and concealing the theme among counter-melodies, etc., that it has taken

even the most expert interpreters and commentators years to discover the secret of the scheme of this movement.

And yet the old *chaconne* form is so strictly carried out that,
from beginning to end, the theme is maintained note for note,
without any transposition into other keys, but only into different
registers, now high, now low. Out of the two hundred and sixty
bars in the whole movement we have only to reckon with twelve
extra ones, which are obtained by extension (*Dehnungen*) from
the figure in the cadential last bar but one, with its downward
leap of an octave (b to B). No detailed analysis of this movement
is possible unless accompanied by a series of musical citations. It is
closely related to the first movement in its deeply serious, mournful, resigned character, and in the delicate intricacy of its writing.
There are variations — for instance the fourth (for strings and
bassoons) — which are clearly reminiscent of the principal subject of the first movement in their intricate part-writing, broken
by rests. From the fourth to the tenth variation the theme lies
in the bass. The eleventh expands the theme into 3/2 time and
in the upper part (flute) dissolves it into sweet, gently lamenting
arabesques and garlands with a softly intricate accompaniment of
chords on the violins, horns, and violas. The twelfth (also in 3/2
time) changes from E minor to E major. The thirteenth conjures up memories of Handel's Hamburg opera *Almira* in a
genuine *chaconne* which, even in its tone-colour (trombones and
bassoons, accompanied by light arpeggios on the 'cellos and
violas), is severely archaistic and full of stately solemnity. With
the fifteenth variation, which once more opens in E minor in
3/4 time, begins the second series of variations, which to some
extent represent further variations on those of the first series.
Of this second series there is a special tour de force in the twenty-
ninth variation: a canon at an interval of a crotchet beat between
the basses and violins. The coda contains one or two simple
cadences in E minor.

The resignation, which keeps increasing in intensity in the
last movement of the Fourth Symphony, assumes a fresh character on the entry of the stately *chaconne*-variation (no. 13),

which is essentially quite similar in feeling to the last movement of the Third Symphony, but with an extraordinary added depth: the autumnal lament over the transitoriness of all earthly things in the first movement of the Fourth Symphony leads up in the last movement, through the stark and monumentally formal thirteenth variation, as through some ominous portal of death, which the stately strains of the trombones invest as it were with a shimmer of antique gold, to an atmosphere of awe before the grave majesty of death. This is tragedy too; but not, as in the First Symphony, conscious tragedy, and therefore lacking in inward foundation and conviction, but unconscious, and therefore deeply real and moving, from both the human and the artistic point of view. And this is why Brahms's Fourth Symphony shines out among its sisters with the white, still radiance of the unapproachable, crowned with the monumental ruggedness of its four strongly characterized movements.

THE VOCAL MUSIC

XXVIII

SONGS, DUETS, AND QUARTETS FOR SOLO VOICES

At this point Dryasdust again has a word to say: out of the hundred and twenty-two works of the composer with opus number, there are thirty-one volumes containing roughly two hundred original songs for solo voice, five volumes (six if we include op. 84) containing twenty vocal duets, and seven volumes (including the *Liebeslieder-Walzer* and *Neue Liebeslieder-Walzer*) containing solo quartets accompanied by the piano. Each of these volumes, again, contains several songs — from four to fifteen. This amounts to a good third of his total work, without counting the *Volkskinderlieder* and the *Deutsche Volkslieder,* which appeared without opus number. Among both amateur and professional performers Brahms is nowadays reckoned as one of the great masters, the classics of German song in the nineteenth century. His extremely strong faculty for self-criticism has had as its result that in this immense collection of songs — though there is naturally some inequality among the individual songs — there is not a single one which is musically valueless; in form and in the technique of composition alike, even the smallest song is worthy of the master. It is now reserved for our further examination to show in detail to what extent Brahms's type of song is comparable to the really great models and masters of German song, not only from the musical point of view, but above all spiritually and intellectually, though in many respects we may point the way to somewhat different conclusions from those of the uncritical enthusiasm of the official works on Brahms.

Our first question is this: Which are Brahms's " great " songs, the most famous of them and the most often sung? The answer is a very interesting one from many points of view. For it shows, on the one hand, that since the seventies and eighties there has been extraordinary shifting of values, and, on the other hand, that each decade has had its own favourites among Brahms's songs, differing in both intellectual and spiritual qualities. As matters stand today, very many songs of Brahms's which were included by past decades among those which were most often sung, most brilliant, and most characteristic of the composer's personality, now occupy a second- or third-rate position in the popular opinion and estimation, while, on the other hand, individual songs out of less well-known books — for instance, op. 43, 46, 49, 57, 63, 72, 84, 85, 86, 94, 96, 97, 105, 106, 121 — which used to be relegated to a secondary place, are nowadays more justifiably reckoned among Brahms's "great" works. Owing to the diversity of personal taste, it is infinitely difficult, if not impossible, to make a selection of those which are most accepted by public opinion and the usage of artists as "great" Brahms songs from any objective general standpoint. Our list, then, can only be of value as an incomplete attempt, which makes no claim to general acceptance. It includes at least the following: *Der Schmied* and *An eine Äolsharfe* from op. 19, *Wie bist du, meine Königin* from op. 32, the *Magelone-Lieder*, op. 33, *Von ewiger Liebe* and *Mainacht* from op. 43, *An die Nachtigall* from op. 46, *O liebliche Wangen* from op. 47, *Wiegenlied* from op. 49, *Unbewegte laue Luft* from op. 57 (to Daumer's words), *Auf dem See* and *Regenlied* from op. 59, *Meine Liebe ist grün* from Book I and *O wüsst' ich doch den Weg zurück* from Book II of op. 63, *Minnelied* from op. 71, *Alte Liebe* from op. 72, *Vergebliches Ständchen* from op. 84, *In Waldeseinsamkeit* from op. 85, *Feldeinsamkeit* from op. 86, *Sapphische Ode* from op. 49, *Der Tod, das ist die kühle Nacht* and *Wir wandelten* from op. 96, *Wie Melodien zieht es*, *Auf dem Kirchhofe*, and *Immer leiser wird mein Schlummer* from op. 105, *Ständchen* from op. 106, *Vier ernste Gesänge*, op. 121. To these may be added the following, which, though less known to the public, are in many ways quite worthy to be ranked with the above in spiritual or musical value: *Liebestreu* from op. 3, *Treue Liebe* and *Heimkehr* from op. 7, *Murrays Ermordung* and *Sonett* from op. 14, *Scheiden und*

Meiden and *In der Ferne* from op. 19, *Das Lied vom Herrn von Falkenstein* from op. 43, *Die Kränze, Magyarisch,* and *Die Schale der Vergessenheit* from op. 46, *Botschaft* and *Sonntag* from op. 47, *Der Gang zum Liebchen* and *Herbstgefühl* from op. 48, *Am Sonntagmorgen, An ein Veilchen,* and *Abenddämmerung* from op. 49, *Wenn du nur zuweilen lächelst* and *Ach, wende diesen Blick* from op. 57, *Schwermut* from op. 58, *Dämmerung senkte sich von oben* and *Nachklang* from op. 59, *An die Tauben* from op. 63, Book I, *Des Liebsten Schwur* and *Mädchenfluch* from op. 69, *Im Garten am Seegestade* and *Lerchengesang* from op. 70, *Es liebt sich so lieblich, An den Mond,* and *Geheimnis* from op. 71, *Sommerfäden* and *O kühler Wald, wie rauschest du* from op. 72, *Sommerabend, Der Kranz,* and *In den Beeren* from op. 84, *Sommerabend* and *Mondenschein* from op. 85, *Therese, Nachtwandler, Über die Heide, Versunken,* and *Todessehnen* from op. 86, *Mädchenlied* and *Der Jäger* from op. 95, *Salamander* and *Meine Lieder* from op. 107.

This is a considerable list, and a general examination of Brahms's type of song must help us to breathe life into the dry bones of these titles and numbers. A general examination, for in no other sphere of Brahms's creative work does the separate examination of each number prove so unprofitable and so distracting from the main point as in the case of the songs. Let us first examine the list of "great" songs once more. We find as the first decisive result of our examination that among them, too, the serious songs predominate.

It is precisely in those passages where love, the eternal poetic theme and inspiration of all true song, assumes a sombre or tragic tinge that Brahms's serious, introspective North German type of sentiment finds its most individual and highest expression. But, fortunately for him, Brahms did not entirely surrender himself to the eroticism which forms the body and substance of modern song. He is equally himself and equally great in passages where nature and man are fused in the universal soul, or where the oppressive memories of care, sorrow, and pain, of old love and lost happiness, threaten to overwhelm one. He drinks it all

in in a very luxury of grief and is as unable and unwilling to give
it up as the Haunted Man in the Christmas Stories of Dickens,
the unique. Brahms is the greatest master of resignation,
pessimism, and *Weltschmerz* even in nineteenth-century song.
His masterpieces in these types of emotion, as, for instance, the
love-songs among the *Magelone-Lieder, An eine Äolsharfe, Von
ewiger Liebe, Mainacht, An eine Nachtigall, Unbewegte laue
Luft, Herbstgefühl, Alte Liebe, Feldeinsamkeit, Auf dem Kirchhofe, Todessehnen, Sapphische Ode, Immer leiser wird mein
Schlummer* and the *Vier ernste Gesänge,* are in Brahms's truest
and greatest manner, such as no other composer could possibly
have written, whether from the musical or the spiritual point
of view. Many of Brahms's songs have features which recall
Hebbel, in their deep, searching reflection, their ghostly atmosphere, as of graveyards by night, and their wild dæmonic spirit;
but by far the larger number display either traits which recall
Theodor Storm — gentle resignation, melancholy that moves one
to tears, or nature in an elegiac mood — or else a playful gaiety and
pensive, subdued cheerfulness reminiscent of Claus Groth. If the
comparatively few mocking, roguish songs and lively, humorous
ones, such as the *Vergebliches Ständchen, Der Schmied,* with its
defiant power, the *Lied vom Herrn von Falkenstein, Tambour-
liedchen,* and *Der Gang zum Liebchen,* among others, have
won greater and more rapid popularity by comparison with
the serious ones, this victory of the lighter and easier style over
the more difficult and intimate is a phenomenon which recurs
with every composer. And with Brahms, too, such fascinating
trifles as these prepared the way for the great, genuine, and
weighty works. But for those who wish to be neither too deeply
and painfully moved nor too lightly and gaily entertained,
Brahms's great love-songs are exactly the right thing. Such
glorious, genuine love-songs, charged with ardent, healthy, sensuous passion, as the *Magelone-Lieder, Wie bist du, meine
Königin,* or *Meine Liebe ist grün* are as genuinely Brahmsian
as his exalted songs of resignation, plaintive sentiment, or forebodings of death, which are far more numerous. And is it not

significant and symbolic that the very first song which caused all hearts on the Rhine to turn towards the young Brahms, the melancholy *Liebestreu,* from op. 3 (" *O versenk, o versenk* "), was precisely a love-lament?

In general character Brahms's songs are thoroughly melodious. It is in his songs, if anywhere, that Brahms may be recognized as a great master of melody. Such broad, boldly traced melodies have only been written before him by Beethoven, Schubert, and Schumann. Like a true northerner, he has a bent towards what is grand and broadly planned, towards rich inspiration welling up from the heart, powerful intensity in both form and feeling, avoidance of minute detail and mere outward effectiveness. Every song of Brahms's is a direct expression of his personality — a personality which did not, indeed, undergo a powerful inner development and which, for all the purely musical variety and distinctiveness of these two hundred odd songs, constantly displays the typically Brahmsian character in a continual repetition of very much the same types of feeling. In his songs, too, in spite of all the extraordinary diversity of material, Brahms moves within a somewhat narrow sphere. None the less, both in intrinsic merit and in number, these songs of his are an inalienable treasure of German song. The few complete cycles among them alone — the " romances " from Tieck's *Magelone,* op. 33, the cycle of songs set to Daumer's words, op. 57, the *Vier ernste Gesänge,* op. 121 — are absolutely unique in their respective kinds among German songs of the nineteenth century. The ecstasy of love in the *Magelone-Lieder,* the sorrows of unhappy love in the Daumer song-cycle and the volume of settings of Platen and Daumer, op. 32, the manly steadfastness with which the forebodings of death and its heart-ache are faced in the deeply resigned *Ernste Gesänge* — all these emotions have been transmuted by Brahms into glorious songs bearing a very personal stamp.

Let us now rapidly review the elements of style, form, and technique which go to make up the Brahmsian type of song. Brahms does not carry on the tradition of Mendelssohn, whom he loyally revered as " the last great master "; Mendelssohn's manner, tender, smooth, and pallid to the verge of effeminacy, is foreign to him. An equally deep gulf separates him from the spirit of Robert Franz, though in his preference for the strophic form and his old-world tinge, going back to old German folk and religious song, he may seem to approximate to him. With Schumann, too, he had from the outset but little in common so far as his songs are concerned — though the case is to some extent different with his piano music. We are conscious of this at once in the entire rejection by Brahms, that master of extreme concentration, of one feature — namely, the introductory and concluding instrumental passages of the accompaniment, which either anticipate or sum up again all that is finest in the song and are so characteristic of Schumann. On the other hand, there is an obvious relation between Brahms's songs and those of Beethoven, and a still more obvious one between them and Schubert's. Schubert was his unattainable ideal in song-writing. "There is not a song of Schubert's from which one can not learn something," as he once said to Jenner. He recommended him to study as minutely as possible all the songs of Franz Schubert, whose acute artistic perception was revealed even in the most modest little song, in order to arrive at a clear idea of where the text admits of the strophic form and where it does not. In his opinion musical form must in all respects reflect the text. If it failed to do so, the fault was due either to a serious deficiency of artistic perception or else to an insufficient insight into the text. It follows that, for all the diversity and richness of his vocal forms, Brahms incomparably preferred the strophic form in a song, both in theory and in practice, and recommended strophic treatment whenever the text would admit of it. And so, when he once said to Jenner: "I am fonder of my little songs than of my big ones," he meant that a successful song in strophic form was more to his taste than any other. But, as his own songs show, this does not exclude a somewhat free handling of his favourite strophic form in the accompaniment, and a varied or modified setting of the different stanzas of the poem. Such free strophic songs of Brahms's then — I may cite as one of the earliest and best-known examples *Wie bist du, meine Königin,* from the period of the *Magelone-Lieder* — form a transition to his larger, freely constructed settings, in which the accompaniment of each strophe varies (*durchkomponierte Lieder*). Brahms's larger songs, and especially his song-cycles, have exercised a good influence in furthering a wholesome reaction against the somewhat regrettable despotism of the short type of song prevalent in the Romantic and post-Romantic periods. In these cycles he was reverting to the way previously indicated by Beethoven in his two song-cycles, *Adelaide* and *An die ferne Geliebte,* and by Schubert in his song-cycles the *Müllerlieder* and *Winterreise,* or in his great so-called "concert-songs" (*Konzertgesänge*) (*Allmacht, Wanderer, Prometheus, Gruppe aus dem Tartarus,* etc.), and pointing forwards to the broadly and freely planned "romance" or the solo cantata. It is not for nothing that "*Lieder und Gesänge*" is found upon the title-page of so many of his collections of songs; it serves as an outward sign that, as regards solo songs with piano accompaniment, he was far from giving his undivided adherence to the narrow strophic form.

In accordance with the similarity of feeling — the somewhat limited emotional range of Brahms's songs, accompanied by a wide diversity and distinctive quality as regards music and form — is the uniform treatment of the piano accompaniments, the composition of which is as a rule to be referred to a few typically Brahmsian technical formulas. The chief and most fundamental of these consists in the use of broken chords in extended position. On the other hand, we find a very wide use of strictly contrapuntal pianoforte accompaniments, often forming a canon with the vocal part — I may cite by way of example *Wie sich Rebenranken schwingen* from op. 3. But the main thing in his eyes was always a clear-cut, beautifully conceived melody, and a decided handling of the bass on good contrapuntal lines. "This is all I read," he said to Jenner on another occasion, smilingly covering the upper stave of the pianoforte accompaniment with one hand, and thus, by reading only the vocal part and the bass, putting the soundness of the composition, both in form and feeling, to a decisive test. "The bass must be a sort of reflection (*Spiegelbild*) of the upper part," as he said to Heuberger. Words expressive of mere "atmosphere" were of as little value in his eyes as accompaniments which merely supplied "atmosphere." He held that the conception of the whole must never be lost sight of in the details. The motto should be: "More out of fullness (*Mehr aus dem Vollen*)." His unerring, severe self-criticism and long, practical experience caused him to set to work slowly and conscientiously, with mature deliberation, even at his songs. "Do you think a single one of my 'few decent songs (*paar ordentlichen Liedern*)' came into my head complete in every detail? I had the deuce of a time with them (*Da hab' ich mich kurios geplagt*)," he confessed to Heuberger. "When an idea comes into your head," was his advice to Jenner, "just go out for a walk. Then you will find that what you took for a perfect idea was only the makings of one." It seemed to him unprofitable to do any of the working-out before the scheme of the whole was completed either in one's head or on paper. But when it came to the working-out, he followed a whole series of golden rules. The first was: a subtle, artistic treatment of the pauses, based on the structure and metre of the verses. The second: a correct handling of the cadences, with special precautions against the choice of untimely six-four chords. The third was: carefully related modulations. The fourth: uniformity of rhythm between the words and music. The fifth: a sound harmonic basis.

Any comprehensive examination of Brahms's songs, including the choral works as well, is incomplete without a rapid glance at the poems on which they were based. "You have a fine collection of *poems* there, at any rate," said the master modestly, early in the eighties, to his Krefeld friend Rudolf von der Leyen, when the latter showed him his collection of Brahms's songs. And fourteen years later, during his last visit to the Rhine, on the occasion of Clara Schumann's funeral, he said to Dr. Gustav Ophüls, one of his circle of friends at Krefeld: "I have often wished I had a collection of the words which I have set to music — both for their own sake and because I am not fond of examining my music too closely, but am very glad at times to let it pass through my head while I read the words." The valuable full collection of all the words set by Brahms, published by Ophüls in a single thick volume, and annotated with philological thoroughness, which Brahms possessed in manuscript before it was printed, was one of the composer's last and greatest joys. And it is also a great joy to all those who love music and the art of Brahms; for the poets' words carry one back to Brahms's melodies, so that one experiences a double pleasure, the music suggesting the words, and the words the music.

Ophüls's book, which is well worth reading, is a unique Brahms anthology. At first sight it appears to be a mere statistical compilation made for a pastime. But this is by no means the case: it goes far beyond a mere dry collection of all the poets whose words were set to music by Brahms. In the first place, it shows us at a glance that Brahms possessed a fastidious and well-defined literary taste and was exceptionally widely read. This is not surprising in a man who, even as a child, knew no greater joy than to lay the foundation of what was to become his large and valuable library, by collecting books which he bought from the itinerant booksellers on the bridges and streets of old Hamburg. In his maturer years the composer had collected round him almost all the German poets, and hardly a single name of worth is missing. The Romantics of the early and middle period preponderate. We find all the dear, familiar names: Arnim, Brentano, Chamisso, Tieck (the songs from *Magelone*), Schenkendorf, Platen, Eichendorff, Hoffmann von Fallersleben, Rückert, Kugler, Kopisch, Simrock, Hölderlin, Uhland, Kerner, Mörike, Hölty, Halm, Heine, Daumer. Among his particular favourites were Rückert, Hölderlin (*Schicksalslied*), Hölty, Eichendorff, Tieck, Schenkendorf, Platen, Halm, and Hoffmann von Fallersleben, and of these, again, he prefers the simple natures, full of homely sentiment, and the elegiac love-poets, such as Hölty, Platen, and Daumer. Goethe, the prince of poets, is naturally the king of his Parnassus. His brother in Apollo, Schiller, is represented by two important pieces, *Abend* and *Nänie*. The name of

Daumer, the melancholy Bavarian erotic and romantic poet, brings us to the rarer and more curious among the poems set by Brahms: those, for instance, of the Alsatian Karl Candidus (*Tambour-liedchen, Jägerlied, Alte Liebe,* etc.), Karl Lemcke, a native of Schwerin, who was a professor at Stuttgart (*Soldatenlieder,* for male choir, *In Waldeseinsamkeit, Verrat,* etc.), C. O. Sternau (*An die Heimat*), the West Prussian Edward Ferrand (Schulz) (*Treue Liebe*), Melchior Grohe, who died in poverty at Naples (*O komme, holde Sommernacht*), Otto Friedrich Gruppe of Danzig (*Das Mädchen spricht*), the Westphalian Friedrich Ruperti (*Es tönt ein voller Harfenklang*), the German-Bohemian Alfred Meissner (*Sie ist gegangen, die Wonnen versanken*). We are already acquainted with his attitude towards modern literature and with his favourite contemporary poets, who were among his friends: Freytag, Heyse, Keller. I may here add Count von Schack and Hermann Lingg of Munich, Bodenstedt, the Balt Hans Schmidt, and the Swiss Adolf Frey.

Unlike Schubert, Schumann, Franz, and Hugo Wolf, Brahms had no particularly favourite poets, whole series and cycles of whose poems he set to music. All that can be said is that he showed a certain preference for Goethe, Schenkendorf, Eichendorff, Uhland, Hölty, Platen, Rückert, Hölderlin, Halm, Hoffmann von Fallersleben, Heine, Daumer, and Heyse, among others, and that in the case at least of Tieck — in the most splendid of his youthful songs, the *Magelone-Lieder,* op. 33 — and Daumer — in the *Acht Lieder und Gesänge,* op. 57 — he composed song-cycles which were settings of their elegiac love-poems. After a careful examination of Ophüls's book one obtains the impression that in choosing words for his songs Brahms was guided far less by the poet than by the atmosphere which he sought from both poem and poet. This was a thoroughly Romantic proceeding and reminds us slightly of Schumann, in that the latter would as a rule complete his piano-pieces first, and not prefix poetical mottoes and titles to them till afterwards.

Brahms's relation to the poets of his own part of the country — namely, Lower Germany, and in particular Schleswig-Holstein

— calls for particular attention. Brahms is by no means a " regional artist " in the modern sense of the word. When he set to music thirteen poems by Claus Groth, a native of his own part of the country, this was mainly due to good, personal reasons of friendship. At any rate, Brahms only very infrequently turned his attention to the great Low German " regional poets " of his own part of the country, Hebbel and Storm, setting three poems by Hebbel and only one by Storm. And the same remark applies to Voss, Geibel, Allmers, and Liliencron. This must arouse some surprise and wonder, when we think how much poets like Hebbel, Storm, Liliencron, and Allmers could have given him — to mention no other Low Germans. And this brings us to the question whether Brahms was always happy in the choice of his words, whether he always managed to select the most characteristic, valuable, and " musical " poem of every poet for setting to music. Unfortunately we cannot answer this question altogether in the affirmative. Brahms's choice of words was often far too much prompted by purely musical considerations and points of view, and too little by purely human considerations, to be always worthy of his uncommonly wide reading and good literary taste.

In two instances, however, Brahms was always particularly happy: in the choice of folk-poetry and of scriptural words. This great man of the people, whose sentimental nature required to be counterbalanced by the naïveté of folk-song, conceived this love for the folk-music of all times, nations, and peoples while still a boy and a young man. It never left him; indeed, it pervades the whole of his art, which, moreover, is only rightly to be understood if regarded as a homogeneous and organic blend of the deepest and most complicated mysteries of art with fresh, simple nature, interpreted in the true German folk-spirit. He wrote to Clara Schumann quite deliberately in January 1860: " Song is at present following such a wrong course that one can not hold up an ideal before one too consistently. And, in my opinion, this ideal is the folk-song." During his apprenticeship at Hamburg he already planned a collection of folk-songs, which he was always trying to increase. When, in 1853, he became

acquainted with student life at Göttingen for the first time, in the
company of his friend Joachim, what fascinated him far more
than all the drinking- and duelling-bouts were the stately patriotic
songs and the jolly students' songs, love-songs and drinking-songs,
in which he joined lustily, and some of which he noted down
for his collection. A generation later, in the *Akademische Festouvertüre,* these splendid days of his youth find a glorified
expression. In the summer of 1858 he begs Clara Schumann for
" songs by Eccard, Schütz, etc., and folk-songs." As a young
man Brahms made his debut in his first two piano sonatas with
variations on old folk-songs and love-songs; in the fifties and
sixties he continued this "folk" note in the collection of songs
forming op. 7, with its six simple songs, which almost produce
the effect of subtly sophisticated Brahmsian folk-songs, in the
Volks-Kinderlieder, for the children of Robert and Clara Schumann, and in the collection of German folk-songs for four-
part chorus dedicated to the Vienna Singakademie; and he remained faithful to it up to the last years of his life, in the great
collection of forty-nine folk-songs in seven books, arranged for
solo voice with piano.

Next to the folk-songs come the settings of scriptural texts.
The chapter on Brahms's songs is not the right place for a closer
appreciation of them, as evidence of a devotion to the Bible which
strikes us nowadays as almost fabulous, for none of the songs
falls under this category but the *Vier ernste Gesänge,* all the
other examples falling under the category of choral or organ
works. But an examination of Ophüls's book moves us to draw
due attention, here again, to the master's merit and delicate discrimination in the choice of his sacred texts from the Book of
books.

If we want to become acquainted with Brahms's personal
idiosyncrasies and place as a song-writer, we shall best find these
in a few of his song-cycles. The first and at the same time the
greatest of the song-cycles, which brought Brahms fame at a
single bound when he was barely thirty years old and placed
him in the front rank of the modern German masters of song-

writing, consists of the five books (op. 33), dedicated to his friend Julius Stockhausen, containing the fifteen uniquely lovely " romances " from Ludwig Tieck's *Wundersame Liebesgeschichte der schönen Magelone und des Grafen Peter aus der Provence* (1796) (*The Wondrous Love-story of the Fair Magelone and Count Peter of Provence*). We must therefore give a brief account here of the varied, adventurous contents of this romantic tale of love and chivalry, in a North German, rather bloodless Eichendorffian style, for the poems scattered through the text, all of which Brahms set to music, with the exception of two, have remained to a large extent incomprehensible, owing to their isolation from the context.

The young Count Peter of Provence wishes to leave his parents' house and go forth into the world. He is confirmed in this intention by a noble wandering minstrel from foreign lands (*" Keinen hat es noch gereut, der das Ross bestiegen "*). Peter follows his advice, takes leave of his parents, and rides off one glorious morning, singing gaily to his lute (*" Traun! Bogen und Pfeil sind gut für den Feind "*). He arrives in the great city of Naples, where there is a King Magelon, with a fascinating young daughter, Magelone; he sees her at a tournament, at which he is twice victorious, falls in love with her, and hurries from the banquet, intoxicated with love by her kindly parting glance, into the solitude of the wondrous summer night (*" Sind es Schmerzen, sind es Freuden, die durch meinen Busen ziehn? "*). Magelone confides to her nurse her deep, silent love for the modest but noble young foreign knight. At the instance of Magelone the nurse questions him in church as to his rank and name, and receives from him one of his mother's precious rings, into which he puts a little roll of parchment, containing words which betray his feelings for Magelone (*" Liebe kam aus fernen Landen "*). Magelone reads them and is deeply moved; she wheedles the ring out of her nurse, who still has scruples on the matter, hangs it round her neck on a fine necklace of pearls, and dreams a beautiful love-dream. The second meeting between the nurse and the knight in church ends with fresh vows of love and the offer of the second ring, with another roll of parchment (" *Willst du des Armen dich gnädig erbarmen?* "). Magelone is enraptured and dreams of her lover far into the night. The nurse meets Peter in church for the third time, makes him swear that his love is chaste and virtuous, and thereupon allows him to have an interview with Magelone in her chamber the next evening. Peter solaces his excess of happiness with song (" *Wie soll ich die Freude, die Wonne denn tragen?* "). He visits her, avows his deep love, gives her the third ring, plights her his troth, and takes his leave, only to confide his happiness once more to his beloved lute on reaching home (" *War es dir, dem diese Lippen bebten?* "). Meanwhile Magelone is to be married to Herr Heinrich von Carpone. Peter conquers Carpone in the joust, and Magelone resolves to flee with him by night to his father. Peter bids farewell to the chamber, the city, and his lute (" *Wir müssen uns trennen, geliebtes Saitenspiel* "). On their flight through wood and wold, Peter lays his weary lady-love to rest in the midday heat beneath the shade of a green tree and sings her softly to sleep (" *Ruhe, Süssliebchen, im Schatten der grünen dämmernden Nacht* "). But destiny is at hand. A black raven has stolen in among the flock of sweet, gentle birds gathered in the boughs above his sleeping love. When Peter discovers, with deep emotion, the three rings carefully wrapped up in a silken kerchief on his lady's breast and lays them beside him on the grass, the raven snatches them from him and flies off seawards, furiously pursued by Peter. It drops them into the water; Peter, beside himself with alarm, rows after it in a boat. A storm suddenly breaks, and drives him, distracted with despair, right out to sea (" *So tönet denn, schäumende Wellen und windet euch rund um mich her* "). Meanwhile Magelone awakes and sees, to her terror, that her lover has abandoned her, but finds the horses still tethered in the wood and then realizes that he is the innocent victim of some adventure. She looses the horses' reins, bids them go free and seek their master, and, after days of toilsome wandering through dense forests, arrives at a lonely shepherd's hut, where she is given a friendly reception by the old couple and tries to beguile her desolation by singing sadly as she spins (" *Wie schnell verschwindet so Licht als Glanz* "). Meanwhile Peter is picked up from his boat by a great ship manned by Moors and pagans, and appointed guardian of a lovely garden by the Sultan, who takes a fancy to him; he now loves to wander about it in solitude, thinking of his beloved Magelone (" *Muss es eine Trennung geben, die das treue Herz zerreisst?* "). The Sultan's lovely daughter, Sulima, falls in love with him; she tries to convince him that Magelone must long since be dead and to persuade him to flee with her. But Peter's fidelity and his unappeasable longing for Magelone win the day. He secretly launches a boat from the shore and rows out to sea, while the song of Sulima, who is waiting for him in vain, floats out from the garden (" *Geliebter, wo zaudert dein irrender Fuss?* "). The song dies away, and Peter is alone on the lonely sea. He lets his boat drift and sings merrily to himself (" *Wie froh und frisch mein Sinn sich hebt* "). In the end Peter's fidelity is rewarded. He is tossed hither and thither on a long and devious course, picked up by a great Christian ship on its way to France, left inadvertently on a desert island, rescued by two fishermen, and directed to an old shepherd who will succour him. This is naturally the old man with whom Magelone is living. He hears her singing, finds the hut and the simple shepherdess Magelone, whom he does not recognize until she appears before him in splendid attire as a king's daughter. Their joy is almost more than they can bear. Peter journeys back to his parents with his newly-found Magelone and marries her. The good old shepherds are royally rewarded, and Peter and his young wife plant a tree on the spot as an everlasting memorial to the miracle of her rediscovery, and revisit it every spring in order to consecrate it anew in song (" *Treue Liebe dauert lange* ").

In these glorious " romances " Brahms's personality, both as man and as artist, wears a most individual guise, revealing itself in a nobly youthful aspect: fresh, open, at times afire with passion, at times dreamy and romantic to the core. In the breadth and amplitude of its plan, construction, and melodic content — which in the very first number herald a departure from the strophic *Lied* form and break its narrow bonds — in the unusually rich flow of its thematic material, in its blending of the dramatic, scenic, and pictorial, on the one hand, with the folk-spirit on the other, the style of the *Magelone-Lieder* again recalls his youthful instrumental works, and especially the piano sonatas. Instead of short, strophic repetitions, he constructs great periods and theme-groups. Other features, as, for instance, the preludes and concluding passages, which are often developed at some length, and at times even based upon new motifs, still recall Schumann. But never does Brahms strike the weak note of a mere minor successor of the Romantics; it is all full of spontaneous inspiration and feeling, all is strong, sound to the core, full of warm humanity, direct, and beautiful.

The easiest way of approaching the characteristic tone of these *Magelone-Lieder* is through those of the songs which treat of the pains and pleasures of love. And what love-songs! We find some, such as the third song, " *Sind es Schmerzen, sind es Freuden,*" which are a blend of sweet intimations of love and an idyllic nature spirit with a youthful turmoil of longing and surging passion. This tone of stormy youthful desire is continued in the fifth, sixth, and seventh songs: " *So willst du des Armen,*" " *Wie soll ich die Freude, die Wonne denn tragen?* " and " *War es dir, dem diese Lippen bebten?* " — in the first in passionate accents of tremulous joy, in the second with more confidence and charm and more romantic feeling (for instance, in the wonderful middle section, in C sharp major, " *Schlage, sehnsüchtige Gewalt,*" with its harmony recalling *Das Rheingold* by its diminished intervals, and the ecstasy, softening to languor, of its concluding section, in F sharp major, " *Ach wie bald* "), in the third in ardent, yearning insistence and accents saturated with emotion. There are also romances like the ninth, " *Ruhe, Süssliebchen, im Schatten,*" which are akin not only to this collection, but to the general type of Brahms's songs, in their division into two parts as regards both form and feeling, in their contrast between the brooding oppressiveness and subdued noonday stillness of nature on the one hand, and the excited imagination and passionate aspiration of the lover towards all that is most glorious on the other. And how homogeneously the second section is developed thematically out of the first! Lastly, we have love-laments, such as the eleventh and twelfth songs, the rapt, plaintive " *Wie schnell verschwindet so Licht als Glanz* " (sung by Magelone), with the delicate figures adorning the accompaniment in a closely knit canon form at the repetition of the principal theme, and the tender, mournful agitation of " *Muss es eine Trennung geben?* " (sung by Peter), with the eloquent, tenderly assuaging piano interlude and concluding passage. The dramatic, scenic quality of so many of these *Magelone* songs is most strongly present in the tenth, entitled *Verzweiflung* (*Despair*) to the words: " *So tönet denn, schäumende Wellen.*" This song, Peter's outburst of impotent fury as he sees himself carried right out to sea in his frail boat, is a uniquely lovely, highly dramatic, and concisely conceived nature-scene, with its plastic musical representation of the tossing sea, in which the turmoil of nature and of the human heart are in such splendid harmony, as in the great sea-scenes in C. M. von Weber's *Oberon;* it may therefore be most fitly grouped with the sea-choruses in Brahms's *Rinaldo,* which were influenced by Weber. The chivalrous note in the romanticism of *Magelone* is stressed in the first two songs only, the stirring " *Keinen hat es noch gereut, der das Ross bestiegen,*" with its horn-calls and " galloping " motif — one can positively see the noble steed galloping off with the young man thirsting for great exploits — and the virile defiance and forceful rhythm of " *Traun! Bogen und Pfeil sind gut für den Feind!* " Brahms has entirely abstained from the use of any oriental local colour; the thirteenth song, *Sulima,* with its Schumannesque rhythms and light, tripping movement, is as German as all the rest. Tone-colour and pictorial effects, too, are only used by Brahms sparingly and with a dignified conventionality. The lute, the troubadour's instrument, is plainly heard in the piano accompaniment only in the third song (" *Sind es Schmerzen* "), and particularly in the eighth (" *Wir müssen uns trennen, geliebtes Saitenspiel* ").

The concluding number of the whole cycle is of wonderfully tranquil and serene beauty, consisting of an animated middle section (" *Errungen, bezwungen von Lieb' ist das Glück* "), which represents the final reunion of the two lovers by a triplet rhythm quivering with joy, set off against a soft, slow principal movement in which " the poet speaks" (*Der Dichter spricht*) in somewhat Schumannesque accents.

As we read in his biography, young Brahms wrote the first book of these *Magelone* songs in the summer of 1862, at Münster am Stein, at the foot of the ruined castle of Ebernburg, where he and Dietrich were staying with Frau Clara Schumann and her children. And so their "local colour" is in general that of the romantic, legéndary Nahetal near Kreuznach, with its towering crags, where we already feel the air of the Rhine.

But just as in the *Magelone-Lieder* we hear the voice of the happy young lover, so in the two books containing eight *Lieder und Gesänge von G. F. Daumer,* op. 57, we hear that of the unhappy lover, and in the *Vier ernste Gesänge,* op. 121, that of the deeply resigned pessimist, coming to terms philosophically with life and death. Daumer (1800–75), a clergyman who taught at the gymnasium at Nuremberg, and whose name we look for in vain in the current histories of literature, was a favourite poet of Brahms's, who set to music fifty-four in all of his original poems or adaptations of foreign folk-poetry. The Daumer cycle may be called Brahms's *Winterreise* or *Dolorosa.* It rings the changes on the theme of unhappy love, in eight poems which their ardently sensuous character and tone render unsuitable for the family circle. On reading them one may perhaps at first be shocked by isolated touches of bombast (" *liebefeuchte Sehe,*" " *Huldgebärden,*" " *mit dem Ätherfuss schweben,*" " *himmlische Genüge geben* "), but the ear will soon grow accustomed to the prevailing tone of this poetry: an ardent, somewhat undisguised sensuality, with a touch of sultry oppressiveness, a romantic sensibility, delicate nature-poetry with the tragically romantic motif, recurring like a ground-bass, of a sensibility intense to the verge of effeminacy, a hopeless, self-pitying, unhappy love, yearning love-agony, and a devouring longing which consumes itself in uncontrolled ardour. In the first book we have the love-lament of the woman, in the second that of the man.

Brahms has not entirely succeeded in avoiding the very characteristic, not very stimulating tone of this poetry even in his music, greatly though this idealizes and transfigures it and brightens it by wonderful nature-scenes. Tender, broken, sultrily subdued colour, iridescent harmonies hovering between major and minor, rich modulations, a strongly chromatic character, and a sometimes morbidly soft and sentimental tendency give the music of this song-cycle an aspect all its own. Songs such as the second ("*Wenn du nur zuweilen lächelst*"), the third ("*Es träumte mir, ich sei dir teuer*"), the sixth ("*Strahlt zuweilen auch ein mildes Licht*"), and the seventh ("*Die Schnur, die Perl' an Perle um deinen Hals gereihte*") might have been written by Adolph Jensen, the tender singer of the *Dolorosa* cycle. In these and other numbers we shall also be irresistibly reminded of Schumann. These songs are in a more miniature style than that of the *Magelone-Lieder,* so their form is naturally incomparably more concise and approximates more nearly to that of the *Lied;* it is only the sombre glow of the famous No. 8, a "night-piece" ("*Unbewegte, laue Luft*"), to the words of Eichendorff, the pearl of this collection, with the faint, silvery plash of its fountains ("*durch die stille Gartennacht plätschert die Fontäne nur*"), that the sharply defined division into two parts (one representing the profound quiet of nature and the other the stormy passion of man), the contrast between the slow and the animated *tempo,* and the ampler form which this requires, recall the first and finest of Brahms's song-cycles. Once only in the first book does this tender sentiment rise by its supreme inward intensity to a tragic grandeur of pathos like that of Beethoven, and that is in the fourth song ("*Ach, wende diesen Blick, wende dies Angesicht!*"), with its magnificently rounded-off form in three sections, in the middle section, in D flat major, at the words: "*wenn einmal die gequälte Seele ruht.*" In the eyes of many this one incomparably lovely page

will be worth more than the whole of the cycle together. Brahms
has deliberately opened it with an idyllic nature-scene (" *Von
waldbekränzter Höhe werf' ich den heissen Blick* "), which in
its more tranquil central section at once plunges this deeply
sensitive human creature into a fresh, bright setting of nature in
springtime.

The *Vier ernste Gesänge,* for solo bass voice with pianoforte
accompaniment, were the master's last work but one and were
published a year before his death. It has often been believed
that they were inspired by the death of his dearest friend and
enthusiastic prophetess, Clara Schumann. But they were already
finished when that noble artist died. In a letter to Frau Schumann's daughters Brahms afterwards alluded to them as follows:
" If a book of *Serious Songs* (*Ernsthafte Gesänge*) arrives shortly,
do not misinterpret the gift. Quite apart from the dear old habit
of writing your name first, the songs also concern you most
seriously. I wrote them in the first week of May [i.e., in 1896,
the year of Clara Schumann's death]; I am often occupied with
words of that kind, but I did not expect to hear worse news of
your mother — but there is often something that speaks and
works deep down in one, almost unconsciously, and at times it
may well clothe itself in sound, as poetry or music. You cannot
try the songs over, for the words would be too moving for you
at present. But I ask you to regard them as really a funeral offering for your dear mother and to lay them aside." On the other
hand, the great Leipzig sculptor and engraver Max Klinger
claims with full justification that they were dedicated to him,
a claim confirmed by a letter to him from Brahms in the June
of that year: " According to Brahms's letter to me, the songs owe
their origin to the purely personal relations between us, and
I am far too proud of it to refrain from stigmatizing the above-
mentioned legend as such [i.e., the origin of the songs after, and
as a result of, Clara Schumann's death]. Besides, Brahms would
have announced quite unequivocally such a cause for their origin
as the death of his most intimate friend would have been, as he
did in dedicating the *Nänie* to Frau Feuerbach."

However this may be, these four songs embody for us one of the master's most important testaments and personal confessions. The trend of ideas in the scriptural texts, selected by Brahms himself, of which they are a setting, can be seen at a glance to be akin to those of the *Deutsches Requiem*. For here, too, they culminate in the last song in a firm, beatific faith in God and the all-subduing power of love: " And now abideth faith, hope, charity, these three; but the greatest of these is charity." But the process by which he attained this serene resignation is quite different; it is a harder and more serious one. He is already deeply, heavily overshadowed by the gnawing doubts and bitter protests of modern man. These *Four Serious Songs* approach even nearer to the first great motet of op. 74 than to the *Deutsches Requiem: Warum ist das Licht gegeben den Mühseligen?* The *Vier ernste Gesänge* are the moving and deeply heart-stirring swan-song of a great artist, who took life harder, perhaps, than any other artist of modern days, whose life was made up of care and toil, and to whom death came, not, as to the needy, aged, and infirm, as a beneficent and longed-for saviour, but as the grim, pitiless destroyer of a rich life, still busied with a thousand plans. A heavy, sombre tone of virile resignation and the most profound *Weltschmerz* underlie this typical work of Brahms's later years; in it, too, " Christian " faith and dogma appear deepened into the " pagan " creed of modern personality. Indeed, the first three songs positively steep themselves, with a painful pleasure, in sombre ideas of the crying contradictions between the ideal world of Christianity and that of modern reality. The first song (Ecclesiastes iii), the content of which forms an absolute pendant to the second movement of the *Deutsches Requiem* (" For all flesh is as grass "), places man on the same level as the beasts in his mortality and transiency (" All are of the dust, and all turn to dust again ") and asks in poignant doubt: " Who knoweth the spirit of man that goeth upward, and the spirit of the beast that goeth downward to the earth?" The second song (ibid., iv) exalts the dead above the living, in its recognition of the injustice born of force, which is going on upon earth at every moment — "Yea, better is he than both they, which hath not yet been." The third song (Sirach xli) praises death as the bitter enemy of those who revel carelessly or thoughtlessly in wealth and luxury, and the gentle benefactor of the miserable, the poor, and the sick. It is not till the fourth song (I Corinthians xiii) that at last, in his bitterest need, he points to faith, hope, and charity as the way out of the fearful labyrinth of these torturing perceptions.

The musical style of these "serious songs" is monumentally rugged and unadorned, this effect being arrived at by the simplest and plainest means. The comparative lack of elaboration in the musical workmanship may at times seem almost poverty-stricken if, as happens only too often in the case of this work, both singer and accompanist approach their task in a superficial spirit and fail to realize its fundamental character, which is that of a gravely weighty, sombre, and virile Old Testament pathos. But when they succeed in striking the right note — and great German singers such as Julius Stockhausen, Karl Scheidemantel, and Felix von Kraus are perhaps the most shining examples of this — its serene tragedy and profound impressiveness can not fail of their effect. Here, too, as in the case of the great choral works with a classical antique tinge, such as the *Schicksalslied,* the way in which Brahms's softer side prevails in the end determines the general effect of the whole. In the beatific serenity of these wonderful strains, magnificent in their amplitude, fluttering downward as on the white wings of angels to a soft harp accompaniment, in which, at the end of the last song, he exalts love, which reconciles all things, we are able, as in hardly any other of his works, to look right into Brahms's good and noble heart — a heart which "gained knowledge through pity (*durch Mitleid wissend*)." There are isolated touches in the preceding songs, too, which also enable us to do so: for example, the passage in the second song, where, in a coloratura passage which springs from the inmost heart, the vocal part bewails those tears which are forced from us by the unjust sufferings of the innocent; or where, in the third song, death appears to the poor and oppressed as a consoler,

accompanied by soft, smooth sequences on the piano, suggestive
of church music.

The *Vier ernste Gesänge* have been called a second *Deutsches
Requiem*. We have already pointed out the contrast and parallel
between the words above. In the music it is displayed most clearly
in the two middle numbers and in the principal theme of the
last song. In these a whole world separates Brahms's latest style
from that of his younger days, when he composed the *Requiem*.
On the other hand, a parallel can certainly be established between
the *Requiem* and the first song, besides the coda of the last
one. The first song may be compared with the funeral march in
the second movement of the *Requiem,* which is treated in the
same rugged way, as a lament over the transience of all flesh;
and the broad, serene melody of the concluding *adagio* — " For
now we see as through a glass darkly (*Wir sehen jetzt durch
einen Spiegel in einem dunkeln Worte*) " — with all those parts
of the *Deutsches Requiem* which combine quiet mourning with
gentle consolation.

Brahms and German folk-song! We have seen above, in examining the folk-poems or scriptural words which he set to
music, how deeply and intimately it is bound up with his work,
how it runs, as it were, like a scarlet thread through his whole
life and production. He began with instrumental variations or
folk-tunes in his three piano sonatas, and with some songs " in the
folk style (*im Volkston*)," op. 7. As a young man he completed
this early folk-music group with the fourteen *Volks-Kinderlieder,*
which he published in 1858 unsigned and without opus number,
and dedicated to the children of Robert and Clara Schumann,
whose intimate circle on the Rhine and at Baden-Baden provides
their setting. Scarcely one of the best-known favourites among
German children's songs is missing: the *Sandmann, Dornröschen,
Heidenröslein, Marienwürmchen, Der Jäger in dem Walde,* and
so on. Equally childlike in its simplicity is the treatment of the
pianoforte accompaniment which he has added. Only in a few
cases has Brahms used it as a musical " commentary," as discreet
as it is lovely, upon the words: in the *Sandmann,* the pearl of the

collection, where we can positively see the little man scattering
the bright, glittering, sleepy drops on the child with his magic
wand; in the *Wiegenlied,* where we can hear the cradle rocking
gently in the bass; in *Das Mädchen und die Hasel,* in which,
in the figure in thirds in the left hand, the little girl seems to
trip daintily up to the spray of roses in the hedge; and in *Marienwürmchen,* in which the right hand illustrates the little wandering light in nimble quavers. In the rest the piano generally follows
the voice in chords.

But the greatest and best-known of Brahms's folk-song cycles
was produced by the composer in his later years, the *Deutsche
Volkslieder,* with pianoforte accompaniment, which appeared
in 1894. They represent the solo counterpart to the *Deutsche
Volkslieder* for mixed choir, which were also published without
opus number. The former comprise seven volumes, containing
in all forty-nine songs; the seventh and last book, containing
seven songs, is arranged, according to the old North German
usage, especially in Schleswig-Holstein and Ditmarsh, for solo
voices and small mixed choir; and thus the end of the composer's
life closes with a meditative backward glance towards its beginning. In it we again find the old, Lower Rhenish folk-song
Verstohlen geht der Mond auf, which served as the theme of
the short variations in the slow movement of the First Piano
Sonata, in C major.

Brahms was much attached to this collection of German folk-
songs. "It is quite the first time," he confessed to Deiters, "that
I have followed any of my productions out into the world with
a fond eye." And in sending it to Professor Bächtold of Zürich,
the biographer of Keller, he says that he does so, "for once in
a way, with particular pleasure." It was to this gifted scholar
and musician, too, that he himself said shortly and concisely
what his intentions had been in this collection: "It is a collection
of German folk-songs with piano accompaniment. I think it will
bring you something new, for if you have taken an interest in
the music of our folk-songs, have Erk and Böhme been your
leaders? They have long since set the tone, and a very Philistine

one it was; my collection takes a completely opposite line." We have already seen, in his collection of folk-songs for mixed choir, in what spirit Brahms arranged the folk-poetry and folk-tunes of the old popular songs, with his infinitely subtle, sympathetic insight into their spirit. These collections of solo folk-songs with piano accompaniment were naturally bound to meet with quite as much sharp disapprobation as enthusiastic approval, owing to the two fundamentally divergent tendencies which existed in the setting of folk-songs: one preferring a plain setting of chords, harmonized on the simplest lines, the other a pianoforte accompaniment skilfully enhanced by subtle delicacy of workmanship in harmonizing, rhythms, and figuration alike. As an artist, Brahms decides for the second, though, with the trustful confidence of the artist in all musical erudition, he used as the source of his own arrangements the collection of *Deutsche Volkslieder mit ihren Originalweisen* published by A. Kretschmer and Zuccalmaglio in 1840, of which he thought very highly, though, as Max Friedländer later pointed out, a small number of the songs in that old collection are not original tunes, but were written, sometimes as parodies, by composers of the old Berlin school of eighteenth-century song-writers, Johann Friedrich Reichardt and Friedrich Nicolai.

Brahms's collections of German folk-songs are miniature gems elaborated with enchantingly finished musical art by the hand of a great master, who, with his heart-felt and loyal devotion, saw concentrated in these immortal melodies, in the clearest and most concise form and with the greatest universality of appeal, the qualities which were entirely lacking in his own art: namely, naïveté and the folk-spirit. He felt it to be his duty to take these diamonds, smooth them, polish them, and skilfully furbish them up, in order to save them for his people by means of his art. This may be open to criticism, but the idea was a fine and noble one, and its execution was even finer and nobler. How fine and noble Clara Schumann's words to the young composer express in the most beautiful way: "But I must indeed beg you, my dear friend, not to give the songs all the credit for what I said to you about folk-songs. One has only to ask oneself the simple questions: What are the songs without accompaniment? And what are they with yours? You yourself must know best of all that such an accompaniment, such a handling of them, such a grasp of the characteristic quality of each and every song, such an intimate interweaving of melody and harmony, often with such fine, delicate touches, in which one is soon unable to think of the one without the other — in short, that none but a genius, a nature that is all poetry and music, is capable of creating such things — and such a one you are, and know that you are!"

The style of Brahms's duets is at first, in the earliest examples, closely related to that of Mendelssohn and Schumann. And this on the whole indicates the musical character of the first book, op. 20, containing three duets for soprano and alto: a pleasing type of music suited for amateur performance, in which the scheme of the two vocal parts does not arise out of the words, as it were by an inward necessity, and which prefers a pleasingly vocal parallel treatment of the voices to an artful blending and interweaving of them. The most Mendelssohnian of the three numbers in this book is the last, *Die Meere* ("*Alle Winde schlafen auf dem Spiegel der Flut*"): a dreamy, swaying barcarole in soft thirds in 6/8 time, something in the style of Mendelssohn's "*Venetianische Gondellieder*" from the *Lieder ohne Worte*. The two others — the exultant hymn to the omnipotence and omnipresence of love in the first number ("*Über die Berge, über die Wellen*"; *Weg der Liebe,* from Herder's *Stimmen der Völker,* I), and its pendant in the second, full of a deep, intense inspiration and quiet concentration ("*Den gordischen Knoten, den Liebe sich band*"), with the lovely contrary movement between the voices and piano — in spite of their parallel treatment of the two vocal parts, in the older manner of Mendelssohn and Schumann, already contain harmonic elements, at least, which are all Brahms's own. But in the next book of duets, op. 28, for alto and baritone, dedicated to Amalie Joachim, the case is already different. From this volume onwards, with its first number, the effective ballad *Die Nonne und der Ritter* (to Eichendorff's words), the Brahms duets take on a wider development, into real songs for two voices, in which each vocal part is treated as an independent personality, being often constructed with the greatest skill — as, for example, in the second section of the first number of the *Klänge,* which is heightened by a canon in contrary motion at a fifth below.

Brahms's duets are more especially a mine of his mocking, roguish humour and include quite a nice little collection of choice and lively pieces: for example, *Vor der Tür* (old German words), *Der Jäger und sein Liebchen* (Hoffmann von Fallersleben) from op. 28; *Die Schwestern,* a slow, pensive dance-tune in simple strophic form, like a folk-song, in which there are two worldly sisters who have an unhappy love for the same young man; and their spiritual counterpart, Justinus Kerner's *Klosterfräulein* from the *Vier Duetten* for soprano and alto, op. 61, who touchingly bewails her cloistered state; the mocking *" Hüt' du dich"* (*Des Knaben Wunderhorn*) from the *Fünf Duetten* for soprano and alto, op. 66, with all kinds of fascinating little rhythmical pitfalls hidden in the piano part; and the jolly *Guter Rat,* the good advice of the mother to her daughter who wants a husband (*Des Knaben Wunderhorn*) from the *Balladen und Romanzen,* op. 75 — but, above all, the *Vergebliches Ständchen,* which has gone all round the world, from the *Romanzen und Lieder* for two voices, op. 84, a collection which may quite well be sung as solos, but were intended as a dialogue, so to speak, for two voices, and are worked up into regular little lyrical scenes.

The majority of serious numbers in these collections of duets sing the pains and pleasures of love. Among them we have exultant pæans full of a tumultuous rush of passion, such as Wenzig's buoyant *Boten der Liebe* from op. 61, pleasing idylls and barcaroles such as Hölty's *Am Strande,* with its charming canon in the middle section (*" Aus fernen, verklungenen Tagen spricht's heimlich mit sanften Stimmen zu mir "*), sombre German forest scenes, such as Candidus's passionate but restrained *Jägerlied* from op. 66, constructed in the terse folk-song form of question (in the major) and answer (in the minor), or songs

of the road, full of deep feeling and overflowing with joy, such
as the Bohemian " *So lass uns wandern,*" from op. 75.

On the other hand, we may see what serious effects may be
achieved in the true duet from numbers such as the two deeply
resigned *Klänge* from op. 66, to the words of Claus Groth, or
the dæmonic *Edward* from op. 75, recalling the piano ballade
of the same name from op. 10, with which it may be compared,
or the fantastic *Walpurgisnacht* (Alexis) from the same volume,
which may be compared with that of Mendelssohn and was
greeted with particular delight by Clara Schumann. The only
tragic Brahms duet, which far surpasses all the other numbers
in these collections, alike in length and importance of content, is
the old Scottish ballad of *Edward* from Herder's *Stimmen der
Völker*. In it the terse, supremely concentrated form of op. 10,
no. 1, is given a broad and powerful rendering in a sort of strophic
form, with a varied accompaniment to each verse of the song
(*durchkomponierte Strophenform*). The rigid, stony calm of the
piano ballade becomes in the song a sombre, uncannily seething
agitation, rising to a high pitch of dramatic intensity in the
murderer's dying shrieks. The note-for-note correspondence between Edward's cry of " O, I hae killed my fadir deir, Mither,
Mither! " (D flat major) and the beginning of the principal
subject of the E flat major Rhapsody for piano (op. 119, no. 4) is
so great and striking that we may perhaps venture to conclude
that there is a conscious reminiscence of this great duet in the
rhapsody, due to a similarity of poetical subject-matter. And on
the other hand, when the composer opens the second of the
deeply mournful numbers in op. 66, set to the words of Claus
Groth (" *Wenn ein müder Leib begraben, klingen Glocken ihn
zur Ruh' *"), by introducing in the bass the beginning of the
theme of the variations from the *andante* of his Second, " Schumannesque," Piano Sonata, op. 2, in F sharp minor, and, by his
treatment of the accompaniment, conjures up the magic of
Schumann's gentle, softly wreathing arabesques, this appears to
me to be another of those many ingenious and mysteriously concealed pieces of musical symbolism (*Tonsymbole*) of which

Brahms was so fond: once again, by a softly melancholy reminiscence, these tolling bells are ringing the knell of his beloved
master and prophet.

It seems bold to include the *Zwei Gesänge für eine Altstimme
mit Bratsche und Pianoforte* (*Two Songs for Contralto Solo
with viola and piano*), op. 91, the sole contribution of the composer to the type of solo song with instrumental accompaniment,
among the Brahms duets. And yet this may be defended, for
in his hands the viola, too, became a noble instrument of song.
The crown of this volume is the second number, E. Geibel's
Geistliches Wiegenlied after the Spanish of Lope de Vega ("*Die
ihr schwebet um diese Palmen*"). This song came into being as
early as the middle sixties; it was the composer's musical gift
to Joseph and Amalie Joachim for the christening of their first
son, Johannes. Elisabeth von Herzogenberg has rightly laid stress
upon the old-world, "legendary tone" of this superb song. Like
Max Reger in our day, in his *Marias Wiegenlied*, Brahms has
with mischievous symbolism freely interwoven his accompaniment with old Calvisius's wonderfully lovely Christmas carol,
dating from the sixteenth century, "*Josef, lieber Josef mein.*"
With dignified discretion Brahms has avoided all attempt to
suggest in his music the rustling palms beneath which the holy
pair are resting; it is not till the middle section, with the growing
gloom of its F minor mood — "*Der Himmelsknabe duldet
Beschwerde; ach, wie so müd' er ward vom Leid der Erde* (The
heavenly Child suffers grievous pain; ah! how weary was he of
the suffering of earth)" — where the sword of burning pain
and anxiety for the future first pierces the Virgin Mother's heart,
that the palms begin to sway softly, as though in sympathy, in
the *legato* quaver triplets. The first number — "*In goldnen
Abendschein getauchet, wie feierlich die Wälder stehn* (Bathed in
the golden evening glow, how solemnly the forests stand)" — is
a setting of Rückert's words, full of yearning longing, transfigured
by the softest, sweetest sadness. The viola and the alto voice sing
their parts in alternation; the piano supplies a background of
tender Brahmsian arpeggio figures.

The collections of solo quartets with pianoforte accompaniment, op. 31, 64, 92, and 112, are, with two exceptions — the *Liebeslieder-Walzer,* op. 52 and op. 65, and the *Zigeunerlieder,* op. 103 — as seldom heard in the concert-hall as the duets. Perhaps it is those numbers in which the composer can dream and rhapsodize in romantic, poetic fashion that speak most directly to our hearts. Among these are particularly included most of the lyrical nature pictures, which are also uniquely beautiful in their tonal effects, in the collections op. 64, *An die Heimat* (to Sternau's words) and *Der Abend* (Schiller); and op. 92, *O schöne Nacht* (Daumer), *Abendlied* (Hebbel), and *Spätherbst* (Allmers). In these compositions we have a precious gem of North German "regional" music in the broadest sense of the word. In his hymn of praise *An die Heimat,* Brahms confesses his ardent love for the soil of his Low German homeland in tender tones saturated with emotion and almost worthy of Schumann; at the very beginning how wonderful is the effect of the two crescendo and diminuendo cries of "*Heimat!*" above the hymnlike, undulating arpeggio passages on the piano; with what ardent aspirations does his heart soar upwards as though on "feathery pinions (*auf befiederten Schwingen*)" in the fugal entries of the four voices; with what blissful, profound tranquillity does he meditate in the evening glow ("*liebende Heimat*") in soulful, *stretto* passages in canon and tender suspensions recalling the style of Franz Abt! In the next number, a setting of Schiller's splendid *Abend* ("*Senke, strahlender Gott*"), this evening peace takes on the mild, august, serene tone of Brahms's choral works in the classical antique style. This composition, with the wonderful, clarified quality of its form, seems to be positively overshadowed by the heavy, oppressive calm of nature thirsting for refreshing rain. Brahms has represented this most graphically by quite simple means in the principal subject, by means of a bass which seems to trail languidly along, with a tone as of *pizzicato* 'cellos, and by overloaded harmonies, densely compressed parts, and strongly chromatic progressions. The middle section represents the apparition of the divine love-bringing Thetis, in a graceful alternating

melody above soft, wave-like arpeggios on the piano. In the
first song of op. 92 we pass from evening into night. As always
happens when he plunges into the erotic atmosphere of Daumer's
poetry, Brahms involuntarily echoes the ecstasy of Wagner's Mid-
summer Night in the *Meistersinger* distantly by his tender, harplike arpeggios, syncopated octave passages on the wood-wind, and
charming nature and tonal effects on the piano, as, for instance,
on the words " *mit Macht im Fliederbusche schlägt die Nachtigall*
(the nightingale in the elder-tree warbles with all its might)."
But what a tender, mysterious emotion fills his heart at the exquisite passage in C major, where " Softly the boy to his beloved
steals (*Der Knabe schleicht zu seiner Liebsten sacht*) " ! The
remaining contribution of this volume to what may be called
the " nocturne (*Notturno*) " for solo quartet, the setting of Hebbel's *Abendlied,* is one of those songs of Brahms's which seem
to defend themselves against superficial intrusion by a certain
reserved coldness and aristocratic colourlessness of inspiration;
but deeper study is richly rewarded by the ecstatic, typically
Brahmsian progressions at the end, as in the passage " *Kommt mir
das Leben ganz wie ein Schlummerlied vor* (Life seems to me
just like a lullaby)," darkened, as it were, by the falling shades
of night. But it is op. 112 that furnishes the last " night-piece "
for solo quartet, in its setting of Kugler's *Nächtens*. It is unique
among Brahms's solo quartets, not only in its strictly worked-
out irregular construction on a five-bar period, but also as a
" character piece " full of sombre, passionate agitation and profound melancholy. We are familiar with such " night-pieces "
of Brahms's, full of an atmosphere of erotic passion, from his
settings of Daumer's words or from the intermezzi and capricci
for piano in minor keys. The restless tremolo on the piano
does not cease for a single bar; the separate verses are preceded,
connected, and followed by a two-bar motif on the piano.

The few remaining songs in these collections (the odd four
" Zigeunerlieder " of op. 112 are dealt with at the same time as
the work of that name, op. 103) maintain the same grave tone
as these evening and night pieces. And here we must particularly

praise Kugler's *Sehnsucht,* from op. 112, as a genuine specimen
of Brahms's elegiac, resigned mood. In the middle section of this
number — "*Du gedenkest der vergangenen Zeit, die liegt so
weit* (Thou dost think of the days that are past, the times that
are far away) " — the ageing composer has subtly introduced
the beginning of the love-theme from *Tristan* into the tenor
part; may this not be a tender, moving reminiscence of the first
and only deep love of his youth on the Rhine?

By far the greater number of the remaining songs in these
books of solo quartets, like so many of the duets, consist of fascinating pearls of teasing, roguish folk humour. To this category
belongs the whole of op. 31, the first two numbers of which
already contain echoes of the *Liebeslieder-Walzer,* with its delightful setting of Goethe's *Wechsellied zum Tanze,* and two
musical folk-poems, the exquisite *Neckereien* (a Moravian air)
and the Bohemian *Gang zum Liebchen,* with its intense feeling,
the words of which he also set later as a solo (op. 48, no. 1). To
this we may add Daumer's *Fragen,* from op. 64, a good half of
which has a tinge of erotic, passionate pathos, in which the solo
quartet inquisitively press the tenor, who is hopelessly and irrevo-
cably in love, with their questions — "'*Mein liebes Herz, was
ist dir?*' '*Ich bin verliebt, das ist mir*' ('Dear heart of mine,
what ails thee?' 'I love; that is what ails me') " — and Goethe's
Warum? from op. 92, in which the vehement questioning at the
beginning, in a sharply staccato rhythm in 4/4 time, is answered
by a gracefully animated motif in 6/8 time, perhaps a little trivial
from the musical point of view.

Of these collections of solo quartets with piano accompaniment two alone have met with universal acceptance in the concert-
halls of the whole world: the *Liebeslieder-Walzer,* op. 52, for
piano duet and voices (solo quartet) *ad libitum,* their continuation, the *Neue Liebeslieder-Walzer,* op. 65, for four voices and
piano duet, and the *Zigeunerlieder,* with accompaniment for
piano duet, op. 103. It is a pleasing and perhaps not altogether
fortuitous accident that the very first of these two splendid
masterpieces among Brahms's works for solo quartet had recourse

to an accompaniment for piano duet. If we recall in this connexion Brahms's two chief brilliant pieces for piano duet only,
the *Walzer,* op. 39, and the *Ungarische Tänze,* three of them give
the light, agreeable impression of music for the intimate circle.
But they are all bathed in the sunshine of the freshest folk-
humour and the most thorough-going *joie de vivre.* The gaiety
of the waltzes for piano duet and the *Liebeslieder-Walzer* has a
predominantly Viennese tinge, with only an occasional touch
of the Magyar spirit; in the Hungarian Dances and *Zigeunerlieder,* on the other hand, it is strongly and thoroughly Magyar.
As in the case of the waltzes for piano duet, op. 39, we will first
hear what Hanslick has to say:

" Brahms and waltzes! The two words stare at each other
in positive amazement on the elegant title-page. The earnest,
silent Brahms, a true younger brother of Schumann, and just as
North German, Protestant, and unworldly as he — writing
waltzes! There is only one word which solves the enigma, and
that is — Vienna. The imperial city induced Beethoven — not, it
is true, to dance, but to write dance-music; it led Schumann into
a carnival prank (*Faschingsschwank*); it might have ensnared
even Bach himself in the mortal sin of writing a *Ländler.*
Brahms's waltzes are the fruit of his residence in Vienna, and
a fruit of the very sweetest kind. It was not for nothing that
this delicate organism was exposed for years to the light, agreeable air of Austria; his waltzes have much to tell us about this.
Even when far from Vienna, he must still have caught echoes
of Strauss's waltzes and Schubert's *Ländler,* our *G'stanzl* and
yodellers, even of Farka's gipsy music, and recalled the pretty
girls, the fiery wine, the wooded hills, and all the rest. Those
who watch with sympathy the development of this straight-
forward and deep but previously, perhaps, one-sided talent will
greet the waltzes as a happy sign of a rejuvenated and refreshed
receptivity, as a sort of conversion to the poetic creed of Haydn,
Mozart, and Schubert — the creed of Hafiz."

Criticism, which already possessed well-known models and
exemplars in Schumann's *Spanischer Liederspiel,* op. 74, for

soprano, alto, tenor, and bass, with accompaniment for piano
solo, and, better still, in his cycle of *Spanische Liebeslieder,* for
four voices with accompaniment for two pianos, was dumb-
founded and perplexed at the appearance of these *Liebeslieder-
Walzer,* not knowing in what pigeon-hole to classify the work.
Was it a solo quartet or a work for two pianos? For here were
real waltzes, quite complete in themselves, though naturally
a little idealized in form, and here was a genuine solo quartet,
which was in no way "tacked on" to these waltzes for piano
duet as a mere accessory and afterthought, but had an independent and sometimes ravishingly lovely melodic life of its
own — for example, in what are perhaps the loveliest, or at any
rate the most popular numbers of op. 52, "*Ein kleiner hübscher
Vogel*" (no. 6), "*Am Donaustrande, da steht ein Haus*" (no. 9).
And what was to be said of numbers such as "*Nein, es ist nicht
auszukommen mit den Leuten*" (no. 11), which for all the truly
Brahmsian quality of its agitated discontent and annoyance, and
its North German cross-grained humour, seemed actually to be
written for solo quartet with an *accompaniment* for piano duet?
And the subtle Brahmsian distinction between the two volumes
in the sub-titles was not very much help to the startled public.
In the first book, the *Liebeslieder-Walzer,* the sub-title, "for
pianoforte duet and vocal parts *ad libitum,*" decidedly gave the
piano part a slight precedence over the four voices; in the second,
on the other hand, the sub-title, "for four voices and piano duet,"
gives the voices a little more prominence. In keeping with this
was the very sparing use of marks of expression in the vocal
parts of op. 52, which was considerably richer in op. 65. But that
is about all, for in each of the two collections will be found
numbers that seem to form exceptions to both these rules.

In this uncertainty which prevailed at the time as to how
to classify them, the *Liebeslieder-Walzer* themselves — which are
for the most part slow Viennese *Ländler* of the Schubertian type
rather than waltzes — hit upon the right solution: they spread
with amazing rapidity, delighting everybody, whether at home
or in the concert-hall, wherever they were well performed with

the right spirit of gaiety, in the right setting, and at the right time, and, together with the *Ungarische Tänze,* won world fame for their composer, leaving it to the sapient critics and the esteemed public to reconcile themselves as their inclination and nature might dictate to this " category " of waltz-songs or dance-songs, which only appeared to be brand-new and independent; for the form of the dance-song, going far back into the depths of the Middle Ages, was naturally well known to Brahms.

And both public and critics, compelled by the irresistibly fresh magic of their melody, did this so quickly and with such a will that only six years later Brahms was able to follow up the eighteen *Liebeslieder-Walzer* of op. 52 with fifteen *Neue Liebeslieder-Walzer,* op. 65. The words of both collections are Daumer's translations and imitations of foreign folk-poetry, mostly Russian, Polish, and Magyar, which are to be found in his *Polydora.* The two cycles form the most charming complement to each other, both poetically and musically. The older *Liebeslieder-Walzer,* op. 52, are filled with an atmosphere of unclouded brightness and happiness, of a peculiarly soft Viennese and voluptuous cast. In them the joy and rapture of love predominates almost exclusively. Only occasionally is a deeper, graver note sounded: for instance, in no. 2, in A minor, with its agitated syncopations (*" Am Gesteine rauscht die Flut "*), in no. 5, with its love-laments, now tender, now passionate (*Die grüne Hopfenranke*), no. 7 (*" Wohl schön bewandt war es vorehe mit meinem Leben "*), and no. 16 (*" Ein dunkler Schacht ist Liebe "*), or in the peevish no. 11, mentioned above (*" Nein, es ist nicht auszukommen mit den Leuten "*). In the *Neue Liebeslieder-Walzer,* op. 65, on the other hand, unfaithfulness, jealousy, rejected love, and misery have crept in. Even those which are perhaps the finest numbers — such as no. 2, in A minor (*" Finstere Schatten der Nacht "*), no. 4, in D minor (*" Ihr schwarzen Augen "*), no. 12, in G minor (*" Schwarzer Wald, dein Schatten ist so düster "*), and no. 14, in A minor (*" Flammenauge, dunkles Haar "*) — emphasize the immeasurably harsher, more passionate, dramatic, and gloomy tone prevailing in this second collection.

In both volumes these qualities are reflected outwardly in the choice of the major or minor key. In the first, out of eighteen numbers, six only are in the minor, while in the second the number is the same out of only fifteen. Enchanting in its loveliness is the quiet, serene note on which the whole of this "lovework" in two parts ends, in the concluding number of the second collection: "*Nun, ihr Musen, genug!*" (Goethe). In it the 3/4 time of the slow *Ländler* is broadened into a peaceful 9/4 time, and the pain and pleasure of love come to a soft conclusion in the sweet gratitude rendered to noble women: "*aber Linderung kommt einzig, ihr Guten, von euch* (but from you alone, who are good, does comfort come)."

The second of Brahms's works for solo quartet to meet with universal acceptance was the *Zigeunerlieder,* op. 103, for four voices with pianoforte accompaniment. Let us once more hear what Hanslick has to say about this masterpiece of Brahms's:

"The *Zigeunerlieder* are a little romance, the events in which we are not told, the persons in which are not named, and yet which we understand perfectly and never forget. The first song (no. 1) begins with a wild cry of: '*He, Zigeuner, greife in die Saiten ein, spiel' das Lied vom ungetreuen Mägdelein!* (Ho, gipsy, strike the strings and sing the song of the faithless maiden).' The tenor sings his solo, the quartet repeats the strophe, blazing up with greater and greater vehemence towards the end. In the following quartet (no. 2), '*Hochgetürmte Rimaflut* (High-piled waters of the Rima),' there is still a lingering echo of the passionate mood. But the gipsy lad seems soon to have found another love: the minor mode is followed by the merry key of D major, furious lamentation by light-hearted love-making (no. 3): '*Wisst Ihr, wann mein Kindchen am allerschönsten ist?* (Do you know when my little one is loveliest?).' Whereupon his lady-love joins in in an equally merry mood (no. 4): '*Lieber Gott, Du weisst ja,*' after which all the voices unite in exuberant jollity (no. 5): '*Brauner Bursche führt zum Tanze sein blauäugig schönes Kind* (The swarthy lad leads out his blue-eyed maiden to the dance).' Next follow two of the loveliest numbers, two gems, one full of playful mockery, the other overflowing with serious, deep feeling. Could anything be daintier than no. 6, the song of the ' *Schönstes Städtchen Kecskemet* (Kecskemet, that fairest of little towns) ' — or anything more full of soul than the following, no. 7, ' *Täusch' mich nicht, verlass' mich nicht* (Deceive me not, oh leave me not) '? An echo of this mood still hovers in the melancholy melody in G minor (no. 8): ' *Horch, der Wind klagt* (Hark, the wind wails),' which opens on such a note of sincerity in the major key, in words of blessing: ' *Gott schütze dich!* ' The next piece (no. 9) displays the same alternation between G minor and G major, but again with quite different colour. It opens wildly and stormily with all the voices singing in unison: ' *Weit und breit schaut niemand mich an* (Far and wide no man beholds me) '; but the mood, which varies so swiftly in these children of nature, changes in a single phrase — ' *Nur mein Schatz, der soll mich lieben* (None but my love shall love me) ' — into the wildest and most exultant csárdás rhythm. Once again longing and heart-ache prevail: a deep, fervent emotion quivers in the song (no. 10): ' *Mond verhüllt sein Angesicht* (The moon veils her face),' the accompaniment of which has a suggestion as of the distant, metallic tremolo of the dulcimer. And now we come to no. 11, the last piece in the collection: ' *Rote Abendwolken ziehen* (Red sunset clouds float overhead).' The melody rushes by, urged on, as it were, at every pause by two powerful, defiant chords. An incomparably poetical conclusion."

We may add the following note on the origin of the *Zigeunerlieder:* Brahms was prompted to compose them by a book of twenty-five Hungarian folk-songs selected by Hugo Conrat from a larger collection by Nagy Zoltán, published by Rószavölgyi at Budapest and arranged by Conrat with a piano accompaniment and German translation. Brahms was delighted with the words of these folk-songs and wrote fresh settings for fifteen of the melodies for solo quartet with piano accompaniment; eleven of these make up op. 103, and four more were afterwards included among the solo quartets of op. 112 (nos. 3–6) as *Vier*

Zigeunerlieder. Eight of the numbers of op. 103 were arranged by Brahms himself for solo voice with piano accompaniment, which greatly encouraged and facilitated their popular circulation, but impaired their original effect. For these *Zigeunerlieder* ought only to be heard in their original version as solo quartets with the piano. It is not till then that, thanks to their intense inspiration and richness of tone, their fiery ardour, and their genuinely Hungarian gipsy local colour, they produce their ravishing effect.

As regards tone, the *Zigeunerlieder,* which Brahms himself described as " a sort of Hungarian *Liebeslieder,*" are among the richest in colour of Brahms's works. Let those who would deny that Brahms has any sense of musical colour only see how subtly he has balanced the tone-colour of these eleven numbers by a variety of technical devices. In the first place, by his choice of the male or female voice to sing the leading part. In nos. 1, 3, 6, 7, 8, and 11 of op. 103 the tenor first sings a verse of the strophe, in no. 4 the soprano, and not till then does the quartet — or the trio, as in no. 6 — make its entry; in no. 3 of op. 112, the passionate *Brennessel* in F minor, it is the tenor who, in the enchanting second section, in F major, first protests that he can easily bear all the envy and hatred of his enemies if only his love remain true to him; in the genuine, racy gipsy music (*presto,* in the key of D minor and in 2/4 time) of no. 4 (" *Liebe Schwalbe, kleine Schwalbe, trage fort mein kleines Briefchen* "), the theme of whose second section, in D major, is so charmingly derived by augmentation from the exultantly rushing no. 1 (" *Himmel strahlt so helle und klar* "), resembling the concluding number of op. 103, it is first the alto, and afterwards the alto and tenor, that beg the " darling swallow, tiny swallow " to bear off the letter of greeting to their beloved. For Brahms knows how to distribute light and shadow in a masterly way by a varied grouping of the voices. In no. 8 the four voices follow one another at the first entry (tenor, alto, soprano, bass) phrase on phrase and line on line; while no. 10 contains a melody sung alternately by the two female and two male voices. Another device is the use of short interludes on the piano, written with all the delicately intricate filigree-like workmanship of Brahms's later manner. And, lastly, the use of nobly conventionalized and idealized imitations of the traditional instruments of gipsy music; in no. 10 of op. 103 the steely quiver of the dulcimer is heard in the bass, in no. 1 of op. 112 (*" Vögleins Lied so lieblich erklingt"*) in the upper register of the piano. As regards form, he prefers the concise, plastic construction of folk-music. No. 3 of op. 103 is consciously modelled on the national dance, the csárdás, with its sharp contrast between a peaceful *allegretto* and a stormy *allegro* in the same key; the *più presto stretto* of the passionately rushing no. 9 (*allegro,* in G minor) is genuine gipsy music. All these devices, indeed, strengthen the Hungarian gipsy " local colour " of the work; but in any case it is thoroughly Hungarian and gipsy, in both music and feeling.

We may venture to assert that Brahms's *Zigeunerlieder,* together with the *Ungarische Tänze* for piano duet, form the most open, splendid, and popular profession of the composer's devotion to Hungarian folk-music. He had already secretly given evidence of this quite early, in the D major Piano Variations on a Hungarian Theme, op. 21, no. 2, in the concluding movements of the two piano quartets, op. 26, and later in many numbers of the waltzes for piano duet, op. 39, in the B minor Capriccio for piano from op. 76, in the slow variation movement of the C major Piano Trio, op. 87, and in many of his remaining works — for instance, in the last movement of the B major Piano Concerto, op. 83 (in the episode in 2/4 time in A minor); and in the *adagio* and finale of the Second String Quintet, op. 111, he has slyly introduced true Hungarian themes and "Zigeuner citations." In both cases he has not merely copied the naturalistic gipsy music, but conventionalized and idealized it, without allowing its fresh, naïve spontaneity, racy of the soil, to evaporate into a mere drawing-room flavour. Those who wish to reassure themselves on this head have only to play through the few enchanting *puszta* idylls of these *Zigeunerlieder,* among which should not be forgotten the ineffably graceful, pleasing no. 2 of the four *Zigeunerlieder* of op. 112 (*" Rote Rosenknospen künden schon des Lenzes Triebe "*), which have unfortunately been so neglected by comparison with op. 103. The passage at the end, where the gipsy lad "*zum ros'gen Mädchen kosen geht* (goes to the caresses of the rosy maiden)," is really as graphic as a picture — first a vehement downward-rushing *forte* passage, followed by a dreamy *piano* and *dolcissimo,* world-forgetting and transported with love.

A comparison at once suggests itself between Brahms and Liszt as composers of gipsy music. In his occasional " parodies " (in the old sense of the word!) of gipsy music Liszt belongs to the naturalistic school; whereas here, too, Brahms remains an idealist. Or, as Hugo Riemann has so strikingly stated the case: "Brahms's gipsies are better trained musicians than Liszt's, without losing anything of their fiery verve in consequence." But the point which must be emphasized above all others is that, even as a "Zigeuner," Brahms remains himself in all points. One of the most wonderful discoveries that one makes in studying Brahms's music is that one is constantly seeing how external musical stimuli and modes of expression become harmoniously fused in Brahms's own personality, both as man and as artist. The *Zigeunerlieder* have a quality which may be characterized in the following terms: " a remarkable wealth of melody, spirited rhythms, fiery, heroic dash, behind an appearance of sullen melancholy, but, side by side with this, occasional flashes of sheer mad gaiety " — that is to say, they are genuine gipsy music, but in every note and every device they are likewise genuine Brahms. In dealing with the Hungarian Dances for piano we saw in greater detail how well Brahms succeeded in preserving the spirit of this gipsy music in spite of the artistic form in which he clothed it, at the same time avoiding all mere imitation.

The immortal theme of love's pains and pleasures, which forms the subject of the *Zigeunerlieder,* tempts one to a comparison with the two sets of *Liebeslieder-Walzer.* The *Zigeunerlieder* naturally surpass them both in their direct and stirring effect, intense local colour, and delicious freshness. But in other respects, too, they are quite different and full of contrast. In the *Liebeslieder-Walzer,* as in the waltzes for piano duet, op. 39, we have the easy, gay old Vienna of Schubert, Lanner, and Strauss; in the other, the broad Hungarian plains; in the one the *Lied,* in the other the "romance" and ballad; in the one an idyllic picture, quite anacreontic in spirit, of the delights of life and love, in the other, passion and its sufferings; in the one the rhythm and measure of the Viennese waltz, in the other a diversity of *tempo,* and a different measure and key in every number. But both require to be finely sung or played, and performed "in gay society" as a sort of idealized "social music (*Gesellschaftsmusik*)."

XXIX

THE LESSER CHORAL WORKS

We may at once divide Brahms's lesser choral works into two classes: sacred and secular. The lesser and small choral works almost all date from the early sixties and were written for his own use, for the female choirs which he directed at Detmold and Hamburg, and are to be judged as the practical artistic result of his close study of early vocal music. It is only these practical considerations that explain Brahms's amazingly rich use of the soft medium of the female-voice choir as opposed to the male-voice choir, with its equally limited range of tone: we have six works from his hand, comprising thirty-six large or small vocal compositions and canons for female choir, with or without accompaniment, but only a single work for male choir!

The oldest of his studies in this kind of composition is the *Ave Maria*, with Latin words, op. 12, for female choir, with orchestral or organ accompaniment. It is scored for a small orchestra consisting of strings, eight wood-wind instruments, and two horns. The character of this piece, which, to quote Clara Schumann's words, is " wonderfully moving in its simplicity," is thoroughly Italian in its type of melody, graceful, tender, and of a folk simplicity. The tender thirds of its themes remind us of an Italian Christmas pastoral rather than of a prayer to the Madonna. The women's voices are divided into two groups — two soprano parts and two alto parts — answering each other antiphonally and imitating each other — as they approach the sacred image in solemn procession. The short middle section, on the words " Blessed art thou," temporarily takes on a more gloomy tinge. At the invocation (" *Sancta Maria, ora pro nobis* ") the voices join in the prayer in unison, and the orchestra then takes up their melody *forte*. The conception is as ingenious as the execution is simple; the effectiveness of this passage, which is the poetical climax of the composition, is extraordinary and full of plastic power. The way in which it dies away at the close, to which the progression of chords, from D flat to F major, in the last bar of the vocal parts, lends a tender, bitter-sweet atmosphere of sorrow, is already thoroughly Brahmsian.

Of far greater importance is the *Begräbnisgesang* (*Funeral Ode*), op. 13, dating from the same period, for choir and wind instruments (two oboes, with a like number of clarinets and horns, three trombones, tuba, and kettledrums). This straight-forward work, which is in the style of a funeral march, and forms, as it were, a preliminary study for the second movement of the *Deutsches Requiem* ("*Denn alles Fleisch, es ist wie Gras*"), was intended, in Brahms's own words, to be performed "in *very* slow" *tempo* at the graveside and is based, as regards both text and music, upon the chorale, with words dating from the six-teenth century, *Nun lasst uns den Leib begraben,* which J. S. Bach used for his four-part setting of the sacred poem *Erhalt' uns, Herr, bei deinem Wort.* From the melody of this chorale Brahms borrows his funeral ode, with its folk simplicity and bareness, the beginning of which follows that of Bach's, note for note. We shrink from reminders of death when they come in such a harsh, stark, gloomy form as this, recalling not only Hebbel's poetry, but also an old woodcut in its archaic musical mannerisms, and foreshadowing the *Gesang der Parzen* in its concise form and pregnant expression. Its colour-scheme is determined by the sombre quality of the wood-wind and brass (two oboes, clarinets, bassoons, and horns, three trombones, and tuba) and of the kettle-drums. The colourless, rigid, gravely deliberate death-melody, stealing about the low C "with an inexorable, almost indifferent gravity, like inevitable fate," as Spitta says, weighs upon the hearer as oppressively and with the same desolate monotony as the second movement of the *Requiem,* which has such a very close affinity with the *Begräbnisgesang.* There is an utter absence of brighter colour; it is a very long time before the soprano enters *forte* on C after the alto — at the first great climax, "*wenn Gottes*

Posaun' wird angehn (when the last trump shall sound) " —
when the heavily brooding composition takes on a little colour
and warmth of tone. As compared with the First Serenade for
orchestra, there is an unmistakable progress in the orchestration,
especially in the scoring of the parts for wind instruments. On
the whole the *Begräbnisgesang* attracts us more by its spiritual
feeling than from the musical point of view, and not least by the
Brahmsian pessimism, which in the sombre passage in unison
" *Erd' ist er und von der Erden, wird auch wieder zu Erd' werden*
(Dust we are and to dust we shall return) " turns to open
pessimism, and the deep, rugged fervour with which the young
composer faces the eternal and insoluble problems of life and
death. As regards the music, the middle section in C major —
" *Sein' Arbeit, Trübsal und Elend ist kommen zu ein'm guten
End* (His labour, affliction, and misery have reached a happy
end) " — contains faint, distant echoes of the great passage in
C major in the *Alto Rhapsody,* in the tranquil crotchet measure
of the voices and the accompaniment in triplets, not to speak
of other places. The finest parts of this profoundly serious work,
and the only ones containing a little warmth and brightness, are
this "trio" in the major key, and the gentle, devout profession
of faith in its terse, interpolated episode — " *Die Seel', die lebt
ohn' alle Klag', der Leib schläft bis am letzten Tag, an welchem
ihn Gott verklären und der Freuden wird gewähren* (The soul
lives apart from all sorrow, the body sleeps until the last day,
when God shall glorify it and transport it into joy) " — but,
above all, the repetition of the lovely progression which closes
this middle section — in Clara Schumann's eyes " the most glorious" in the whole of this work, which stirred her to the depths —
" *in ewiger Freude und Wonne leuchten wie die schöne Sonne*
(shine like the glorious sun in everlasting joy and bliss)," to which
the oboes, a favourite instrument of Brahms's for expressing
resignation, lend such an uplifted and moving quality by their
arabesques of triplets, closely followed by the repetition of the
sombre funeral march, after that of the eloquent little interlude.

Immeasurably warmer and more inviting in aspect are the

next two short sacred choral works, which are decidedly of the nature of studies: the *Marienlieder,* op. 22, for four-part mixed choir, unaccompanied, and *Psalm XIII* (*"Herr, wie lange willst du mein so gar vergessen"*), op. 27, for three-part female choir with organ or piano accompaniment. The *Marienlieder* (episodes from the life of the Virgin), with German words, belong to the category of sacred legends with a Catholic tendency. Musically they have their origin in the old German sacred choral songs of such composers as Eccard, Senfl, Praetorius, Schröter, Hasler, and Schein, rather than in the old Roman and Netherlandish unaccompanied polyphonic works of Palestrina or Orlando di Lasso. And this not only in their general style and manner of composition, or in isolated technical traits, but also in their whole atmosphere. Brahms's *Marienlieder* are a specimen of the old choral music of the sixteenth century rendered into the Brahmsian idiom. The first choral song, " *Der englische Gruss* (The Angelic Salutation)," at once strikes the note of the whole collection, which is one of folk simplicity accompanied by a soft tinge of archaism. It starts *con moto* with chords in fifths on the horns, and the sopranos in contrary movement, and closes with an archaistic cadential passage, and pure, clear progressions of triads from A flat through B flat major, C, F, G minor, and D flat major to E flat major. In the second number, " *Marias Kirchgang,"* the melody is given to an inner part, the alto, after the manner of the old tenor part. This number is certainly the most lovely, as an enchanting experiment in choral tone-painting in the naïve style, with the simple resources of the early composers. The Virgin Mary sets sail across the deep lake for the little church, accompanied by the young boatman, who, as a recompense, desires in vain to have her as his helpmeet. When they are out in the middle of the lake, " all the bells begin to ring " (in fifths in the bass — E flat, B flat — and fourths in the soprano — B flat, E flat). The last song in the first book, *"Marias Wallfahrt,"* with its lovely archaic closing cadence passing from F major through B flat, C, and D to G major (with E instead of E flat), at the words " *so fern in's fremde Land, bis sie Gott den Herren fand*

(so far away in distant lands, until they found the Lord God),"
and the sorrowful overclouding suggested by the introduction of
the minor at the end — " *dass das Himmelreich leidet Gewalt!*
(for the kingdom of heaven suffereth violence) " — maintains the
austere, yet at the same time charming and softly unobtrusive
archaizing character of this collection. The first number in the
second book, " *Der Jäger,*" corresponds to a certain extent with
the same number of the first book, being equally unadorned and
like a folk-song. The pearl of this book is certainly the second
number, the " *Ruf zur Maria* (Invocation to Mary)," fervent,
sustained, and devout in tone in its *poco adagio,* with its moving,
plaintive refrain, " *Bitt' für uns, Maria* (Pray for us)." The following number, " *Magdalena,*" stirs even deeper emotions. On this
page alone, and for the first time in the whole collection, Brahms
speaks to us in his own idiom, in soft combinations of thirds and
sixths. The final number, " *Marias Lob* (Praise of Mary) " is in
a joyous, buoyant, rushing *allegro.* Brahms's *Marienlieder* are a
most beautiful testimony to the young composer's delicately artistic cult of the Virgin; perhaps, in addition to his studies of
ancient vocal music at Detmold and Hamburg, his previous
residence in the Catholic Rhineland was not altogether without
influence upon his development.

The musical character of *Psalm XIII* (not *XXIII,* as we find
in almost all Brahms catalogues, biographies, and programs, in
consequence of a printer's error), a work for three-part female
choir with organ or pianoforte accompaniment, the plan of which
was sketched out at a single sitting one Sunday evening, has no
relation whatever to the pleasingly graceful, languorous type
which practically held the field at the time when it was composed and is represented by the settings of the Psalms by Mendelssohn and his school. Even in form, consisting as it does of a
series of short sections following one another without a pause,
as well as in a variety of particular traits — such, for example, as
its somewhat frequent use of the bare fifth in the cadence, its
thematic imitation, and its austere ecclesiastical cadences — it is
far more akin to the old Italian cantatas of the seventeenth and

eighteenth centuries and the German cantatas of the Italianizing school. In the last great section (*" Ich hoffe aber darauf, dass du so gnädig bist "*) this psalm already foreshadows the fourth movement (*"Wie lieblich sind deine Wohnungen"*) of the *Deutsches Requiem*. The text, with its many words, is treated with extraordinary conciseness. The wealth of themes and motifs recalls the ancient motets. The first section, the invocation, with its forceful modulations expressive of anxious, uneasy questioning, remains rugged, austere, and gloomy, as the text demands. The second is on softer and more flowing lines (*" Wie lange soll sich mein Feind über mich erheben? "*), introducing a tone of true psalmody in a wonderfully natural way at the words *" Schaue doch und erhöre mich, Herr, mein Gott. Erleuchte meine Augen, dass ich nicht im Tode entschlafe."* In the quite short third movement (*" Dass nicht mein Feind rühme, er sei mächtig worden"*) the parts imitate each other with aggressive vigour. But it is the fourth, which aroused the delighted praise of Clara Schumann and contains the musical climax of the work, the wonderful cantilena passage *" Ich hoffe aber darauf, dass Du so gnädig bist,"* soaring above the peaceful crotchet accompaniment on the organ, which, with its broad *"*duplets (*Duolen*) *"* worked against triplets, and exquisite progressions on the words *" Ich will dem Herren singen, dass er so wohl an mir tut,"* forms a superb final climax on broad, well-defined lines.

On the other hand, the next of these works, which is also in the nature of a study, and a step towards the renaissance of the sacred choral song, the *Drei geistliche Chören* (*Three Sacred Choruses*), op. 37, for female voices unaccompanied, may most fittingly be grouped with the *Marienlieder*. Like the latter, but to a far greater and more exclusive extent, they are the artistic reaction caused by Brahms's earnest study of the unaccompanied, polyphonic style of the old Roman school of the sixteenth century, which we are in the habit of calling the style of Palestrina, after its greatest master. This time the words are Latin. The two first choruses — *O bone Jesu* and *Adoramus te, Christe* — are taken from the *improperia* of Holy Week; the third — *Regina cœli* —

belongs to Eastertide. The form is unusually strict, and all three
of the numbers are devoted to solving the most difficult problems
of canon form. The first number, *O bone Jesu,* groups the four
female voices in pairs — first soprano and first alto, second soprano and second alto — and contains a canon *in motu contrario*
(by inversion) between the first soprano and second alto. The
second number, *Adoramus,* is a rather long, strictly worked-out
four-part canon, the voices entering at intervals of a bar; it is not
till the close, at the invocation of the Deity and the "*Miserere,*"
that the four voices join in simple Palestrinian triad harmonies.
The finest, most rich in content, and most beautiful in tone is
the third, the *Regina cœli.* The first section consists of a canon
by inversion between solo soprano and solo alto, full of rich
colour in the treatment of the melody, while the four-part chorus
interjects short, joyful alleluias. In the second section, or "*Re-
sponsorium,*" the four-part chorus is divided into two groups,
each of two parts, and proceeds to develop a canon in similar
fashion. It is not till the close (the "*Alleluia*") that both the solo
voices unite with it in a *stretto* passage in canon, leading up to
simple and majestic four-part harmonies.

These three sacred choruses for female voices are strictly of the
nature of studies, to an even greater extent than the *Marienlieder,*
which have an almost folk simplicity and easiness of compre-
hension. As a collection of specimens of the most difficult forms
of canon, they form a continuation of another small study in
sacred composition, started a few years earlier, during the Detmold and second Hamburg period: namely, the *Geistliches Lied,*
a setting of Paul Flemming's "*Lass dich nur nichts nicht dauren,*"
op. 30, for four-part mixed choir with organ or pianoforte accompaniment. As an exceptionally skilful study in canon form (it
is a so-called double canon at the ninth below, between soprano
and tenor on the one hand, and alto and bass on the other), it
may most suitably be classed with the *Drei geistliche Chören,*
op. 37, which were written after it. But on the whole it has shaken
off the dust of the academic style far more than they have. The
form is clear and simple, consisting of three sections, with short

Bach-like interludes on the organ between them, with tranquil crotchet figures in an *alla breve* bar; it has warmth and suavity of feeling, and tenderness and beauty of tone, but in the concluding *"Amen"* passage it becomes absolutely uplifted in its deeply soothing, Bach-like, subdominant effect (the D flat in particular is superbly effective), which is already conceived on broad, clearly defined lines which are truly Brahmsian. This piece is pre-Bachian, almost old Netherlandish indeed, in its astounding mastery of the most difficult problems of counterpoint, but Bach-like in tone, character, and harmonizing, and still more so in the fact that the uninitiated can detect nothing of all this amazing ingenuity of composition; on the contrary, in spite of Clara Schumann's startled and uneasy fear lest the " effect might prove stiff (*steifen Klanges*)," it all seems to blend in the most natural way in sweet melody and sentiment.

On the other hand, Brahms's great motets, for unaccompanied mixed choir, far transcend this purely or predominantly technical character of studies. We have, in all, three collections of them, spread over all his periods of production: op. 29, op. 74, and op. 110. The number of parts varies: in op. 29 there are five, in op. 74 four or six, in op. 110 four or eight. They all date from his years in Vienna and belong to the category of German chorale-motets with uninterrupted *canto fermo*. Brahms's motets, even more than his sacred and secular choral works, are in the sharpest contrast with the motets of Mendelssohn and his school, to whose Italianizing, languorous character, in which the setting and style follow the text word for word and syllable for syllable, Brahms opposes the incisive austerity and style of Bach's old motets and those of the German masters who preceded him — a style in which all the words and syllables are like mere wavelets merged in a surging ocean of long, majestic waves of sound, now crossing one another, now crowding one upon the other in emulation. Brahms's motets are another superb contribution to the master's high endeavour to infuse his own new and thoroughly individual vitality and feeling into the grand old vocal art of the early masters by means of the resources of modern times. In Brahms's motets, then, we shall be able to trace not only Johann Sebastian Bach, but his great German and Italian predecessors as well.

The two five-part motets of op. 29, dating from the year 1864, were written by Brahms at the age of thirty, when he was director of the chorus at the Vienna Singakademie; they are the precious fruit of long years of deep immersion in the great vocal works of Bach and practical experience of them, and, viewed in the light of his position as instructor in choral singing, an ideal "*pièce d'occasion.*" Both these motets — *Es ist das Heil uns kommen her* and *Schaffe in mir, Gott, ein rein' Herz!* — are grandiose masterpieces in a difficult contrapuntal style, which revels in the most elaborate possibilities of the chorale, simultaneous double augmentation of values in the *canto fermo,* imitation and inversion of themes, augmentations, and strictly fugal concluding sections.

We may take the first motet, *Es ist das Heil uns kommen her,* as an example. It opens with the chorale arranged for five parts, quite in the manner of Bach. This is followed by the development of the chorale in the form of a strict five-part fugue. The *canto fermo* is given to the first bass. The other voices lead up to its entry, which takes place each time in a majestic *forte,* by developing each of the seven different lines of the chorale in mutual imitations. The *canto fermo,* doubly augmented and therefore written for the most part in heavy minims, forms a splendid rhythmical contrast with their mobile crotchets and quavers in mutual imitation.

The second motet, *Schaffe in mir, Gott, ein rein' Herz,* from Psalm li, " a masterpiece in every part," as Clara Schumann says, brings up still heavier contrapuntal artillery. The introductory chorale in the first motet has as its counterpart in the second an opening *andante moderato* in G major, distantly reminiscent of Mendelssohn in its languorous beauty of tone and its apparently quite simple setting in chords. We say " apparently," for the second bass, which enters simultaneously with the soprano, is almost throughout a strictly worked-out imitation of the soprano part with the time-values increased — that is to say, a canon by augmentation. The four-part fugue which follows (" *Verwirf mich nicht von deinem Angesicht* ") is, in spite of its vigour, more than ordinarily ingenious, omitting neither inversion nor augmentation of the theme, nor transformation of its rhythm. While the rather shorter first motet of op. 29 can show only one big fugue, the second also contains a fiery concluding fugue, written in the manner of Handel rather than of Bach, and with a touch of brighter colour (" *und der freudige Geist erhalte mich* "). But between these two fugues, as at the beginning, Brahms once more places a tranquil, sustained movement in five or sometimes six parts, which again conceals within it a contrapuntal secret, disguised in a masterly way: it is a canon at the seventh below, between the tenor and second bass, on the words " *Tröste mich wieder mit deiner Hilfe.*" The tonal effect of this movement is wonderful; the preponderance of the male voices gives it a sombre and intense warmth of tone-colour. The women's lighter voices do not enter till the tenth bar; the two groups of voices are handled separately throughout.

All these features, intensified by supreme contrapuntal skill, appear in the two great motets, op. 74, written fifteen years later in Vienna and significantly dedicated to Philipp Spitta, the great Berlin expert on Bach, and a friend of Brahms's: *Warum ist das Licht gegeben den Mühseligen* and *O Heiland, reiss die Himmel auf*. Spiritually, too, owing to the fact that they were written in memory of Hermann Goetz's premature death, they seem if possible more mature, intellectual, and poetical in every way. In these works the words seem to point us from the church into the world, while the music points us back from the world and the concert-hall into the church. At the same time it is music which would be as much in place in St. Peter's, Rome, as in St. Thomas's, Leipzig. The first of these two motets, in four parts, is on the whole more varied in feeling and richer and freer in expression and form. Its treatment of the opening question is so poetical that Billroth calls it outright the " *Warum?* (Why?) motet." He places it next in importance to the *Deutsches Requiem* and justly attributes part of its unique beauty to the words, " at once so human and so divine, yet outside all creeds (*konfessionslos*). Childlike questionings, the wisdom of old age, the doubts of maturity — all these are to be found in it." It was this " unsectarian " quality that Brahms had in mind when he jestingly asked Elisabeth von Herzogenberg for some fresh words to set as motets, as those in the Bible did not seem to him " pagan (*heidnisch*) " enough. The motet is in four divisions. The first, in four sections, is the most impressive of them and once more takes up and elaborates the cry of desolation in the last number of op. 62 — " *Vergangen ist mir Glück und Heil* (My happiness and joy are past)." As regards its words, it is among the harbingers of the *Vier ernste Gesänge*. For the first time Brahms stands before us as the great interpreter of world-weary pessimism, of the longing of the wretched and afflicted for death, for which they yearn as a welcome end to their earthly sorrows and mortifications, and displays all the Low German's profound and melancholy conception of life. " Why is light and life granted to the heavy-laden? Why? " asks the composer, repeating the double question three times in a tone of doubt, bitterness, and sorrow. This " *Warum?* " breaks up the first division into three sections. The first is in fugal form, with an uneasy questioning in its agitated intervals and chromatic part-writing. The second — " *Die des Todes warten kommt nicht* (They that wait for death that comes not) " — depicts in broad, oppressive syncopations the dull, resigned expectation of those who long for death. The third, with the uncertain, hesitating gropings of its unison passages, is meant to represent the perplexed wanderings of the man whose way God hides from him. The second division, in six sections, seeks an issue out of this grey misery, by urging man to prayer with the words " *Lasset uns unser Herz samt den Händen aufheben zu Gott* (Let us lift up our hearts and hands to God)." The form is that of a strict canon; the theme is derived from the *Benedictus* of Brahms's youthful mass in the contrapuntal style. In its first division the third section, also with six vocal parts, weaves a close polyphonic tissue round the words " *Siehe, wir preisen selig* (Lo, we call them blessed)," after which it proceeds directly to the second division, with its antiphonal character — " *Die Geduld Hiob habt ihr gehört* (Ye have heard of Job's patience) " — which at its close — "*denn der Herr ist barmherzig und Erbarmer* (for the Lord is merciful and full of compassion) " — once more introduces the suave conclusion of the second division, with the soft subdominant effect of which Brahms was so fond. Just as the first motet of op. 29 begins with a four-part, lightly figured chorale division, in the manner of Bach, so the first of op. 74 closes with a similar one — " *Mit Fried' und Freud' ich fahr dahin* (In peace and joy I pass away)." And so this motet, full of bitter doubt, gentle protest, and pitying sorrow for the often undeserved misery of the world, its hard injustice and brutal egoism, completes the whole cycle of spiritual development, passing through prayer to a joyous trust in God.

The second of the two motets of op. 74, *O Heiland, reiss die Himmel auf,* is again akin to the first number of op. 29 (*Es ist das Heil uns kommen her*) in the form and treatment of its arrangement of this old Advent hymn. Like that number, it is also in the form of a chorale-motet without solo parts, with a continuous *canto fermo*. It is doubly astonishing that these narrow formal limitations, to which Brahms voluntarily subjected himself, positively heighten the wealth of spiritual effect, instead of decreasing it. But over all is cast a splendid Bach-like mantle of subtly wrought counterpoint. The *canto fermo* is found in a different part in each of the five strophes. In the first and second it is given to the soprano, while the other parts imitate it; in the third to the tenor, in the fourth to the bass; the fifth strophe (" *Da wollen wir all' danken dir* ") is a double fugue. A brightly figured " *Amen* " closes the work, as in the later *Fest- und Gedenksprüche.*

The third and last collection of motets, op. 110, for unaccompanied four- and eight-part choir, the words of which are profoundly serious in tone throughout, adds yet another novel feature and individual touch taken from early vocal music: namely, the use of the double choir. They may at once be grouped with the *Fest- und Gedenksprüche,* op. 109, for unaccompanied eight-part

mixed choir, which appeared immediately before them, in 1890,
and in which, as we saw in the biographical part of the book,
Brahms expressed in musical form to His Magnificence the Burgomaster of Hamburg, Dr. Carl Petersen, his acknowledgment of
the freedom of the city which had been conferred upon him.
Both these typical works in Brahms's later manner reveal by the
consistent uniformity of their prevailing atmosphere, the unadorned austerity and conciseness of their form, and the supreme
art of their marvellously delicate and firm vocal texture the fact
that by this time Brahms has assimilated, digested, and fused in
his own personality not only Bach, but also Schütz and the great
old Italian and Venetian masters of composition for double choir,
above all the two Gabrielis and Lotti. The words of the first
motet in op. 110 (*Ich aber bin elend und mir ist wehe*) and of
the three *Fest- und Gedenksprüche* (*Unsere Väter hofften auf
dich — Wenn ein starker Gewappneter seinen Palast bewahret —
Wo ist ein so herrlich Volk?*) were again chosen from the Bible
by the composer himself, who was so well grounded in the
Scriptures, and we may remember that he took particular credit
for those of the *Fest- und Gedenksprüche*.

The three motets for unaccompanied four- and eight-voice
choir, op. 110, display the characteristics of Brahms's "last manner" in their unusually sombre and rugged character. The first
(*Ich aber bin elend*) is in eight parts and is of peculiar beauty in
its extremely sharp contrasts, crowded into the narrowest space,
between harsh austerity ("*Herr, Herr Gott!*") and gentle consolation ("*Barmherzig und gnädig und geduldig*"). It at once
strikes the old-world, archaistic note of these three motets quite
clearly and consciously, not only harmonically, but also in rhythm
and measure. The second motet, in F minor, *Ach, arme Welt,
du trägest mich,* with the rugged Dorian colour of its D instead
of D flat in the key of F minor, is even harsher, but unusually
concise and unadorned in its use of the strophic form in two
sections. It is the simplest and shortest of all Brahms's motets.
Its close is tenderly poetical: it is not till the word "*Frieden
(peace)*" that the major key introduces a serene mood. The third

and longest of the motets in this collection, *Wenn wir in höchsten Nöten sein,"* in C minor, is among the most repellent and harsh works, offering the greatest vocal difficulties, that Brahms ever wrote for a choir. Once more our thoughts go back to the two previous "cries of affliction *(Elendklagen)* " of op. 62, no. 7, and op. 74, no. 1; *"steh' uns in unsrem Elend bei* (be with us in our affliction) " runs the second strophe. But here the case is to a certain extent simpler, and there is no scope for pessimistic doubts and protests, as there was in the first movement of op. 74, no. 1. The way in which Brahms depicts the grievous distress of life, in which we often hardly know which way to turn, though we may worry from morning till night, and the trustful appeal to God for salvation, have as their natural result the two sharply contrasted thematic divisions. For the former he has chosen a theme in C minor, which ascends and descends within two bars, crowded together as though under constraint, and illustrating very finely and convincingly the restlessly urgent perplexity of tortured humanity, as does also the *stretto* entry of the male voices of the second choir. In the latter, at the words *" So ist das unser Trost allein, dass wir zusammen ingemein dich rufen an, O treuer Gott,"* he introduces a strongly rhythmical and closely knit theme on a vigorous harmonic scheme. The intermediate parts represent in the style of the early masters, with a bustling monotony, the uneasy perplexity, the vain, unremitting anxieties of men and the stern constraint of their obedience to God. Much subtle psychological discrimination, much quiet self-knowledge, lies hidden in them. How the fugal arrangement of the voices makes them seem positively to crowd upon each other in their distraction! How emulously they repeat this effect at the words *" Sorgen früh und spät* (Vex themselves early and late) "! With what Old Testament rigour and submissiveness the two choirs, treated at this point quite antiphonally, zealously assure each other of their obedience to God's word! In this concluding section, which is quite peculiarly moving, lies the key and solution of the composer's reading of the words of this motet. Anyone who sees with emotion how the second " theme of faith " makes its first entry

in F minor and continues in this minor key even on its last
appearance, at the words "*Dich allzeit preisen hier und dort*
(Praise Thee at all times, here and there)," only in the end to
rise with a note of positive agony into the major, in the contrary
motion in thirds of the middle parts, divines at once, from his
knowledge of Brahms's nature, what the composer meant by this.

Only the first and last numbers in this collection are motets
in the grand style; and once again the concluding one stands out
far above all the preceding ones in inward significance and
mastery of form and treatment. It is the final link in the chain
connecting the motets directly with the *Fest- und Gedenksprüche,*
op. 109, for unaccompanied eight-part mixed choir.

Brahms's thoroughly German spirit, what we may call his
"*treuer Eckart*" side, as illustrated by the cautioning, admonitory, warning note of the words of the *Fest- und Gedenksprüche,*
with its imposing eight-part setting, causes it to rank with the
Triumphlied as evidence of the overflowingly patriotic emotions
called forth in the composer by the victorious issue of the Franco-
German war of 1870–1 and of their reaction on him. There is
perhaps no work of Brahms's whose words have such "actuality"
as these *Fest- und Gedenksprüche,* intended by him "for such
celebrations as that of Sedan, etc."; none in which he again
appears so amazingly "modern" as here. From the opening
words: "*Unsere Väter hofften auf dich; und da sie hofften, halfst
du ihnen aus* (Our fathers trusted in Thee, and as they trusted,
Thou didst aid them)," through the middle number: "*Wenn ein
starker Gewappneter seinen Palast bewahret, so bleibet das Seine
in Frieden. Aber ein jeglich Reich, so es mit ihm selbst uneins
wird, das wird wüste, und ein Haus fället über das andere* (When
a strong man armed keepeth his palace, his goods are in peace.
Every kingdom divided against itself is brought to desolation;
and a house divided against a house falleth)," down to the concluding words: "*Hüte dich nur und bewahre deine Seele wohl,
dass du nicht vergessest der Geschichte, die deine Augen gesehen
haben. Und dass sie nicht aus deinem Herzen komme all dein
Lebelang. Und sollt deinen Kindern und Kindeskindern kund-*

tun (Take good care and give heed to thy soul, that thou forget not the things that thine eyes have seen. And that they abide in thine heart all the days of thy life. And that thou tell them unto thy children and thy children's children) " — do not these words seem to have been written, not only for the Germany of 1870–1, but also for that of 1914–18, and in particular, alas! for that of the years following 1918 and of today? So terribly has the fatality of the German national failing of internal dissension and ruinous fraternal discord been fulfilled in the great catastrophe — a fatality perhaps secretly dreaded and foreseen by that great patriot and Bismarckian Brahms.

Not only in their eight-part setting, but also in their style and treatment, the *Fest- und Gedenksprüche* contain hidden echoes of the *Triumphlied.* All three pieces are themselves in three divisions, and further based on strong contrasts, especially of a dynamic order. The rich and strikingly graphic way in which coloratura effects in the choral parts are used for purposes of tone-painting and characterization, at the words: " *und wurden errettet und wurden nicht zuschanden* " in the first piece, and " *seinen Palast bewahret* " in the second, reminds us of Schütz, Bach, and Handel; while it is the old Venetian masters of two-choir composition who are more particularly suggested by the brilliance of the passages in a more solemn, sustained strain, written in a more homophonic style in chords — a brilliance with the rich lustre of old gold and a wonderful warmth and splendour. All three pieces are severely archaic in their harmony and part-writing, as well as in the broad treatment, recalling the early masters, of the " *Aber* " passage, which forms a bridge between one section and the other in the second piece, formed by two G minor triads in minims with an opening crotchet rest in 3/4 time; the result is once again unmistakably and typically Brahmsian in the stately and fierily spirited animation which runs through the great contrapuntal sections, and in the simple, insistent, heart-felt admonition and pleading which runs through the more homophonic parts. The German indications of *tempo* —" *Feierlich bewegt* " (*maestoso*) for no. 1, " *Lebhaft und entschlossen*" (*allegro risoluto*) for no. 2, "*Froh bewegt*" (*allegro giocoso*) for no. 3 — seem, indeed, symbolic of the whole work: it is truly festal music, coming from a heart full of festive and joyful emotion; but at the same time music which, for all its predominantly virile and vigorous character, is unlike the last collection of motets in that it is filled with a fine, heart-felt, spiritual warmth. And, finally, the tonal effects are also reminiscent of the early masters. In some places they display an intoxicating beauty in the handling of the double choir, and the most subtle balance between the passages in which the two four-part choirs sing alternately or together. In the alternating passages Brahms is fond of resorting to yet another technical device borrowed from the early methods of choral writing: for instance, at the very beginning of the first piece, where in the massive, unison passage ("*Unsere Väter*") in minims, introduced immediately afterwards in inversion, at the words "*hofften auf dich*," he makes the first choir accompany the second choir's three notes (minims), F, C, A, sung in unison, in a crotchet passage in which these notes are embellished with passing notes.

But much as we may admire the "dense (*dicht*)," majestic fullness of the parts for both choirs, or the rare but brilliant and characteristic touches of tone-painting — the fugal *stretto* passage at the words "*Ein jeglich Reich, so es mit ihm selbst uneins wird*," or the *stretto* passage at "*und ein Haus fället über das andere*" in the second piece — the deepest and most Brahmsian qualities are to be found in the "quiet" parts for only one choir, or even half of one. Among these I should place above all the concluding section of the first piece, "*Der Herr wird seinem Volk Kraft geben, der Herr wird sein Volk segnen mit Frieden*," with its homophonic chord setting, which opens with the entry of the male voices of both choirs on a note of such wonderful mildness, sombre solemnity, and warmth. I would add the passage in the second piece where the terrible consequences of inward dissension are depicted ominously *piano* and in an insistent moving tone of wailing reproach ("*Das wird wüste*"); and, lastly, almost the whole of the third piece, in which the composer implores his beloved countrymen from the bottom of his heart never to forget their country's history or the great and noble things which their eyes have seen. The heartfelt warmth that permeates this piece, opening so magnificently with the F major triad in the tenor, immediately afterwards imitated in the soprano part, is irresistible and even nowadays still produces a particularly profound effect at the place where, at the beginning of the second section, on the words " *Hüte dich nur und bewahre deine Seele wohl,*" a *stretto* passage in simple chords adjures the people, *piano,* not to forget their glorious past. But the most splendid passage in the whole of the three pieces comes right at the end: the stately grandeur of the " *Amen,*" with its consummate polyphonic structure, working up with wonderful breadth and tranquillity to a climax which closes the whole work on a note of uplifted solemnity.

Of Brahms's shorter *secular* choral works the larger number, which, like the sacred ones, are again decidedly of the nature of studies, date from his Detmold and Hamburg days. Here, too, the greater number are written for female choir, and once again the young composer seeks in the early masters the foundation, pattern, and model for the renaissance of choral song which was his aim. Such a revival was as important and necessary in the choral song, whether unaccompanied or accompanied, as in the accompanied solo song. Both of these branches of art were cumbered by the accumulated trash produced by the lesser followers of Mendelssohn, with their effeminate, sickly, sleek style. Brahms started from totally different principles. Here too he began as a Romantic, but he at once blended with his romanticism a good, sound admixture of the ancient spirit. The *Ave Maria,* which opens the series of the lesser sacred choral works, has as its pendant the *Vier Gesänge* for three-part female choir, op. 17, with accompaniment for two horns and harp, which dates from the following year and opens the secular series. In the romantic and charming character of their tonal effects these " wonderful, poetic harp-songs " (Clara Schumann) may be grouped with the two serenades for orchestra. As always with Brahms, the choice of the accompanying instruments arises intimately and inevitably out of the words. The first choral song, *Es tönt ein voller Harfen-klang,* calls for rushing harp arpeggios, rising and falling now softly, now strongly. To these is added a horn in deep C, which, by its persistent Schumann motif, G, C, D, G, gives a certain thematic homogeneity to the aerial tissue of this superb tone-study, with its suggestion of free improvisation. The two middle pieces are of less importance: the fool's song from Shakspere's *Twelfth Night* (" Come away, death "), which has, however, a wonderful close on the words " *Treu hält es* (No one so true) . . . *Und weine* (To weep there) "; and a setting of Eichendorff's *Gärtner,* with its sweet, charming sentiment (" *Wohin ich geh' und schaue* "), which treats this " lovely, exalted poetry " in the tender spirit of Mendelssohn. But in this collection, too, it is the last number, the *Gesang aus Fingal,* of Ossian, with its Nordic character, that is by far the most important. It is Nordic not only in its tonal effects — the two horns in deep C in particular lend it quite a characteristic and genuinely Nordic tone-colour — but also in character and atmosphere. It is written in the key of C minor, used by Gade in his settings of Ossian. Its subject is the lament of the lovelorn maid of Inistore over the fallen young hero Trenar by the rock of the raging winds. This dirge is conceived as a simple folk-melody in the style of a funeral march in 2/4 time. In the exquisite middle section (alternating section in A flat major) the lament, at first stark in its rigidity, takes on a sweet and moving melodic quality, but it is soon tinged with a pale, Nordic, spectral atmosphere when the murdered man's grey hounds break into howls as they see his spirit floating past to his house (short steps of a second), while in the ominous unison passage for the voices a deathly stillness gradually casts its shadow more deeply over hall and heath, thus leading naturally to the repetition of the principal subject. And here, in the closing passage in C major, all the grief of the maid of Inistore breaks forth once more in repeated heart-rending and desperate out-cries, but grows softer and more tranquil amid the closing con-solations of the chorus.

The *Lieder und Romanzen,* op. 44 (two books), for four-part female choir, unaccompanied, or with pianoforte accompaniment *ad libitum,* have the simplicity of folk-songs both in content and in form and are also fresh and full of melody. Each book contains a pearl. The first has young Fidelin's *Barkarole* from the Italian (" *O Fischer auf dem Fluten* "), the second Uhland's *Märznacht.* In the *Barkarole* the Italian local colour is delightfully caught in the passages in which the solo singers and *tutti* alternate, and by passages in tender thirds and sixths. The *Märznacht* brings up its heavy contrapuntal artillery within restricted limits: the first soprano and first alto on the one hand, and the second soprano and second alto on the other, represent a raging, stormy night in wailing chromatic passages in a canon at the fifth, entering at an interval of half a bar after each other; but as the belated wanderer is seized by a " feeling of shuddering sweetness," caused by the intimations of approaching spring, the gloomy B flat minor changes into the cheerful B flat major, and the harsh canon at the fifth becomes a soft canon at the sixth, with sweetly sad accents (the G flat in the chord of the subdominant). The remaining numbers in this collection are weaker, though not a single one of them is entirely weak. The four songs from Heyse's *Jungbrunnen* in the second book strike quite a novel and individual note, for all the folk simplicity of their content and form. The palm must be given to the *Und gehst du über den Kirchhof,* with its deep feeling, the elemental effect of its juxtaposition of minor and major, and its pensive citation of Schumann at the beginning. In the first book we would draw attention to the setting of the elder Voss's *Minnelied,* with its touch of quaint archaism, its three-bar periods and unusual rhythm, the setting of Eichendorff's bright *Bräutigam,* with its echoing horn-calls, and of Uhland's *Nonne,* producing the effect of a plaintive folk-song with its touching close; in the second book to Wilhelm Müller's *Braut,* bewailing the death of her drowned betrothed, which opens in the elastic 3/2 measure and seems, indeed, with its slight Slavonic tinge, to come from Moravia rather than from the island of Rügen.

The third and last choral work for women's voices is a late work from the year 1891 and bears the formidable title of *Dreizehn Kanons für Frauenstimmen* (*Thirteen Canons for Female Voices*), op. 113. These " summer fruits " perform their difficult task of providing admirable material for training female choirs unobtrusively, and at the same time with feeling and humour, in the shape of a variety of melodies borrowed from the treasury of folk-songs and children's songs. Goethe opens the collection with the first two numbers; the remaining eleven are devoted to the older Romantics, and especially to Rückert, of whom Brahms was so fond. The numbers arranged as canons are as simple as possible. The playful numbers are either borrowed or imitated from North German or Austrian folk-songs or children's songs. They include: the arch four-part song *Sitzt a schön's Vögerl auf'm Dannabaum,* with its piquant measure based on a three-bar period, the three-part *Schlaf', Kindlein, schlaf',* and the playful little *Wille wille will, der Mann ist kommen,* which trips daintily by as though on tiptoe — three productions which already appear under other titles as solos among the *Volks-Kinderlieder.* In spite of the narrow fetters of their strict form, the last three mournful numbers among these canons, to Rückert's words, are of particular beauty and typically Brahmsian. And here the last and longest number, *Einförmig ist der Liebe Gram,* merits particular attention. This arrangement of Schubert's *Leiermann* is a canon for four soprano parts, with a drone-like bass in fifths on the tonic and dominant in the two alto parts, again in canon. Most of the rest, with the exception of Eichendorff's jovial rhymed proverb, *Ein Gems auf dem Stein,* arranged as a four-part canon, are dedicated to the god of love and contain among them some ingenious settings: for instance, the sixth song, in four parts, *So lange Schönheit wird bestehn* (Hoffmann von Fallersleben), a most natural, flowing canon by inversion between the two sopranos and altos. Equally ingenious is the last number, *An's Auge des Liebsten fest mit Blicken dich ansauge* (Rückert), a double canon at the fifth between the first soprano and first alto, and the second soprano and second alto. No. 10, in four

parts, *Leise Töne der Brust* (Rückert), is already known to us
from no. 1 (*Nachtwache*) of the *Fünf Gesänge für gemischten
Chor,* op. 104. A little group apart, with a Greek classical tinge,
is formed by the first two numbers, which are settings of Goethe's
words: one an invocation of the god of sleep (*Göttlicher Morpheus*), with charming touches of colour, the other a love-lament
full of tender feeling (*Grausam erweiset sich Amor an mir*).

The *Jungbrunnen* of Paul Heyse, the Munich writer of exquisitely finished short stories with an Italian atmosphere, for
whom Brahms had a heart-felt admiration, was the source of the
four choral songs included in op. 62, *Sieben Lieder,* for unaccompanied four-part mixed choir, as well as of op. 44. Like
the rest of the composer's collections of secular songs for unaccompanied mixed choir — the *Drei Gesänge* for six-part unaccompanied choir, op. 42, the six four-part *Lieder und Romanzen,*
op. 93a, the setting of Eichendorff's *Tafellied* ("*Dank der
Damen*"), op. 93b, for six-part chorus with piano accompaniment, and the *Fünf Gesänge,* op. 104, for six-part choir — they
show that during every period of his production Brahms remained true to his aim of regenerating the German choral song —
which had been degraded by Mendelssohn's innumerable followers to a dead level of effeminate bourgeois sentimentality and
anæmic sickliness — by a renaissance of the old German choral
song, especially that of the sixteenth century, in a modern spirit.
And he does so in the only fitting and right way for a modern
composer: he recalls the spirit and tone of early days in those
places alone where it appears to arise inevitably out of the
text.

This can be admirably studied in all these collections of
choral songs, and in the first place in the *Drei Gesänge,* op. 42,
for unaccompanied six-part choir. The hand of the director of
choral singing at the Vienna Singakademie can clearly be traced
in these. In tonal effect they are among the loveliest and tenderest
of Brahms's choral songs. No. 1, Clemens Brentano's *Abendständchen* ("*Hör', es klagt die Flöte wieder*"), full of an enchantingly lovely eventide atmosphere, reveals the fact that it is

based on ancient models in the division of the six-part choir into
two three-part groups (of both male and female voices), which
imitate each other, in its free treatment, with a preference for
strongly marked metrical accentuation of the words (on *"Hör',"*
for instance), and in its impatience of the rigid restraint of modern
bar-lines. No. 2, *Vineta* (W. Müller), which is steeped in an
equally tender beauty of tone, has no touch of archaism and,
though not very remarkable for its invention, is quite wonderfully beautiful in the tender, " cerulean (*lichtblau*) " translucence
of its colour suggestion. It enchants one by its subtle, unobtrusive
division into five bar-periods; only at the cadences of all the main
sections of this poem on the wonderful old sunken city on the
island of Rügen are these periods prolonged for a bar by a device
of syncopation. The pearl of this collection, no. 3, is once more
Herder's rendering of a Nordic, Ossianic poem, *Darthulas Grabes-*
gesang. Our memory at once goes back to the *Gesang aus Fingal,*
the last number of the *Vier Gesänge,* op. 17, for female choir with
two horns and harp. This funeral song is also a dirge, sung by
the men and women assembled at the grave of the fair maid of
Kola, Darthula, the last descendant of the house of Thrutil. Here
again the tone, character, and atmosphere of the piece have a
Nordic tinge. Less so, perhaps, in the graceful " Awake " addressed
to Darthula in the G major middle section, with its slightly
Mendelssohnian colour: *" Wach' auf, Darthula, Frühling ist*
draussen," which develops in the charming passage at the end
into an antiphonal song between the male and female voices, than
in the first and last sections in G minor, which form a pendant
to each other. Here Brahms has produced the sombre, grey, " old
Nordic " character by simple means, but in an astonishingly individual way: by antiphonal passages between the alto and male
voices, the brighter soprano not entering till later; or by a
monotonous chanting tone (*" Mädchen von Kola, du schläfst "*),
old-world harmonies, a free treatment of rhythm (alternate use of
2/2 and 3/2 bar), and harsh, unadorned colour, which only takes
on a more emotional quality in the sorrowing despair and
abandonment of grief towards the end of the first section,

where, at the words *" nimmer kommt dir die Sonne weckend an deine Ruhestätte,"* the voices strive upwards in groups of three.

The seven choral songs of op. 62 are evidently treated as simply and easily as possible in content, form, and composition. But we at once notice that they fall into two groups, according as they are in the new or the old style. In those whose words follow ancient models, Brahms is consciously archaic. The very first number, *Rosmarin* (from *Des Knaben Wunderhorn*), at once strikes the naïve folk note of the Middle Ages in a way which rings delightfully true, with just a slight touch of Schumannesque colour. The second, *Von alten Liebesliedern,* from the same source, with its lulling refrain, *" Trab, Rösslein, trab für und für,"* is full of the light elegance, courtesy and charming gaiety of the good old days. The fifth, *All' meine Herzgedanken,* from Heyse's *Jungbrunnen,* might almost be by Eccard, with its division of the voices into two groups, one of men, the other of women, and its strictly treated cadences. But the last, *Vergangen ist mir Glück und heil* (old German traditional words) is so archaic in treatment and enters with such fine intuition into the spirit and musical idiom of old German choral music, in both harmony and measure (4/2 bar), that Brahms's own personality falls entirely into the background; while in Heinrich Isaak's other lament, *Innsbruck, ich muss dich lassen,* we have the old imperishable model tangibly before us.

In the remaining pieces in this and the other collections enumerated above, with an admixture of secular choral songs, we find in particular, side by side with Brahms's typically melancholy resignation and mysterious communion with nature, very much that is beautiful, individual, and wonderfully melodious. To this category belong, for example, the two woodland scenes included among the four songs from Heyse's *Jungbrunnen,* op. 62. With what wonderful, German depth of feeling, steeped in intense emotion, almost in the manner of Mendelssohn, are we surrounded in the cool *Waldesnacht* (no. 3), and with what romantic tone and colour! How simple and poetic is the contrast in no. 6 (*Es geht ein Wehen*), where we first hear the tempest sweeping through the forest, kept close to earth, as it were, by the heavy, persistent minims in the bass, in the uncanny, subdued, restrained minor mode, followed by the bright major quality expressive of love's sweet hopes, with the soprano and tenor answering each other in soft, imitative passages!

In op. 93a and op. 104, which are in Brahms's late and still more resigned manner, we find, above all, Achim von Arnim's *O süsser Mai,* from op. 93a, full of intense grief, the two splendid night-pieces of Rückert's *Nachtwache* ("*Leise Töne der Brust*" —"*Ruhn sie? rufet das Horn des Wächters*"), Kalbeck's *Letztes Glück,* steeped in the sweet, gentle sorrow of quiet hopelessness, Wenzig's *Verlorene Jugend,* and Claus Groth's deeply melancholy *Herbst* ("*Ernst ist der Herbst*"), all belonging to the same category of laments. It is very characteristic of Brahms that these choral songs are among the loveliest things he ever wrote. This is true of the songs from Rückert's *Nachtwache* in particular, the brilliantly ornate gem of op. 104. The first of these two choruses ("*Leise Töne der Brust*") is a tender dialogue, a touching love-lament, between the two three-part groups of the six-part choir; the second, which was sung at the composer's funeral, in 1897, is a marvellous piece, full of the romance of night, more in the mood of Eichendorff than of Rückert. "*Ruhn sie?* (Are they at rest?) " —the question rings out in the still solemnity of the night like a horn-call and rises from the tonic to the dominant as one watchman passes it on to another; then comes the equally soft, grave answer: "*Sie ruhn* (They rest)," descending again from the dominant to the tonic and dying away on a note of soft, gentle peace. The whole thing is so magnificent that one would gladly pass such a "night-watch" as this ten times over. The remaining numbers of this collection are on the same extraordinarily high level, at least in the technique of their composition. This is particularly true of the art with which the imitative part-writing is handled in Wenzig's *Verlorene Jugend,* in five parts, with its canon in G minor between soprano and alto and afterwards between the first bass and the soprano. As regards content, the four-part setting of Claus Groth's *Herbst* rises, at its highest, to the level of the *Nachtwache,* transformed into accents of passionate emotion and of the deepest, sweetest resignation.

The four-part *Lieder und Romanzen* of op. 93a are not quite on the same high level, but are conceived on the whole with greater simplicity. Indeed, they, too, have an occasional admixture of a lighter folk-tone. One of them belongs to the Rhineland, the jolly *Der bucklichte Fiedler,* and two are Serbian, *Das Mädchen* and *Der Falke.* The wonderful tale of the hump-backed fiddler who is rewarded for his good playing by a lovely lady of Frankfurt, who removes his hump, is told with much verve as well as a suitable degree of realism — for instance, the ominous *Walpurgisnacht* suggestion, obtained by a bare fifth, in the representation of the great revels at the feast. The Serbian *Mädchen* — which also appeared later in op. 95 as a solo — enchants us, like all such productions of Brahms's with a Slav cast, by its individual combination of 3/4 and 4/4 time, producing a natural, unconstrained effect, and its naïve, lively folk-tone. The Serbian *Falke* is more reserved and restrained; but again the elastic and varied rhythm lends it a decidedly Slav character and folk-tone. The next number, Rückert's *Fahr' wohl!* is closely akin to Arnim's *O süsser Mai.* These two ravishing pages breathe the whole soft, sweet pain of parting which we feel on the departure of late summer and the migration of the birds. But the gem of this collection is the concluding number, Goethe's *Beherzigung,* a powerful and tellingly effective four-part double canon, with a sculptural quality, between soprano and tenor, alto and bass. This piece, combining the simplest construction in two parts with a consummate art which escapes the notice of the uninitiated — what a subtle touch is the inverted entry of the double canon in the tonic major at the beginning of the second part! — is at the same time a revelation of Brahms's own human experience.

The *Tafellied* ("*Dank der Damen*"), op. 93b, for six-part mixed choir with piano accompaniment, calls for a short separate examination. The title-page, adorned with garlands of vine-leaves, bears the dedication: "To my friends at Krefeld, January 28,

1885." We learn from Rudolf von der Leyen's little book on
Brahms that the work was first performed on that date, at a
festival concert of the Krefeld Konzertgesellschaft, and that
Brahms presented the manuscript to Rudolf von der Leyen's
brother-in-law, Alwin von Beckerath, and his sister Marie. This
"occasional" piece, in the best sense of the word, is one of the
least known of Brahms's compositions, but at the same time one
of the most charming and gay. Eichendorff's poem represents
a delicately polished dialogue between the ladies and gentlemen
at a banquet. The ladies archly reproach the men with doing
homage to other gods than their own sex — namely, red and
white wine. The men, not at all abashed, hastily instruct them
in the right way to fill a glass, and soon mollify them by the
gallant assurance that, even if they have no particular person
in mind as they sip their wine, they drink to the praise of all
beauty in general. The argument is conclusive, and both ladies and
gentlemen unite at the end in mutual thanks. As regards form,
Brahms has preserved the spirit of the dialogue with extraordinary
homogeneity by means of a vigorously rhythmical, jovial, and
buoyant theme, nor has he omitted to supplement it by a finely
written pianoforte accompaniment. At the end the two choirs,
which have so far been handled separately, unite in a brilliant
six-part passage, heightened, if possible, by a slightly fugal
treatment ("*Sänger, Frau'n, wo die im Bunde*"). It is also
a drinking-song, but one more suited for an intimate, festive
circle than for a great concert-hall. It requires rather too well
trained a choir for the former, while for the latter the piano
accompaniment is on rather too small a scale. Perhaps this is
one material reason for the regrettable fact that — even in the
books on Brahms — this *Tafellied* is still treated almost as an
apocryphal work.

As regards works for male-voice choir, German music unfortunately only owes one to Brahms, but a very important one,
the *Fünf Lieder,* op. 41, dating from the late sixties. The fact
that this splendid work has not yet become a leading feature in
the repertory of male-voice choirs is merely evidence of the

more and more commonplace, sentimental, effeminate, artificial
modern spirit which has affected the style of German male-voice
choirs. These songs, indeed, offer no languishing serenades to
coo, no lullabies for a hundred voices to hum, no old Teutonic
battle-pieces or grisly ballads about spectres to be realistically
represented with a heavy brush. But they set themselves to solve
the real, inherent problems of handling male-voice choirs: first
comes an old German *Jägerlied* ("*Ich schwing' mein Horn in's
Jammertal*"), with a setting of austere, old-world harmonies based
on the triad; next come settings of four of Carl Lemcke's soldier
songs, full of the pithy, blunt humour native to the German
soldier. No. 1, about a love-lorn young huntsman — which we
also know as a solo, *Ich schell' mein Horn,* from op. 43 — will be
no surprise to us; the adoption of the austere style and serious
tone of the old German choral song, particularly in compositions
for male choirs, with their sombre tone-colour, was sure to appeal
to Brahms. The remaining four numbers reveal his patriotic side.
We know from the reminiscences of Widmann, Jenner, and
Ferdinand Schumann what an enthusiastic soldier Brahms would
have been. Here he also reveals it in his music, and it is to be
hoped and desired that, in spite of all internal and external
cataclysms, these songs will keep alive and preserve what is good
and sound in the militarism of the German soldier people for
better times in the future. The first and best-known of these four
martial pieces, the *Freiwillige, her!* is certainly not the most
remarkable musically, but it produces a stirring effect by its
brisk, rousing, declamatory rhythm and its virile, steely character. The thoughtful, gentle side of the honest German soldier
is shown in the following number, *Geleit,* in which Brahms shows
him blessing the lowered coffin in the tender refrain at the end
of every strophe: "*Auf Wiedersehn,*" from Mendelssohn's popular
farewell song, *Es ist bestimmt in Gottes Rat.* The next number,
the fourth, *Marschieren,* is a fine piece, with its youthful, tur-
bulent, progressive humour, its good-humoured, blunt insubor-
dination to all tactless seniors, and its full, popular conclusion.
The last number, *Gebt Acht!* like the first and second, is serious

in spirit. For the first time Brahms appears, as he was to do much
later, in the *Triumphlied* and the *Fest- und Gedenksprüche,* as
the *" treuer Eckart"* of the German people. A good ten years
before the outbreak of the war with France, he raised his warning, admonitory voice, cautioning his countrymen to be on their
guard against the external enemies secretly threatening them on
all sides; this rousing, sharp, peremptory clarion call in fifths
and fourths runs through the whole of this piece, producing
an elemental effect. Nowadays its impression will be felt to
be tragically heart-rending, recalling the grudging envy with
which Germany's coming greatness was already regarded at that
time, and heralding a new and better race. And now once again
we may sum up the character of this unique book of Brahms
songs, shortly and in general terms, as good, solid fare for
German male-voice choirs, full of sound, virile strength, and
standing poles apart from all the feeble, snivelling efforts of
provincial choral societies.

A special place among Brahms's lesser choral works is taken
by a small set of songs which appeared about the middle of the
sixties without opus number: *Deutsche Volkslieder,* arranged
for four-part chorus. Here again, as in the *Ungarische Tänze,*
the word " arranged " emphasizes the fact that the melodies are
by another hand: they are taken from F. M. Böhme's old German
song-book, and rearranged by Brahms, in the manner of the
old German collections of songs made by Finck, Forster, Ott,
and others in the sixteenth century, with the finest sympathetic
insight into early folk art, some with polyphonic elaboration,
some with homophonic simplicity. As a discriminating and
thorough connoisseur of old vocal music, he has done his work
with incomparable tact and understanding. But fortunately he
has turned these melodies not only into something new, but into
something truly Brahmsian. Whoever plunges deep into the
serious numbers in these collections, permeated by a profound
resignation — such, for instance, as *In stiller Nacht* or *Schnitter
Tod* — will know what we mean by this.

XXX

THE *DEUTSCHES REQUIEM*

It was the *Deutsches Requiem,* op. 45, Brahms's most important choral work and the most widely known composition of the mass type since Beethoven, that really laid the foundation of his world-wide fame. This triumph is to be explained by its character, in which emotion and sentiment are given strong prominence, and also by the wonderful melodious magic of its tender themes, which are thoroughly singable and have a superb amplitude of line. Its ideal of beauty is the classical one: not classical with the wide, free intellectual horizon of a Bach, a Handel, or a Beethoven, but classicistic, comparable in the eneffably moving loveliness of its grief and mourning with the art of a Thorwaldsen.

In spite of the entirely unsectarian choice and applicability of its words, Brahms's *Deutsches Requiem* is not a Catholic mass for the dead, but a fundamentally Protestant one. The Protestant quality lies not so much in the fact that the words are German — "a German text such as this may please you as well as the accustomed Latin one," wrote the composer to Clara Schumann — or that the *Requiem* entirely departs from the well-known form in five movements of the Roman mass for the dead, as because its spirit is totally different. And this fundamental divergence is due to a different conception of death and of the life after death. In the Roman Catholic mass for the dead the foreground and middle distance are occupied by the *Dies Iræ,* the day of wrath, the last judgment, which threatens the departed with purgatory and the pains of hell, and is only turned into a day of eternal beatitude through the intercession of the saints and the fervent supplications of those who are left behind. The Protestant *Requiem,* on the other hand, professes a gentler faith in a blissful resurrection and reunion through the atoning death of Jesus Christ. Its underlying idea is somewhat as follows: Blessed are they which mourn, for they shall be comforted. It is true that all flesh is as grass and all the glory of man like the flower of grass; it is true that every man must die one day. But death is not an eternal annihilation; the redeemed of the Lord shall obtain everlasting joy and gladness, and sorrow and sighing shall flee away. And, therefore, we say in the end: Blessed are the dead who die in the Lord from this time on. For death leads us into a better life; those who led a god-fearing and upright life on earth, shall see their dear ones again in heaven, and rest from their cares and labour, for their works follow them.

Thus the Roman liturgical and dogmatic ceremonial office for the dead is transformed into the German funeral ceremony, accessible to all creeds and stages of belief, universally human, and transfigured by music, whose deeply moving emotional effect is due by no means least to the comforting, sanguine mildness of its underlying conception, to the possibility of reconciling the terrible discrepancy between the nothingness and transitoriness of things earthly, between the terrors of the last judgment on the one hand, and celestial glory on the other. Only once, in the sixth movement, does the "hour of the last trump," the older conception of the *Dies Iræ,* predominate for a brief and terrifying moment. The planning and carrying out of this deep conception of reconciliation in words freely chosen from the Holy Scriptures were Brahms's own, thoroughly personal work. None but he, who confessed to his friend Rudolf von der Leyen that, like a true North German, he longed for the Bible every day, never let a day go by without it, and could lay his hand on his Bible in his study even in the dark — who, from childhood upwards, was a devoted believer in the Bible — none but he could have succeeded so beautifully, and with such subtle discrimination, in realizing his conception so perfectly in the fitting-together of the words, in a way that has never been sufficiently appreciated. Later, in his greater choral works, the *Schicksalslied* and the *Gesang*

der Parzen, he often rang the changes on these eternal, fundamental ideas, on the everlasting antithesis between the earthly
and the heavenly life, between transiency and misery on the one
hand, and eternity on the other — between life and death.

The *Deutsches Requiem* consists of seven movements. Only
three of them, the third, fifth, and sixth, have solo parts interwoven with them, all the others are purely choral. In spite of
the brief *Dies Iræ* episode in the sixth movement, it is permissible
to divide the whole into two parts, based on its inward feeling.
The first half — the first to the third movements — is devoted
almost entirely to earthly suffering, lamentation and mourning
over the transitoriness and nothingness of human life, rather than
to the consolation and the everlasting bliss of the redeemed.
In the second half — the fourth to the seventh movements —
mourning is gradually transformed, passing through the stages
of pious faith, consolation, and joy in the living God, to celestial
bliss and triumphant resurrection.

Each separate movement of the *Deutsches Requiem* has its
own definite and special character, with an unmistakable and
clearly defined stamp, that is carried out even down to its individual tonal scheme. This latter is also North German and
Brahmsian in its preference for sombre colour. How beautiful
and how eloquent is the rejection of the bright tone-colour of
the violins in the first movement: " *Selig sind, die da Leid
tragen* (Blessed are they that mourn, for they shall be comforted) "! The same factors as those which lend the second
Brahms serenade its suggestion of mystery and night — the division of the violas into groups, and the soft use of the harps —
impart to the first movement of the *Requiem* a character of
heart-rendingly sublime and quiet grief. We forget that earlier
composers, such as Méhul (in his *Uthal*), Cherubini, Hauptmann,
etc., omitted the violins from their dramatic and religious compositions, or in similar cases of a sombre spiritual mood, and feel
this subtle touch of Brahms's as something new and original,
owing to its poetic inspiration. But the same is the case with
the tonal scheme of the remaining movements. They are

conceived with such genius, yet at the same time so simply, that they at once reveal how little ground there is for the opinion that Brahms had no skill in instrumentation. We may here cite a few very characteristic examples: in the second movement — "*Denn alles Fleisch, es ist wie Gras, und alle Herrlichkeit des Menschen wie des Grases Blume* (For all flesh is as grass) " — we have a contrast in tone between the chorus and the orchestra; the former, with its distant old-world reminiscences of the chorale *Wer nur den lieben Gott lässt walten,* is sung in unison by the choir, and passes by rigid and inexorable as one of the riders in the Apocalypse, while the orchestra drags along in a heavy funeral-march rhythm. It is also in contrast with the mighty pæan of rejoicing in the concluding section: "*Die Erlöseten des Herrn* (And the redeemed of the Lord shall come to Zion with songs and everlasting joy upon their heads)." This unison passage for the choir has as its thematic germs, from which it is derived by diminution into crotchets and quavers, the principal subject of the B minor scherzo of the B major Piano Trio, op. 8, and the principal subject of the finale of the E flat major Horn Trio, op. 40. In the third movement — "*Herr, lehre doch mich, dass es ein Ende mit mir haben muss* (Lord, show me mine end) " — we have the same sharp contrast between the curiously open and thin scoring of the orchestral parts, and the words of the solo baritone, tossed up and down by unrest and anguish of soul, and broken into short phrases, on the one hand, and the compactly constructed, exultant concluding fugue, on the words " *Der Gerechten Seelen sind in Gottes Hand* (The souls of the righteous are in God's hand)," with its strict counterpoint and the resonant pedal point on D continuing for thirty-six double bars, on the other. In the third, with its Mendelssohnian grace — " *Wie lieblich* (How lovely are Thy dwellings, O Lord God of Sabaoth) " — we have the rich use of the suave wood-wind and horns, scored in the most open way. In the *Dies Iræ* section of the sixth movement we note the compact choral writing, distractedly huddled together in close harmony at narrow intervals — " *Denn es wird die Posaune schallen* (The trumpet shall sound) " — and in the seventh and last, at the words " *Ja, der Geist spricht* (Yea, the Spirit also maketh utterance)," the use of the trombones to give an awe-inspiring or mystically visionary atmosphere to certain passages.

Behind the tonal effects stand the form and content. The form of the *Deutsches Requiem,* like the selection of the Biblical passages, is a masterpiece in itself both as a whole and in its parts. The form of the separate numbers consists, as a rule, of two sections, for the most part based upon abrupt contrasts of both spirit and form — for instance, between grief and joy (first movement), between earthly anguish and the everlasting bliss of heaven (second movement), between the uneasy doubts, perplexity, and moral suffering of man and divine repose and steadfastness (third movement), between mourning and consolation (fifth movement), between death, the grave, and the last judgment, on the one hand, and the resurrection on the other (sixth movement). Thematically the form of the whole forms a complete cycle, the choir singing: " *Selig sind die Toten* (Blessed are the dead which die in the Lord)," in the last movement, to the theme which in the first movement accompanies the words " *Selig sind, die da Leid tragen* (Blessed are they that mourn)."

The well-defined, separate character of each individual movement, on which we have laid stress above, makes any comparison of the movements among themselves somewhat unprofitable. On the whole, it may be said that in this work, too, Brahms always has the most beautiful and personal message to give when his aim is to express in music serene resignation, mild, grave consolation, a deep *Weltschmerz,* sorrowful lamentation, deeply agitated moral unrest, an exquisitely idyllic atmosphere, or mystic visionary absorption. To such moods, for instance, belong the whole of the first and last movements, with the wonderful nobility of their ample melodic line and suave cantilena passages, and, again, the rigid, gloomy passage in the form of a funeral march in the second movement, the prayerful passage of the third movement, which only gradually and painfully regains its composure after tortures of moral suffering, the soft, Biblical idyll of the fourth, or, lastly, the melancholy mingling of grief and consolation in the fifth, and the powerful imaginative conceptions of death, the grave, the last judgment, and the resurrection in the sixth movement. Perhaps, indeed, it is precisely these inexorably harsh, wild, and gloomy imaginative passages in the second and sixth movements which form the crown of the whole work, both spiritually and musically. In individual quality, on the other hand, though by no means in contrapuntal mastery, inward fervour, and outward brilliance, the mighty choral movements and fugues of the second, third, and sixth movements, dealing with the resurrection, the blissful ecstasy and exultant joy of the redeemed in Zion, the glory and worship of God, are inferior to these. They are derived from Handel (in his oratorios), Bach (in his Passions and B minor Mass), and Beethoven (in his *Missa Solennis* and Ninth Symphony), and it is mainly in them, with their lavish but unobtrusive use of all the resources of the contrapuntal art of the early masters, that the archaizing elements in the *Requiem* are chiefly to be found. Two of them rise to towering and giddy heights: the Handelian D major fugue, with the famous pedal point at the words " *Der Gerechten Seelen sind in Gottes Hand* (The souls of the righteous are in God's hand)," at the close of the third, and the powerful, rock-hewn, monumentally Bach-like fugue in C major on the words " *Herr, du bist würdig, zu nehmen Preis und Ehre und Kraft* (Worthy art Thou, O Lord, to receive blessing and honour and strength)," in the sixth movement, which is even more grandiose in style. The typically Brahmsian features in the great choral fugues which form the climax of these movements consist in the tranquil, gravely contemplative, or beatific episodes enshrined in them: for instance, the passage " *Ewige Freude wird über ihrem Haupte sein* (Everlasting joy shall be upon their heads)," in the great choral section of the second, at the words " *Die Erlöseten des Herrn werden wiederkommen* (The redeemed of the Lord shall return to Zion) "; or the passage " *Denn du hast alle Dinge erschaffen* (For Thou hast created all things)," in the great C major choral fugue of the sixth movement.

To sum up: Brahms's *Deutsches Requiem* stands in the front rank of the great masterpieces of Protestant church music, with an appeal for all creeds, which point the way from Bach and Handel, through Beethoven's *Missa Solennis* and Mendelssohn's oratorios, into modern times. But just as in the case of Mendelssohn, it is the comparatively less important middle movements — the fourth, " *Wie lieblich sind deine Wohnungen* (How lovely are Thy dwellings) " — composed after the rest, and in Brahms's own opinion " certainly the weakest piece of choral writing in the *Requiem* " — and the fifth, " *Ihr habt nun Traurigkeit,*" with its celestially serene soprano solo — that have been admitted to the repertory of church choirs and sacred concerts even in quite small towns; and this is indicative of the character of Brahms's art, which was in the noblest sense bourgeois, full of human sentiment, and North German in its type of emotion. But it is also significant of all the due and obvious interval which separates him from the corresponding great works of Bach and Handel in oratorio form, which serve more and more as a criterion for judging Brahms's *Deutsches Requiem*. If, for instance, we have now arrived at a different and somewhat cooler estimate of the fugal movements of the *Deutsches Requiem,* which used to be placed on the same level as those of the great old masters — if, again, even the famous great organ-point in " *Der Gerechten Seelen* " no longer seems to grip us quite so much, this at least shows that perhaps the palmy days of Brahms's *Requiem* are already over, that by lapse of time Brahms's reputation as a symphony-writer has outstripped his reputation as a vocal-composer. But this naturally in no way detracts from the great importance and unique beauty of the *Deutsches Requiem* itself, which far transcends the judgment of a single age.

XXXI

THE LARGER CHORAL WORKS

Of Brahms's larger choral works four — the *Rinaldo,* the *Alto Rhapsody,* from Goethe's *Harzreise im Winter,* the *Schicksalslied,* and the *Triumphlied* — came into being during the years 1869–72; two, the *Nänie* and the *Gesang der Parzen,* some ten years later, between 1881 and 1889. This can be detected especially in the form and style: the later the date, the more concentrated, concise, and austere these become. But as regards subject the *Schicksalslied,* the *Gesang der Parzen* and the *Rinaldo* belong to the first or classical antique group, the *Alto Rhapsody* and the *Rinaldo* to the second or Goethean group, the *Triumphlied* to the third or patriotic group.

Of all these the *Schicksalslied,* for mixed choir and orchestra, op. 54, is the most nearly akin to the *Deutsches Requiem,* in both spirit and form. This " Little Requiem," as it has been called, likewise deals with the eternal contrast between life and death, between the cruel sufferings of struggling mankind and the gods enjoying celestial peace and bliss, between the uncertain and transitory on the one hand and the eternal on the other. It treats this contrast as expressed in a poem by Friedrich Hölderlin, romantic in its splendid pictures of the heavenly beings on high treading the soft floor of heaven in eternal light, drawing their breath as unconscious of destiny as the sleeping infant, and gazing in rapture into the tranquil atmosphere of eternal brightness; and then of suffering man, falling from hour to hour down into the unknown and tossed like water from rock to rock; classical, for all its tenderness, for all its deep undertone of mild reconciliation and compassion, in its pitiless recognition and rendering of that power of fate which overshadows pagan antiquity. Among the eternal gods there is neither destiny nor compassion nor pity.

Merciless and desolate — so run the concluding verses — nothing abides eternally among men save their wretched destiny and the uncertainty as to their ultimate bourne.

Brahms is no Hyperion; in him, as we shall see confirmed even more clearly in the *Gesang der Parzen,* nothing is to be found of that antique grandeur, that conception of life as dominated by the power of fate, which belongs to really great artists — to Bach, Handel, Mozart, or Beethoven, or even to Schubert, in spite of his simple humanity and inferior culture, as compared to that of Brahms. There is a surging rush of compassion and pity for the tortured human race at the end, where the composer attempts to mitigate and, so far as possible, to eliminate the pitiless classical conception of fate, with a tender sensibility that is as German as it is characteristically Brahmsian. Yet, by so doing, he only reveals the fact that he lacks that universality of feeling that is the heritage of none but very great artists and is inseparable from real greatness. And this was not due to any lack of culture, for Brahms was one of the most highly cultivated composers of all time, but simply because the ancient Greek conception of fate remained foreign to his nature.

Thus Brahms does not see it as his principal task to bring out the dread contrasts in this poem between heaven and earth, gods and men, in equally pitiless, inflexible, and inexorable music, with all the antique fatality of this conception of eternity, but rather to veil it in compassion and pity and, to the best of his power, to keep it in the background. His conception is neither antique, universal, nor grandly conceived, but it is honest, full of human beauty and nobility, and typically Brahmsian and provides yet another fine and instructive piece of evidence against the theory of Brahms's alleged harshness. He achieves his purpose in a manner as simple as it is full of genius and eloquence, by repeating at the end in C major (*adagio*) the wonderful, nobly ecstatic, yearning, and blissfully serene orchestral introduction in E flat major (*langsam und sehnsuchtsvoll*) like a dreamy, tender vision, and so leads back the listener, who has been harrowed by the human life-struggle which has gone before, to peace, gentle melancholy, tranquillity, and hope.

But this is also accompanied by a deep perception which, as it were, interprets the antique in terms of Christianity: he satisfies earthly longing by promises of heaven, suggesting that, in spite of all, a better fate awaits mankind than the terrible doom depicted by the poet. Accordingly, the supreme beauty and individuality of the music are to be found rather in all the parts characterized by longing and hope, soft melancholy, and tranquil, serenely uplifted joy than in the dramatically and dæmonically graphic and striking representation of the hopeless striving and fall of suffering mankind, which he sometimes elects to express in broad, harsh, rugged unison passages in the choral part, accompanied by wildly agitated quaver figures in the orchestra, sometimes in a polyphonic handling of the vocal parts, tranquilly fugal in style and full of softly submissive and mournful resignation, sometimes in outcries of passionate despair — as at the word " *blindlings* (blindfold) " — sometimes in wailing chromatic progressions, sometimes in broken, distracted falterings — as at the words " *in's Ungewisse hinab* (downwards into the unknown)." To the former order belong the instrumental prologue and epilogue, the lightly hovering representation of the realm of the gods and of the celestial beings treading its soft ground in beatitude, over which he throws the bright, tender colour of the wood-wind (flutes) in the orchestral accompaniment — in the passage where the alto choir sings: " *Ihr wandelt droben im Licht* (Ye walk above in the light) " — and the whole of the middle section, from the melody which unfolds itself so magnificently to a celestial accompaniment of harps on the words " *wie die Finger der Künstlerin heilige Saiten* (as the harper's fingers the holy strings)," to the lovely unaccompanied concluding passage, which shows the gods gazing blissfully into the tranquil brightness of eternity. In such parts as these alone is to be found the classical antique element of the *Schicksalslied,* as well as its spiritual and musical affinity with similar lyrical movements and sections of the *Deutsches Requiem,* which is at times very close: we may compare in particular the soothing, ecstatic final cadence of the " *der Künstlerin heilige Saiten* " section with that on the words " *Ewige Freude wird über ihrem Haupte sein* " in that great religious work. There, as here, a mighty rush of emotion is followed by a perfectly tranquil conclusion, full of introspective and devotional sentiment. There, as here, Brahms strikes his deepest and most moving note of grief and consolation. In the *Schicksalslied* this occurs at the place where the second and last representation of the fall of the mortals dies down and expires amid a prolonged, muffled roll of kettledrums and shuddering laments and sighs in bare unison passages for each pair of vocal parts in turn (" *in's Ungewisse hinab* "); whereupon the serenely visionary orchestral epilogue to which we have alluded draws, as it were, a gentle veil of Christian pity and sympathy over the pitiless rigour of this scene of antique fatality and its powers.

Both poetically and musically the *Gesang der Parzen* (from Goethe's *Iphigenie*), op. 89, for six-part choir and orchestra, stands in the same relation to the *Schicksalslied* as the latter does to the *Deutsches Requiem*. As regards poetic content, the two are linked together by their underlying idea, that of the harsh contrast between the beatific repose of the gods, on the one hand, and mortal humanity, which they have cast down pitilessly and indifferently " *in nächtliche Tiefen* (into the abysses of night)," as a punishment for its dissensions, where it waits in vain for a just judgment and is visited by the gods with curses and exile even to remote generations. On the one hand are the glorious peace of heaven, with thrones standing round golden tables on the rocks and clouds, and eternal feasting; on the other hand, the grim battle between Titans and men in the depths of the abyss, the ban laid upon their children and children's children, and their exile to gloomy caverns. The musical affinity between the *Gesang der Parzen* and the *Schicksalslied* is quite obvious — most of all, perhaps, where similar words — " *auf Klippen und Wolken sind Stühle bereitet* (thrones are made ready on crag and on cloud) " — are the occasion for similar writing of the vocal parts, interspersed with pauses in a way that is, as it were, a modern revival of the "hoketus" of mediæval music. In the *Schicksalslied* the four parts sing together, crotchet chords alternating with crotchet rests; in the *Gesang der Parzen* the three female voices and the three male voices answer each other antiphonally in a *stretto* passage. The affinity is also evident in the following passage, depicting the eternal realm of the gods. For the rest, the *Gesang der Parzen* is incomparably more concise as regards its musical form and is much more homogeneous and lapidary in character than the *Schicksalslied*.

This extreme conciseness recalls the art of classical antiquity. There is also an antique flavour, both in music and in character, about all those elements which suggest the lofty unapproachableness, the pitiless rigour and unfeeling indifference, of the eternal gods, and mankind's dread of them. Witness the strict *legato,* the massiveness combined with deeply suffering agitation, of the orchestral introduction in D minor (*maestoso*), witness the "leading theme (*leitthema*)" of the whole of the principal section, upon which the two separate groups of male and female voices declaim antiphonally the lament: "*Es fürchte die Götter das Menschengeschlecht* (Let the race of mankind fear the gods)," to an accompaniment of muffled, rolling kettledrums and in a spirit of profound resignation, broken, as it were, and paralysed before a fearful power. Witness the imposing passage expressive of the dread power of the gods, in Handelian dotted rhythms ("*Auf Klippen und Wolken sind Stühle bereitet um goldene Tische*"), or of their divine unconcern and festal rejoicing — "*Sie aber, sie bleiben in ewigen Festen an goldenen Tischen* (But they remain at their golden tables, feasting for ever and ever)" — or of the hideous downfall of the mortals whom they have spurned — "*Erhebet ein Zwist sich, so stürzen die Gäste, geschmäht und geschändet, in nächtliche Tiefen* (Should discord arise, the guests are hurled down to abysses of gloom, contemned and dishonoured)" — with a music almost Bach-like in the stern symbolism of its tone, and homogeneously derived from the "leading theme" in the development of the rebellious *stretto* passage, modulating wildly as though in transports of rage.

But classicistic is not the same thing as classical. Goethe's conception of the inexorable and pitiless power of fate is entirely classical. The more classical — in the Hellenic and Goethean sense of the word — a composer's sense of it is, the more inexorable and pitiless will be his setting of the poem; most of all in those words in the last strophe but one which determine the whole character of the poetical scheme: "*Es wenden die Herrscher ihr segnendes Auge von ganzen Geschlechtern, und meiden, im Enkel die ehmals geliebten, still redenden Züge des Ahnherrn zu sehn* (But the rulers on high avert their favouring eye from whole generations, nor deign to behold in the young the traits that silently tell of their once loved sire)." But Brahms does not do this. He modifies the end of the *Gesang der Parzen*, as he does that of the *Schicksalslied*, softening it and introducing a feeling of pity and compassion for the mortals hurled down by the gods from on high. Once again we must repeat that this is not classical, not really great and universal in the Greek sense as reflected in Goethe; but it has a human nobility and beauty which command our entire respect and are truly Brahmsian. And, again, this is not a quality which can be acquired by culture, however lofty, or by any intellectual process of the understanding; it must be an organic part of the nature and feeling of the man and artist. Brahms did not possess it, nor did he profess to be able to do justice to such subjects, such conceptions of eternity, in form at least. And so he merges and steeps the whole of this second concluding section — which, as we said before, opens with the six-part chorus unaccompanied — in gentle melancholy and soft lamentation, in a spirit of bitter-sweet memory of the happy days that are no more, which is intrinsically wonderful, deeply soothing and serene in its effect. And at the end it is in the same spirit that he sets the words of the final strophe, which throw, as it were, a veil of legendary unreality over the whole with the words: "*So sangen die Parzen; es horcht der Verbannte in nächtlichen Höhlen, der Alte, die Lieder, denkt Kinder und Enkel und schüttelt das Haupt* (So sang the three Fates; the old man in exile in his gloomy caverns gives ear to their songs and thinks of his children and his children's children and shakes his head sadly)." He produces this effect by the perfectly plain, subdued chant-like psalmody of the choral parts, which now sing separately, now two or three at a time, and gradually die away *pianissimo* into nothingness.

Brahms was very fond of both these two works, which were the first of his to be tinged with the classical antique spirit. In the first section of the present work we saw the account in Dietrich's reminiscences of how the first draft of the *Schicksalslied* was sketched out on the sea-shore at Wilhelmshaven, and the special stress which he laid on the fact that the composer was "stirred to his depths" by Hölderlin's poem. Von der Leyen has told us how, at the first performance of the *Gesang der Parzen* at Krefeld, Brahms "had great tears of emotion and joy running down his cheeks." This is very characteristic and confirms what we said above about the temperamental reasons which inspired Brahms's "twisting (*Umbiegung*)" of the concluding parts of both works.

The third of this group of what may be called Brahms's choral works of classical Greek inspiration is his setting of Schiller's *Nänie,* op. 82, for chorus and orchestra (with harp *ad libitum*), as an elegy on the premature death of his friend the painter Anselm Feuerbach, dedicated to the artist's mother, Frau Hofrat Henriette Feuerbach, who survived her son and died in 1880. The explanation of the title is to be found in classical literature: *neniæ* were the laments for the dead sung at their funerals, originally by the surviving relatives, but later by hired female mourners, who beat their breasts and arms in sign of grief as they sang. Schiller's *Nänie,* set by Brahms, is an ode to Death, as personified by the Greeks. He is represented as a kindly young divinity, the twin brother of Sleep, with his torch reversed. Softly he extinguishes the flame of life; the dead man is laid in a sarcophagus or burnt, and his ashes preserved in an urn, both ceremonies taking place at some distance outside the city, with the sacred funerary roads leading out into the open country and lined with tombs. Both mausoleum and tombstone are adorned with graceful reliefs representing the life, calling, and activities of the dead man and are not in the least ashamed to preserve some echo of the gayer side of life.

The *Nänie* of Schiller and Brahms had its origin in this spirit of the Greek and Roman dirges of " pagan " antiquity. It is a gem of musical charm, tenderness, gentleness, and suavity, transforming grief into tender melancholy, lamentation into consolation, mourning into sweetly sad memory and friendly reconciliation. " *Auch das Schöne muss sterben* (Even the beautiful must die)," sing the mourners in the broad, tranquil opening chorus, in 6/4 time, which flows on in exquisite progressions, with no poignant accents of grief, despair, or lamentation, in a simple fugal form, ending on a note of growing tranquillity and consolation: " *Auch ein Klaglied zu sein im Mund der Geliebten ist herrlich* (Even to be a lament in the mouth of the loved one is glorious)." It is no mere chance that the " mouth of the beloved " once again echoes the *Deutsches Requiem*: it is in the grave, mild, tender tones of its grief and consolation, in the Thorwaldsen-like expression of supreme grace and charm even in grief for the beloved dead, that the *Nänie* is most deeply and intimately akin to the first and last movements of the *Deutsches Requiem*. In both of them the words and atmosphere of the poem determine even the tonal scheme of the composition. The tender, soft colour of the wood-wind and horns, the open scoring of the strings, the sombre colour of the three trombones, the light colour of the harps, which are used in a number of places, in order to give, so far as possible, a Greek suggestion, are predominant throughout. How sparingly and yet how subtly, for instance, are the trombones introduced; they form the sole accompaniment to the highly agitated battle-scene, in which the divine Achilles " *am skäischen Tor fallend, sein Schicksal erfüllt* (falls at the Skæan gate, fulfilling his destiny)," and they mingle their grave tones softly and solemnly in the deep lament " *dass das Vollkommene stirbt, das Schöne vergeht* (that the perfect should die, that the beautiful passes away)."

The underlying character of the Schiller-Brahms *Nänie* is

one of grief restrained by a tranquil, antique grace. It is only in the passage where the foam-born goddess Aphrodite rises from the sea with all the daughters of Nereus and raises a lament over her glorified son that the sun breaks for a moment through the clouds, which are dark, but nowhere heavy, in the brilliant key of F sharp major and the broad, full melody of the lament, in 4/4 time, with a rushing harp accompaniment. The theme of the concluding section once more recalls the first; it takes on a little warmth once again in a few short, magnificent unaccompanied bars — on the words "*im Mund der Geliebten* (in the mouth of the loved one) " — then concludes in a blissfully uplifted tone on the word "*herrlich* (glorious)," repeated softly several times. And thus the music of Brahms's *Nänie* becomes at the same time splendidly symbolic of the art of him whose premature end it laments: namely, Anselm Feuerbach, the great reviver of the classical antique in a modern spirit.

A second group of Brahms's larger choral works, set to words by Goethe, which is far less often heard, is formed by the *Alto Rhapsody,* from Goethe's *Harzreise im Winter,* and the *Rinaldo.* The *Rhapsody,* op. 53, for alto solo, male choir, and orchestra, requires a short explanation of its poetic subject, which is hard to understand without recalling Goethe's travels in the Harz Mountains in the winter of 1777, upon which he was induced to start out, as he told Charlotte von Stein, by a desire to visit the Brocken and to pursue his geological researches in the mines, but most of all by a desire to make the personal acquaintance of young Plessing, who had taken refuge in correspondence with him from his misanthropic, self-tormenting, Wertherian mood. He was accompanied by his own gloomy, passionately agitated thoughts, by oppressive memories and a turmoil of emotion. All of this still quivers in this glorious poem. Brahms, the modern master of *Weltschmerz* and resignation in music, was of all people the one who was most likely to be tempted to set it to music. He chose three stanzas from it, on which are based the three sections of his work, which follow on directly, one after the other. The first, "*Aber abseits, wer ist's* (But who is that who walks apart?)," *adagio,* in C minor and 4/4 time, in which the orchestra plays the leading role, depicts, by the simplest and most vivid musical devices, the unhappy young man, at odds with himself and the world, wandering aloof and solitary through the wintry desolation of the mountains; by a sighing theme in the bass, descending step by step heavily into the depths, by stabbing *sforzati,* bleak tremolos on the muted strings, overloaded chords, abrupt alternations of dynamic power, and blank bars, filled only by the bass and the solo voice, which depicts the situation feelingly in a few sparing touches, sometimes in a regular melody, sometimes half in declamatory style. The whole is a sombre instrumental piece, with obbligato solo voice, full of intense feeling, and at first indicating the general background. In the second section, " *Ach, wer heilet die Schmerzen dess, dem Balsam zu Gift ward* (Ah, who shall heal the pain of him to whom the healing balm becomes a poison?)," *poco andante* in C minor, 6/4 time, we change from the general to the particular and subjective. The voice now laments in sympathy with the unhappy young man, with a tranquil, broadly traced melodic line, and an outward composure expressed by the calm minims above a firm bass; but this composure is only achieved by an effort, as is revealed by the wide, spasmodic leaps of the voice and the inward agitation, which becomes almost dramatically intense at the word " *Menschenhass* (hatred of mankind)." The orchestra falls into the background, acting as a mere accompaniment, and only occasionally sustaining an independent role for a short time, as, for instance, at the words " *aus der Fülle der Liebe trank* (drank deep draughts of love)," where it endeavours, by a suave melody in thirds and suspensions charged with emotion, to introduce a softer and more pleasing tone into this sombrely agitated section. The third section, " *Ist auf deinem Psalter, Vater der Liebe, ein Ton seinem Ohr vernehmlich* (If his ear can catch a note from thy lyre, O father of love)," *adagio* in C major, 4/4 time, is a glowing, fervent, humble prayer that he may find refreshment and healing. Here for the first time the male choir enters, *pianissimo* and *mezza voce,* with a profoundly moving effect, and the alto solo, soaring above it, joins it in a melody full of deep and painful emotion and restrained melancholy, expressive of devout faith and ardent prayer, of a type peculiar to Brahms, above an accompaniment of *pizzicato* triplets on the basses. Here again the nobly uplifted note of love and longing in Beethoven's song-cycles is once more struck. How nobly and with what over-flowing warmth is the conclusion — " *erquicke sein Herz* (refresh his heart) " — built up, like some miraculous little shrine, in a final imitative passage, and in what simple, elevated, and beatific accents does it die away in the heavenly serenity of the key of C major! The man who could write such passages as these was a man of real goodness and feeling. There are few passages in Brahms's works in which the composer has laid bare his inmost heart so directly and beautifully as in this third section of the *Alto Rhapsody*.

But not only is this rhapsody truly Brahmsian; we may almost say that it breathes the very spirit of the Harz Mountains. It is Nordic in character, with a grave, melancholy beauty and the calm, grand lines of the mountains. And when, at the beginning of the third strophe, the alto and male choir appear, as it were, by their wonderful song of supplication to dispel the oppressive, heavy gloom of the two preceding strophes, the genuine atmos-phere of the Harz Mountains is once more suggested, just as when, in late summer, the mild, subdued evening sun breaks through the tender, transparent, silvery mist, transfiguring and reconciling all things.

Brahms was particularly attached to this rhapsody, with its strongly defined and deeply fervent character, for it was a piece after his own heart. The words with which he sent it to Dietrich are, indeed, curt and dry enough: " Conductors will not exactly fight for this opus; to you at least it may perhaps be gratifying that I do not always express myself in the frivolous 3/4 time " (an allusion, no doubt, to the *Liebeslieder-Walzer,* which had ap-peared shortly before). But he did also say to Dietrich on one occasion that he was " so fond of this work that he could not help putting it under his pillow at night, so as to have it always

with him." And this very intimate avowal is in keeping with
the effect of these " wonderful, deeply earnest, heart-stirring accents," this " marvellously intimate, profoundly moving piece "
upon Clara Schumann, in whom it produced " deep agitation," in
the year of its origin, as we are expressly informed by Eugenie
Schumann. Just at that time, when Julie Schumann was marrying
and leaving home, and signs of incurable mental derangement
had appeared in Clara's eldest son, Ludwig, Brahms had indeed
given her a most painful and moving surprise by offering this
rhapsody as *his* " bridal song."

The male chorus of the *Rhapsody* is also used in the cantata
Rinaldo, op. 50, for tenor solo, male choir, and orchestra, which
appeared a year earlier. Goethe's poem, which, with two others
of similar form (*Idylle* and *Die erste Walpurgisnacht*), was
written expressly for setting to music, as a great concert cantata,
treats of the episode in Tasso's *Gerusalemme Liberata* in which
the valiant hero Rinaldo is delivered from the seductive embraces
of the sorceress Armida, who sinks into the earth with her magic
garden amid thunder and lightning, thanks to the diamond shield
held before him as a mirror and to the prayer of the crusaders.
We at once think of Gluck's opera of the reformed type *Armide,*
Wagner's Parsifal and Kundry, Klingsor's magic castle and garden. Goethe's poem, with the cold, abstract, intellectual quality
of its language and presentation of the subject, is unfortunately
very lacking in dramatic vigour. The sorceress Armida does not
herself appear as a protagonist; it is only from the words of the
chorus that we hear how she first laments and bewails the loss
of Rinaldo, then, by a change of mood, turns, raging " like a
demon " in her wrath and fury, against her own palace. The
culminating dramatic incident — the annihilation of Armida's
magic power by the holding up to her of the diamond shield, and
the prayer of the crusaders — is touched upon by dignified allu-
sions rather than pictorially and graphically represented. The
appearance of this shield, which is to reflect to Rinaldo his own
deep degradation, is represented by mysterious fanfares of wind
instruments in the orchestra, but so abruptly that the listener

who is unfamiliar with the subject cannot at once grasp this decisive inward crisis and change in the poem. Again, the effect of the "prayers of the faithful," which finally break the charm and bring about the collapse of the palace and garden, is only slightly indicated by a short section for vocal quartet and is at once interwoven with the summons to return, which follows it.

Brahms's music was bound, too, to suffer considerably from these inward weaknesses of the poem, in spite of all its wonderful beauty of detail. It has never been popular, least of all among the great male-voice choral societies, with a view to which it was written; indeed, it is chiefly for this reason that it has been classed among Brahms's weaker works — that is to say, those which have not "come off." There is some truth in this, if we expect to find in it a contribution to the great *dramatic* type of choral cantata. For, however much Clara Schumann may have praised the "extraordinary dramatic fire" of this cantata, and great as are the beauty, warmth of feeling, and even dramatic effectiveness that may be found in it in detail, as a whole this work, in which Goethe had already made all the action take place inwardly, in the soul and spirit of the hero, shows quite unmistakably that Brahms did not possess real dramatic genius or the sense of the theatre. Hence it is, in my opinion, needless to deplore the fact that the projects for an opera, pursued with touching persistence by Brahms for a few years, remained no more than projects and finally came to nothing. As late as March 1870 he writes to Clara Schumann: "Wagner would not hinder me in the least from going in for opera with the greatest pleasure. Moreover, among the many things I wish for, this opera comes, for instance, even before a position as musical director." His friend Widmann championed the claims of Gozzi's *Re Cervo* or Calderon's *El Secreto a Voces* in Gozzi's translation, as a possible libretto for an opera. What we learn about Brahms's attitude towards opera from the chapter in Widmann's reminiscences of Brahms entitled *"Eine Oper?"* — what we should have been justified in expecting of Brahms in opera — is, in any case, not a continuous (*durchkomponierte*) modern music drama, as conceived by

Wagner, and in his style, but a regular "number opera (*Nummernoper*)" in the old style, with dialogue, *recitativo secco*, arias, and ensembles, the libretto of which he would most likely have taken from some romantic legend with a magic or faerie element.

Like Grieg's *Olav Trygvason*, Brahms's *Rinaldo* was a dramatic fragment for the concert-room. The music is divided into seven sections. The most important and valuable part of the work lies in Rinaldo's three great love-songs, full of deep, tender passion, when he is trying unsuccessfully to tear himself away ("*Stelle her der gold'nen Tage Paradiese noch einmal*," "*Mit der Turteltaube Locken lockt zugleich die Nachtigall*," "*Zum zweitenmale seh' ich erscheinen*"), and next to these comes the great chorus of the crusaders. The consoling, healing elements in the poem are to a certain extent contained in these choruses, but they also contain, to a still larger extent, all that aims at rousing the hero's courage and inducing him to return home, by spurring him to energy and reminding him of his duty as he remains irresolute, entangled in the bonds of love. The first ("*Zu dem Strande! Zu der Barke!*") and the last ("*Segel schwellen*") form a pendant to each other. These are the actual seafaring- and sea-choruses of the cantata. Purer and grander than these is the final chorus, "*Auf dem Meere*," the use of which as a separate number Brahms himself expressly sanctions in a letter to his friend von der Leyen, and which suggests in a fresh, animated, grandly conceived and strikingly picturesque fashion a sea-voyage and its wonders. The remaining choruses break in abruptly in a warning tone on Rinaldo's rather effeminate love-laments. The first ("*Sachte kommt!*") is peculiarly romantic in colour, with its tender pity and gentle consolation; the second ("*Nein! nicht länger ist zu säumen*") opens vehemently and is vigorously developed in fugal style in a broad 3/2 measure; the third ("*Zurück nur! zurücke durch günstige Meere*") with the different voices alternating in a light, merrily buoyant 2/4 measure; the fourth ("*Schon sind sie erhöret*"), with a similar setting, in a tone of devout supplication. Choral and solo singing predominate. The orchestra has but little to say on its own account; its most important appearance is in the short introduction, in which Armida's siren calls on the wood-wind blend with Rinaldo's strongly chromatic laments in soft thirds and sixths on the oboe and with the syncopated figure of the crusaders urging and pressing him to return; next in the brief appearance of the diamond shield, and lastly in the picture of the sorceress, first softly lamenting, then raging with fury, and in the dramatic climax of the sudden collapse of the magic palace and garden, which is only sketched in in a few brief touches. The general style tries to approximate to opera, especially in the use and development of a few *Leitmotiven,* among which Armida's siren call, with its upward leaps of an octave, is the most important. We are often reminded of Beethoven's *Fidelio,* and even more of Weber's *Oberon,* most irresistibly so in the alternating choral quartet " *Wie sie kommen! Wie sie schweben!* " in the great concluding chorus, with its suave, melodious sixths.

What was it that attracted Brahms to Goethe's *Rinaldo?* In the first place, as in the *Schicksalslied,* the *Gesang der Parzen,* and the *Nänie,* the classical setting, the " land of the *Æneid,*" as Richard Voss once called it, the blue skies, the southern seas, the luxuriant bloom of the magic garden. And, secondly, the deep ethical background: the victory over lax sensuality and self-forgetfulness through manly self-control. And, lastly, the wealth of beautiful and truly musical situations and atmosphere in the poem, which in its incorporeal insubstantiality and sombre language somewhat approximates to the style of the second part of *Faust,* the Pandora passage: the sea-voyage, Armida's magic garden, the apparitions of demons, the romance of the crusades. And it is these wonderful scenic passages which form the musical backbone of the whole work. It is too stately, intellectual, and restrained in expression on the one hand, and makes too great demands on the tenors, as regards both volume and compass in the high register, on the other, for there to be much prospect of its coming into its own among male choral societies in Germany.

A special place in the range of Brahms's larger choral works with orchestra is occupied by the *Triumphlied,* op. 55, for eight-part choir and orchestra (organ *ad libitum*). We have already read in the composer's biography of the circumstances which led to its inception, of its triumphal progress through all German-speaking countries, and Billroth's impressions of its first performance in Vienna: Brahms, who was full of deep and impassioned patriotism, wrote it under the immediate impression of the German victory in the Franco-German war of 1870-1, " in honour of the triumph of the German arms," to quote the words originally inscribed upon the title-page, and " humbly dedicated to H.M. the German Emperor William I." His reward was grudging enough, being merely a cold, official acknowledgment. As in the case of the *Deutsches Requiem* and the *Fest- und Gedenksprüche* ten years later, the composer himself, whose knowledge of the Scriptures was so profound, selected the words from Revelation xix, from the passage about the fall of Babylon. But to Brahms, who hated and despised the French deeply and cordially, the Babylon of the Apocalypse meant Paris, the modern Babylon on the Seine.

The work is a true festival composition, a mighty choral hymn for massed choirs, patriotic musical festivals, and vast spaces, in the manner and form of the great Handel anthems in three parts, the Utrecht and Dettingen *Te Deums*. It appears from Brahms's own words to Reinthaler — " If I could do it, and, what is more, had the courage to do it, I should write a good Te Deum and then go off to Germany " — that his original idea had even been to emulate Handel by adopting the form of a Te Deum. It is also Handelian in style and composition, in its grand, simple plan, the predominance of the choral element, the monumental vividness with which the most important passages of the text are illustrated in the music; as, for instance, at the words: " *denn wahrhaftig und gerecht sind seine Gerichte*," " *hiess Treu und Wahrhaftig*," " *und er tritt die Kelter des Weins*," " *ein König aller Könige*" (" for true and righteous are His judgments," " called steadfast and faithful," " and He trod the winepress," " a King of kings "). The first of the three mighty movements is a highly animated, joyous, festal great choral fantasia on a slightly conventionalized version of the Prussian national anthem, *Heil dir im Siegerkranz,* closing with an eight-part " *Hallelujah.*" The second movement culminates in the introduction of the chorale *Nun danket alle Gott* (*Now thank we all our God*) on the wind instruments, to the words "*Lasset uns freuen* (Let us rejoice)," sung by the choir in a soft, melodious, antiphonal setting; then, to quote Brahms's own words to Widmann, all the bells peal in sign of victory, and a festal Te Deum rings out through the land. The third movement works up from the entry of the soloists (bass and baritone) to the ecstatic and exultant jubilation of the concluding chorus.

As in Handel's *Te Deums,* it is a whole nation exulting and giving thanks to the Lord of Battles in grand, mighty choruses. Brahms's treatment, like that of Handel, alternates between the manner of a motet, in which the words are dismissed rapidly, and an amply developed fugal manner which dwells on certain phrases and words at some length. And, as in the mighty choral fugues of the *Deutsches Requiem,* Brahms speaks with the tongue of Handel when his aim is to rejoice in the universal emotion of a whole people, to exult with it and join in its praise and thanks for the great victory. Brahms's own accents are far too little heard in this monumental composition — only in passing, indeed, in passages such as the conclusion of the second section, where jubilation is softened to an overflowing, tranquil emotion of thanksgiving and happiness. This is very characteristic: the art of Brahms, like that of Gluck, has its roots in the gloomier side of life. Brahms's music, like that of Gluck, contains no gospel of joy; he is the introspective, melancholy exponent of virile, restrained resignation, sorrow, and *Weltschmerz.* In both the brighter colour is tempered by a more sombre cast.

The words used by Brahms to Dietrich, in sending a hearty greeting to the Oldenburg "*Freiwillige*" (volunteers) for the first performance at Bremen — "It is not heavy, only *forte* " — emphasize the condition necessary for a successful performance of the *Triumphlied:* namely, a massed choir. For the outward effect of this rather slowly moving, imposing, and spectacular piece of music is always, to use Dietrich's words, " overwhelming and grandiose." It was a thousand times more so in those days of Germany's triumphant exultations; nowadays we find it quite hard to recall the astonishing fact that, as late as the eighties, the *Triumphlied* was rated by many competent judges above the *Deutsches Requiem,* or at least on the same level.

XXXII

CONCLUSION

And now that we have become acquainted with Brahms's
creative work in all its branches, I will sum up briefly in asking
the question: What was Brahms's position in musical history in
the eyes of his contemporaries — that is, in the nineteenth century
— and what is it in ours — that is, in the twentieth? Brahms is
undoubtedly the most remarkable creative personality, besides
Wagner, in the later German music of the nineteenth century.
In both the external and the internal features of their work they
are two utterly and fundamentally different representatives of the
same age and cultural period, and yet, in spite of this diversity,
they have their roots in the same soil — somewhat in the same
way as Bach and Handel, Gluck and Hasse, Mozart and Haydn,
Beethoven and Napoleon, Schiller and Goethe, Goethe and Byron,
Hebbel and Ludwig. If, for more than a decade, the war-cry
"Wagner versus Brahms" drowned the other cry "Bruckner
versus Brahms" in Vienna, there are good reasons for this.
There is no single German composer in the second half of the
nineteenth century belonging to the anti-Wagnerite camp whose
name can compare with that of Brahms in importance and
weight: Brahms is in very truth by far the most important of
Wagner's competitors, even if we include the sphere of poetry —
in spite of Gottfried Keller — and painting — in spite of Böcklin
and Klinger.

In the chapter entitled "Friends and Foes" we have already
seen how the old opposition, Brahms *versus* Wagner, which led
to so much confusion and ill feeling, has long since been harmoniously resolved in the equation: Brahms *and* Wagner. By
which we mean to say that nowadays we love, understand, and
perform Brahms and Wagner equally; we are justifiably delighted

at the fact that the ninteenth century has presented us with two such entirely different and remarkable creative minds, both of whom reached the most consummate development and maturity and brought German musical Romanticism to full perfection; finally, we must feel deeply thankful that, side by side with such a wonderful, mighty, and exceptional phenomenon as Wagner and his artistic achievement in music drama, it was also possible for a neo-classical composer of what is known as " absolute " music, such as Brahms, to produce a great and intense effect upon the spiritual and musical life of Germany. German spiritual and musical culture in the nineteenth century would have remained terribly one-sided if it had, so to speak, said its first and last word in Wagner. Brahms acted as a salutary and absolutely necessary complement to him.

Wagner was the mightiest culmination and consummation of that pan-Germanism which collapsed in the World War with the wreck of Bismarck's heritage, of the " German Idea " of Rohrbach, so far as this concerned Germany's position and significance as a world-power. Wagner's art conquered the world — particularly in all the peoples of Latin stock, in spite of their violently opposing tendencies — in a way which had never fallen to the lot of any artist before. But if this " German Idea " is to preserve its inward soundness and vitality, it requires, as a contrast to the vast dramatic power of Wagner, which looks outward, the tranquil, intimate, absolute strength of Brahms, which looks inward. Only by this means will a harmonious balance of power be arrived at in the German music of the nineteenth century. This is quite plainly to be seen in connexion with Brahms: whereas Wagner compelled the recognition and admiration of the whole world, Brahms has produced his deepest impression, outside Germany, on the Germanic peoples alone, hardly at all on the Latin races — and that in spite of the fact that both masters are equally Germanic. The wide appeal of the stage, as opposed to the concert-room, has undoubtedly had a great deal to do with this. In comparison with Wagner's mighty musical frescoes, the art of Brahms produces an intimate and almost domestic effect.

But it is the further development and deepening of just such powers as these of which we Germans of today stand urgently in need. At no period has this been more true than today, and for this reason perhaps this book may prove to have appeared at the right time. For Brahms is the last great representative of this important and beautiful introspective side of German intellectual life in modern music. Wagner and Brahms may be taken as symbolical of the German people before the World War, and we may rejoice with all our hearts that, in his own style, Brahms by no means comes off second-best in the comparison with Wagner.

Brahms's position in musical history for us and future ages is not so easy to define. For here any clear view is clouded for the present by the dense incense of the uncritical and unqualified cult of Brahms. It is only by comparison with the really great masters of music that we shall arrive at a just estimate both of Wagner's peculiar greatness and of the undeniable limitations of Brahms's spiritual endowments, intellectual horizon, and outlook upon life. At the present day the cult of Brahms is at the height of its bloom, and all that is written about Brahms bears the stamp of an uncritical apotheosis. There can be no doubt that in course of time the judgment pronounced on him will become far more objective, and will undergo considerable revision, when it has to stand before the judgment-seat of musical history. But this may very well happen without in any way detracting from our deep love and lofty veneration for the best part of his life-work. If this book has made a few solid contributions to that fresh examination of Brahms in the future and laid a solid foundation for it, it will have fulfilled its aim in the best possible way.

APPENDICES

I. BRAHMS'S WORKS

Arranged in order of opus number. Brackets contain: name of publisher, year of composition (c.), year of publication (p.).

Opus 1. (First) Sonata in C major for pianoforte, dedicated to Joseph Joachim (Simrock, c. and p. 1853). (a) Allegro. (b) Andante. (c) Scherzo (Allegro molto e con fuoco). (d) Finale (Allegro con fuoco).

Opus 2. (Second) Sonata in F sharp minor for pianoforte, dedicated to Frau Clara Schumann (Simrock, c. 1852, p. 1853). (a) Allegro non troppo ma energico. (b) Andante con espressione. (c) Scherzo (Allegro). (d) Finale (Introduzione [Sostenuto] and Allegro non troppo e rubato).

Opus 3. Six Songs (*Gesänge*) for tenor or soprano solo with pianoforte accompaniment, dedicated to Bettina von Arnim (Simrock, c. 1852–3, p. 1854). (1) Liebestreu. (2) Liebe und Frühling, I. (3) Liebe und Frühling, II. (4) Song from Bodenstedt's *Ivan*. (5) In der Fremde. (6) Lied.

Opus 4. Scherzo in E flat minor for pianoforte, dedicated to Ernst Ferdinand Wenzel (Simrock, c. 1853, p. 1854).

Opus 5. (Third) Sonata in F minor for pianoforte, dedicated to the Countess Ida von Hohenthal, née Countess Seherr-Thoss (Senff,[1] c. 1853, p. 1854). (a) Allegro maestoso. (b) Andante espressivo. (c) Scherzo (Allegro energico). (d) Intermezzo (Rückblick). (e) Finale (Allegro moderato ma rubato).

Opus 6. Six Songs (*Gesänge*) for soprano or tenor solo with pianoforte accompaniment, dedicated to Fräulein Luise and Minna Japha (Senff, c. and p. 1853). (1) Spanisches Lied. (2) Der Frühling. (3) Nachwirkung. (4) Juchhe! (5) Wie die Wolke nach der Sonne. (6) Nachtigallen schwingen.

Opus 7. Six Songs (*Gesänge*) for solo voice with pianoforte accompaniment, dedicated to Albert Dietrich (Simrock, c. 1853, p. 1854).

[1] Works originally published by Senff are now published by N. Simrock.

(1) Treue Liebe. (2) Parole. (3) Anklänge. (4) Volkslied. (5) Die Trauernde. (6) Heimkehr.

Opus 8. (First) Trio in B major for pianoforte, violin, and violoncello (Simrock, c. before 1853–4, p. 1859; revised edition by the composer, 1891). (a) Allegro con moto (revised edition: Allegro con brio). (b) Scherzo (Allegro molto). (c) Adagio non troppo (revised edition: Adagio). (d) Finale (Allegro molto agitato; revised edition: Allegro).

Opus 9. Variations in F sharp minor for pianoforte on a theme by Robert Schumann, dedicated to Frau Clara Schumann (Simrock, c. 1853, p. 1854).

Opus 10. Four Ballades for pianoforte, dedicated to Julius O. Grimm (Simrock, c. after 1854, p. 1856). (1) Andante (D minor, "Edward"). (2) Andante (D major). (3) Intermezzo (Allegro, B minor). (4) Andante con moto (B major).

Opus 11. (First) Serenade in D major for full orchestra (Simrock, c. 1857, p. 1860). (a) Allegro molto. (b) Scherzo (Allegro non troppo). (c) Adagio non troppo. (d) Menuetto, I. (e) Menuetto, II. (f) Scherzo (Allegro). (g) Rondo (Allegro).

Opus 12. Ave Maria for female choir, with orchestral or organ accompaniment (Rieter-Biedermann,[2] c. 1858, p. 1861).

Opus 13. Begräbnisgesang for choir and wind instruments (Rieter-Biedermann, c. before 1860, p. 1861).

Opus 14. Eight Songs and Romances (*Lieder und Romanzen*) for solo voice with pianoforte accompaniment (Rieter-Biedermann, c. 1856–7, p. 1861). (1) Vor dem Fenster. (2) Vom verwundeten Knaben. (3) Murrays Ermordung. (4) Ein Sonett. (5) Trennung. (6) Gang zur Liebsten. (7) Ständchen. (8) Sehnsucht.

Opus 15. (First) Concerto in D minor for pianoforte with orchestra (Rieter-Biedermann, c. after 1853, p. 1861). (a) Maestoso. (b) Adagio. (c) Rondo (Allegro non troppo).

Opus 16. (Second) Serenade in A major for small orchestra (Simrock, c. 1858–9, p. 1860; new and revised version, 1875). (a) Allegro moderato. (b) Scherzo (Vivace). (c) Adagio non troppo. (d) Quasi Menuetto. (e) Rondo (Allegro).

Opus 17. Songs (*Gesänge*) for female choir with accompaniment of two horns and harp (Simrock, c. before 1860, p. 1862). (1) Es tönt

---

[2] Works originally published by Rieter-Biedermann are now published by N. Simrock.

ein voller Harfenklang. (2) Lied von Shakespeare. (3) Der Gärtner. (4) Gesang aus Fingal.

Opus 18. (First) Sextet in B flat major for two violins, two violas, and two violoncellos (Simrock, c. 1860, p. 1862). (a) Allegro ma non troppo — Poco più moderato. (b) Andante, ma moderato (Theme with variations). (c) Scherzo (Allegro molto — Trio: Animato). (d) Rondo (Poco Allegretto e grazioso).

Opus 19. Five Poems (*Fünf Gedichte*) for solo voice with pianoforte accompaniment (Simrock, c. 1857, p. 1862). (1) Der Kuss. (2) Scheiden und Meiden. (3) In der Ferne. (4) Der Schmied. (5) An eine Äolsharfe.

Opus 20. Three Duets for soprano and alto with pianoforte accompaniment (Simrock, c. 1857, p. 1861). (1) Weg der Liebe, I. (2) Weg der Liebe, II. (3) Die Meere.

Opus 21. Variations in D major for pianoforte (Simrock, c. after 1854, p. 1861). (1) On an original theme. (2) On a Hungarian song.

Opus 22. Marienlieder for mixed choir (Rieter-Biedermann, c. before 1860, p. 1862). (1) Der englische Gruss. (2) Marias Kirchgang. (3) Marias Wallfahrt. (4) Der Jäger. (5) Ruf zur Maria. (6) Magdalena. (7) Marias Lob.

Opus 23. Variations in E flat major on a theme by Robert Schumann for pianoforte duet, dedicated to Fräulein Julie Schumann (Rieter-Biedermann, c. 1861, p. 1866).

Opus 24. Variations and Fugue in B flat major on a theme by Handel for pianoforte (Simrock, c. 1861, p. 1862).

Opus 25. (First) Quartet in G minor for pianoforte, violin, viola, and violoncello, dedicated to Baron Reinhard von Dalwigk (Simrock, c. 1856, p. 1863). (a) Allegro. (b) Intermezzo (Allegro ma non troppo). (c) Andante con moto. (d) Rondo alla Zingarese (Presto).

Opus 26. (Second) Quartet for pianoforte, violin, viola, and violoncello, dedicated to Frau Dr. Elisabeth Rösing (Simrock, c. 1856, p. 1863). (a) Allegro non troppo. (b) Poco Adagio. (c) Scherzo (Poco Allegro). (d) Finale (Allegro).

Opus 27. Psalm XIII (" Herr, wie lange willst du mein so gar vergessen ") for three-part female choir with organ or pianoforte accompaniment (Cranz, c. about 1860, p. 1864).

Opus 28. Four Duets for alto and baritone with pianoforte accompaniment, dedicated to Frau Amalie Joachim (Cranz, c. 1860-2,

p. 1864). (1) Die Nonne und der Ritter. (2) Vor der Tür. (3) Es rauschet das Wasser. (4) Der Jäger und sein Liebchen.

Opus 29. Two Motets for five-part mixed choir unaccompanied (Simrock, c. before 1860, p. 1864). (1) Es ist das Heil uns kommen her. (2) Schaffe in mir, Gott, ein rein' Herz (from Psalm li).

Opus 30. Sacred Song (*Geistliches Lied*) by Paul Flemming ("Lass dich nur nichts nicht dauren") for four-part mixed choir with organ or pianoforte accompaniment (Simrock, c. 1856-7, p. 1864).

Opus 31. Three Quartets for four solo voices with pianoforte (Simrock, c. 1859-63, p. 1864). (1) Wechsellied zum Tanze. (2) Neckereien. (3) Der Gang zum Liebchen.

Opus 32. Nine Songs (*Lieder und Gesänge*) by A. v. Platen and G. F. Daumer, set to music for solo voice with pianoforte accompaniment. Two books (Rieter-Biedermann, c. 1863 and earlier, p. 1864). Book I: (1) Wie rafft' ich mich auf in der Nacht. (2) Nicht mehr zu dir zu gehen beschloss ich. (3) Ich schleich' umher. (4) Der Strom, der neben mir verrauschte. Book II: (5) Wehe, willst du mich wieder, drohende Fessel, umfangen? (6) Du sprichst, dass ich mich täuschte. (7) Bitteres zu sagen, denkst du. (8) So stehn wir, ich und meine Weide. (9) Wie bist du, meine Königin.

Opus 33. Fifteen Songs (*Romanzen*) from L. Tieck's *Liebesgeschichte der schönen Magelone und Grafen Peter von Provence* for solo voice with pianoforte accompaniment, dedicated to Julius Stockhausen. Five books (Rieter-Biedermann, c. after 1861, p. Books 1, 2, 1865, Books 3-5, 1868). Book I: (1) Keinen hat es noch gereut, der das Ross bestiegen. (2) Traun! Bogen und Pfeil sind gut für den Feind. (3) Sind es Schmerzen, sind es Freuden, die durch meinen Busen ziehn? Book II: (4) Liebe kam aus fernen Landen. (5) So willst du des Armen dich gnädig erbarmen? (6) Wie soll ich die Freude, die Wonne denn tragen? Book III: (7) War es dir, dem diese Lippen bebten? (8) Wir müssen uns trennen, geliebtes Saitenspiel. (9) Ruhe, Süssliebchen, im Schatten der grünen, dämmernden Nacht. Book IV: (10) Verzweiflung ("So tönet denn, schäumende Wellen"). (11) Wie schnell verschwindet so Licht als Glanz. (12) Muss es eine Trennung geben, die das treue Herz zerbricht. Book V: (13) Sulima ("Geliebter, wo zaudert dein irrender Fuss?"). (14) Wie froh und frisch mein Sinn sich hebt. (15) Treue Liebe dauert lange.

Opus 34a. Quintet for pianoforte, two violins, viola, and violoncello, dedicated to H. R. H. Princess Anna of Hesse (Rieter-Biedermann. First version as a string quintet, c. 1861–2; second version as sonata for two pianos, see below op. 34b; third version as piano quintet, c. 1864; p. 1865). (a) Allegro non troppo. (b) Andante, un poco Adagio. (c) Scherzo (Allegro). (d) Finale (Poco sostenuto — Allegro non troppo — Presto, non troppo).

Opus 34b. Sonata for two pianofortes (arranged from the quintet op. 34) (Rieter-Biedermann, c. 1864, p. 1872).

Opus 35. Studies for the pianoforte: Variations on a theme by Paganini. Two books (Rieter-Biedermann, 1866).

Opus 36. (Second) Sextet in G major for two violins, two violas, and two violoncellos (Simrock, c. 1864, p. 1866). (a) Allegro non troppo — Un poco sostenuto. (b) Scherzo (Allegro non troppo — Trio: Presto giocoso). (c) Poco Adagio. (d) Poco Allegro.

Opus 37. Three Sacred Choruses for female voices unaccompanied (Rieter-Biedermann, c. 1859–63, p. 1866). (1) O bone Jesu. (2) Adoramus. (3) Regina cœli.

Opus 38. (First) Sonata in E minor for pianoforte and violoncello, dedicated to Herr Dr. Joseph Gänsbacher (Simrock, c. 1865, p. 1866). (a) Allegro non troppo. (b) Allegretto quasi Menuetto. (c) Allegro.

Opus 39. Waltzes for pianoforte duet, dedicated to Dr. Eduard Hanslick (Rieter-Biedermann, c. 1865, p. 1867). (1) Tempo giusto (B major). (2) E major. (3) G sharp minor. (4) Poco sostenuto (E minor). (5) Grazioso (E major). (6) Vivace (C sharp major). (7) Poco più Andante (C sharp minor). (8) B flat major. (9) D minor. (10) G major. (11) B minor. (12) E major. (13) B major. (14) G sharp minor. (15) A flat major. (16) C sharp minor.

Opus 40. Trio for pianoforte, violin, and horn (or viola or violoncello) (Simrock, c. 1865, p. 1868). (a) Andante. (b) Scherzo (Allegro). (c) Adagio mesto. (d) Finale (Allegro con brio).

Opus 41. Five Songs (*Lieder*) for four-part male choir (Rieter-Biedermann, c. before 1860, p. 1867). (1) Ich schwing' mein Horn. (2) Freiwillige her! (3) Geleit. (4) Marschieren. (5) Gebt acht!

Opus 42. Three Songs (*Gesänge*) for six-part choir unaccompanied (Cranz [Spina], c. before 1860–1, p. 1868). (1) Abendständchen. (2) Vineta. (3) Darthulas Grabesgesang.

Opus 43. Four Songs (*Gesänge*) for solo voice with pianoforte accompaniment (Rieter-Biedermann, c. 1857, p. 1868). (1) Von ewiger Liebe. (2) Die Mainacht. (3) Ich schell' mein Horn. (4) Das Lied vom Herrn von Falkenstein.

Opus 44. Twelve Songs (*Lieder und Romanzen*) for female choir unaccompanied, or with pianoforte ad libitum (Rieter-Biedermann, c. 1857–9, p. 1866). Book I: (1) Minnelied. (2) Der Bräutigam. (3) Barkarole. (4) Fragen. (5) Die Müllerin. (6) Die Nonne. Book II: (1–4) Four Songs from *Der Jungbrunnen*. (5) Die Braut. (6) Märznacht.

Opus 45. A German Requiem (*Ein Deutsches Requiem*) to words from the Holy Scriptures, for solo voices, chorus, and orchestra (organ ad libitum) (Rieter-Biedermann, c. 1857–66, p. 1868). (I) Selig sind, die da Leid tragen. (II) Denn alles Fleisch, es ist wie Gras. (III) Herr, lehre mich doch. (IV) Wie lieblich sind deine Wohnungen. (V) Ihr habt nun Traurigkeit. (VI) Denn wir haben hier keine bleibende Statt. (VII) Selig sind die Toten.

Opus 46. Four Songs (*Gesänge*) for solo voice with pianoforte accompaniment (Simrock, c. after 1864, p. 1868). (1) Die Kränze. (2) Magyarisch. (3) Die Schale der Vergessenheit. (4) An die Nachtigall.

Opus 47. Five Songs (*Lieder*) for solo voice with pianoforte accompaniment (Simrock, c. after 1864, p. 1868). (1) Botschaft. (2) Liebesglut. (3) Sonntag. (4) O liebliche Wangen. (5) Die Liebende schreibt.

Opus 48. Seven Songs (*Lieder*) for solo voice with pianoforte accompaniment (Simrock, c. after 1864, p. 1868). (1) Der Gang zum Liebchen. (2) Der Überläufer. (3) Liebesklage des Mädchens. (4) Gold überwiegt die Liebe. (5) Trost in Tränen. (6) Vergangen ist mir Glück und Heil. (7) Herbstgefühl.

Opus 49. Five Songs (*Lieder*) for solo voice with pianoforte accompaniment (Simrock, c. after 1864, p. 1868). (1) Am Sonntagmorgen. (2) An ein Veilchen. (3) Sehnsucht. (4) Wiegenlied. (5) Abenddämmerung.

Opus 50. Rinaldo. A cantata by Goethe, for tenor solo, male choir, and orchestra (Simrock, c. 1863, p. 1869). (1) Orchestral introduction (Allegro) and chorus ("Zu dem Strande"). (2) Tenor solo ("Stelle her der gold'nen Tage Paradiese noch einmal") with chorus ("Sachte kommt!"). (3) Tenor solo ("Mit der Turteltaube Locken") and chorus ("Nein! nicht länger ist zu säumen! "). (4) Chorus ("Zurück nur! zurücke, durch günstige Meere "). (5) Tenor solo with chorus ("Zum zweitenmale seh' ich erscheinen "). (6) Chorus with tenor solo ("Schon sind sie erhöret "). (7) Final chorus: Auf dem Meere ("Segel schwellen! ").

Opus 51. Two Quartets for two violins, viola, and violoncello, dedicated to "his friend Dr. Theodor Billroth in Vienna" (Simrock, c. after 1865, p. 1873). No. I in C minor. (a) Allegro. (b) Romanze (Poco adagio). (c) Allegretto molto moderato e comodo (Trio: Un poco più animato). (d) Allegro. No. II in A minor. (a) Allegro non troppo. (b) Andante moderato. (c) Quasi Menuetto, moderato (Second section: Allegretto vivace). (d) Finale (Allegro non assai).

Opus 52. Love-songs (*Liebeslieder*), words from Daumer's *Polydora*. Waltzes for pianoforte duet and vocal parts (four solo voices) ad libitum (Simrock, c. 1869, p. 1869). (1) Rede, Mädchen, allzu liebes. (2) Am Gesteine rauscht die Flut. (3) O die Frauen, o die Frauen, wie sie Wonne tauen! (4) Wie des Abends schöne Röte. (5) Die grüne Hopfenranke. (6) Ein kleiner, hübscher Vogel nahm den Flug. (7) Wohl schön bewandt war es vorehe. (8) Wenn so lind dein Auge mir und so lieblich schauet. (9) Am Donaustrande, da steht ein Haus. (10) O wie sanft die Quelle sich durch die Wiese windet. (11) Nein, es ist nicht auszukommen mit den Leuten. (12) Schlosser auf! (13) Vögelein durchrauscht die Luft. (14) Sieh, wie ist die Welle klar. (15) Nachtigall, sie singt so schön. (16) Ein dunkler Schacht ist Liebe. (17) Nicht wandle, mein Licht. (18) Es bebet das Gesträuche.

Opus 52a. Waltzes for pianoforte duet, after the Liebeslieder op. 52 (Simrock, c. 1868–9, p. 1869).

Opus 53. Rhapsody from Goethe's *Harzreise im Winter* ("Aber abseits, wer ist's? ") for alto solo, male choir, and orchestra (Simrock, c. 1869, p. 1870).

Opus 54. Song of Destiny (*Schicksalslied*) by Friedrich Hölderlin ("Ihr wandelt droben im Licht auf weichem Boden, selige Genien") for chorus and orchestra (Simrock, c. 1868, p. 1871).

Opus 55. Triumphlied ("Halleluja! Heil und Preis, Ehre und Kraft sei Gott, unserm Herrn! ") for eight-part chorus and orchestra (organ ad libitum), dedicated to H. M. the German Emperor William I (Simrock, c. 1870, p. 1872).

Opus 56. Variations on a theme by Joseph Haydn in B flat major
(a) for orchestra (Simrock, c. 1872, p. 1874); (b) for two pianofortes (Simrock, c. 1872, p. 1873).

Opus 57. Eight Songs (*Lieder und Gesänge*) by G. F. Daumer, for
solo voice with pianoforte accompaniment. Two books (Rieter-
Biedermann, c. 1868–9, p. 1871). Book I: (1) Von waldbekränzter
Höhe werf' ich den heissen Blick. (2) Wenn du nur zuweilen
lächelst. (3) Es träumte mir, ich sei dir teuer. (4) Wenn einmal
die geqüalte Seele ruht. Book II: (5) In meiner Nächte Sehnen.
(6) Strahlt zuweilen auch ein mildes Licht. (7) Die Schnur, die
Perl' an Perle. (8) Unbewegte laue Luft.

Opus 58. Eight Songs (*Lieder und Gesänge*) for solo voice with
pianoforte accompaniment. Two books (Rieter-Biedermann, c.
1868–70, p. 1873). Book I: (1) Blinde Kuh. (2) Während des
Regens. (3) Die Spröde. (4) O komme, holde Sommernacht!
Book II: (5) Schwermut. (6) In der Gasse. (7) Vorüber. (8)
Serenade.

Opus 59. Eight Songs (*Lieder und Gesänge*) for solo voice with pianoforte accompaniment. Two books (Rieter-Biedermann, c. 1871–3,
p. 1873). Book I: (1) Dämmerung senkte sich von oben. (2) Auf
dem See. (3) Regenlied. (4) Nachklang. Book II: (5) Agnes. (6)
Eine gute, gute Nacht pflegst du mir zu sagen. (7) Mein wundes
Herz verlangt nach milder Ruh. (8) Dein blaues Auge hält so
still.

Opus 60. (Third) Quartet in C minor for pianoforte, violin, viola,
and violoncello (Simrock, c. 1859–75, p. 1875). (a) Allegro non
troppo. (b) Scherzo (Allegro). (c) Andante. (d) Finale (Allegro
comodo).

Opus 61. Four Duets for soprano and alto with pianoforte accompaniment (Simrock, c. and p. 1874). (1) Die Schwestern. (2) Klosterfräulein. (3) Phänomen. (4) Die Boten der Liebe.

Opus 62. Seven Songs (*Lieder*) for mixed choir unaccompanied (Simrock, c. and p. 1874). (1) Rosmarin. (2) Von alten Liebesliedern.
(3) Waldesnacht. (4) Dein Herzlein mild. (5) All' meine Herzgedanken. (6) Es geht ein Wehen. (7) Vergangen ist mir Glück
und Heil.

Opus 63. Nine Songs (*Lieder und Gesänge*) for solo voice with pianoforte accompaniment. Two books (Peters, c. after 1873, p. 1874).
Book I: (1) Frühlingstrost. (2) Erinnerung. (3) An ein Bild. (4)

An die Tauben. Book II: (5) Junge Lieder, I. (6) Junge Lieder, II. (7) Heimweh, I. (8) Heimweh, II. (9) Heimweh, III.

Opus 64. Three Quartets for four solo voices with pianoforte (Peters, c. after 1862, p. 1874). (1) An die Heimat. (2) Der Abend. (3) Fragen.

Opus 65. Neue Liebeslieder. Waltzes for four solo voices and pianoforte duet. Words from Turkish, Persian, Lettish-Lithuanian, Russian-Polish, Sicilian, Spanish, Malay, and Serbian folk-poems (Simrock, c. 1874, p. 1875). (1) Verzicht', o Herz, auf Rettung. (2) Finstere Schatten der Nacht. (3) An jeder Hand die Finger hatt' ich bedeckt mit Ringen. (4) Ihr schwarzen Augen, ihr dürft nur winken. (5) Wahre, wahre deinen Sohn, Nachbarin, vor Wehe. (6) Rosen steckt mir an die Mutter. (7) Vom Gebirge Well' auf Well'. (8) Weiche Gräser im Revier. (9) Nagen am Herzen fühl' ich ein Gift mir. (10) Ich kose süss mit der und der. (11) Alles, alles in den Wind sagst du mir, du Schmeichler. (12) Schwarzer Wald, dein Schatten ist so düster! (13) Nein, Geliebter, setze dich mir so nahe nicht! (14) Flammenauge, dunkles Haar. (15) Zum Schluss (Epilogue): " Nun, ihr Musen, genug! " (Goethe).

Opus 65a. Waltzes for pianoforte duet, after the Neue Liebeslieder-Walzer, opus 65 (Simrock, p. 1877).

Opus 66. Five Duets for soprano and alto with pianoforte accompaniment (Simrock, c. after 1874, p. 1875). (1) Klänge, I. (2) Klänge, II. (3) Am Strande. (4) Jägerlied. (5) Hüt' du dich.

Opus 67. (Third) Quartet in B flat major for two violins, viola, and violoncello, dedicated to " his friend Professor Th. W. Engelmann of Utrecht " (Simrock, c. 1875 [?], p. 1876). (a) Vivace. (b) Andante. (c) Agitato (Allegro ma non troppo). (d) Poco Allegretto con Variazioni-Doppio Movimento.

Opus 68. First Symphony in C minor for full orchestra (Simrock, c. 1854–76, p. 1877). (a) Un poco sostenuto — Allegro. (b) Andante sostenuto. (c) Un poco Allegretto e grazioso. (d) Finale (Adagio — Più Andante — Allegro ma non troppo e con brio).

Opus 69. Nine Songs (*Gesänge*) for solo voice with pianoforte accompaniment. Two books (Simrock, c. 1876, p. 1877). Book I: (1) Klage, I. (2) Klage, II. (3) Abschied. (4) Des Liebsten Schwur. (5) Tambourliedchen. Book II: (6) Vom Strande. (7) Über die See. (8) Salome. (9) Mädchenfluch.

Opus 70. Four Songs (*Gesänge*) for solo voice with pianoforte accompaniment (Simrock, c. 1876, p. 1877). (1) Im Garten am Seegestade. (2) Lerchengesang. (3) Serenade. (4) Abendregen.

Opus 71. Five Songs (*Gesänge*) for solo voice with pianoforte accompaniment (Simrock, c. 1876, p. 1877). (1) Es liebt sich so lieblich im Lenze. (2) An den Mond. (3) Geheimnis. (4) Willst du, dass ich geh? (5) Minnelied.

Opus 72. Five Songs (*Gesänge*) for solo voice with pianoforte accompaniment (Simrock, c. 1876, p. 1877). (1) Alte Liebe. (2) Sommerfäden. (3) O kühler Wald. (4) Verzagen. (5) Unüberwindlich.

Opus 73. Second Symphony in D major for full orchestra (Simrock, c. 1877, p. 1878). (a) Allegro non troppo. (b) Adagio non troppo. (c) Allegretto grazioso quasi Andantino. (d) Allegro con spirito. .

Opus 74. Two Motets for mixed choir unaccompanied (Simrock, c. 1877, p. 1879). (1) Warum ist das Licht gegeben den Mühseligen. (2) O Heiland, reiss' die Himmel auf.

Opus 75. Four Ballads and Songs (*Balladen und Romanzen*) for two voices with pianoforte accompaniment, dedicated to "his friend Julius Allgeyer" (Simrock, c. after 1876, p. 1878). (1) Edward. (2) Guter Rat. (3) So lass uns wandern. (4) Walpurgisnacht.

Opus 76. Piano Pieces (*Klavierstücke*). Two books (Simrock, c. after 1877, p. 1879). Book I: (1) Capriccio (F sharp minor, Un poco agitato). (2) Capriccio (B minor, Allegretto non troppo). (3) Intermezzo (A flat major, Grazioso). (4) Intermezzo (B flat major, Allegretto grazioso). Book II: (5) Capriccio (C sharp minor, Agitato, ma non troppo presto). (6) Intermezzo (A major, Andante con moto). (7) Intermezzo (A minor, Moderato semplice). (8) Capriccio (C major, Grazioso ed un poco vivace).

Opus 77. Concerto in D major for violin with orchestral accompaniment, dedicated to Joseph Joachim (Simrock, c. after 1877, p. 1879). (a) Allegro non troppo. (b) Adagio. (c) Allegro giocoso, ma non troppo vivace.

Opus 78. (First) Sonata in G major for pianoforte and violin (Simrock, c. 1878, p. 1880). (a) Vivace non troppo. (b) Adagio. (c) Allegro molto moderato.

Opus 79. Two Rhapsodies for the pianoforte, dedicated to Frau Elisabeth von Herzogenberg (Simrock, c. after 1878, p. 1880). (1)

Agitato (B minor). (2) Molto passionato, ma non troppo allegro (G minor).

Opus 80. Academic Festival Overture (*Akademische Festouvertüre*) in C minor for orchestra (Simrock, c. 1880, p. 1881).

Opus 81. Tragic Overture (*Tragische Ouvertüre*) in D minor for orchestra (Simrock, c. 1880, p. 1881).

Opus 82. Nänie ("Auch das Schöne muss sterben") by Friedrich Schiller, for chorus and orchestra (harp ad libitum), dedicated to Frau Hofrat Henriette Feuerbach (Peters, c. 1880, p. 1881).

Opus 83. (Second) Concerto in B flat major for pianoforte with orchestral accompaniment, dedicated to "his dear friend and teacher Eduard Marxsen" (Simrock, c. after 1878, p. 1882). (a) Allegro non troppo. (b) Allegro appassionato. (c) Andante. (d) Allegretto grazioso.

Opus 84. Five Songs (*Romanzen und Lieder*) for one or two voices with pianoforte accompaniment (Simrock, c. after 1877, p. 1882). (1) Sommerabend. (2) Der Kranz. (3) In den Beeren. (4) Vergebliches Ständchen. (5) Spannung.

Opus 85. Six Songs (*Lieder*) for solo voice with pianoforte accompaniment (Simrock, c. after 1873, p. 1882). (1) Sommerabend. (2) Mondenschein. (3) Mädchenlied. (4) Ade! (5) Frühlingslied. (6) In Waldeseinsamkeit.

Opus 86. Six Songs (*Lieder*) for a low voice with pianoforte accompaniment (Simrock, c. after 1873, p. 1882). (1) Therese. (2) Feldeinsamkeit. (3) Nachtwandler. (4) Über die Heide. (5) Versunken. (6) Todessehnen.

Opus 87. (Second) Trio in C major for pianoforte, violin, and violoncello (Simrock, c. after 1880, p. 1883). (a) Allegro. (b) Andante con moto (Thema mit Variationen). (c) Scherzo (Presto). (d) Finale (Allegro giocoso).

Opus 88. (First) Quintet in F major for two violins, two violas, and violoncello (Simrock, c. 1881, p. 1883). (a) Allegro non troppo ma con brio. (b) leading on to (c) Grave ed appassionato — Allegretto vivace — Tempo primo. (d) Finale (Allegro energico).

Opus 89. Song of the Fates (*Gesang der Parzen:* "Es fürchte die Götter das Menschengeschlecht!") by W. von Goethe, for six-part chorus and orchestra, "most respectfully dedicated to H. H. Duke George of Saxe-Meiningen" (Simrock, c. 1882, p. 1883).

Opus 90. Third Symphony in F major for full orchestra (Simrock, c.

1883, p. 1884). (a) Allegro con brio. (b) Andante. (c) Poco Allegretto. (d) Allegro.

Opus 91. Two Songs (*Gesänge*) for alto solo with viola and pianoforte (Simrock, c. after 1863, p. 1884). (1) Gestillte Sehnsucht. (2) Geistliches Wiegenlied.

Opus 92. Four Quartets for soprano, alto, tenor, and bass with pianoforte (Simrock, c. 1882, p. 1884). (1) O schöne Nacht. (2) Spätherbst. (3) Abendlied. (4) Warum?

Opus 93a. Six Songs (*Lieder und Romanzen*) for four-part mixed choir unaccompanied (Simrock, c. 1882, p. 1884). (1) Der bucklichte Fiedler. (2) Das Mädchen. (3) O süsser Mai. (4) Fahr wohl! (5) Der Falke. (6) Beherzigung.

Opus 93b. Tafellied ("Dank der Damen ") for six-part mixed choir and pianoforte, dedicated to " his friends at Krefeld for January 28, 1885 " (Simrock, c. 1884, p. 1885).

Opus 94. Five Songs (*Lieder*) for a deep voice with pianoforte accompaniment (Simrock, c. in part before 1880, p. 1884). (1) Mit vierzig Jahren. (2) Steig auf, geliebter Schatten. (3) Mein Herz ist schwer. (4) Sapphische Ode. (5) Kein Haus, keine Heimat.

Opus 95. Seven Songs (*Lieder*) for solo voice with pianoforte accompaniment (Simrock, c. in part before 1880, p. 1884). (1) Das Mädchen. (2) Bei dir sind meine Gedanken. (3) Beim Abschied. (4) Der Jäger. (5) Vorschneller Schwur. (6) Mädchenlied. (7) Schön war, was ich dir weihte.

Opus 96. Four Songs (*Lieder*) for solo voice with pianoforte accompaniment (Simrock, c. in part before 1881, p. 1886). (1) Der Tod, das ist die kühle Nacht. (2) Wir wandelten, wir zwei zusammen. (3) Es schauen die Blumen alle. (4) Meerfahrt.

Opus 97. Six Songs (*Lieder*) for solo voice with pianoforte accompaniment (Simrock, c. in part before 1880, p. 1886). (1) Nachtigall. (2) Auf dem Schiffe. (3) Entführung. (4) Dort in den Weiden steht ein Haus. (5) Komm' bald. (6) Trennung.

Opus 98. Fourth Symphony in E minor for full orchestra (Simrock, c. 1884–5, p. 1886). (a) Allegro non troppo. (b) Andante moderato. (c) Allegro giocoso. (d) Allegro energico e passionato (Passacaglia).

Opus 99. (Second) Sonata in F major for violoncello and pianoforte (Simrock, c. 1886, p. 1886). (a) Allegro vivace. (b) Adagio affettuoso. (c) Allegro passionato. (d) Allegro molto.

Opus 100. (Second) Sonata in A major for violin and piano-forte (Simrock, c, 1886, p. 1887). (a) Allegro amabile. (b) Andante tranquillo. (c) Vivace. (d) Allegretto grazioso (quasi Andante).

Opus 101. (Third) Trio in C minor for pianoforte, violin, and violoncello (Simrock, c. after 1880, p. 1887). (a) Allegro energico. (b) Scherzo (Presto non assai). (c) Andante grazioso. (d) Allegro molto.

Opus 102. Concerto for violin and violoncello (known as the Double Concerto), with orchestral accompaniment (Simrock, c. 1887, p. 1888). (a) Allegro. (b) Andante. (c) Vivace non troppo.

Opus 103. Gipsy Songs (*Zigeunerlieder*) for four voices with piano-forte accompaniment. (Eight of them are arranged for various solo voices.) (Simrock, c. 1887, p. 1888.) (1) He, Zigeuner, greife in die Saiten ein. (2) Hochgetürmte Rimaflut. (3) Wisst ihr, wann mein Kindchen am allerschönsten ist? (4) Lieber Gott, du weisst, wie oft bereut ich hab. (5) Brauner Bursche führt zum Tanze. (6) Röslein dreie in der Reihe blüh'n so rot. (7) Kommt dir manch-mal in den Sinn. (8) Horcht, der Wind klagt in den Zweigen traurig sacht. (9) Weit und breit schaut niemand mich an. (10) Mond verhüllt sein Angesicht. (11) Rote Abendwolken zieh'n am Firmament.

Opus 104. Five Songs (*Gesänge*) for mixed choir unaccompanied (Simrock, c. 1888 and earlier, p. 1889). (1) Nachtwache, I. (2) Nachtwache, II. (3) Letztes Glück. (4) Verlorene Jugend. (5) Im Herbst.

Opus 105. Five Songs (*Lieder*) for low voice with pianoforte accom-paniment (Simrock, c. in the late eighties, p. 1889). (1) Wie Melo-dien zieht es. (2) Immer leiser wird mein Schlummer. (3) Klage. (4) Auf dem Kirchhofe. (5) Verrat.

Opus 106. Five Songs (*Lieder*) for solo voice with pianoforte accom-paniment (Simrock, c. in the late eighties, p. 1889). (1) Ständchen. (2) Auf dem See. (3) Es hing der Reif im Lindenbaum. (4) Meine Lieder. (5) Ein Wanderer.

Opus 107. Five Songs (*Lieder*) for solo voice with pianoforte accom-paniment (Simrock, c. in the late eighties, p. 1889). (1) An die Stolze. (2) Salamander. (3) Das Mädchen spricht. (4) Maien-kätzchen. (5) Mädchenlied.

Opus 108. (Third Sonata in D minor for violin and pianoforte, dedicated to "his friend Hans von Bülow" (Simrock, c. 1887, p. 1889). (a) Allegro. (b) Adagio. (c) Un poco presto e con sentimento. (d) Presto agitato.

Opus 109. Festival and Commemoration pieces (*Fest- und Gedenksprüche*) for eight-part mixed choir unaccompanied, "respectfully dedicated to His Magnificence Dr. Carl Petersen, Burgomaster of Hamburg" (Simrock, c. 1889, p. 1890). (1) Unsere Väter hofften auf dich. (2) Wenn ein starker Gewappneter seinen Palast bewahret. (3) Wo ist ein so herrlich Volk.

Opus 110. Three Motets for four- and eight-part choir unaccompanied (Simrock, c. 1889, p. 1890). (1) Ich aber bin elend, und mir ist wehe. (2) Ach, arme Welt, du trügest mich. (3) Wenn wir in höchsten Nöten sein.

Opus 111. (Second) Quintet for two violins, two violas, and violoncello (Simrock, c. 1890, p. 1891). (a) Allegro non troppo, ma con brio. (b) Adagio. (c) Un poco Allegretto. (d) Vivace ma non troppo presto.

Opus 112. Six Quartets for soprano, alto, tenor, and bass with pianoforte (Peters, c. 1890, p. 1891). (1) Sehnsucht. (2) Nächtens. (3–6) Four Gipsy Songs (*Zigeunerlieder*): (3) Himmel strahlt so helle und klar. (4) Rote Rosenknospen künden schon des Lenzes Triebe. (5) Brennessel steht am Wegesrand. (6) Liebe Schwalbe.

Opus 113. Thirteen Canons for female voices (Peters, c. 1890 [1856], p. 1891). (1) Göttlicher Morpheus. (2) Grausam erweiset sich Amor an mir! (3) Die Nachtigall ("Sitzt a schön's Vögerl auf'm Dannabaum"). (4) Wiegenlied ("Schlaf', Kindlein, schlaf'!"). (5) Der Mann ("Wille wille will, der Mann ist kommen"). (6) So lange Schönheit wird besteh'n. (7) Wenn die Klänge nah'n und fliehen. (8) Ein Gems auf dem Stein. (9) An's Auge des Liebsten fest mit Blicken dich ansauge. (10) Nachtwache, I ("Leise Töne der Brust"). (11) Ich weiss nicht, was im Hain die Taube girret? (12) Wenn Kummer hätte zu töten Macht. (13) Einförmig ist der Liebe Gram.

Opus 114. Trio in A minor for pianoforte, clarinet (or viola), and violoncello (Simrock, c. 1891, p. 1892). (a) Allegro. (b) Adagio. (c) Andantino grazioso. (d) Allegro.

Opus 115. Quintet for clarinet (or viola), two violins, viola, and violoncello (Simrock, c. 1891, p. 1892). (a) Allegro. (b) Adagio. (c)

Andantino. (d) Presto non assai, ma con sentimento. (e) Con moto — un poco meno mosso.

Opus 116. Fantasias for pianoforte (*Fantasien*). Two books (Simrock, c. 1892 and earlier, p. 1892). Book I: (1) Capriccio (D minor, Presto energico). (2) Intermezzo (A minor, Andante). (3) Capriccio (G minor, Allegro passionato). Book II: Intermezzo (E major, Adagio). (5) Intermezzo (E minor, Andante con grazia ed intimissimo sentimento). (6) Intermezzo (E major, Andantino teneramente). (7) Capriccio (D minor, Allegro agitato).

Opus 117. Three Intermezzi for pianoforte (Simrock, c. and p. 1892). (1) E flat major ("Schlaf sanft, mein Kind, schlaf sanft und schön!" Andante moderato). (2) B flat minor (Andante non troppo e con molto espressione). (3) C sharp minor (Andante con moto).

Opus 118. Piano pieces (*Klavierstücke*) (Simrock, c. and p. 1893). (1) Intermezzo (A minor, Allegro non assai, ma molto appassionato). (2) Intermezzo (A major, Andante teneramente). (3) Ballade (G minor, Allegro energico). (4) Intermezzo (F minor, Allegretto un poco agitato). (5) Romanze (F major, Andante). (6) Intermezzo (E flat minor, Andante, largo e mesto).

Opus 119. Piano pieces (*Klavierstücke*) (Simrock, c. and p. 1893). (1) Intermezzo (B minor, Adagio). (2) Intermezzo (E minor, Andantino un poco agitato). (3) Intermezzo (C major, Grazioso e giocoso). (4) Rhapsodie (E flat major, Allegro risoluto).

Opus 120. Two Sonatas for clarinet (or viola) and pianoforte (Simrock, c. 1894, p. 1895). No. I: (a) Allegro appassionato. (b) Sostenuto ed espressivo. (c) Andante un poco Adagio. (d) Allegretto grazioso. (e) Vivace. No. II: (a) Allegro amabile. (b) Allegro appassionato. (c) Sostenuto. (d) Andante con moto. (e) Allegro.

Opus 121. Four Serious Songs (*Vier ernste Gesänge*) for solo bass voice with pianoforte accompaniment, dedicated to Max Klinger (Simrock, c. and p. 1896). (1) Denn es gehet dem Menschen wie dem Vieh. (2) Ich wandte mich und sahe an alle, die Unrecht leiden unter der Sonne. (3) O Tod, wie bitter bist du. (4) Wenn ich mit Menschen- und mit Engelszungen redete.

Opus 122. Eleven Chorale-Preludes for organ. Two books. Posthumous work (Simrock, c. 1896 and earlier, p. 1902). Book I: (1) Mein Jesu, der du mich zum Lustspiel ewiglich dir hast erwählet. (2) Herzliebster Jesu, was hast du verbrochen. (3) O Welt, ich muss dich lassen, I. (4) Herzlich tut mich erfreuen die schöne Sommerzeit. Book II: (5) Schmücke dich, o liebe Seele. (6) O wie selig seid ihr doch, ihr Frommen. (7) O Gott, du frommer Gott. (8) Es ist ein Ros' entsprungen. (9) Herzlich tut mich verlangen, I. (10) Herzlich tut mich verlangen, II. (11) O Welt, ich muss dich lassen, II.

WORKS WITHOUT OPUS NUMBER

Fourteen Children's Folk-songs (*Volks-Kinderlieder*), with the addition of a pianoforte accompaniment, dedicated to the children of Robert and Clara Schumann (Rieter-Biedermann, p. 1858). (1) Dornröschen. (2) Die Nachtigall. (3) Die Henne. (4) Sandmännchen. (5) Der Mann. (6) Heideröslein. (7) Das Schlaraffenland. (8a, b) Beim Ritt auf dem Knie. (9) Der Jäger in dem Walde. (10) Das Mädchen und der Hasel. (11) Wiegenlied. (12) Weihnachten. (13) Marienwürmchen. (14) Dem Schutzengel.

Fourteen German Folk-songs (*Deutsche Volkslieder*), arranged for four-part choir, dedicated to the Vienna Singakademie (Rieter-Biedermann, p. 1864). (1) Von edler Art. (2) Mit Lust tät ich ausreiten. (3) Bei nächtlicher Weil. (4) Vom heiligen Märtyrer Emmerano, Bischoffen zu Regensburg. (5) Täublein weiss. (6) Ach, lieber Herre Jesu Christ'. (7) Sankt Raphael. (8) In stiller Nacht. (9) Abschiedslied ("Ich fahr' dahin, wenn es muss sein"). (10) Der tote Knabe. (11) Die Wollust in den Mayen. (12) Morgengesang ("Wach' auf, mein Kind"). (13) Schnitter Tod. (14) Der englische Jäger ("Es wollt' gut Jäger jagen").

Fugue in A flat minor for organ (Supplement to *Allgemeine Musikalische Zeitung,* 1864, No. 29. Now Simrock, new edition, 1883).

Mondnacht, by Eichendorff ("Es war, als hätt' der Himmel"), for solo voice with pianoforte accompaniment (In the collection *Albumblätter* [Göttingen, G. H. Wigand, 1854], afterwards Raabe and Plothow, p. 1872).

Hungarian Dances (*Ungarische Tänze*) arranged for pianoforte duet. Four books (Simrock, Books I and II, p. 1869; III and IV, p. 1880). Also arranged for orchestra. Book I: (1) G minor (Allegro molto). (2) D minor (Allegro non assai). (3) F major (Allegretto). (4) F minor (Poco sostenuto). (5) F sharp minor (Allegro). Book II:

(6) D flat major (Vivace). (7) A major (Allegretto). (8) A minor (Presto). (9) E minor (Allegro non troppo). (10) E major (Presto). Book III: (11) A minor (Poco Andante). (12) D minor (Presto). (13) D major (Andantino grazioso). (14) D minor (Un poco Andante). (15) B flat major (Allegretto grazioso). (16) F minor (Con moto). Book IV: (17) F sharp minor (Andantino). (18) D major (Molto vivace). (19) B minor (Allegretto). (20) E minor (Poco Allegretto). (21) E minor (Vivace).

Chorale-Prelude and Fugue on *O Traurigkeit, o Herzeleid* for organ (Supplement to 13th year of issue [1881] of the *Musikalisches Wochenblatt*, E. W. Fritzsch, now Deutsche Brahms-Gesellschaft).

Fifty-one Exercises (*Einundfünfzig Übungen*) for pianoforte. Two books (Simrock, c. 1880, p. 1893).

German Folk-songs (*Deutsche Volkslieder*) with piano accompaniment. Seven books (Books I–VI for solo voice, Book VII for solo voices and small chorus) (Simrock, p. 1894). Book I: (1) Sagt mir, o schönste Schäf'rin mein. (2) Erlaube mir, fein's Mädchen. (3) Gar lieblich hat sich gesellet. (4) Guten Abend. (5) Die Sonne scheint nicht mehr. (6) Da unten im Tale. (7) Gunhilde lebt' gar still und fromm. Book II: (8) Ach, englische Schäferin. (9) Es war eine schöne Jüdin. (10) Es ritt ein Ritter wohl durch das Ried. (11) Jungfräulein, soll ich mit euch geh'n. (12) Feinsliebchen, du sollst nicht barfuss geh'n. (13) Wach' auf, mein Hort. (14) Maria ging aus wandern. Book III: (15) Schwesterlein, Schwesterlein, wann geh'n wir nach Haus? (16) Wach' auf, mein' Herzensschöne. (17) Ach Gott, wie weh tut scheiden. (18) So wünsch' ich ihr ein' gute Nacht. (19) Nur ein Gesicht auf Erden lebt. (20) Schönster Schatz, mein Engel. (21) Es ging ein Maidlein zarte. Book IV: (22) Wo gehst du hin, du Stolze? (23) Der Reiter spreitet seinen Mantel aus. (24) Mir ist ein schön's braun's Maidelein. (25) Mein Mädel hat einen Rosenmund. (26) Ach, könnt' ich diesen Abend noch einmal freien gehen. (27) Ich stand auf hohem Berge. (28) Es reit' ein Herr und auch sein Knecht. Book V: (29) Es war ein Markgraf über'm Rhein. (30) All' mein' Gedanken, die ich hab', die sind bei dir. (31) Dort in den Weiden. (32) So will ich frisch und fröhlich sein. (33) Och Mod'r, ich well en Ding han! (34) We kumm' ich dann de Pooz erenn. (35) Soll sich der Mond. Book VI: (36) Es wohnet ein Fiedler. (37) Du mein einzig Licht. (38) Des Abends kann ich nicht schlafen gehn. (39) Schöner Augen, schöne Strahlen. (40) Ich weiss mir'n Maidlein. (41) Es steht ein' Lind' in jenem Tal. (42) In stiller

Nacht. Book VII: (43) Es stunden drei Rosen auf einem Zweig. (44) Dem Himmel will ich klagen. (45) Es sass ein schneeweiss' Vögelein. (46) Es war einmal ein Zimmergesell. (47) Es ging sich uns're Fraue. (48) Nachtigall, sag'. (49) Verstohlen geht der Mond auf.

Scherzo (movement of a sonata) in C minor for violin and pianoforte. From the sonata composed for Joseph Joachim with Schumann and Dietrich in 1853 (posthumous, Deutsche Brahms-Gesellschaft, p. 1906).

Regenlied ("Regentropfen aus den Bäumen fallen") by Claus Groth, second version; for the first see opus 59, No. 3 (posthumous, Deutsche Brahms-Gesellschaft).

UNPUBLISHED POSTHUMOUS WORKS

Two Folk-songs arranged for soprano, alto, tenor, and bass. (1) Wach' auf, mein' Herzensschöne. (2) Dort in den Weiden steht ein Haus.

Two Songs (*Lieder*) for soprano, alto, tenor, and bass after opus 44, Nos. 5 and 6. (1) Die Müllerin (Chamisso). (2) Die Nonne (Uhland).

Three "Puzzle Canons" (*Rätselkanons*). (1) Töne, lindernder Klang (for soprano, alto, tenor, and bass). (2) Mir lächelt kein Frühling (for four female voices). (3) Wann hört der Himmel auf zu strafen (Uhland) (for soprano and alto).

Two Canons for four female voices unaccompanied (Studies for opus 113, Nos. 2 and 1). (1) Grausam erweiset sich Amor an mir. (2) Göttlicher Morpheus!

Canon for soprano, alto, tenor, and bass ("Zu Rauch muss werden der Erde Schmelz und des Himmels Azur") (Rückert).

ARRANGEMENTS, ETC.

Studies for the Pianoforte. Five books (Senff; Books I and II, p. 1869, Books III–V, p. 1879). (I) Étude after Fr. Chopin. (II) Rondo after C. M. von Weber. (III, IV) Presto after J. S. Bach, in two arrangements. (V) Chaconne by J. S. Bach, for the left hand alone.

Gavotte in A major from Gluck's *Paris and Helen,* arranged for pianoforte and dedicated to Frau Clara Schumann (Senff, p. 1871).

Schumann's Piano Quartet, opus 47, arranged for piano duet (Fürstner), and Piano Quintet, opus 44, in a similar arrangement (unpublished).

Overture to Shakspere's *Henry IV* by Joseph Joachim, arranged for two pianos (posthumous, Simrock).

Two Cadenzas for Beethoven's Piano Concerto in G major (posthumous, Deutsche Brahms-Gesellschaft).

Ellen's Second Song from Scott's *Lady of the Lake* (opus 52, No. 2), arranged for soprano solo, female choir, and wind instruments (posthumous, Deutsche Brahms-Gesellschaft).

Arrangements of Schubert's *Gruppe aus dem Tartarus* and *An Schwager Kronos,* for one-part male choir with orchestra (unpublished).

EDITIONS OF OLDER WORKS IN WHICH BRAHMS COLLABORATED

François Couperin, Piano works (*Klavierwerke*) (in Chrysander's *Denkmäler der Tonkunst,* Vol. II; Bergedorf, 1871; reprinted by Augener & Company, London, 1888).

Handel, Kammerduette (Leipzig, ed. Peters).

Phil. Em. Bach, Sonatas for piano and violin (*Sonaten für Klavier und Violine*) (Leipzig, Rieter-Biedermann).

Wilh. Friedemann Bach, Sonatas for two pianos.

Mozart, Complete Edition (*Gesamtausgabe*), Series 24 (Revision of the Requiem).

Schubert, Complete Edition, Series 1 (Symphonies and posthumous piano-pieces).

Schumann, Complete Edition, Series 14 (Supplementary Volume, and critical advice given to Clara Schumann in preparing the complete edition for publication) (Breitkopf and Härtel).

Chopin, Complete Edition (mainly the Sonatas, Mazurkas, the Fantasie, opus 49, and Barcarolle, opus 60).

YOUTHFUL WORKS

(With the exception of the first, unpublished or lost)

Souvenir de la Russie, transcriptions in the form of a fantasia on Russian and Bohemian airs, for piano duet (under the name G. W. Marks, for August Cranz, Hamburg).

Fantasia (*Fantasie*) on a favourite waltz for pianoforte (played in Hamburg).

Duet for piano and violoncello, under the name Karl Würth (played in Hamburg, July 5, 1851).

Trio for piano and strings, under the name Karl Würth (played in Hamburg, July 5, 1851).

Mass in canon form, a four-part Benedictus from which is mentioned in letters to Clara Schumann and Joachim.

Movements from piano sonatas, songs, sonatas for piano and violin, string quartets, folk-songs for male choir, etc.

II. BRAHMS'S ARRANGEMENTS OF HIS OWN WORKS

Opus	Work	Arranged as
11	First Serenade for full orchestra	Piano duet
12	Ave Maria for female choir, with orchestral or organ accompaniment	Piano score with words
13	Begräbnisgesang for choir and wind instruments	Piano score with words
15	First Piano Concerto (in D minor) with orchestra	Piano duet, for one and two pianos
16	Second Serenade for small orchestra	Piano duet
17	Songs for female choir with two horns and harp	Piano score with words
18	First String Sextet (in B flat major)	Piano duet
25	First Piano Quartet (in G minor)	} Piano duet
26	Second Piano Quartet (in A major)	
29	Two Motets for five-part mixed choir unaccompanied	Piano score for use at choir practices
34b	Sonata for two pianos (in F minor)	Piano quintet (in F minor), opus 34a
36	Second String Sextet (in G major)	Piano duet

Opus	Work	Arranged as
39	Waltzes for piano duet	Piano solo
42	Three Songs for six-part choir unaccompanied	Piano score for use at choir practices
44	Songs (*Lieder und Romanzen*) for female voices unaccompanied	Piano accompaniment ad libitum for use at choir practices
45	German Requiem for solo voices, chorus, and orchestra	Piano score with words, also for piano duet without words
50	Rinaldo. Cantata for tenor solo, male choir, and orchestra	Piano score with text
51	Two String Quartets (in C minor and A minor)	Piano duet
52	Liebeslieder-Walzer for piano duet with vocal parts ad libitum	Waltzes for piano duet (opus 52a)
53	Rhapsody for alto solo, male choir, and orchestra	Piano score with text
54	Song of Destiny (*Schicksalslied*) for chorus and orchestra	Piano score with words
55	Triumphlied for eight-part choir and orchestra	Piano score with words, and for piano duet
56a	Variations on a theme by Joseph Haydn for orchestra	Two pianos, opus 56b
65	Neue Liebeslieder, waltzes for four voices with piano duet	Piano duet, opus 65a
67	Third String Quartet (in B flat major)	Piano duet
69	First Symphony (in C minor) for full orchestra	Piano score for piano duet
73	Second Symphony (in D major) for full orchestra	Piano score for piano duet
80	Academic Festival Overture (in C minor) for full orchestra	Piano score for piano duet
81	Tragic Overture (in D minor) for full orchestra	Piano score for piano duet
82	Elegy (Nänie) for chorus and orchestra	Piano score with words

Opus	Work	Arranged as
83	Second Piano Concerto (in B flat major)	Piano duet, for two pianos
88	First String Quintet (in F major)	Piano duet
90	Third Symphony (in F major) for full orchestra	Piano duet, for two pianos
98	Fourth Symphony (in E minor) for full orchestra	Piano duet, for two pianos
103	Gipsy Songs (*Zigeunerlieder*) for four voices with piano accompaniment	For solo voice with piano (Nos. 1–7 and 11)
109	Fest- und Gedenksprüche for eight-part mixed choir unaccompanied	Piano score for use at choir practices
110	Three Motets for four- and eight-part choir unaccompanied	Piano scores for use at choir practices
111	Second String Quintet (in G major)	Piano duet
120	Two Sonatas for clarinet and piano	Violin and piano
Without opus no.	Hungarian Dances (*Ungarische Tänze*) for piano duet	Piano solo (Books I and II) and for orchestra (Nos. 1, 3, 10)

III. BIBLIOGRAPHY OF THE PRINCIPAL GERMAN WORKS ON BRAHMS

BIOGRAPHIES

MAX KALBECK: *Johannes Brahms* (8 vols.). Berlin, 1904–14, &c., Deutsche Brahms-Gesellschaft

A. THOMAS-SAN GALLI: *Johannes Brahms*. Munich, 1912 &c., R. Piper

SMALLER BIOGRAPHIES

HERMANN DEITERS: *Johannes Brahms* (in *Graf Waldersees Sammlung musikalischer Vorträge*). Leipzig, 1880 (I) and 1898 (II), Breitkopf & Härtel

LOUIS KÖHLER: *Johannes Brahms und seine Stellung in der Musikge-schichte*. Hanover, 1880, Arnold Simon

BERNHARD VOGEL: *Johannes Brahms* (in the series *Musikheroen der Neuzeit*, IV). Leipzig (now Berlin), 1888, Max Hesse

HEINRICH REIMANN: *Johannes Brahms* (in the series *Berühmte Musiker*, I). Berlin, 1897, &c., Harmonie-Verlag; now Breslau, Schlesische Verlagsanstalt

A. STEINER: *Johannes Brahms*. Allgemeine Musikgesellschaft, Zürich, New Year Nos. 86 (1898) and 87 (1899)

EMIL KRAUSE: *Johannes Brahms in seinen Werken* (with lists of all the instrumental and vocal works). Hamburg, 1892, Lucas Gräfe & Sillem

JULIUS SPENGEL: *Johannes Brahms. Eine Charakterstudie* (in the series *Hamburgische Liebhaberbibliothek*, ed. Alfr. Lichtwark). Ham-burg, 1898, Commetersche Kunsthandlung

RICHARD BARTH: *Johannes Brahms und seine Musik* (collected lectures). Hamburg, 1903, Otto Meissner

WALTER PAULI: *Johannes Brahms* (in the series *Moderne Geister* ed. Hans Landsberg, Nos. 2, 3). Berlin, 1907, now Munich, Pan-Verlag

RICHARD VON PERGER: *Johannes Brahms* (in the series *Musiker-Bio-graphien*, Universal-Bibliothek, No. 27). Leipzig, 1908, Phil. Reclam

WILLIBALD NAGEL: *Johannes Brahms* (in the series *Musikalische Volks-bücher*, ed. Adolf Spemann). Stuttgart, 1923, J. Engelhorns Nachf.

LUDWIG MISCH: *Johannes Brahms* (in the series *Velhagen und Klasing's Volksbücher*, No. 79). Bielefeld and Leipzig, 1922, Velhagen and Klasing

PHILIPP SPITTA: *Johannes Brahms* (in *Sechzehn Aufsätze zur Musik*), Berlin, 1892

HERMANN KRETZSCHMAR: *Johannes Brahms* (1884), in *Gesammelte Aufsätze*, I (a collected edition of his articles in the *Grenzboten*). Leipzig, 1910, Fr. Wilh. Grunow, now Breitkopf & Härtel

—: *Das deutsche Lied seit Robert Schumann* (1880). Same publisher.

—: *Das deutsche Lied seit dem Tode Richard Wagners* (1897), in *Gesammelte Aufsätze*, II (articles reprinted from Peters's *Jahr-buch*). Leipzig, 1911, C. F. Peters

LEOPOLD SCHMIDT: *Johannes Brahms*, in *Meister der Tonkunst im 19. Jahrhundert*. Berlin, 1908, Julius Bard

A. WOLFGANG THOMAS (SAN GALLI): *Johannes Brahms. Eine musikpsy-*

chologische Studie in 5 Variationen. Strassburg, 1905, J. H. Ed. Heitz (Heitz & Mündel)

MAX CHOP: *Johannes Brahms,* in *Zeitgenössische Tondichter,* I. Leipzig, 1888–90, Rossberg

WILLIBALD NAGEL: *Johannes Brahms als Nachfolger Beethovens.* Leipzig and Zürich (1892), Gebrüder Hug

LA MARA (MARIE LIPSIUS): *Johannes Brahms,* in *Musikalische Studienköpfe,* III. Leipzig, 1878, etc., Breitkopf & Härtel

STUDIES

BERTHOLD LITZMANN: *Clara Schumann–Johannes Brahms, Briefe aus den Jahren 1853–1896, im Auftrage von Marie Schumann herausgegeben* (2 vols.). Leipzig, 1927, Breitkopf & Härtel

EUGENIE SCHUMANN: *Erinnerungen,* in the series *Musikalische Volksbücher.* Stuttgart, I. Engelhorns Nachf., 2nd ed. 1927

KARL GOLDMARK: *Erinnerungen aus meinem Leben.* Vienna, etc., 1922, Rikola-Verlag

HERMINE SCHWARZ: *Ignaz Brüll und sein Freundeskreis* (reminiscences of Brüll, Goldmark, and Brahms). Vienna, etc., 1922, Rikola-Verlag

FRANZ LUDWIG: *Julius Otto Grimm (Ein Beitrag zur Geschichte der musikalischen Spätromantik).* Bielefeld and Leipzig, 1925, Velhagen & Klasing

MONIKA HUNNIUS: *Mein Weg zur Kunst.* Heilbronn, 1925, Eugen Salzer

MEMOIRS

ALBERT DIETRICH: *Erinnerungen an Johannes Brahms in Briefen, besonders aus seiner Jugendzeit.* Leipzig, 1899f., Otto Wigand

J. V. WIDMANN: *Johannes Brahms in Erinnerungen.* Berlin, 1898f., Gebr. Paetel

— : *Sizilien und andere Gegenden Italiens (Reisen mit Johannes Brahms).* Frauenfeld, Switzerland, 1897f., Huber & Co.

WALTER HÜBBE: *Brahms in Hamburg* (" *Hamburgische Liebhaberbibliothek* "). Hamburg, 1902

RUDOLF VON DER LEYEN: *Johannes Brahms als Mensch und Freund.* Düsseldorf and Leipzig, 1905, K. Rob. Langewiesche

GUSTAV JENNER: *Johannes Brahms als Mensch, Lehrer und Künstler.*
Marburg, 1905, N. G. Elwert

GUSTAV OPHÜLS: *Erinnerungen an Johannes Brahms.* Berlin, 1921,
Deutsche Brahms-Gesellschaft

PAUL KUNZ and ERNST ISLER: *Johannes Brahms in Thun.* Paper written
for the 16th general meeting of the Schweiz. Tonkünstler Verein at
Thun. Zürich, July 10, 1915; Gebr. Hug

COMMENTARIES ON THE WORKS

HERMANN KRETZSCHMAR: *Führer durch den Konzertsaal.* Leipzig, 1886f.,
Breitkopf & Härtel. Also in separate parts

HUGO RIEMANN: *Symphonien,* etc., in Bechtold's *Der Musikführer.* In
separate parts. Now Berlin, Schlesinger

MAX BURKHARDT: *Johannes Brahms. Ein Führer durch seine Werke.*
Berlin, Globus-Verlag

MAX CHOP: *Brahms' Symphonien* (Reclam's *Universal-Bibliothek,* No.
6309). Leipzig, 1921

WALTER HAMMERMANN: *Johannes Brahms als Liedkomponist* (thesis).
Leipzig, 1912, Spamersche Buchdruckerei

WILLIBALD NAGEL: *Die Klaviersonaten von Johannes Brahms. Tech-
nischästhetische Analysen.* Stuttgart, 1915, C. Grüninger

MAX FRIEDLÄNDER: *Brahms' Volkslieder.* In Peters's *Jahrbuch,* Leipzig,
1902

— : *Brahms' Lieder. Einführung in seine Gesänge für eine und zwei
Stimmen.* Berlin and Leipzig, 1922, N. Simrock

PAUL MIES: *Stilmomente und Ausdrucksformen im Brahms'schen Lied.*
Leipzig, 1923, Breitkopf & Härtel

LETTERS

Brahms' Briefwechsel. Berlin, 1907, etc., Deutsche Brahms-Gesellschaft
Vol. 1, 2, with Heinrich and Elisabeth von Herzogenberg (Max
Kalbeck)

" 3 " Reinthaler, Bruch, Rudorff, Deiters, Heimsoeth, Reinecke, Bernhard and Luise Scholz (Wilhelm Altmann)

" 4 " J. O. Grimm (Heinrich Barth)

" 5, 6 " Joachim (Andreas Moser)

Vol. 7 with Levi, Gernsheim, and the Hecht and Fellinger families (Leopold Schmidt)
" 8 " Widmann, Vetter, Schubring (Max Kalbeck)
" 9/12 " P. Jos. and Fritz Simrock (Max Kalbeck)
" 13 " Theod. Wilh. Engelmann (Julius Röntgen)
" 14 " his publishers: Breitkopf & Härtel, Senff, Rieter-Biedermann, Peters, Fritzsch, Lienau (Wilhelm Altmann)
" 15 " Franz Wüllner (Ernst Wolff)
" 16 " Spitta and Dessoff (Karl Krebs)

ALMANACS, ALBUMS, ETC.

Des jungen Kreislers Schatzkästlein (sayings of poets, philosophers, and artists, collected by Brahms), edited with an introduction by Karl Krebs. Berlin, 1909, Deutsche Brahms-Gesellschaft

Brahms-Kalender. Berlin, 1909, Schuster & Loeffler

VIKTOR MILLER ZU AICHHOLZ: *Ein Brahms Bilderbuch,* with explanatory text by Max Kalbeck. Vienna, 1905, R. Lechner

MARIE FELLINGER: *Brahms-Bilder.* Vienna, 1900, privately published; since 1911, Leipzig, Breitkopf & Härtel

COLLECTION OF WORDS

GUSTAV OPHÜLS: *Brahms-Texte, Vollständige Sammlung der von Johannes Brahms komponierten und musikalisch bearbeiteten Dichtungen.* Berlin, 1897, etc., Deutsche Brahms-Gesellschaft

ANALYSES AND MINIATURE SCORES

Thematisches Verzeichnis sämtlicher im Druck erschienener Werke von Johannes Brahms. Nebst systematischem Verzeichnis und Registern (a thematic analysis of all the published works, with indices, etc.). Berlin, 1897, etc., Simrock

Miniature scores of Brahm's symphonies, concertos, chamber-music, choral works, etc. Payne and Eulenberg's *Kleine Partituren-Ausgaben.* Leipzig, Ernst Eulenberg, with introductions by Arthur Smolian

Philharmonia Taschen-Partituren, Wiener Philharmonischer Verlag, by permission of N. Simrock, Berlin (larger choral works and some others)

IV. BIBLIOGRAPHY OF THE PRINCIPAL ENGLISH WORKS ON BRAHMS

FLORENCE MAY: *The Life of Johannes Brahms* (2 vols.). London, E. Arnold, 1905

JOHN ALEXANDER FULLER-MAITLAND: *Brahms.* London, Methuen, 1911

— : *Masters of German Music;* pp. 1–95. London, Osgood, McIlvaine & Co., 1894; New York, Scribner, 1894

EDWIN EVANS: *Handbook to the Vocal Work of Brahms. Historical, descriptive and analytical account of the entire works.* New York, Scribner, 1912

HENRY COPE COLLES: *Brahms.* London, John Lane, 1908; New York, Brentano's, 1908

J. LAWRENCE ERB: *Brahms,* in The Master Musicians series. London, Dent; New York, Dutton, 1905

ERNEST MARKHAM LEE: *Brahms; the Man and his Music.* New York, Scribner, 1916

JEFFREY PULVER: *Johannes Brahms.* London, K. Paul, Trench, Trubner & Co., 1926

SIR CHARLES VILLIERS STANFORD: *Brahms.* New York, Frederick A. Stokes, 1912

SIR GEORGE HENSCHEL: *Personal Recollections of Johannes Brahms.* New York, *Century Magazine,* LXI, pp. 725–36; London, Roy. Inst. of Gt. Brit. Proc., XVIII, pp. 136–51 (1906)

— : *Musings and Memories of a Musician.* London, Macmillan, 1918

JAMES GIBBONS HUNEKER: *Mezzotints in Modern Music.* New York, Scribner, 1899, 1905

DANIEL GREGORY MASON: *From Grieg to Brahms.* New York, Outlook Co., 1902

WILLIAM HENRY HADOW: *Studies in Modern Music.* Second Series. London, Seeley, 1895

INDEX OF NAMES

INDEX OF REFERENCES TO WORKS
IN THE TEXT